THE EPIC JOURNEY IN GREEK AND ROMAN LITERATURE

This volume explores journeys across time and space in Greek and Latin literature, taking as its starting point the paradigm of travel offered by the epic genre. The epic journey is central to the dynamics of Classical literature, offering a powerful lens through which characters, authors, and readers experience their real and imaginary worlds. The journey informs questions of identity formation, narrative development, historical emplotment, and constructions of heroism – topics that move through and beyond the story itself. The act of moving to and from "home" – both a fixed point of spatial orientation and a transportable set of cultural values – thus represents a physical journey and an intellectual process. In exploring its many manifestations, the chapters in this collection reconceive the centrality of the epic journey across a wide variety of genres and historical contexts, from Homer to the moon.

THOMAS BIGGS is Assistant Professor of Classics at the University of Georgia. He specializes in Roman literature and culture, especially poetry and poetics, and is completing a book on the First Punic War, the representation of history in Latin literature, and the development of the epic genre.

JESSICA BLUM is Assistant Professor of Classical Studies at the University of San Francisco. Her research focuses on imperial Latin poetry and the epic tradition, and she is completing a monograph on the interaction of visual effects, genre, and discourses of exemplarity in Valerius Flaccus' *Argonautica*, with a particular focus on the character of Hercules.

VOLUME XXXIX

THE EPIC JOURNEY IN GREEK AND ROMAN LITERATURE

EDITED FOR THE DEPARTMENT OF CLASSICS BY

THOMAS BIGGS

Assistant Professor of Classics at the University of Georgia

JESSICA BLUM

Assistant Professor of Classical Studies at the University of San Francisco

CAMBRIDGE
UNIVERSITY PRESS

University Printing House, Cambridge CB2 8BS, United Kingdom

One Liberty Plaza, 20th Floor, New York, NY 10006, USA

477 Williamstown Road, Port Melbourne, VIC 3207, Australia

314–321, 3rd Floor, Plot 3, Splendor Forum, Jasola District Centre, New Delhi – 110025, India

79 Anson Road, #06–04/06, Singapore 079906

Cambridge University Press is part of the University of Cambridge.

It furthers the University's mission by disseminating knowledge in the pursuit of education, learning, and research at the highest international levels of excellence.

www.cambridge.org
Information on this title: www.cambridge.org/9781108498098
DOI: 10.1017/9781108628129

© Cambridge University Press 2019

This publication is in copyright. Subject to statutory exception and to the provisions of relevant collective licensing agreements, no reproduction of any part may take place without the written permission of Cambridge University Press.

First published 2019

Printed in the United Kingdom by TJ International Ltd. Padstow Cornwall

A catalogue record for this publication is available from the British Library.

Library of Congress Cataloging-in-Publication Data
NAMES: Biggs, Thomas, editor. | Blum, Jessica, editor.
TITLE: The epic journey in Greek and Roman literature / edited for the Department of Classics by Thomas Biggs, Jessica Blum.
DESCRIPTION: Cambridge : Cambridge University Press, 2019.
IDENTIFIERS: LCCN 2018045902 | ISBN 9781108498098 (hardback : alk. paper) | ISBN 9781108702898 (pbk. : alk. paper)
SUBJECTS: LCSH: Travel in literature. | Greek literature–History and criticism. | Latin literature–History and criticism.
CLASSIFICATION: LCC PA3015.T7 E75 2019 | DDC 880.9/32–DC23
LC record available at https://lccn.loc.gov/2018045902

ISBN 978-1-108-49809-8 Hardback

Cambridge University Press has no responsibility for the persistence or accuracy of URLs for external or third-party internet websites referred to in this publication and does not guarantee that any content on such websites is, or will remain, accurate or appropriate.

Contents

List of Illustrations	*page* vii
Notes on Contributors	viii
Acknowledgments	xi
List of Abbreviations	xiii

1 Introduction   1
 Thomas Biggs and Jessica Blum

PART I ODYSSEAN JOURNEYS   9
 Introduction   9

2 In and Out of the Golden Age: A Hesiodic Reading
 of the *Odyssey*   11
 Egbert J. Bakker

3 *Pompē* in the *Odyssey*   31
 Alexander C. Loney

4 "What Country, Friends, is This?" Geography and
 Exemplarity in Valerius Flaccus' *Argonautica*   59
 Jessica Blum

PART II GENDERED MAPS   89
 Introduction   89

5 Wandering, Love, and Home in Apollonius of Rhodes'
 Argonautica and Heliodorus' *Aethiopica*   91
 Silvia Montiglio

6 Heroes and Homemakers in Xenophon   108
 Emily Baragwanath

7 Women's Travels in the *Aeneid*   130
   Alison Keith

PART III ROME'S JOURNEY: CONSTRUCTIONS OF
ROME THROUGH TRAVEL   145
   Introduction   145

8 Epic Journeys on an Urban Scale: Movement and
   Travel in Vergil's *Aeneid*   151
   Timothy M. O'Sullivan

9 Roman and Carthaginian Journeys: Punic *Pietas* in
   Naevius' *Bellum Punicum* and Plautus' *Poenulus*   170
   Thomas Biggs

10 Defining Home, Defining Rome: Germanicus' Eastern Tour   194
   Cynthia Damon and Elizabeth Palazzolo

11 Odyssean Wanderings and Greek Responses to Roman Empire   211
   Andrew C. Johnston

PART IV UNEARTHLY JOURNEYS   241
   Introduction   241

12 From Rome to the Moon: Rutilius Namatianus and the
   Late Antique Game of Knowledge   243
   Martin Devecka

13 Looking Back in Wonder: Contemplating Home
   from the *Iliad* to *Pale Blue Dot*   263
   Karen ní Mheallaigh

References   292
Index Locorum   314
General Index   319

Illustrations

1. The first ever photograph of Earth, taken by *Lunar Orbiter 1* in August 1966 — *page* 272
2. *Earthrise*, December 24, 1968 — 273
3. *The Blue Marble*, December 7, 1972 — 274
4. *Pale Blue Dot*, February 14, 1990 — 286
5. *The Day the Earth Smiled*, July 19, 2013 — 289

The color plate section can be found between pages 274 and 275.

Contributors

EGBERT J. BAKKER is the Alvan Talcott Professor of Classics at Yale University. His latest books are *The Meaning of Meat and the Structure of the* Odyssey (Cambridge 2013) and *A Companion to the Greek Language* (Malden, MA 2010). He is currently working on a commentary on Book 9 of the *Odyssey*.

EMILY BARAGWANATH is Associate Professor in the Classics Department at the University of North Carolina at Chapel Hill. Her publications include *Motivation and Narrative in Herodotus* (Oxford 2008), articles on the literary techniques employed by the Greek historians, and the co-edited volumes *Myth, Truth, and Narrative in Herodotus* (Oxford 2012) and *Clio and Thalia: Attic Comedy and Historiography* (*Histos* Supplement 2017). At present she is writing a monograph on the fourth-century Athenian writer Xenophon.

THOMAS BIGGS is Assistant Professor of Classics at the University of Georgia. He is currently writing a book on the First Punic War and Latin literature. He has articles and reviews recently published and forthcoming in *CJ, AJP, CP, Latomus*, and *Trends in Classics*, as well as chapters in several edited volumes.

JESSICA BLUM is Assistant Professor of Classics at the University of San Francisco. She is currently writing a monograph on the interaction of visual effects, genre, and discourses of exemplarity in Valerius Flaccus' *Argonautica*, with a particular focus on the character of Hercules. She has recently published articles in *CJ* and *CO* on Valerius Flaccus, Ovid, and Vergil, and has several forthcoming on generic interfaces in the *Argonautica*.

CYNTHIA DAMON is Professor of Classical Studies at the University of Pennsylvania. She is the author of *The Mask of the Parasite: A Pathology of Roman Patronage* (Ann Arbor 1997), a commentary on Tacitus,

Histories I (Cambridge 2003), a translation of Tacitus' *Annals* in the Penguin series (2013), and, with Will Batstone, *Caesar's Civil War* (Oxford 2006). She recently published an OCT of Caesar's *Bellum civile*, a companion volume on the text of the *Bellum civile* (2015), a new Loeb edition of Caesar's *Civil War* (2016), and a variorum commentary on Tacitus' *Agricola* (Dickinson College Commentaries 2017). She is currently preparing a pilot edition of the *Bellum Alexandrinum* for the Library of Digital Latin Texts.

MARTIN DEVECKA is Assistant Professor at the University of California, Santa Cruz. His work focuses on the cultural history of Rome and of the ancient world more generally. He is currently completing a comparative history of premodern ruins.

ANDREW C. JOHNSTON is Associate Professor of Classics and History at Yale University. His first book explores the experiences of local communities of the western provinces under Roman rule (*The Sons of Remus: Identity in Roman Gaul and Spain*, Harvard 2017); he is currently writing a book on the origins and development of the fear of kingship in Roman culture. His other research interests include the imagination and representation of selves and others at Rome, especially as relates to ethnography and geography, and the archaeology of central Italy, specifically the Latin city of Gabii.

ALISON KEITH has written extensively on gender and genre in Latin literature and Roman culture. She is the author of books on Ovid's *Metamorphoses*, women in Latin epic, and Propertius, and the co-editor of volumes on Roman dress and women and war in antiquity. She is Director of the Jackman Humanities Institute at the University of Toronto and co-editor of the Phoenix Supplementary Series with the University of Toronto Press. Current research projects include a volume on Vergil for I. B. Tauris in their series Understanding Classics; a commentary on the fourth book of Ovid's *Metamorphoses* for Cambridge University Press; and a SSHRC-funded project on the reception of Ovid's *Metamorphoses* in Flavian epic.

ALEXANDER C. LONEY is Associate Professor of Classical Languages at Wheaton College. He has written on Homer, Hesiod, and Greek lyric poetry. He is the author of *The Ethics of Revenge and the Meanings of the* Odyssey and the *Oxford Handbook of Hesiod* (co-edited with Stephen Scully). His current research focuses on hope, nostaligia, and temporality in Greek poetry, as well as a further work on revenge in Greek culture.

KAREN NÍ MHEALLAIGH is Professor of Greek at the University of Exeter in the UK. Her research explores the ways in which ancient fictions engage with their contemporary intellectual, textual, and material cultures, especially the culture of wonders. Her recent monograph examines Lucian of Samosata as both a writer of fiction and a literary theorist (*Reading Fiction with Lucian: Fakes, Freaks and Hyperreality*, Cambridge 2014), and she has just completed a second monograph about the moon in the ancient imagination.

SILVIA MONTIGLIO is the Basil L. Gildersleeve Professor of Classics at the Johns Hopkins University. She has written extensively on several aspects of ancient literature, including journeying (*Wandering in Ancient Greek Culture*, Chicago 2005) and related themes (*From Villain to Hero: Odysseus in Ancient Thought*, Ann Arbor 2011; *Love and Providence: Recognition in the Ancient Novel*, New York 2013). Her most recent book is *The Myth of Hero and Leander: The History and Reception of an Enduring Greek Legend* (London 2017).

TIMOTHY M. O'SULLIVAN, Professor of Classical Studies at Trinity University, is the author of *Walking in Roman Culture* (Cambridge 2011). He has also written articles on Vergil's *Aeneid*, Statius' *Silvae*, Apuleius' *Metamorphoses*, and on Roman attitudes to floor and ceiling decoration. His current project is a study of the ideology of movement in the Augustan age.

ELIZABETH PALAZZOLO received her Ph.D. in Classical Studies from the University of Pennsylvania in 2016. Her dissertation examined the Roman cultural memory of the conquest of Latium, and her broader research interests include Greek and Roman historiography, Roman cultural history, and material culture. She is currently a Visiting Assistant Professor in the Classics Department at Saint Anselm College.

Acknowledgments

From the Editors

We wish to thank first and foremost all of the contributors for their patience and inspiring work throughout the editorial process. This volume, and the conference with which it originated, are greatly indebted to the Department of Classics at Yale University and the Edward J. and Dorothy Clarke Kempf Fund for their generous sponsorship. Many colleagues at Yale – too many to mention individually – contributed their time and feedback; we are particularly grateful to Andrew Johnston and Alexander Loney, who organized a yearlong colloquium at Yale on "Home" in the ancient world and from whose collaboration this project benefited greatly, and to Kirk Freudenburg and Christina S. Kraus for their help and support. We also wish to thank Damien Nelis for being an integral part of the conference and conversations that went into this volume.

We also extend warm thanks to Michael Sharp and the editorial staff at Cambridge University Press for ushering this project through the publication process. Both we and our contributors are grateful to the anonymous readers, whose detailed and insightful feedback improved the book immensely.

We both would like to thank family, friends, and all those who have helped us along the way for their ongoing support and enthusiasm. We could not have brought this project to fruition without them.

Jessica Blum

I am very grateful to the Department of Modern and Classical Languages at the University of San Francisco, and the Departments of Classics at Wabash College and the University of California, Irvine. My students and colleagues at all three have been a great source of inspiration for this project. I also wish to thank the Fondation Hardt in Vandoeuvres, Switzerland for two invaluable research stays in the course of preparing the volume. I am especially grateful to the Yale Department of Classics for the opportunity to undertake both conference and volume, and Tom Biggs for venturing on this journey with me. Above all, I thank my family – my parents, Peter and Sarah, my brothers, Chris and Christian – for their support and encouragement.

Thomas Biggs

I am greatly indebted to the Department of Classics at the University of Georgia for supporting my research and teaching during the years this volume has been in preparation. To my colleagues and especially to the students of my courses in ancient epic: thank you! In one way or another, you have all made a positive impact on this project. I thank the Willson Center for the Humanities at the University of Georgia and the Fondation Hardt in Vandoeuvres, Switzerland for providing me with research fellowships. I also thank the Centre for Classical and Near Eastern Studies of Australia and the Department of Classics and Ancient History at the University of Sydney for selecting me as an Apollo Fellow in 2017. The intellectual environment in Sydney was extremely motivating for the completion of my contribution to this volume. Countless thanks are owed to my co-editor, not in the least for putting up with my dislike of scheduling. And most of all I thank my parents, Rich and Michele, and my Sarah.

Abbreviations

Abbreviations for ancient authors and works generally follow those used in *The Oxford Classical Dictionary* (4th edn, ed. Simon Hornblower, Antony Spawforth, and Esther Eidinow; Oxford 2012). Abbreviations for academic journals and periodicals follow those used in *L'Année philologique*.

Anth. Lat.	*Anthologia Latina*, ed. A. Riese, F. Buecheler, and E. Lommatzsch (Leipzig: B. G. Teubner, 1869–1926)
BNJ	*Brill's New Jacoby*: available at http://referenceworks.brillonline.com/browse/brill-s-new-jacoby
CAH	*Cambridge Ancient History* (Cambridge: Cambridge University Press, 1924)
*CAH*2	*Cambridge Ancient History*, 2nd edn (Cambridge: Cambridge University Press, 1970–2005)
CIG	*Corpus Inscriptionum Graecarum*, ed. A. Boeckh et al. (Berlin: Königlich Preussische Akademie der Wissenschaften zu Berlin, 1828–77)
CIL	*Corpus Inscriptionum Latinarum*, ed. T. Mommsen et al. (Berlin: Königlich Preussische Akademie der Wissenschaften zu Berlin, 1893–)
FGrH	*Die Fragmente der griechischen Historiker*, ed. F. Jacoby (Berlin/Leiden: Weidmann/Brill, 1923–)
FPL	*Fragmenta poetarum Latinorum epicorum et lyricorum*, ed. J. Blänsdorf et al. (Berlin/New York: De Gruyter, 2011)
IG II^2	*Inscriptiones Graecae. Vol. II et III. Inscriptiones Atticae Euclidis anno posteriores. Editio altera*, ed. J. Kirchner (Berlin: De Gruyter, 1913–40)
IG XII.2	*Inscriptiones Graecae XII. Inscriptiones insularum maris Aegaei praeter Delum, 2. Inscriptiones Lesbi, Nesi, Tenedi*, ed. W. R. Paton (Berlin: De Gruyter, 1899)

IGR	*Inscriptiones Graecae ad res Romanas pertinentes*, ed. R. Cagnat (Paris: E. Leroux, 1901–27)
IMT	*Inschriften Mysia und Troas*, ed. M. Barth and J. Stabber (Munich: Leopold Wenger-Institute, 1993)
IvAssos	*Die Inschriften von Assos*, ed. R. Merkelbach (Bonn: Habelt, 1976)
IvO	*Die Inschriften von Olympia*, ed. W. Dittenberger and K. Purgol (Berlin: Asher, 1896)
L&S	C. T. Lewis and C. Short, *A Latin Dictionary* (Oxford: Clarendon Press, 1879)
LfgrE	*Lexikon des frühgriechischen Epos* (Göttingen: Vandenhoeck & Ruprecht, 1979–2010)
OGI	*Orientis Graeci Inscriptiones Selectae. Supplementum Sylloges inscriptionum graecarum*, ed. W. Dittenberger (Leipzig: S. Hirzel, 1903)
OLD	*Oxford Latin Dictionary* (Oxford: Oxford University Press, 1968–82)
P.Oxy.	*Oxyrhynchus Papyri* (1898–): available at https://onlinebooks.library.upenn.edu/webbin/serial?id=ocyrhynchus
RE	*Realencyclopädie der classischen Altertumswissenschaft*, ed. A. Pauly, G. Wissowa, W. Kroll, et al. (Stuttgart: J. B. Metzler, 1893–1980)
RG	*Res Gestae Divi Augusti*
RIC I²	H. Mattingly, E. A. Sydenham et al. (eds.), *The Roman Imperial Coinage*, 2nd ed., vol. I, ed. C. H. V. Sutherland and R. A. G. Carson (London: Spink, 1984)
RPC	*Roman Provincial Coinage*, vols. I and II, ed. A. Burnett, M. Amandry, P. Ripollès, and I. Caradice (London/Paris: British Museum Press/Bibliothèque Nationale, 1992 and 1999)
SEG	*Supplementum Epigraphicum Graecum*, vols. XXX, LII, LVI, LX (Leiden/Boston: Brill, 1983–2014)
Th	W. Theiler (ed.), *Die Fragmente Poseidonius* (Berlin and New York: de Gruyter, 1982)
TLL	*Thesaurus Linguae Latinae* (Leipzig: De Gruyter, 1900–)
VE	R. F. Thomas and J. M. Ziolkowski (eds.), *The Virgil Encyclopedia* (Malden, MA: Wiley-Blackwell, 2014)

CHAPTER I

Introduction

Thomas Biggs and Jessica Blum

This volume explores journeys across time and space in Greek and Latin literature, taking as its starting point the paradigm of travel offered by the epic genre. In light of a recent wave of research concerning space, time, and landscape, both in epic poetry and farther afield, this collection approaches the journey as an essential but often overlooked feature of Classical literature. Since antiquity, detailed scholarly attention has been paid to the far-reaching influence of epic poetry, but a single volume has yet to be dedicated to the epic journey itself in the field of Classical studies. In the significant scholarship on travel and homecoming (*nostos*) in ancient literature, the centrality of the journey has been taken for granted. Accordingly, the journey remains a concept largely treated in disparate works, one that calls for interaction with a growing body of nuanced critical perspectives.

The factors that make the journeys explored in this volume specifically "epic" are manifold, but circulate around a set of key themes, formal features, and influences. Each act of motion, whether depicted in Archaic Greek hexameter verse or Imperial Latin prose, gestures toward the structure and content of the ur-journey as defined by Homer. Homeric epic, particularly the *Odyssey*, is therefore an anchor for the volume. As the chapters show, however, Odysseus' voyage spawned a variety of parallel and peripheral acts of literary movement, often with little visible trace of their Greek literary origins. In fact, those built upon the voyage of the Argo display different understandings of time and space, of travel as quest, in contrast to or in conjunction with the journey as *nostos*. Homer's journey is thus both route and point of departure for its many descendants.

Beyond their derivation from benchmark "epic journeys," the non-epic voyages in this volume appropriate elements of the epic genre, including elevated tone and register, heroic expectations and characterizations, laborious obstacles, and even the vastness of space itself. It is most frequently an epic lens through which the volume's characters create meaning from the landscapes they negotiate. Epic space presents a world against which reality can crash, a world that often appears as a series of imaginary cartographies drawn up in contrast to lived and experienced space. But at times, these seemingly distinct planes of existence appear to coalesce, as actors – both mythic and historic – traverse and perceive topographies of the real through those of the impossible. At their core, acts of departing and returning home were always already bound to epic features, since it is in epic that the first attempts were taken to define these central human concepts in literary terms. As this volume shows in detail, therefore, the epic journey offers a powerful framework for talking about "home" and its antitheses. With such an outsized influence attributed to the genre in the cultures of Greece and Rome, the epic journey perhaps unsurprisingly emerges as intrinsic to questions of identity both collective and individual; to the development of narrative; to historical emplotment; and to constructions of heroism. This collection seeks to elucidate these various aspects in isolation and in interaction, offering a wide-ranging discussion of the epic journey from a number of different angles.

In the course of conceptualizing this volume, several questions emerged as shared points of investigation throughout the contributions. By applying the model of the epic journey to a variety of generic contexts and historical periods, our contributors explore how the nature of the journey creates its multiplicity of functions. Specifically, by examining the structure of the journey within different generic frameworks, the chapters reveal the journey's function as a point of departure and of cohesion as each work situates itself against epic templates. Translated into different genres, the journey provides a vehicle for identifying and authorizing the protagonists of the various texts under consideration. Mapped onto community, kingdom, or empire, it enables these protagonists to assert knowledge, and therefore power, over the spaces they trace and traverse. By its very nature, the journey raises questions of agency and leadership, informing the relationship between individual and community, male and female, parent and child, but also destabilizing these most rudimentary binaries: the journey links while it creates distance – it always functions in multiple dimensions.

In order to understand the journey in its many facets, this volume reflects broadly on ideas of home, displacement, and the dialogue between the two created by the act of traveling.[1] While the array of topics under analysis may

---

[1] The discussion of "home" here is indebted to a colloquium series organized by Andrew C. Johnston and Alexander Loney at Yale University in 2014.

appear to range far from one another, the contributions find shared ground not only in their focus on epic travel and its influence, but also in their consistent return to the most common and powerful point of departure. As the ideological center of a community, "home" is both a fixed point of orientation and a transportable set of cultural values.[2] As Kirsten Jacobson suggests,

> Just as our bodies and our ability to find orientation through our bodies serve to open us up onto the world and varying spatial levels, the home is also responsible for providing a form of habituated orientation for us insofar as it is intimately tied up with these developments of our body. In and through our homes (especially those of our childhood), we develop certain ways of doing and perceiving things, and we carry these tendencies with us into our future homes as well as into the world.[3]

Gaston Bachelard's reflections on the retrospective impact of "home" in *The Poetics of Space* underscore the centrality of home for the shaping of the self:

> The successive houses in which we have lived have no doubt made our gestures commonplace. But we are very surprised, when we return to the old house, after an odyssey of many years, to find that the most delicate gestures, the earliest gestures suddenly come alive, are still faultless. In short, the house we were born in has engraved within us the hierarchy of the various functions of inhabiting. We are the diagram of the functions of inhabiting that particular house, and all the other houses are but variations on a fundamental theme.[4]

We see here the role of home in the making of a "home" in the world, of constructing a zone of familiarity while "abroad."[5] "Home," in fact, is not

---

[2] Cf. Jacobson 2012. On "home" and the creation of political subjects, see Kirsten Jacobson's very useful discussion in Jacobson 2010. Through engagement with Gilles Deleuze and Félix Guattari's treatment of home and beyond, Jacobson argues that "although leaving home is essential to our experience of home *as* home, it is an activity that we win, so to speak, through effort and ultimately through the established security of the home" (Jacobson 2010: 220). She continues, "[t]o be public is to improvise on the basis of a foundation—a homestead," noting elsewhere that, "[b]eing an individual must be a development that relies on our being first *with* others, on our having departed from a secure base—from a home" (Jacobson 2010: 230; 242). Cf. esp. Deleuze and Guattari 1987. For the foundational idea of "being-at-home," see Jacobson 2009.
[3] Jacobson 2010: 228. She here engages with Steinbock 1995.
[4] Bachelard 1964: 15. See discussion of the quotation at Jacobson 2010: 221.
[5] The political dimensions of the spatial construction of the city (*polis*-space) have exercised numerous thinkers. Arendt's claim in *The Human Condition* is particularly relevant: "men's life together in the form of the *polis* seemed to assure that the most futile of human activities, action and speech...would become imperishable. The organization of the *polis*, physically secured by the wall around the city and physiognomically guaranteed by its laws...is a kind of organized remembrance" (Arendt 1998: 198). See discussion at Willis 2011: 6. For "home" and human movement, see also Virilio 1997.

always left behind: it can be used to negotiate collective and cultural identity upon reaching a foreign destination. The idea of "home" also has its darker side. It excludes, separating inside from outside, distinguishing "us" from "them"; even within the home, boundaries of gender, age, and social status are constructed and negotiated. "Home" can be represented as a place, a perspective, a language, through which the idea of travel can be explored, not just as a physical journey but also as an intellectual process. A journey can be conceptualized in similarly metaphorical terms, as translation, conquest, or self-definition, as a process of movement away from or through an ideological home as much as a geographical one: famously, the journey is itself a "metaphor we live by."[6] In a consideration of the impact that mobility and movement have on ideas, cultures, cities, and peoples, Stephen Greenblatt has observed that "the reality, for most of the past as once again for the present, is more about nomads than natives."[7] Hence, whether one looks to Greek colonists conceptualizing their westward journeys through the lens of the *Odyssey* or Vergil's composition of the *Aeneid* as a homecoming achieved through civil conquest, the journey, mobility in action, emerges as intrinsic to the construction of "home."[8]

Recent research in Classics has devoted significant attention to place, space, liminality, boundaries, and their transgression. It has been some time since Michel Foucault (1986) proclaimed the coming "spatial turn" in cultural analysis (cf. Tally 2013) and Henri Lefebvre theorized the cultural and political dimensions of the "production of space," particularly that of the city. For Lefebvre, the individual's relationship with environmental systems and spatial networks help scholars articulate a vision of the participant as viewer and creator, one who inhabits the interstitial zone between active and passive. Such theories continue to influence contemporary understanding of a variety of ancient contexts, concepts, and figures, from the Ovidian flâneur to Augustan architectural intervention in Rome's urban ebb and flow.[9] Within the fields of Classics and Comparative Literature space and spatiality have been increasingly prominent in scholarly inquiry for nearly twenty years, serving as "objects" of analysis and as lenses for

---

[6] Lakoff and Johnson 1980. [7] Greenblatt 2010: 6.
[8] Jacobson discusses the role of home in Biblical and Homeric texts, concluding that stories of homes lost and regained, of hospitality offered and perverted, "emphasise the ways in which our homes establish our participation in human community–both family and nation–and the conflicts and responsibilities that emerge within and between such communities" (Jacobson 2012: 178).
[9] See Lefebvre 1970 and 1991. Also of significance is the treatment of urban motion in de Certeau 1984. In this volume, see O'Sullivan's discussion of movement in Ch. 8.

Introduction 5

viewing and interrogating literary and cultural production. The cartographic impulse of many ancient genres and the key role of "place" in texts as disparate as Greek pastoral and Propertian elegy have led Classicists to undertake the study of landscape (real and imaginary) within the subfields of history, archaeology, literary studies, and well beyond (Alcock 1993; Shipley and Salmon 1996; Alcock, Cherry, and Elsner 2001; Spencer 2010; Scott 2013). Roman literary studies offer a well-known example: work on Latin literature and the palimpsestic landscape of monumental Rome has often broken new ground concerning the impact of place on interpretation (and that of interpretation on the construction of place) (Edwards 1996; Jaeger 1997; Welch 2005). The narratological implications of thinking spatially – a methodology that our focus on the journey may bring out more fully – have also received more attention in recent years. Among Classical scholars, De Jong 2012 heralded space as the overlooked companion of time in literary interpretation, a call already heeded by Heirman and Klooster 2013.[10] The afterlife of the Odyssean journey, one of the better-studied paradigms of epic travel (Stanford 1954; Malkin 1998; Hartog 2001), has recently given rise to a significant volume of reception studies (Gardner and Murnaghan 2014). Indeed, the epic genre – and to a lesser degree the epic journey – has lately been treated in terms of space, landscape, and geography (Skempis and Ziogas 2013). The chapters in this volume aim to complement this rapidly growing body of scholarship.

An example that demonstrates the centrality of the epic journey across genres is Emily Gowers' 1994 reading of Horace *Satires* 1.5, in which the epic journey provides a point of reference and departure for the satirist's travels. Reversing, in some sense, Aeneas' foundational journey to Rome, Horace depicts himself bumbling along the route to Brundisium with none other than Vergil himself. As Gowers points out, his progress is "a series of negative choices. The roads not taken on this journey are as much part of the picture as those that are."[11] Horace flips his epic counterpoint's geographical and historical teleology, denying his audience both the site and sight of Augustan Rome and the political inner circle they crave. Another significant example of spatial research, this time focused on reading the epic genre itself, is found in William Thalmann's 2011 study of Apollonius Rhodius' *Argonautica*. Its introduction offers a detailed survey of place, space, and spatiality as conceptualized in current literary theory and Classical studies. For Thalmann, space is essential to the poem, and the *Argonautica* offers "a richly suggestive portrayal of space, the

---

[10] Cf. Purves 2010a with bibliography.   [11] Gowers 1994: 50.

physical world as it is experienced, shaped, and imagined by human beings in their social and cultural interactions."[12] It is such inherent yet often-overlooked elements of epic's textualized relationships between human actors and the physical world, in this case within a poem that is itself about movement through spaces and places, that render Thalmann's readings and methodological propositions a springboard for further interpretation. As he well puts it, "space as a concept ... encompasses geography as emplotment and measurement and in some ways relies on it; but it includes much more: in particular, human experience."[13] This potted formulation points toward the core of what the present collection is about. For our authors, space is always crafted by human experience, never a static given; it is always caught up in the transformative journey to which it is subjected through the construction of "place." And movement through literary space on epic terms allows for its measurement in ways that serve not only to imbue it with meaning, but also to define the self.

The contributions to this volume represent a first step toward filling a scholarly gap by looking at the "epic journey" with a wide lens, but with particular focus on journeys taken to and from home. Individual chapters discuss authors as distinct as Homer (Bakker, Loney) and Rutilius Namatianus (Devecka), Tacitus (Damon and Palazzolo) and Lucian (ní Mheallaigh). The voyage of the Argo is explored in Apollonius of Rhodes, in comparison with the *Aethiopica* of Heliodorus (Montiglio), and in the *Argonautica* of Valerius Flaccus (Blum). From Rome to the moon (Devecka, ní Mheallaigh), the journeys in this volume span the space between *oikos* and *oikumene*, *urbs* and *orbis* (Baragwanath, Johnston, O'Sullivan). Journeys provide the means to negotiate Greek identity in the shadow of Rome (Johnston) and to conceptualize periods of transition in Hesiodic time (Bakker). Such journeys take numerous forms: whether the foundational story of *nostos* presented in the *Odyssey* (Loney); its redirection as the structure that underlies Aeneas' (or Dido's) journey from east to west (Keith, O'Sullivan, Biggs); or Xenophon's Odyssean *nostos* in the *Anabasis* (Baragwanath). The epic journey not only provides the road map for the heroic quest, but as a framework may also be coopted into historiographical accounts, such as Germanicus' voyage to the periphery of the Roman Empire (Damon and Palazzolo) or Xenophon's account of his own return (Baragwanath). The analysis of what this generically encoded structure does in a range of literary environments enables us to better understand still-underserved topics that are as essential to the heroic

[12] Thalmann 2011: 9.   [13] Thalmann 2011: 14.

quest as a hero in motion, such as the impact of gender on the epic narrative: after all, it is not only male heroes who undertake epic voyages, nor is the home from which one travels necessarily a male-dominated sphere (Keith, Baragwanath). With such a wealth of examples, the journey emerges as a vital subject of investigation in its own right.

An understanding of the journey as a process of construction – of self, space, or society – also provides a common theme throughout the volume. What emerges from this thread of investigation is a series of interconnections that maps literary intertextuality onto the historical and geographical *loci* depicted by the ancient authors. These textualized constellations tell the story of the epic journey from Odysseus' wanderings to modern-day voyages to the moon. Through a retrospective lens, Homer becomes "home" – a point of departure to which later authors, implicitly or explicitly, return in a sort of literary *nostos*. Part I, focusing on the *Odyssey* and its reception, locates the journey in a temporal as well as spatial continuum as it traces the origins and parameters of the Iron Age present. Part II develops the idea of characterization and "home" through gendered journeys, examining in particular the relationships between different travelers and the different teleologies they posit for their journey. Part III takes the idea of the journey as a *locus* for the construction of national identity to Rome, where the movements – willing or unwilling – of various travelers define Rome's place in the wider world. Part IV, too, explores the interaction of distance and definition in the Roman Empire, examining how the spaces across which one journeys locate the center in a cosmic scheme. Each part begins with a summary and discussion of the chapters it includes. These brief editorial treatments are designed to highlight points of continuity and contrast between the various themes throughout the volume. We have decided upon these localized engagements in lieu of a frontloaded survey in the general introduction: by distributing our comments throughout the book, we hope to offer readers some waystations for reflection as they travel through its pages.

Many of the chapters in this volume are based on papers given at a conference organized by Thomas Biggs and Jessica Blum at Yale University on 25–26 April 2014. The event, entitled "Home and Away: The Epic Journey," was the first step in the reevaluation of the journey that we now aim to realize in the pages that follow. The conversations that took place between the contributors have given rise to the vast yet cohesive scope of this volume. In addition to the conference, several of the volume's chapters derive from a yearlong colloquium also held at Yale on the concept of "home," organized by Andrew C. Johnston and Alexander Loney, and from the papers delivered at a symposium on poetic journeys held at Yale in March 2014. Together, they bring into dialogue a wide range of texts, methodologies, and focal points, offering numerous pathways for the interpretive journey.

Lastly, a note on format and the use of critical editions. As editors we have crafted a level of consistency throughout the volume. Nevertheless, to provide our contributors with the scope to express their views as desired, we have allowed individual authors to use distinct forms of transliteration and some freedom in the presentation of the ancient languages for emphasis. For example, although consistency is maintained within each chapter, Hellenists have on the whole elected to maintain a form of transliteration closer to the Greek (e.g. Phaiakians), while the Latinized forms appear more often in the contributions of Romanists. In most cases contributors employ the standard critical texts as defined by the current scholarly consensus, but in some instances an author firmly believed in the need to engage with a different edition. These editorial decisions reflect our belief in the strength of the arguments as they are presented.

PART I

Odyssean Journeys

Introduction

We begin our exploration of the journey and of "home" with a look at the original epic journey, Odysseus' homeward voyage to Ithaca. The three chapters in this part explore different constructions of *nostos* (homecoming) in time as well as space, reading (the model of) Odysseus' journey as a process that shapes both the individual hero and the world around him. The first two chapters focus on the *Odyssey* itself, examining the interactions between the hero and those he encounters along his route. In both, the hero's journey provides a point of contact between the worlds of men, monsters, gods, and, through this interaction, locates the human race in a wider moral universe. The first and last chapters focus on the temporal significance of the journey, mapping chronological progress onto the spatial dimension. Both take as their starting point the shift between the different Ages of Man in, first, the *Odyssey* (Bakker) and, second, the *Argonautica* of Valerius Flaccus (Blum). For all three chapters, the framework of the journey offers a space in which the hero's (or heroes') response to a changing world reflects and encodes the proper bounds of human behavior.

Egbert Bakker's contribution discusses the *Odyssey* as a narrative of transition between the Golden and Iron Ages. Encompassing both historical and Hesiodic constructions of the Ages of Man, he brings to light the tensions between chronological periods mapped onto the geography of Odysseus' journey. Bakker shows how the contrasts between opulence and scarcity, Iliadic heroes and daily violence, trace the transition from the Bronze to the Iron Age via the Golden Age landscapes that appear along his route. Odysseus' return from Troy, then, ushers in a new world, bringing both protagonist and audience into a harsh present through the hero's *nostos* narrative. Odysseus' homecoming and reunion with his family represent the new realities of human life, bridging the gap between the heroic world of Troy and the historical audience viewing it from afar. Odysseus' journey defines the Iron Age parameters of the post-Homeric world.

In the next chapter, Alexander Loney addresses the narrative and thematic device of *pompē* (conveyance) as an essential aspect of Odysseus' homecoming. Defining conveyance as a cooperative exercise, he examines instances of failed or delayed homecomings through the lens of Odysseus' relationships with those he encounters. Through these case studies Loney shows the mutual good faith required on both sides in order to achieve homecoming, suggesting that Odysseus' final, successful *pompē* is an indication of his ethical as well as geographical progress. As for Bakker, the interactions that shape Odysseus' journey trace out a new moral code for the post-Iliadic world by demonstrating the importance of reciprocal relationships.

In the final chapter, Jessica Blum takes the concept of the journey as a space that defines ethical boundaries into the Latin epic tradition, examining Valerius Flaccus' *Argonautica* as an imperial Roman response to the *Odyssey*. She suggests that the Argonauts' imitation of their (literary) ancestral *exempla* represents a fruitless desire to return to the lost world of Homeric epic, and that this desire operates in tension with Jupiter's plans for forward progress: the behavioral models of the past do not necessarily translate into the present. In effect, Valerius' Argonauts experience the same temporal disjuncture as Odysseus during his return home from the Trojan War. Using the multiple generic teleologies embedded in the Argonautic myth – epic triumph, elegiac romance, tragic violence – Blum shows how the Argonauts' *imitatio* of martial-epic models may lead to unexpected outcomes in their changing world. Like Odysseus, the Argo's crew confronts a world in transition from heroic past to Iron Age present; and their journey to Colchis thereby calls into question the value of heroic and literary *imitatio*.

The first part of the volume thus brings to light a number of fault lines in the *Odyssey*'s paradigm of the epic journey: the tensions between progress and regress; the possibility of alternate generic frameworks coexisting alongside the "epic"; the ethical implications of journeys across space and time. The three chapters anticipate many points of discussion that will animate the following parts, including questions of temporality, genre, and the structure of the epic journey as a performance space for heroes, villains, and the wider social and literary communities in which they participate.

CHAPTER 2

In and Out of the Golden Age: A Hesiodic Reading of the Odyssey

Egbert J. Bakker

The *Odyssey* is a poem of travel and movement, from outbound (away from Troy) to inbound (back to Ithaca). The world of Odysseus is a world full of wanderers, traveling merchants, adventurers, and pirates. As commentators from Finley to Malkin have noticed, this world of people on the move, including the poem's principal character, owes much to the post-Mycenaean reality of the Dark Ages and early Archaic Age, with the Phoenicians roaming the Mediterranean and the Greeks beginning their first colonial experiments. In mythico-historical time this is a world in which the Age of Heroes is coming to an end, in which the Trojan War is already fading into the past, in the process of becoming a subject for epic song.[1]

For the archaeologists this is the Iron Age, following on the second-millennium Bronze Age: the age of the palatial societies of Mycenaean Greece; of the height of Hittite civilization in the East; and the New Kingdom in Egypt. Recent paleobotanical research seems to have produced evidence for climate change – severe and prolonged drought in the Eastern Mediterranean basin – as a leading factor in the collapse of all these advanced civilizations, to which subsequent centuries would look back as a time of heroes, a heroic age enjoying more prosperity than their own "Iron Age" could ever dream of.[2]

Now metals, bronze and iron, or even gold, are not the exclusive prerogative of the archaeologists, and we can use them also to mark periods not in archaeological time, but in mythical time. The motivation to do this comes from Hesiod, of course, where at the beginning of the *Works*

---

[1] A classic statement of the *Odyssey*'s self-conscious awareness of being "post-war," representing a world in which *kleos* has to be taken in the second degree, is Segal 1994: 85–109 ("*Kleos* and its Ironies").
[2] For climate change, see Kaniewski et al. 2010, Neumann 1993. A suggestive ancient testimony is Arist. *Metaph.* 352a7–17 (on Mycenae being fertile at the time of the Trojan War and barren in Aristotle's time). In Bakker 2013 I argue that the thematic importance of meat in the *Odyssey* reflects an Iron Age sensibility of its relative scarcity, as opposed to the unproblematic availability of meat animals in the (heroic) *Iliad*.

and *Days* (ll. 109–78) we encounter the mythical history of mankind in terms of the five races of man, from Gold through Silver and Bronze via the race of Heroes, the fourth race, to the Iron race of the present, the fifth and last.

In this chapter I will use the symbolism of metals as a navigational tool to chart Odysseus' return in the *Odyssey*, a poem of and about the Iron Age. The Iron Age is an era that is not merely suggested in the *Odyssey*, with its realistic descriptions of agricultural realities: the return of Odysseus marks as such the end of the Heroic Age. The *Odyssey* enforces the beginning of the Iron Age, performatively, in and through the telling of its story.[3] In departing from Troy Odysseus leaves the Heroic Age, which is for modern archaeology the Bronze Age. But the homebound journey is not straight sailing into the Iron Age, the world of Ithaca *and* that of the *Odyssey*'s historical audiences; Odysseus arrives in fantastic, enchanting, and terrifying places for which gold, rather than bronze or iron, is the appropriate metallic label. Odysseus' travels take place not only in space but also in time; they are sandwiched as a Golden Age between the heroic Bronze Age of the *Iliad* and the Iron Age of his longed-for homeland.

In Hesiod the Golden race of men is distinguished from the race of Heroes, but there are a number of ways in which these two races, numbers one and four in Hesiod's temporal sequence, are not so different as they might seem at first sight.[4] Let us first look at the way in which the Golden race of men is described in Hesiod:

Χρύσεον μὲν πρώτιστα γένος μερόπων ἀνθρώπων
ἀθάνατοι ποίησαν Ὀλύμπια δώματ' ἔχοντες.
οἳ μὲν ἐπὶ Κρόνου ἦσαν, ὅτ' οὐρανῷ ἐμβασίλευεν·
ὥστε θεοὶ δ' ἔζωον ἀκηδέα θυμὸν ἔχοντες
νόσφιν ἄτερ τε πόνων καὶ ὀιζύος, οὐδέ τι δειλὸν
γῆρας ἐπῆν, αἰεὶ δὲ πόδας καὶ χεῖρας ὁμοῖοι
τέρποντ' ἐν θαλίῃσι, κακῶν ἔκτοσθεν ἁπάντων·
θνῆσκον δ' ὥσθ' ὕπνῳ δεδμημένοι· ἐσθλὰ δὲ πάντα
τοῖσιν ἔην· καρπὸν δ' ἔφερε ζείδωρος ἄρουρα
αὐτομάτη πολλόν τε καὶ ἄφθονον· οἳ δ' ἐθελημοὶ
ἥσυχοι ἔργ' ἐνέμοντο σὺν ἐσθλοῖσιν πολέεσσιν.
(Hes. *Op.* 109–19)

First it was the golden race of mortal men
that the immortal gods made, who dwell on Olympos.

---

[3] For a reading of the *Odyssey* as "end point" with emphasis on Telemachus, see Martin 1993.
[4] Cf. Scodel 1982: 38–9, on the basis of a reading of Hes. fr. 204.99–100 M-W (Zeus intent on annihilating the race of the ἡμίθεοι in connection with *Il.* 12.23).

These men were in the time of Kronos, when he was king in the sky;
like gods they lived with a spirit free of cares
far from toil and misery, nor came helpless
old age upon them, and always equal in the strength of their feet and hands
they delighted in feasts, far from all that is harmful.
They would die as if subdued by sleep; everything good
was their share, and it carried fruit, the barley-giving field,
all of its own accord, plentiful and unstinting. And willingly
they lived on their land in quiet and peace, blessed with many excellent
   possessions.

We see that this was a time before the reign of Zeus, when Kronos was king in the sky; there was no disease, as people died peacefully in old age; there was continuous feasting (ἐν θαλίῃσι); and there was natural agricultural abundance – no toil was needed to have a rich harvest, and the barley-giving earth carried fruit all of its own accord (καρπὸν δ' ἔφερε ζείδωρος ἄρουρα). These living conditions for the Golden race of humans are strikingly similar to those of the heroes of the fourth race in their afterlife, on the Isles of the Blessed:

> τοῖς δὲ δίχ' ἀνθρώπων βίοτον καὶ ἤθε' ὀπάσσας
> Ζεὺς Κρονίδης κατένασσε πατὴρ ἐς πείρατα γαίης.
> καὶ τοὶ μὲν ναίουσιν ἀκηδέα θυμὸν ἔχοντες
> ἐν μακάρων νήσοισι παρ' Ὠκεανὸν βαθυδίνην,
> ὄλβιοι ἥρωες, τοῖσιν μελιηδέα καρπὸν
> τρὶς ἔτεος θάλλοντα φέρει ζείδωρος ἄρουρα.
>   (Hes. Op. 168–73)

For them he provided livelihood and an abode far away from humans,
father Zeus the son of Kronos, and he established them at the edges
   of the earth.
And these live there with a spirit free of care,
on the Isles of the Blessed beside Okeanos of the deep eddies,
happy heroes, for whom <it is> honey-sweet fruit
flowering three times in the year <that> the barley-giving field carries.

Again there is the ζείδωρος ἄρουρα formula, this time to bring out the fact that the earth bears fruit *thrice* per year for these blessed heroes. From other sources, such as Pindar's second *Olympian Ode*, we learn that this is where Kronos still is lord, even though he has been vanquished by Zeus, and removed from earth, where Iron Age conditions now obtain.[5]

---

[5] Pind. *Ol.* 2.68–73; note that Hesiod describes the "just city" in terms reminiscent of the description of the life of the Golden race: *Op.* 225–37, esp. 231 (θαλίῃς δὲ μεμηλότα ἔργα νέμονται) and 237 (καρπὸν δὲ φέρει ζείδωρος ἄρουρα).

Now the Golden Age is more than an "objective" period in historical or mythical time; it is good to think with: it can function as the projection of any number of wishes and fantasies. For the distressed Iron Age subsistence farmer it becomes a time preceding agriculture, when the field was αὐτομάτη and the produce grew without the need of human intervention or toil. Occurring before the introduction of sacrifice, the prime religious ritual of the Iron Age, the Golden Age becomes a place of plenty, a land of Cocagne, where meat is limitlessly available; or alternatively, it becomes a time *before* meat eating, a land without blood sacrifice and without the killing of domesticated animals.[6]

And because of its being such a desirable object of utopian fantasy the Golden Age tends to be thought of as something you can actually attain or experience. A public festival with sacrifices and abundant meat for everyone can be framed as a temporary return of the Golden Age; this is particularly obvious in the case of the Kronia, the festival of Kronos, during which the established order would be temporarily reversed, with masters serving slaves and abundant food and drink for everyone.[7] A more informal occasion for smaller groups, but no less important, would be the symposium, the temporary relief from cares and sorrows in the wine-induced *euphrosúnē* that can be felt as a temporary return of the Golden Age – or, conversely, one can construe the Golden Age as a permanent state of sympotic bliss (think of the *thaliai* in Hesiod's description of the life of the Golden race).[8] Consider in this respect the wish of the Theognidean symposiast:

> ὧδ' εἶναι καὶ ἄμεινον· εὔφρονα θυμὸν ἔχοντας
> νόσφι μεριμνάων εὐφροσύνως διάγειν
> τερπομένους, τηλοῦ δὲ κακὰς ἀπὸ κῆρας ἀμῦναι
> γῆράς τ' οὐλόμενον καὶ θανάτοιο τέλος.
> (*Theogn.* 765–8)

(I wish it could be) like this or better: that we could pass the
time in *euphrosúnē*
with festive spirit far from all cares,
enjoying ourselves; and that we could fend off far from us the evil spirits,
and accursed old age and the end point of death.

---

[6] For utopian fantasies of Golden Age plenty in comedy, see Ceccarelli 1996; vegetarian paradise: Emp. B128 DK.
[7] See Versnel 1987.
[8] On the symposium seen in terms of past life and practice (including the Golden Age), see Topper 2012.

In the symposium one can temporarily forget about old age, diseases, sorrow, and misfortunes to attain for the moment the condition of the members of the Golden race.

But the Golden Age is not blissful without problems or complications. As H. S. Versnel has demonstrated, the figure of Kronos and the character of the Golden Age he inhabits are deeply ambiguous, in systematic ways.[9] Opposed to the idea of the wise and good king who governs peacefully over a land of easy abundance free of labor and toil is the image of the infanticide, the teknophagous monster that swallows his own offspring in a reign of lawlessness and terror. The Golden Age in this way embodies the deep ambiguity of the idea "lawless": it equally applies to a situation where there is no *need* for laws, a precultural peaceful and harmonious situation, and to what happens when there *are* neither laws nor justice. The lack of hardship and toil is indissolubly linked with a lack of laws and rules, and so the Golden Age in its double-edged nature comes to be the reverse of human civilization as a compromise: scarcity and toil in justice is negatively mirrored by carefree abundance in lawlessness.

Such ambiguity is especially acute in the symposium, where the wine not only creates the euphoria of *euphrosúnē*, but also increases the likelihood of brawls and violence. This double-edged situation seems to be what is envisaged in Xenophanes' metasympotic elegy (1W), which after a description of an idealized sympotic setting turns in the second half to prescription and to reflection on good and bad sympotic behavior:[10]

> χρὴ δὲ πρῶτον μὲν θεὸν ὑμνεῖν εὔφρονας ἄνδρας
> εὐφήμοις μύθοις καὶ καθαροῖσι λόγοις,
> σπείσαντάς τε καὶ εὐξαμένους τὰ δίκαια δύνασθαι
> πρήσσειν· ταῦτα γὰρ ὦν ἐστι προχειρότερον,
> οὐχ ὕβρεις· πίνειν δ' ὁπόσον κεν ἔχων ἀφίκοιο
> οἴκαδ' ἄνευ προπόλου μὴ πάνυ γηραλέος.
> ἀνδρῶν δ' αἰνεῖν τοῦτον ὃς ἐσθλὰ πιὼν ἀναφαίνει,
> ὡς ἦι μνημοσύνη καὶ τόνος ἀμφ' ἀρετῆς,
> οὔ τι μάχας διέπειν Τιτήνων οὐδὲ Γιγάντων
> οὐδὲ < > Κενταύρων, πλάσμα<τα> τῶν προτέρων,
> ἢ στάσιας σφεδανάς· τοῖς οὐδὲν χρηστὸν ἔνεστιν·
> θεῶν <δὲ> προμηθείην αἰὲν ἔχειν ἀγαθήν.
> (Xenophanes 1.13–24W)

Men in sympotic bliss need first of all to hymn the god
with propitious tales and pure speech,

---

[9] See in detail Versnel 1987.
[10] On Xenophanes 1W in terms of "metasympotics," see Hobden 2013: 25–8.

> after libation and prayer to be able to do
> what is just, for that is the obvious thing to do,
> not brawls. Drink as much as you are able to hold and still
> get back home without a servant, unless you are very old.
> Of men praise that one who produces words of value even when
>   drinking heavily,
> so that there be mindfulness and competition over excellence.
> Do not in any way engage in the battles of Titans or of Giants,
> nor of the Centaurs, figments of the imagination of past generations,
> nor in violent strife. There is nothing of use in such practices.
> Hold the gods in great consideration.

The Titanomachy, Gigantomachy, and Centauromachy are not merely subjects of song; the songs are sympotic action of a questionable nature, action that can easily get out of hand.[11] Too much narrated violence coupled with too much wine can easily spill over into real violence. The Centaurs are thematically even more tightly linked to the sympotic context than the Titans and the Giants, as their violence is unleashed precisely by an excess of wine. Centaurs are the mythical template for the bad symposiast. The apex of their anti-sympotic behavior is the way they disrupted the wedding feast of Perithous, which leads to the Centauromachy, the battle of Centaurs and Lapiths, that Xenophanes is referring to.

By being a good symposiast, then, you can bring the Golden Age closer – or in misbehaving you can act out the violent side of the Golden Age. The other way to (re)gain contact with Golden Age condition is to move in space, to travel to the edges of the world; the farther you travel in space, the closer you will come back in time to the Golden Age. The Aethiopians in Homer and Herodotus come to mind, the ἔσχατοι ἀνδρῶν who still dine with the gods, just as the human race in general did in the Golden Age; or the Hyperboreans and the "milk-drinking Abioi, who are the most just of humans" (*Il.* 13.6).[12]

The *Odyssey* presents Odysseus as both a (proto-)symposiast and a cosmopolitan traveler. Odysseus has seen and experienced what the average Greek in his homeland can only dream about. He has dined with Aiolos, whose never-ending steak dinner enjoyed on his floating island is every beef-hungry Greek's ultimate food fantasy; he has seen the Lotus-Eaters, whose carefree existence is in stark contrast with the restless and

---

[11] On the poem's moral and "philosophical" outlook, see Marcovich 1978; Granger 2007. Xenophanes precedes Plato in singling out Gigantomachies as undesirable subjects for poetry: cf. Pl. *Resp.* 378C.
[12] Aethiopians: *Il.* 1.423; *Od.* 1.22–3; Hdt. 3.20–5.

In and Out of the Golden Age

dangerous life on the high seas that is so typical of the Iron Age merchant; he has enjoyed the disquieting and supernatural abundance in Circe's palace, where animals and their flesh may not be what they seem to be; but the adventure richest in themes pertaining both to Golden Age and the symposium is his encounter with Polyphemos the Cyclops.[13]

That adventure resonates with the context in which it is presented. At the court of Alkinoos the king of the Phaeacians a banquet – a symposium – is held in Odysseus' honor. The Cyclops story is part of Odysseus' great after-dinner speech at that occasion, the *Apologoi*. Odysseus begins the speech by describing the festive sympotic setting in lines that are even more essential for sympotic harmony and poetics than Xenophanes' poem:[14]

Ἀλκίνοε κρεῖον, πάντων ἀριδείκετε λαῶν,
ἦ τοι μὲν τόδε καλὸν ἀκουέμεν ἐστὶν ἀοιδοῦ
τοιοῦδ᾽, οἷος ὅδ᾽ ἐστί, θεοῖσ᾽ ἐναλίγκιος αὐδήν.
οὐ γὰρ ἐγώ γέ τί φημι τέλος χαριέστερον εἶναι
ἢ ὅτ᾽ ἐϋφροσύνη μὲν ἔχῃ κατὰ δῆμον ἅπαντα,
δαιτυμόνες δ᾽ ἀνὰ δώματ᾽ ἀκουάζωνται ἀοιδοῦ
ἥμενοι ἑξείης, παρὰ δὲ πλήθωσι τράπεζαι
σίτου καὶ κρειῶν, μέθυ δ᾽ ἐκ κρητῆρος ἀφύσσων
οἰνοχόος φορέῃσι καὶ ἐγχείῃ δεπάεσσι·
τοῦτό τί μοι κάλλιστον ἐνὶ φρεσὶν εἴδεται εἶναι.
(*Od.* 9.2–11)

Lord Alkinoos, illustrious among the people,
I tell you this is the peak of beauty, to listen to the singer,
such as this man here is, equal to the gods in his voice.
No, I think there is nothing that has more grace and charm
than when <u>sympotic festivity</u> holds sway over the entire population,
and the table guests around the house listen to the singer,
being seated in a row, and nearby the tables are loaded
with bread and meat, and drawing the wine from the crater
the wine-pourer carries it around and fills up the goblets.
That is what seems to me in my mind to be the most beautiful
   thing that exists.

These lines were known in antiquity as the Golden Verses, and they were recited at symposia, libations, and other festive occasions.[15] Odysseus certainly does justice to this extraordinary event, which contrasts so starkly

---

[13] An anthropological background for reading the Circe episode, which is compatible with later allegorizing readings of the passage, is offered in Bakker 2013: 80–91.
[14] For a reading of this passage against the background of Greek sympotic culture, see Ford 1999. Wecowski 2002 discusses the sympotic elements in Homer.
[15] *Cert. Hom. et Hes.* 90–4.

with the diseased symposium that will later take place in his own palace at Ithaca: he is a gifted storyteller, an ideal symposiast, whose tale will be praised by the audience as being equal to that of a real poet (11.367–9). But he does violate Xenophanes' rule about not bringing up subjects that are inappropriate at the symposium, since he tells the tale of his violent dealings with the worst symposiast imaginable, Polyphemos the Cyclops, drinker of milk and eater of cheese – and human flesh. Odysseus' account reconfirms the deeply ambiguous nature of the Golden Age. He introduces the Cyclopes and their society as follows:

> Κυκλώπων δ' ἐς γαῖαν ὑπερφιάλων ἀθεμίστων
> ἱκόμεθ', οἵ ῥα θεοῖσι πεποιθότες ἀθανάτοισιν
> οὔτε φυτεύουσιν χερσὶν φυτὸν οὔτ' ἀρόωσιν,
> ἀλλὰ τά γ' ἄσπαρτα καὶ ἀνήροτα πάντα φύονται,
> πυροὶ καὶ κριθαὶ ἠδ' ἄμπελοι, αἵ τε φέρουσιν
> οἶνον ἐριστάφυλον, καί σφιν Διὸς ὄμβρος ἀέξει.
> τοῖσιν δ' οὔτ' ἀγοραὶ βουληφόροι οὔτε θέμιστες,
> ἀλλ' οἵ γ' ὑψηλῶν ὀρέων ναίουσι κάρηνα
> ἐν σπέεσι γλαφυροῖσι, θεμιστεύει δὲ ἕκαστος
> παίδων ἠδ' ἀλόχων, οὐδ' ἀλλήλων ἀλέγουσι.
> (*Od.* 9.106–15)

> It was the land of the Cyclopes, <u>overweening and lawless</u>
> that we now reached; these, trusting the gods immortal,
> do not plant crops with their hands, nor do they plow the earth;
> no, unsown and unplowed everything grows for them:
> wheat, barley, and vines that carry
> wine from rich grapes, and <u>the rain from Zeus</u> makes everything thrive.
> For these no assemblies where council is made, nor custom of law;
> instead, they inhabit the peaks of tall mountains,
> living in hollow caves, and each of them lays down the law
> for his wife and children, nor do they care about each other.

This description is a prime example of the typical Greek habit of cultural self-definition through polarity. The negative characterization of Cyclopean society – no agricultural labor and no collective decision making – highlights by contrast the conventional Greek conception of culture that we see in the Hesiodic *Works and Days*: agriculture with political organization aimed at justice.[16]

Some ancient readers, such as Porphyry, place emphasis on the detail that the Cyclopes are trusting in the immortal gods (θεοῖσι πεποιθότες

---

[16] On the Golden Age overtones of the Cyclops habitat, see Kirk 1970: 167–8; Mondi 1983: 19; Vidal-Naquet 1986: 21–2; Nieto-Hernández 2000: 349–50.

ἀθανάτοισιν) and read the passage as a positive description of the Cyclops community as a simple and god-fearing society; they have no laws or assemblies because they don't *need* any, being naturally just.[17] Only Polyphemos, they argue, is a dangerous, blasphemous cannibal. In modern scholarship this line of thought is picked up by Philip Mondi, who argues that these Cyclopes are in fact the same as the Cyclopes of the Hesiodic *Theogony*, who helped Zeus in his battle with Kronos and the Titans by crafting the thunderbolt for him; for this they were rewarded with this pleasant retirement. Odysseus' opponent is seen as the intrusion of the well-known folktale motif of the blinded ogre into an independent mythical conception.[18]

It is true that the text informs us that Polyphemos is a loner who lives apart from his fellow Cyclopes (9.188–9); but there is no gain in assuming that the other Cyclopes, whom we never get to see anyway, are just and law-abiding. And the lawlessness of this utopian pastoralist community fits in very well with the ambiguous, double-edged nature of the Golden Age as described by Versnel. We could add that the adjective used to characterize the Cyclops community – ὑπερφίαλος – may have sympotic overtones: "what exceeds the rim of the φιάλη, the drinking vessel," a sympotic term denoting excess in wine consumption.[19]

Before Odysseus encounters the inhabitants of this land, he disembarks on an island of which he gives an instructive description. The Cyclopes cannot reach it, because they have no ships (9.125) – this is a continuation of the catalog of negated features; the absence of navigation is in fact another telltale feature of the Golden Age: seafaring and traveling is for anxious, greedy, and restless Iron Age people.[20] Odysseus looks at this land, which he reaches by ship, with the eyes of the colonist, the city-founder: he sees grassy meadows good for cattle-grazing; he sees deep and fertile plow land; and an excellent natural harbor – the way he describes all this suggests that the poem's audience was invited to look at it as the place

---

[17] Porph. *Quest. hom.* 9.106 ff.; schol. *Od.* 9.106–7. This reading also involves understanding ὑπερφιάλων not in a moral sense, but as referring to the Cyclopes' body size (τῶν μεγαλοφυῶν τῷ σώματι).
[18] Mondi 1983: 23–4; Hesiodic Cyclopes: Hes. *Theog.* 139–46; the Cyclops as instantiation of the folktale motif of the blinded ogre: Hackman 1904; Frazer 1921, vol. II: 404–55; Germain 1954: 55–65; Glenn 1971. Overviews of the folktale complex can be found in Page 1955: 3–20; Cook 1995: 93; and Burgess 2001: 94–5.
[19] Cf. πεπληρωμέναις φιάλαις as gloss on ὑπερφιάλοισιν (schol. Q ad *Od.* 16.271).
[20] Note that the inhabitants of the "just city" in the *Works and Days* do not board ships (*Op.* 236–7); cf. n. 5 above.

to found a city.[21] But the most conspicuous thing about this island is the wildlife. The place teems with wild goats that are "stirred up" by their guardians the nymphs (9.154) in order to be caught.[22] After an easy and comfortable hunt there is an extended feast on the beach:

ὣς τότε μὲν πρόπαν ἦμαρ ἐς ἠέλιον καταδύντα
ἥμεθα δαινύμενοι κρέα τ' ἄσπετα καὶ μέθυ ἡδύ.
(*Od.* 9.161–2)

This way the whole day till sunset
we sat there feasting on limitless meat and sweet wine.

This is a vision of the Golden Age; not an existence free of agricultural toil but as a land of Cocagne, a place where the fish and other delicacies jump into the frying pan of their own accord, eager to be cooked and consumed; where there is unproblematic, unencumbered abundance and its happy and unembarrassed consumption.

Such conditions can never last, and if there is anyone who knows this, it is Odysseus. Even when he and the Companions are gorging on the "innumerable meats," the κρέα ἄσπετα, of the wild goats, he hears the bleating of the domesticated sheep of the Cyclopes on the other side of the strait (9.166–7). This is not a gesture of decadence, the creation of new cravings when all needs have been fulfilled; this is progress. Odysseus the restless seafarer and wanderer is the man of the Iron Age. He knows that limitless meat acquired through hunting, meat that cannot be sacrificed to the gods, is less desirable than the strictly limited meat of domesticated animals that need to be sacrificed. And the owner of those farmed, essential animals is Polyphemos the Cyclops, the object of Odysseus' expedition.

Polyphemos, it is hard to believe, is a vegetarian. There is no suggestion whatsoever in Odysseus' tale that the Cyclops eats his sheep. He talks to them, which can lead to mock-epic effects, as when he addresses his ram with the phrase μακρὰ βιβάς "making great strides," which is also applied to heroes such as Ajax in the *Iliad*.[23] But we can also see this as a consequence of the pre-sacrificial stage of development, when the boundaries between humans and animals (as well as between humans and gods) were not yet clear-cut.

---

[21] Kirk 1970: 165; Vidal-Naquet 1986: 21; Dougherty 1993: 21; Malkin 1998: 160; Bakker 2013: 60.
[22] The nymphs can be seen as mistresses of animals in a (from a Greek point of view) pre-sacrificial vision of human existence as a hunt; see Bakker 2013: 60–2, 80–4.
[23] *Od.* 9.450; cf. *Il.* 7.213; 15.307, etc. Cf. *Od.* 9.308: κλυτὰ μῆλα.

The vegetarian lifestyle of Polyphemos, who does not eat the animals of his flock, is a reflex of his Golden Age existence. But his is a precarious Golden Age, which he upholds at his own peril, because Kronos is now no longer king in the sky. Zeus is, and it is the "rain of Zeus" (Διὸς ὄμβρος, 9.111) that makes Polyphemos' plants grow, as we saw. The pre-sacrificial stage is now over, because Zeus is the god of sacrifice. By the sacrificial logic of the Iron Age, not eating meat is not sacrificing, and not sacrificing is rejecting communication with Zeus and the Olympians. And this is exactly what Polyphemos says he does, when he answers Odysseus' attempts to establish some sort of relationship with him under the tutelage of the laws of Zeus Xeineios, Zeus the protector of guests and travelers:

ἀλλ' αἰδεῖο, φέριστε, θεούς· ἱκέται δέ τοί εἰμεν.
Ζεὺς δ' ἐπιτιμήτωρ ἱκετάων τε ξείνων τε,
ξείνιος, ὃς ξείνοισιν ἅμ' αἰδοίοισιν ὀπηδεῖ.'
   ὣς ἐφάμην, ὁ δέ μ' αὐτίκ' ἀμείβετο νηλέϊ θυμῷ·
'νήπιός εἰς, ὦ ξεῖν', ἢ τηλόθεν εἰλήλουθας,
ὅς με θεοὺς κέλεαι ἢ δειδίμεν ἢ ἀλέασθαι.
οὐ γὰρ Κύκλωπες Διὸς αἰγιόχου ἀλέγουσιν
οὐδὲ θεῶν μακάρων, ἐπεὶ ἦ πολὺ φέρτεροί εἰμεν·
οὐδ' ἂν ἐγὼ Διὸς ἔχθος ἀλευάμενος πεφιδοίμην
οὔτε σεῦ οὔθ' ἑτάρων, εἰ μὴ θυμός με κελεύοι.
               (Od. 9.269–78)

"Please show reverence for the gods, my friend; we are suppliants.
Zeus is the avenger of suppliants and strangers,
Zeus Xeinios, the companion of strangers who deserve respect."
This is how I spoke, and he replied to me immediately, with merciless spirit:
"You are a fool, stranger, or else you come from far away,
in telling me to fear or shun the gods.
You should know that the Cyclopes do not care about Zeus who holds
   the aigis,
nor about the other blessed gods, because, I'm telling you, we are
   far stronger.
I would never spare you or your companions just to avoid the hostility
   of Zeus.
No, I would only spare you if I wanted to."

And the Cyclops makes good on his words by snatching two of Odysseus' companions, smashing them to the ground, and devouring them raw.

If this is the Golden Age, then this is obviously its violent, lawless side. Polyphemos' vegetarianism is at the same time peaceful and rustic *and* a direct defiance of Zeus and his reign. Polyphemos is as ambiguous as Kronos. In fact, he is beginning to look like Kronos, as he devours his adversaries, just as Kronos swallowed his own children.[24] We may think of even that gruesome act as inherently ambiguous, for wasn't Kronos trying to prevent his offspring from overthrowing his just and peaceful Golden Age kingdom? Polyphemos, too, by ingesting Odysseus' companions is initiating the end of his private paradise, which falls apart as a violent and failed symposium.

Odysseus has the weapon of the wine, the sympotic defense par excellence. Wine is one of the principal attainments from the Iron Age, the very substance of the *euphrosúnē* produced in and by the symposium. Wine, in fact, is the substitute for the Golden Age in the symposium – and just as double-edged as the happy condition it is meant to represent. We may perhaps infer that in the Greek conception the men of the Golden Age did not need, or even know, wine. Herodotus' Aethiopians are scornful and dismissive of all the tokens of civilization that Cambyses' messengers show them, except for the wine, which they do not know and like immensely (Hdt. 3.22.3–4). The Cyclops likewise is very pleased with Maron's wine.[25] Even though the Cyclopes are said to have "wine from rich grapes" in Odysseus' description (see above), it is not clear that they know anything beyond grapes as fruit that grows through the "rain of Zeus." In any case Polyphemos does not seem to be familiar with its workings. And in addition he commits the serious breach of symposium etiquette by drinking this very potent wine pure, circumventing the essential *kratêr*, where the wine is mixed with water. But it becomes worse when he puts his vinous pleasure into words:

> καὶ γὰρ Κυκλώπεσσι φέρει ζείδωρος ἄρουρα
> οἶνον ἐριστάφυλον, καί σφιν Διὸς ὄμβρος ἀέξει·
> ἀλλὰ τόδ' ἀμβροσίης καὶ νέκταρός ἐστιν ἀπορρώξ.
> (*Od.* 9.357–9)

> Also for the Cyclopes does the barley-giving field bear
> wine from rich grapes, and the rain from Zeus makes everything thrive;
> but this here is pure ambrosia and nectar.

Polyphemos confuses all kinds of categories; he uses Golden Age language (φέρει ζείδωρος ἄρουρα – cf. Hes. *Op.* 117, 173, 237) for his own world, where everything depends on the rain of Zeus; and then he mistakes Maron's wine, a blend of nature and of human culture, for the food of

---

[24] See Nieto-Hernández 2000: 351.
[25] *Od.* 9.353 ἥσατο δ' αἰνῶς; cf. Hdt. 3.22.3 ὑπερησθεὶς τῷ πόματι.

the gods: nectar and ambrosia. The rest is history, of course, when Polyphemos falls victim to Odysseus' naming trick, passes out in drunken stupor, loses his eye, and has a rude awakening: one disastrous symposium took him from the Golden Age into the bleak reality of the Iron Age. Of particular interest here are the words with which his Cyclopian neighbors walk away when they have heard from Polyphemos inside his cave that "nobody" is killing him:

> εἰ μὲν δὴ μή τίς σε βιάζεται οἶον ἐόντα,
> νοῦσόν γ' οὔ πως ἔστι Διὸς μεγάλου ἀλέασθαι
> (*Od.* 9.410–11)
>
> Well, if nobody harms you and you are alone in your cave,
> there is no way to avoid the disease of great Zeus.

The neighbors remind Polyphemos that not only do they enjoy the rain of Zeus, but they are also subject to the reign of Zeus: there is no way to escape the disease that comes from Zeus. Disease is in fact a signature feature of the Iron Age – the Golden race didn't yet know disease: we saw in Hesiod's description that the members of the Golden race of men died peacefully in their sleep, far from all suffering (*Op.* 115–16). We are reminded here of the story that precedes the account of the five races, the story of Pandora, the first woman, who opened the fateful jar sent by Zeus and the other Olympian gods, and so released the diseases that oppress mankind in the Iron Age:

> ἄλλα δὲ μυρία λυγρὰ κατ' ἀνθρώπους ἀλάληται·
> πλείη μὲν γὰρ γαῖα κακῶν, πλείη δὲ θάλασσα·
> νοῦσοι δ' ἀνθρώποισιν ἐφ' ἡμέρῃ, αἳ δ' ἐπὶ νυκτὶ
> αὐτόματοι φοιτῶσι κακὰ θνητοῖσι φέρουσαι
> σιγῇ, ἐπεὶ φωνὴν ἐξείλετο μητίετα Ζεύς.
> οὕτως οὔ τί πη ἔστι Διὸς νόον ἐξαλέασθαι.
> (Hes. *Op.* 100–5)
>
> And a myriad of further grievous afflictions swirl around all of humanity;
> the earth is full of evils, full is the sea:
> diseases come to visit humans, in the day, and some at night,
> all of their own accord, carrying woes to mortals –
> silently, since Zeus of the councils has taken their voice away.
> Thus there is no way to avoid the mind of Zeus.

Whereas for the Golden race the earth is *automatos*, carrying fruit, for Pandora's descendants it is the diseases that are *automatoi*, carrying evil and suffering. The final verse of the Pandora episode (*Op.* 105) resonates with the advice that the Cyclopes give to their wounded neighbor: the *nóos* of

Zeus becomes the *nósos* of Zeus, but from the point of view of the Iron Age this amounts to the same thing.[26]

Polyphemos' blinding, then, puts an end to his Golden Age. If he came to occupy the role of Kronos, the displaced king of the Golden Age, then Odysseus comes to play the role of Zeus, as is argued by Pura Nieto-Hernández.[27] Both Zeus and Odysseus achieve their victories through a combination of violence and ruse, *bía* and *mētis*. In line with this Odysseus presents himself as the instrument of the punishment of the gods when he taunts the Cyclops from the relative safety of his boat:

> Κύκλωψ, οὐκ ἄρ' ἔμελλες ἀνάλκιδος ἀνδρὸς ἑταίρους
> ἔδμεναι ἐν σπῆϊ γλαφυρῷ κρατερῆφι βίηφι.
> καὶ λίην σέ γ' ἔμελλε κιχήσεσθαι κακὰ ἔργα,
> σχέτλι', ἐπεὶ ξείνους οὐχ ἅζεο σῷ ἐνὶ οἴκῳ
> ἐσθέμεναι· τῶ σε Ζεὺς τείσατο καὶ θεοὶ ἄλλοι
> (*Od.* 9.475–9)

> Cyclops, you now know that in your hollow cave and with your brute force
> you were not going to eat the companions of a man without defense.
> Bad things were going to hit you,
> you terrible brute, since you did not stand back in awe from eating the strangers in your house. That is why Zeus has taken revenge on you and also the other gods.

The Cyclops was not just a brute, a sinner; he got it completely backward as regards the age he was living in. Odysseus ends his Golden Age violently, just as Zeus ended the Golden Age of Kronos.

Now the visit of Odysseus to the cave of the Cyclops and its consequences have strong thematic relations with another visit of the hero. We saw that the Cyclopes were characterized as ὑπερφιάλων ἀθεμίστων, "overbearing and lawless" (*Od.* 9.106); these same terms, which can be used to denote the violent and failed symposium, are used many times for characters elsewhere in the poem, who live, not in some exotic, supernaturally fertile land at the edge of the world, but in a rural corner of Greece, the rocky island of Ithaca.

---

[26] In drawing attention to the thematic link between Hes. *Op.* 105 and *Od.* 9.411 I do not mean to imply that the poet of the *Odyssey* actually refers or alludes to a specific line of the Hesiodic *Works and Days* as we have it. Rather, the intertextuality (or "interformularity," see Bakker 2013: 157–69) is a matter of the evocation of phraseology associated with a given traditional and recognizable theme. The impossibility of outsmarting Zeus certainly qualifies as such a theme. On this, see further Burgess (2011: 168): "an oral epic reusing phraseology that has become associated with specific mythological situations as they were traditionally articulated in the oral epic tradition."

[27] Nieto-Hernández 2000: 351, 362–4.

In and Out of the Golden Age

The Suitors' crime is often considered to be the harassment of Queen Penelope, but they are also out to destroy Odysseus' estate by literally eating it, slaughtering all his animals.[28] The meat-crazy Suitors are the complete opposite of the vegetarian Cyclops. But in their carnivorous frenzy they become aligned with the Cyclops because they never sacrifice to the gods.[29] By sacrificial logic, as we saw, not eating meat is not sacrificing, is rejecting the gods; but eating the meat of domestic animals without sacrifice is even worse. The Suitors and the Cyclops are polar opposites, but they become united in being equidistant from the norm.

Just like the Cyclops the Suitors have it completely backward as to the world they live in. They create for themselves the illusion of a heroic context, in which animals are ritually and proportionally divided among the warriors, like the spoils of a sacked city. They also create the malicious illusion of the limitless abundance of the Golden Age, feasting day in and day out on a seemingly endless supply of meat. They add criminal intent to a decadent illusion of Golden Age plenty. Their gathering is a diseased symposium, one based on violence, with violent brawls possible at any moment.[30]

The worst brawl is the last one, and it is instantly and completely lethal. Odysseus emerges from the past like an avenging Centaur from another age. In fact, ironically, Antinoos had likened the anonymous beggar to the Centaurs as spoilers of the symposium, when the beggar asked if he could also try out the bow:

οἶνός σε τρώει μελιηδής, ὅς τε καὶ ἄλλους
βλάπτει, ὃς ἄν μιν χανδὸν ἕλῃ μηδ' αἴσιμα πίνῃ.
οἶνος καὶ Κένταυρον, ἀγακλυτὸν Εὐρυτίωνα,
ἄασ' ἐνὶ μεγάρῳ μεγαθύμου Πειριθόοιο,
ἐς Λαπίθας ἐλθόνθ'· ὁ δ' ἐπεὶ φρένας ἄασεν οἴνῳ,
μαινόμενος κάκ' ἔρεξε δόμον κάτα Πειριθόοιο.
ἥρωας δ' ἄχος εἷλε, διὲκ προθύρου δὲ θύραζε
ἕλκον ἀναΐξαντες, ἀπ' οὔατα νηλέϊ χαλκῷ

---

[28] On the crimes of the Suitors, see Saïd 1979; Bakker 2013: 43–8, 91–5.
[29] E.g. *Od.* 14.94 (Eumaios). The verb ἱερεύειν is sometimes used for the slaughter (e.g. 17.180–1, 535; 20.250, 391), but as Saïd (1979: 36) notes, this need not imply actual sacrifices (as does the more explicit ἔρδειν/ ῥέζειν ἱερά): in a culture in which any animal slaughtered for human consumption is a sacrifice, the verb may come to be used loosely for any killing in the absence of a vocabulary for butchery proper. See Bakker 2013: 47 n. 25.
[30] On cyclopean traits of the Suitors, see Bakker 2013: 53–7, 69–73. Odysseus functions as *akletos* ("uninvited guest," cf. Fehr 1990) at the symposium of the Suitors, acting as entertainer (e.g. the Iron scene) or catalyst of disruption (e.g. 18.351–409).

ῥῖνάς τ' ἀμήσαντες· ὁ δὲ φρεσὶν ᾗσιν ἀασθεὶς
ἤϊεν ἣν ἄτην ὀχέων ἀεσίφρονι θυμῷ.
ἐξ οὗ Κενταύροισι καὶ ἀνδράσι νεῖκος ἐτύχθη,
οἷ δ' αὐτῷ πρώτῳ κακὸν εὕρετο οἰνοβαρείων.
ὣς καὶ σοὶ μέγα πῆμα πιφαύσκομαι, αἴ κε τὸ τόξον
ἐντανύσῃς·
(*Od.* 21.293–306)

The honeysweet wine is hurting you; it does harm to others
as well, whoever gulps it and drinks beyond measure.
Wine also blinded the Centaur, famous Eurytion,
in the halls of great-hearted Peirithoos,
when he came to the Lapiths. And he, when he had blinded his
    brain with wine,
he went mad and did terrible things all over the house of Peirithoos.
The heroes were pained, sprang to their feet, and right through
    the forecourt
they dragged him outside; with pitiless bronze they mowed off
his ears and nose; but he was still blinded in his brain,
and went about carrying his delusion in his witless spirit.
Since then there has been war between Centaurs and humans,
but he found grievous pain first of all for himself, as he was weighed
    with wine.
Just like that I announce great grief to you too, if you string that bow.

This is one of the fullest accounts of the Centauromachy, the battle of men and Centaurs, which as we saw became the ultimate mythical template for the failed symposium, especially among the symposiasts themselves.[31] The speech is full of irony. Antinoos likens the beggar to an unruly, party-spoiling Centaur, but in actuality he is the Centaur himself. Another irony is that the misbehavior of Eurytion the Centaur took place at a wedding feast, and this is what the perverted symposium of the Suitors has become, now that Penelope has announced that she is ready to remarry. Little does Antinoos realize that he is talking to the bridegroom, whose wedding he is disrupting.

When the beggar in fact does string the bow, many sympotic elements come into play. The hero stringing his bow is likened to a singer stringing his lyre in the famous simile:

ὡς ὅτ' ἀνὴρ φόρμιγγος ἐπιστάμενος καὶ ἀοιδῆς
ῥηϊδίως ἐτάνυσσε νέῳ περὶ κόλλοπι χορδήν,
ἅψας ἀμφοτέρωθεν ἐϋστρεφὲς ἔντερον οἰός,

---

[31] In addition to Xenophanes 1.22W (above), see *Theogn.* 541–2.

ὡς ἄρ' ἄτερ σπουδῆς τάνυσεν μέγα τόξον Ὀδυσσεύς.
δεξιτερῇ δ' ἄρα χειρὶ λαβὼν πειρήσατο νευρῆς·
ἡ δ' ὑπὸ καλὸν ἄεισε, χελιδόνι εἰκέλη αὐδήν.
(*Od.* 21.406–11)

Just as when a man who is <u>expert in the lyre and in song</u>
easily fastens a string on the new peg,
fastening on either side the well-twisted sheep gut:
so then, without effort, did Odysseus string the great bow
and taking it with his right hand he tested the string,
and it sang a beautiful tune, similar to the song of the swallow.

The bow and the lyre: both are stringed instruments, both sing, and, as Odysseus goes on to say with grim humor, the lyre – his great bow – is the ideal accompaniment of the banquet:[32]

νῦν δ' ὤρη καὶ δόρπον Ἀχαιοῖσιν τετυκέσθαι
ἐν φάει, αὐτὰρ ἔπειτα καὶ ἄλλως ἑψιάασθαι
<u>μολπῇ καὶ φόρμιγγι</u>· τὰ γάρ τ' ἀναθήματα δαιτός.
(*Od.* 21.428–30)

Now it's the moment to prepare the Achaeans a meal
in the sunlight; and thereafter to amuse ourselves in other ways,
<u>with song and the lyre</u>; for those are the delights of the banquet.

Odysseus casts himself as a singer at the symposium – a lethal singer, whose lyre will cause the death of all the symposiasts. At the ideal symposium of the Phaeacians, where his contribution was words and tales, he was compared by the king to a singer (11.367–9); here at the perverted symposium of the Suitors he becomes a singer again, whose song, sung by his lyre, will be a song of death.

His first victim is Antinoos. When he shoots him through the throat, a thick spurt of blood comes out of his nose, which is expressed in a curious way:

ἐκλίνθη δ' ἑτέρωσε, δέπας δέ οἱ ἔκπεσε χειρὸς
βλημένου, αὐτίκα δ' <u>αὐλὸς</u> ἀνὰ ῥῖνας παχὺς ἦλθεν
αἵματος ἀνδρομέοιο·
(*Od.* 22.17–19)

He bent forward, and the goblet fell from his hand,
As he was hit, and immediately a thick <u>"pipe"</u> of blood came
through his nose.

---

[32] For connections of this passage to Helios, another cattle owner whose animals were illegally eaten, see Bakker 2013: 109–13.

The word αὐλός is usually understood as a "spurt," a "pipe" of blood, but the word is known to the Homeric tradition in its musical sense (*Il.* 18.495), and we may perhaps entertain the possibility that the quintessentially sympotic musical instrument is referred to here as well. This would mean that Antinoos "plays" the aulos at the moment of his death in and through the symposium.

The slaughter of the Suitors can be seen at two levels. At one level there is personal revenge, with Odysseus becoming, in a simile, like a bloodthirsty lion engaging in a killing spree (22.401–6); the result is extreme social unrest, even civil war, when the relatives of the dead Suitors take up arms to avenge the murder of their kinsmen.

But on another level the killing of the Suitors is not a matter of personal vendetta, but of divine retribution. This is how Odysseus himself presents the matter when the nurse Eurycleia is about to ululate over the bodies of the slain Suitors:

> τούσδε δὲ μοῖρ' ἐδάμασσε θεῶν καὶ σχέτλια ἔργα·
> οὔ τινα γὰρ τίεσκον ἐπιχθονίων ἀνθρώπων,
> οὐ κακὸν οὐδὲ μὲν ἐσθλόν, ὅτίς σφεας εἰσαφίκοιτο·
> (*Od.* 22.413–15)

> These men, the doom of the gods subdued them as well as their
>   own awful deeds,
> for they did not honor anyone of the earth-dwelling humans,
> neither base nor noble, whoever would come in contact with them.

We should compare these words with Odysseus' address to the Cyclops at 9.475–9 (above). Once more Odysseus frames the punishment as a matter not between himself and his enemies, but between them and Zeus the protector of travelers, the typical function of the typical god of the Iron Age.

The Suitors were in fact even more delusional than Polyphemos. Their unstable paradise was not only a travesty of heroic life; it was also a perverted illusion of the Golden Age. Continuous feasting and never-ending sympotic cheer may be a collective wish fantasy of humans in the Iron Age, a fantasy that the historical Colophonians were attempting to act out, as they were partying from dawn till dusk.[33] But this fantasy is dangerous, and the demise of Colophon became a topic of sympotic wisdom, the retribution for acts of *hubris*.[34] The Suitors, in addition to their sympotic hubris and excess, suppress all acts of sacrifice, treating Odysseus' farmed animals as if they are game on the hunting-grounds of the Golden Age, an act of defiance of

---

[33] Ath. 12.31. [34] *Theogn.* 1103–4.

Zeus and the Olympians no less preposterous than the boasting of Polyphemos that the Cyclopes are stronger than Zeus.

The Suitors in their confusion of categories and periods are precariously placed in the liminal space between the end of the Heroic Age and the beginning of the Iron Age, between the end of the Trojan War and the homecoming of Odysseus. That homecoming, in fact, effectively ends the Heroic Age, just as Odysseus puts an end to the Golden Age illusion of the Cyclops.

We may think in this connection of the conception of the Trojan War as a cataclysmic event of extinction. This idea goes back to the cyclical *Cypria* (though it may well be older), of which we have a fragment that talks about this as the "plan of Zeus," the Διὸς βουλή:

> ἦν ὅτε μυρία φῦλα κατὰ χθόνα πλαζόμεν' αἰεὶ
> <ἀνθρώπων ἐπίεζε> βαρυστέρνου πλάτος αἴης,
> Ζεὺς δὲ ἰδὼν ἐλέησε καὶ ἐν πυκιναῖς πραπίδεσσι
> κουφίσαι ἀνθρώπων παμβώτορα σύνθετο γαῖαν,
> ῥιπίσσας πολέμου μεγάλην ἔριν Ἰλιακοῖο,
> ὄφρα κενώσειεν θανάτῳ βάρος. οἱ δ' ἐνὶ Τροίῃ
> ἥρωες κτείνοντο, Διὸς δ' ἐτελείετο βουλή.
>
> (*Cypr.* fr. 1)
>
> There was a time when numerous tribes of man, roaming
> all over the land were oppressing the surface of broad-chested earth.
> And Zeus saw it and took pity, and in his deep dense mind
> he resolved to unburden all-feeding earth of the weight of men,
> fanning up the great conflict of the Trojan War,
> so as to empty the burden through death. And those in Troy,
> the heroes they were killed, and the plan of Zeus was fulfilled.

The last generation of heroes fights itself to death on the Trojan plain, and the survivors go on to re-people the world by founding cities in the far West and East, moving from the barren Greek homeland to more fertile shores far away. Severe drought under changing climatic conditions may have been a factor in these migrations.[35] In the telescoping mythico-historical imagination of the Greeks remaining in the heartland the resulting colonization finds a prototype in the fantastic travels of Odysseus to fabulously fertile and exotic lands, lands that he rejects in favor of returning home.

We can now, at the end of this chapter, reformulate the way in which Odysseus' *nostos*, his homebound quest, is traditionally understood: we

---

[35] Cf. Hdt. 7.171 (the survivors of the Cretan contingent in the Trojan War being confronted with famine upon their return).

commonly see the hero's *nostos* as an urge to reach his home and renew his marriage with the mortal Penelope in preference over the immortal existence that Calypso offered him. But as the combined Prometheus and Pandora myths in Hesiod teach us, marriage is one of the signature features of the Iron Age, along with sacrifice, agriculture, and disease. Odysseus rejects carefree abundance in favor of scarcity and toil, and violently terminates the seemingly carefree existence of others. His homecoming enforces the beginning of a new age for a new race of men. In this way the *Odyssey* is a true epic; it unites its audience as a people with a common culture. It defines the Greeks as men of the Iron Age.

CHAPTER 3

Pompē *in the* Odyssey

Alexander C. Loney

The final stage in Odysseus' epic journey is accomplished through *pompē*, "conveyance." Odysseus' *pompē* is the agenda of the central third of the poem, from the divine council at the opening of Book 5 that announces Odysseus' return by way of Scherie to the Phaiakians' punishment in Book 13 for conveying him home. And yet *pompē*, considered as a thematic and narrative device, has received little scholarly attention, especially when compared to the related theme of *nostos*. Such an analysis is important because *pompē* – a mode of travel requiring cooperation and trust – reveals important aspects of Odysseus' character as an agent engaged in his journey home. The collaborative nature of *pompē* and its pivotal role in his return journey inform us about the sort of an epic hero Odysseus is. When he finally reaches Ithaca he is neither an independent journeyer, determining his own course, nor a mere object of fate, driven ashore by divine or natural forces. The poet underscores right away in the proem that neither of these two polarities of agency, of purely active or purely passive action, allow Odysseus to return home. On the one hand, Odysseus is a passive victim, "driven far" (μάλα πολλὰ πλάγχθη, *Od.* 1.1–2), who "suffered many pains upon the sea" (πολλὰ δ' ὅ γ' ἐν πόντῳ πάθεν ἄλγεα, 4). On the other hand, he actively tried to exercise his will: he "wished" (ἱέμενός, 6) to protect his companions and he "tried to save" (ἀρνύμενος, 5) them and himself. The proem thus presents the audience with a picture of Odysseus as one who has not yet achieved *nostos*, either actively by his own will or passively by the will of another. Odysseus' own efforts have come to naught – at this point in the narrative he is detained by a goddess on her island – and being "driven" is essentially synonymous with being away and kept from home.[1]

I would like to thank the editors of this volume for their invitation to contribute this chapter, which develops an idea I was unable to include in my forthcoming book, *The Ethics of Revenge and the Meanings of the Odyssey* (Oxford 2019).

[1] Louden 1999: 71–90 has shown how the verb πλάζω, which is emphasized in the proem in the form of the enjambed participle πλάγχθη, is a thematically important term, serving as an "index of divine

When Odysseus finally achieves his return it comes through a mode of travel that is a mixture of these polarities – *pompē*.

In this chapter I consider what it means in the *Odyssey* to be "conveyed," and how this mode of travel fits in the themes and structure of the poem. I conclude that the key elements of Odysseus' eventual, successful conveyance by the Phaiakians, the elements that distinguish it from the other failed cases, are cooperation, trust, and promise-keeping: successful *pompē* requires Odysseus to be dependent upon others who will fulfill their promises. This chapter proceeds as follows: first, by reviewing the previous scholarship on *pompē* and establishing its basic meaning; second, by examining various instances of *pompē* in the poem as comparanda for Odysseus' own conveyance; third, by considering *pompē* in the narrative structure of the *Odyssey*; fourth, by considering Odysseus' unsuccessful attempts at obtaining *pompē*; lastly, by showing how the Phaiakians' *pompē* succeeds when Odysseus relies on them as helpers and they, out of their abundant generosity, give him conveyance at the cost of their own destruction.

3.1 The Nature of *Pompē*

Relatively few scholars have examined *pompē* in the *Odyssey*. It is transparently cognate with the verb πέμπω, "to send," though the etymology of that verb is unknown.[2] The most straightforward usages of the noun refer to the "conveying" of persons in need to their destination, usually their home (e.g. Alkinoös' offer of *pompē* to Ithaca for Odysseus: *Od.* 11.352). A few scholars have given cursory treatments of *pompē* in the service of arguing other points. Jonathan Burgess has noted that, while literally meaning "a sending," *pompē* can be used flexibly.[3] In every case, however, it ultimately refers to the act of conveying persons, though different aspects of the action are emphasized and can take different forms. For instance, Kalypso plans Odysseus' *pompē* (5.233) by giving him tools and instructions on how to build a raft (5.234–61); at other points the emphasis falls on the agent or

---

disfavor" (71), signaling "a god's wrath visited upon a mortal who has committed offense" (72). Because of divine wrath, such mortals are made to wander. Cook 1999 argues that Odysseus combines both passive and active strategies to achieve his goals: see esp. 151 on the proem.

[2] See Chantraine 1999 and *LfgrE* s.v. πέμπω.

[3] Burgess 2012: 279–80: "[*pompē*] is a flexible word that most literally means 'send-off,' but its connotations include 'directions,' 'means for travel,' or 'conveyance,' depending on the circumstances ... The range of the term *pompē* is wide indeed, including material for Odysseus' raft, the right wind for their ships, and even a magic ship itself" (280).

force giving *pompē* – winds (4.362, 10.18), humans (3.325, 5.16–17), or gods may act as "conveyers" (πομπῆες, 3.376); at yet other points, *pompē* consists of directions for the path to take to get home (10.490–540). A. F. Garvie has observed that the term is part of the vocabulary and themes of *nostos* poetry.[4] Others have discussed *pompē* as the final element in a larger narrative structure, either of *nostos* or of *xenia*.[5] Still others have taken up its connection with *xenia* and considered how granting *pompē* can confer recognition and status, which may change depending on the form the conveyance takes.[6] The most extended discussion of *pompē* is by Hans Kilb, who has described it as the "central theme" of Books 5–12. Kilb, however, is mostly interested in defending the integrity of the transmitted text of Book 7 against the criticisms of analysts, and does not define in any detail what the characteristics of *pompē* are.[7] None of these studies has systematically analyzed the meaning and significance of *pompē* for the *Odyssey*, although several make valuable points to which I shall refer in the course of this study.

In order to establish the significance of conveyance in the *Odyssey*, an overview of terminology is in order. The key term is πομπή. It appears twenty-five times in the *Odyssey*, but only once in the *Iliad*. This difference in frequency alone is significant. The balance for the cognate verb πέμπω and its compounds ἀποπέμπω and ἐκπέμπω is also weighted toward the *Odyssey*, though less strongly: ninety-four to forty-one times. The other cognate terms follow this pattern – πομπεύς and πομπεύω are found only in the *Odyssey*, five times and once respectively – with the exception of πομπός, which appears more frequently in the *Iliad* (eight times, to four in the *Odyssey*). This imbalance results in part from the different narrative situations of the poems. The action of the *Iliad* takes place entirely at Troy, so there is little occasion to tell of a hero's journey. The one instance of πομπή in the *Iliad* comes in a mythological allusion to Bellerophon's journey to Lycia (see n. 10 in this chapter). All instances of πομπός in the *Iliad* occur in circumstances associated with the conveyance of the dead. The Trojan warrior Deïphobos gloats that by killing the Achaian warrior Hypsenor he has provided a "guide" (πομπόν, *Il.* 13.416) for the slain Trojan Asios on his journey to Hades. Sleep and Death are "guides" (πομποῖσιν, *Il.* 16.671, 81) for the body of Sarpedon, bringing it back to

---

[4] Garvie 2014: 122–3; 1994: 153, 201.
[5] *nostos*: Bonifazi 2009: 484. *xenia*: Most 1989: 28–9; Reece 1993: 39; de Jong 2001: 170.
[6] Murnaghan 1987: 111–12; Van Wees 1992: 398.
[7] Kilb 1973: 34–42, 46–9: "The central theme of the Phaiakian episode ... is the conveyance home, the πομπή, of Odysseus" (34). Kilb here is countering the analytical arguments of Schadewaldt, esp. 1959.

Lycia for burial. Most prominently, Hermes is five times referred to as a πομπός for Priam, guiding him safely to Achilles' tent (*Il.* 24.153, 182, 437, 439, 461). This scene deploys many of the conventions of a heroic *katabasis*, and thus Hermes' actions recall his traditional role as *psychopompos*.[8] This restricted usage is peculiar to the *Iliad*. In the *Odyssey*, πομπός is used of Nestor's son Peisistratos (*Od.* 4.162) and Athena (4.826) as guides of Telemachos, and generically of the Phaiakians (8.566=13.174): its meaning and usage hardly differ from πομπεύς.

I draw some preliminary conclusions from this survey of usage. Terms built on the o-grade of the root **p(e/o)mp-* always denote conveyance.[9] But terms built on e-grade have more varied meaning. While they can denote conveyance (e.g. 13.39, 48, 52, etc.), they need not always do so: e.g. Telemachos contemplates "sending away" (ἀπὸ ... πέμψω, 2.133) his mother against her will. In that scenario, Penelope would not cooperate in the conveyance – a key feature of *pompē*, as we shall see. Accordingly, *pompē* and its o-grade cognates form a technical vocabulary for "conveyance" in the *Odyssey*.

What does it mean for a subject to receive *pompē*, to be conveyed? As I alluded to in the opening paragraph, it is not a purely active mode of motion by the recipient. There must be another agent who does the conveyance. If we consider that *pompē* is a verbal noun, related to the verb πέμπω, the agent of conveyance is the grammatical subject of the verb or of the implied action of the noun. In the *Odyssey* we find a range of agents: "a god" or "gods" generically (e.g. 5.32);[10] a specific divinity (Kalypso,

---

[8] See de Jáuregui 2011: esp. 44–5. The epithet *psychopompos*, "spirit-guide," is a relatively late description for Hermes (first appearing in Euripides), though its roots are archaic: notably in *Od.* 24 Hermes guides the souls of the dead suitors down to Hades. See Sourvinou-Inwood 1995: 104–6, who takes *Od.* 24 as a late seventh- or early sixth-century addition to the poem. Regardless of whether the second *nekuia* in the *Odyssey* and Hermes' role as *psychopompos* are latter additions to the poem – points debated already by Aristarchus – Hermes' role as a guide to and from Hades for the living is attested elsewhere in Homer (*Od.* 11.626).

[9] Although there is manifestly a systematic relationship between words with an internal -o- vowel like πομπή and the verb πέμπω, the etymology of these words is unknown: see Chantraine 1999: 879–80. The verb πέμπω also has an -o- grade in the perfect πέπομφα, but none of these forms are found in texts before the fifth century.

[10] Although I do not discuss the *Iliad* in this present argument, it is worth noting that the only example of *pompē* in the *Iliad*, Bellerophon's conveyance to Lycia, has this sort of agent. "Gods" give Bellerophon "harmless conveyance" (ἀμύμονι **πομπῇ**, *Il.* 6.171) to Lycia – a journey that Proitos intended to result in his death. Though it is never made explicit in this condensed version of the story, Bellerophon's successful journeys – not only to Lycia, but also to other sites where he might perform dangerous labors at the bidding of Proitos – may have depended upon the favor of the gods. (Note that Bellerophon "trust[s] in the portents of the gods" [θεῶν τεράεσσι πιθήσας, 6.183] and is recognized as "an offspring of a god" [θεοῦ γόνον, 6.191].) Eventually, he will at any rate lose that favor and "become hateful to all the gods" (ἀπήχθετο πᾶσι θεοῖσιν, 6.200). As Alden

5.173, 233; Athena, 1.93); mortals or "sailors" generically (4.560, 5.32); a specific mortal or mortals (Alkinoös, 6.290; Arete, 7.151; the Phaiakians, 7.191–3, 317; Menelaos, 4.589, 15.15, 53, 63; Nestor, 3.369; son[s] of Nestor, 3.325); winds (4.362, 586). This is not an exhaustive list of every case of *pompē*. But in every instance it means that the recipient moves through the agency of another, a sender. This sender has a special position of power and authority in the situation, while the recipient is dependent upon the sender. This is true even in cases where the recipient is the social superior of the sender – as when the companions are referred to as Odysseus' senders. In several cases, multiple senders can work simultaneously to convey the recipient: a god may "send" a mortal by ordering the winds to "send" his ship or persuade another mortal to "send" the recipient. Thus, the agent doing the sending may seem different to the recipient, depending on the perspective adopted. In each case the recipient either participates in or at least willingly accepts the offer: he may pilot a ship that is set in motion by rowing sailors or blowing winds; use tools given to build a raft (5.233); take and drive an offered chariot (3.369). Regardless, the one conveyed and the one conveying cooperate to convey the recipient to his destination.

This consideration of agency is at the core of the significance of *pompē*, and what distinguishes it from another, purely passive and dependent, mode of travel. This other mode is typical of persons in exile or made to wander. For instance, as is typical for a homicide, Theoklymenos "flees" and "wanders among men" (φεύγω ... κατ' ἀνθρώπους ἀλάλησθαι, 15.276) in order to escape facing retribution. He is not a willing subject in his travel. Furthermore, we may note that his travel is motivated by an outward force, away from a threat. This we may contrast with *pompē*, which is directed toward a goal, with the subject often passing *through* threats to reach it. We may also contrast situations in which traveling subjects assert their complete independence, usually with disastrous consequences. For example, Lokrian Ajax is shipwrecked on his return from Troy and rescued from the sea by Poseidon (4.499–501). But, ignoring both the wrath of Athena and Poseidon's help, he boasts that he saved himself "apart from the will of the gods" (ἀέκητι θεῶν, 4.504). For this boast, Poseidon kills him (4.505–11). In contrast to these cases, *pompē*, in its proper form, is distinguished by cooperation.

(2000: 138–40) has argued, this vagueness about the cause of both divine favor and anger emphasizes the arbitrariness of the gods' will toward mortals – in my view, a thoroughly Iliadic sentiment that fits the *Odyssey* less well.

Zeus foretells in the beginning of Book 5 that Odysseus will achieve successful *pompē* to Ithaca from the Phaiakians. Before that happens in Book 13, the audience will hear of several cases of *pompē* that do not bring Odysseus home. Each negatively reflects the Phaiakians' proper *pompē*. Elsewhere in the poem other characters receive successful *pompē*, and these cases also inform its thematic significance. First, I turn to the important examples of other characters' successful *pompē*, and then to Odysseus'.

3.2 Minor Cases of *Pompē*

The first instance of *pompē* in the poem is Telemachos' conveyance by Athena to Pylos and Sparta. The journey is described in advance and in summary fashion by Athena:

πέμψω δ' ἐς Σπάρτην τε καὶ ἐς Πύλον ἠμαθόεντα
νόστον πευσόμενον πατρὸς φίλου, ἤν που ἀκούσῃ,
ἠδ' ἵνα μιν κλέος ἐσθλὸν ἐν ἀνθρώποισιν ἔχῃσιν.
(*Od.* 1.93–5)

I shall send him to Sparta and to sandy Pylos
in order to learn of the homecoming of his dear father, if somehow
 he should hear of it,
and in order that good renown among men might be his.[11]

In this initial description, Telemachos' journey is directed by a divine power. Athena is the explicit agent of conveyance from this overall, programmatic perspective. She executes her plan by persuading him to set out and convincing him that such a journey would solve his domestic problems (1.279–92). Thus, Telemachos cooperates with Athena in his conveyance: he gathers the provisions for the journey (2.410), while she obtains and outfits a ship (2.382–92); he commands his companions to sail (2.422–30), while she provides the wind (2.420–1). As the narrative of Telemachos' journey unfolds, other agents provide him with conveyance from one stage of his journey to the next. Nestor gives him conveyance from Sparta to Pylos:

σὺ δὲ τοῦτον, ἐπεὶ τεὸν ἵκετο δῶμα,
πέμψον σὺν δίφρῳ τε καὶ υἱέϊ· δὸς δέ οἱ ἵππους,
οἵ τοι ἐλαφρότατοι θείειν καὶ κάρτος ἄριστοι.
(*Od.* 3.368–70)

---

[11] Unless otherwise noted, I follow von der Mühll's 1962 Greek text of the *Odyssey*. All translations are my own.

> But since this man has come to your house,
> Send him with a chariot and your son. Give to him horses,
> the ones of yours which are swiftest in running and best in strength.

Athena speaks these lines to Nestor, who has already offered his chariot, horses, and sons as "conveyers" (πομπῆες, 3.325). Athena's conveyance consists, in part, of using others' offers of conveyance – or persuading them to make an offer of conveyance – from one point to another, which she puts in the service of her larger goal of bringing Telemachos to Pylos, Sparta, and back again to Ithaca. Menelaos also "sends" Telemachos on his way (4.589), after Athena urges Telemachos to have Menelaos do so (15.15, 53, 63).

When Odysseus learns that Telemachos set out in search of news about him, he is concerned about Telemachos' fate, even wondering whether Athena wanted him to suffer as Odysseus has:

> ἦ ἵνα που καὶ κεῖνος ἀλώμενος ἄλγεα πάσχῃ
> πόντον ἐπ' ἀτρύγετον, βίοτον δέ οἱ ἄλλοι ἔδωσι;
> (*Od.* 13.418–19)

> Was it in order that perhaps that man too, wandering, might suffer pains upon the barren sea, and that the others might devour his livelihood?

The language here echoes the descriptions of Odysseus' own situation: in the thematically weighty words of the proem, Odysseus "suffered many pains on the sea" (ἐν πόντῳ πάθεν ἄλγεα, 1.4);[12] as Athena had just told Odysseus, the suitors "are devouring [his] livelihood" (βίοτον κατέδουσιν, 13.396).[13] The closest comparandum comes in Odysseus' interview with Penelope, when he adopts the ironically appropriate persona of a Cretan who "wander[s] among many cities of mortals, suffering pains" (πολλὰ βροτῶν ἐπὶ ἄστε' ἀλώμενος, ἄλγεα πάσχων, 19.170). The audience is presented, thus, with a scenario in which Telemachos could have faced a journey full of woe – an *Odyssey* – but Athena assures Odysseus this is not the case:

> αὐτή μιν **πόμπευον**, ἵνα κλέος ἐσθλὸν ἄροιτο
> κεῖσ' ἐλθών· ἀτὰρ οὔ τιν' ἔχει πόνον, ἀλλὰ ἔκηλος
> ἧσται ἐν Ἀτρεΐδαο δόμοις, παρὰ δ' ἄσπετα κεῖται.
> (*Od.* 13.422–4)

---

[12] Cf. 5.13 et al.
[13] Cf. 1.160, 14.377, et al. On the suitors' consumption of Odysseus' household, see Bakker, Chapter 2 in this volume.

I myself was conveying him, in order that he might gain noble renown
having gone there. And he does not have any toil, but sits secure
in the home of the son of Atreus, and numberless goods lie beside him.

Because Athena has acted as conveyer she has ensured that Telemachos will be safe. When Penelope is similarly worried about Telemachos' journey, the phantom of her sister also reassures her that Telemachos is protected because Athena is his "conveyer" (πομπός, 4.826). Athena does this by providing advice to Telemachos about how to avoid the suitors' ambush (15.27–42) and sending a fair wind (15.292–4). Antinoös recognizes the role a divinity played in saving Telemachos from their ambush (16.364–70). Athena's role as a πομπός for Telemachos is likewise evident to Nestor after she leaves Telemachos' side in the form of an eagle (3.371–84). Telemachos' *pompē*, therefore, is the most important example in the *Odyssey* apart from Odysseus' own. But there are a few other examples worth noting in brief.

Menelaos is involved in several cases of *pompē*. He is waylaid on his journey home from Troy by the absence of conveyance, resulting from divine anger. After a lengthy stay in Egypt he makes it to the island of Pharos, where he is stuck because he does not have winds favorable for sailing home:

> ἔνθα μ' ἐείκοσιν ἤματ' ἔχον θεοί, οὐδέ ποτ' οὖροι
> πνείοντες φαίνονθ' ἁλιαέες, οἵ ῥά τε νηῶν
> **πομπῆες** γίνονται ἐπ' εὐρέα νῶτα θαλάσσης.
> (*Od.* 4.360–2)

> There the gods held me for twenty days, and there never appeared
> blowing, sea-gusting winds, which for ships
> are conveyers upon the wide back of the sea.

Menelaos lacks "conveyors" and, for this reason, cannot reach his home, even though he is "eager to return" (μεμαῶτα νέεσθαι, 4.351). Menelaos' situation is thus parallel to Odysseus' on Ogygia, who is also "in need of return" (νόστου κεχρημένον, 1.13). As others have noted, Menelaos' wanderings parallel Odysseus' in many aspects, but the similarity of their plight on their respective islands underscores the need for *pompē*.[14] And in both cases the hero is dependent on another to provide it. Menelaos learns from Proteus that he does not have the winds he needs because the gods are angry

---

[14] Lord 1960: 165–9; Powell 1970 emphasizes the parallel between Menelaos' last stop on his journey, the island of Pharos, and Odysseus' Scherie. This may be the strongest parallel, but, as we shall see, at each of Odysseus' stopping points – Ogygia, Aiaia, Aiolia – he confronts the same need for conveyance.

with him. He had neglected to perform a sacrifice before setting out from Egypt, and so must first return there and perform the sacrifice to gain their goodwill and conveyance home (4.351–3, 472–80).[15] Proteus also tells Menelaos that later in life he will have a final conveyance: the gods "will send" (πέμψουσιν, 4.564) him to the Elysion plain – a kind of paradise the gods allow him to enjoy because of his status as a husband to Helen.[16]

Finally, the conditions on Ithaca before Odysseus arrives illustrate how proper conveyance can be lost or corrupted if a generous lord is absent (19.312–16). The suitors even mockingly offer to "send away" (ἐκπέμψασθε, 20.361) the "guest" (ξεῖνος, 360) Theoklymenos in a distortion of the practice, who retorts he has no need of their "conveyers" (πομπῆας, 364).

3.3 The *Pompē* of Odysseus and the Program of the Poem

The *Odyssey* opens with Zeus' complaint that mortals blame the gods for the troubles that actually come by their own fault. Athena counters that Odysseus, however, does not deserve to be abandoned on an island and held there by Kalypso. She even goes so far as to blame Zeus for Odysseus' grief: "Why do you give him such pains?" (τί νύ οἱ τόσον ὠδύσαο, 1.62). Zeus responds that it is really Poseidon, angered over Polyphemos' blinding, who is behind Odysseus' plight. Nonetheless, he proposes they now consider Odysseus' *nostos*. At this point, Athena sets forth a program of action that becomes the agenda for the first half of the poem:

Ἑρμείαν μὲν ἔπειτα, διάκτορον Ἀργεϊφόντην,
νῆσον ἐς Ὠγυγίην ὀτρύνομεν, ὄφρα τάχιστα
νύμφῃ ἐϋπλοκάμῳ εἴπῃ νημερτέα βουλήν,
νόστον Ὀδυσσῆος ταλασίφρονος, ὥς κε νέηται.
αὐτὰρ ἐγὼν Ἰθάκηνδε ἐλεύσομαι, ὄφρα οἱ υἱὸν
μᾶλλον ἐποτρύνω καί οἱ μένος ἐν φρεσὶ θείω,
εἰς ἀγορὴν καλέσαντα κάρη κομόωντας Ἀχαιοὺς
πᾶσι μνηστήρεσσιν ἀπειπέμεν, οἵ τέ οἱ αἰεὶ
μῆλ' ἁδινὰ σφάζουσι καὶ εἰλίποδας ἕλικας βοῦς.
πέμψω δ' ἐς Σπάρτην τε καὶ ἐς Πύλον ἠμαθόεντα

---

[15] Nestor tells Telemachos that Apollo (3.279) and Zeus (3.288) hindered Menelaos' *nostos*, though he has no way of knowing of their involvement. This is a typical inference of divine causation for otherwise unexplained disastrous events: see Jörgensen 1904.
[16] Menelaos also "conveys" (πέμπε[ν], 4.5, 8) his daughter to Neoptolemos to be his wife. And one of Menelaos' attendants suggests as a proper way of receiving strangers "conveying" (πέμπωμεν, 4.29) them on to another host.

> νόστον πευσόμενον πατρὸς φίλου, ἤν που ἀκούσῃ,
> ἠδ' ἵνα μιν κλέος ἐσθλὸν ἐν ἀνθρώποισιν ἔχῃσιν.
> (*Od.* 1.84–95)
>
> Then rouse Hermes, the guide, Argeïphontes,
> to go to the island Ogygia, in order that swiftly
> he may tell the nymph of goodly locks the unerring plan –
> the homecoming of stout-minded Odysseus, how he may return.
> But I shall go to Ithaca, in order that I may rouse his son
> and put in his heart strength,
> that, having summoned the long-haired Achaians into an assembly,
> he may speak out against all the suitors who continually
> slaughter his thick-thronging sheep and his shambling,
>   spiral-horned cattle.
> I shall send him to Sparta and to sandy Pylos,
> so that he may learn of his father, if ever he hears of him,
> and so that noble glory may hold him among men.

Athena outlines two threads to her plan. Hermes is to handle Odysseus' return; Athena herself is to deal with matters on Ithaca and the journey of Odysseus' son. The second thread becomes the plot of the next four books of the poem. Of the first thread, we hear nothing until Book 5. Hermes does not appear until then; Odysseus' captivity on the island is mentioned a handful of times, but only to give the characters (principally Telemachos) hope that he is still alive and may return (1.196–204; 4.498, 551–60). The poet holds back any further explanation of the details of the "unerring plan." There is a pronounced juncture between 1.87 and 1.88 – so much so that many scholars of an analytical inclination have seen this point as the division between an original kernel of a *nostos* epic, resumed in Book 5, and an interpolated Telemachy.[17] Although few now would accept such conclusions, it is striking how, after six days have passed, Zeus resumes announcing the gods' plan for Odysseus right where Athena left off at 1.87. The one difference is that, in Book 5, the poet puts the program for Odysseus' return in Zeus' mouth. The poem's audience now hears what it was promised in Book 1: Zeus commissions Hermes, who is to bear the message of the gods' plan to Kalypso:

> Ἑρμεία· σὺ γὰρ αὖτε τά τ' ἄλλα περ ἄγγελός ἐσσι·
> νύμφῃ ἐϋπλοκάμῳ εἰπεῖν νημερτέα βουλήν,
> νόστον Ὀδυσσῆος ταλασίφρονος, ὥς κε νέηται,
> οὔτε θεῶν **πομπῇ** οὔτε θνητῶν ἀνθρώπων·

---

[17] See, e.g., Kirchhoff 1879: 196–8. For a recent discussion, see West 2014: 106–13, 147.

ἀλλ' ὅ γ' ἐπὶ σχεδίης πολυδέσμου πήματα πάσχων
ἤματι εἰκοστῷ Σχερίην ἐρίβωλον ἵκοιτο,
Φαιήκων ἐς γαῖαν, οἳ ἀγχίθεοι γεγάασιν·
οἵ κέν μιν περὶ κῆρι θεὸν ὣς τιμήσουσι,
πέμψουσιν δ' ἐν νηΐ φίλην ἐς πατρίδα γαῖαν,
χαλκόν τε χρυσόν τε ἅλις ἐσθῆτά τε δόντες,
πόλλ', ὅσ' ἂν οὐδέ ποτε Τροίης ἐξήρατ' Ὀδυσσεύς,
εἴ περ ἀπήμων ἦλθε, λαχὼν ἀπὸ ληΐδος αἶσαν.
ὣς γάρ οἱ μοῖρ' ἐστὶ φίλους τ' ἰδέειν καὶ ἱκέσθαι
οἶκον ἐς ὑψόροφον καὶ ἑὴν ἐς πατρίδα γαῖαν.
(*Od.* 5.29–42)

Hermes, as you are the messenger in all other matters,
tell the nymph of goodly locks the unerring plan –
the homecoming of stout-minded Odysseus, how he may return,
not by the conveyance of gods or mortal men.
Instead, upon a well-bound raft, suffering harms,
on the twentieth day he will arrive at fertile Scherie,
the land of the Phaiakians, who are near the gods.
They will honor him greatly in their hearts, like a god,
and they will send him in a ship to his dear ancestral land,
having given him bronze and gold in abundance and clothing,
so much as Odysseus never would have carried off from Troy,
even if he had returned unharmed, having obtained his allotment of loot.
For thus is it fated for him to see his dear ones and reach
his lofty-roofed home and his ancestral land.

Lines 5.30–1 repeat 1.86–7 verbatim, with the one change (εἰπεῖν for εἴπῃ) now that the thought comes as a command. The two speeches, spread out with four books intervening, complement one another so well that the same analysts who thought that the Telemachy was separable from an original *nostos* poem believed that the two divine council scenes were originally one. Zeus completes the thought begun by Athena: we could *almost* imagine 5.32–42 following right after 1.87. Almost, I write, because Athena cannot deliver the content of the gods' "plan" (βουλή, 1.86, 5.30) – a word of important programmatic significance – but only Zeus can.[18] Since Zeus does not immediately answer Athena's proposal in 1.80–95, the audience is left in suspense until the opening of Book 5 about how exactly Odysseus will come home. The manner of Odysseus' return is an open item in the agenda of the poem that will not begin to be filled in

---

[18] On the motif of Διὸς βουλή, see, among others, Kullmann 1955; Nagy 1979: 81; Clay 1999; Marks 2008: 4, 8–13, 132–46, *passim*; Elmer 2013: 155–66.

until this second council scene, where, with the same two lines introducing the topic, it becomes the central preoccupation of the next eight books.[19]

The very next line, in which Zeus begins to reveal his plan, introduces for the first time in the poem the term *pompē* – though, somewhat oddly, in the negative. Odysseus will go on his way to Ithaca "without a conveyance by gods or mortals" (οὔτε θεῶν **πομπῇ** οὔτε θνητῶν ἀνθρώπων, 5.32). This is something of a puzzle, since a few lines later Zeus says the Phaiakians will "send" (πέμψουσιν, 37) – i.e. "convey" – him to Ithaca. Furthermore, Kalypso will shortly plan for Odysseus' *pompē* (5.233) from her island and "send" (πέμπ', 5.263) him on his way. Evidently, as the contrastive ἀλλ' that begins line 33 indicates, Zeus has in mind the interval of eighteen days during which Odysseus sails entirely on his own without assistance. As a result of lack of *pompē*, Odysseus will suffer yet more "pains" (πήματα, 33) when he is left unprotected from a final attack by Poseidon (5.282–381). Therefore, even after the gods set in motion Odysseus' *nostos*, he still must obtain *pompē* before he can make it to Ithaca. Indeed, Zeus is circumspect about the nature of the "pains" Odysseus will first suffer. He implies this will occur "upon a well-bound raft" and makes no mention of Poseidon. As it happens, after facing the initial storm sent by Poseidon that wrecks his raft, Odysseus will actually suffer most of his "pains" on this leg of his journey *off* his raft, swimming in the water. The dramatic storm and Odysseus' difficult salvation from the sea, rescued with the help of the nymph Leukotheë, Athena, and a river god, point to the impossibility of Odysseus' making it home unaided, without *pompē*.

The desperation of Odysseus' situation on Ogygia is underscored in a recurring set of formulaic lines:

... νύμφης ἐν μεγάροισι Καλυψοῦς, ἥ μιν ἀνάγκῃ
ἴσχει· ὁ δ' οὐ δύναται ἣν πατρίδα γαῖαν ἱκέσθαι·
οὐ γάρ οἱ πάρα νῆες ἐπήρετμοι καὶ ἑταῖροι,
οἵ κέν μιν **πέμποιεν** ἐπ' εὐρέα νῶτα θαλάσσης.

(*Od.* 4.557–60)

... in the halls of the nymph Kalypso, who, by force, restrains him. He is unable to reach his fatherland. For there are not available oared ships and companions who could send him upon the wide back of the sea.

---

[19] This piece-by-piece, gradual revelation in a series of divine pronouncements of Zeus' βουλή regarding Odysseus' return parallels the way Zeus' βουλή for the Trojan War is gradually revealed throughout the *Iliad*. See Allan 2008: 207–10; de Jong 2001: 126–7 and xvi under the term "paralipsis" for earlier scholarship.

These four lines repeat verbatim twice more (5.14–17, 17.143–6, quoting 4.557–60) and on another occasion the final two lines repeat (5.141–2). In each of these cases, we have a god – Proteus, Athena, or Kalypso – asserting with divine authority that Odysseus needs sailors to help him complete his journey. Only companions (ἑταῖροι) can "send" (πέμποιεν) him home – i.e. provide *pompē*. But he has at this point lost his companions, so he will need to find new ones who can be his "conveyers." On Scherie he will find the sailors, the "conveyers" he needs.

Odysseus is thus in a similarly extreme state of need when he first arrives on Scherie. He possesses nothing, not even clothes. He does not know where he is, nor to whom he should appeal for aid, nor even whether he ought to seek help, for fear that the inhabitants are as dangerous as the violent and wild men and monsters he has encountered before. After departing Troy with a full complement of ships, men, and loot, he has been gradually reduced to an animalistic state of poverty. And yet the poem's audience had learned in the previous book that Odysseus will, as a result of his stay on this island, receive a conveyance home that enriches him to an even greater extent than when he first departed Troy (5.36–40). The next third of the poem explains how he achieves this goal.

3.4 Odysseus' Failed Cases of *Pompē*

Before Odysseus arrives on Scherie, he faces a number of situations where the topic of *pompē* arises but does not result in his obtaining a proper conveyance home. Each of these presents a distorted mirror to Odysseus' eventual, successful *pompē* from the Phaiakians.

In Polyphemos' cave, Odysseus and his companions encounter several reversals of proper *xenia*, as others have noted.[20] Providing conveyance is one part of this larger custom of hospitality, and Polyphemos corrupts this too. Conveyance is first mentioned when Odysseus, trapped in the cave, tries to scheme his way out by getting Polyphemos drunk. He offers him wine, couching his offer in terms of an appeal for *pompē*:

σοὶ δ' αὖ λοιβὴν φέρον, εἴ μ' ἐλεήσας
οἴκαδε **πέμψειας**· σὺ δὲ μαίνεαι οὐκέτ' ἀνεκτῶς.
(*Od.* 9.349–50)

---

[20] Reece 1993: 123–43; see also Bakker, Chapter 2 in this volume.

> To you, in turn, I was bringing a drink offering, in the hope that,
>   having pity on me,
> you would send me homeward. You are raging intolerably.

This is hardly a sincere request. Though Odysseus desires conveyance home, he does not now suppose that he will get it from Polyphemos. Odysseus addresses Polyphemos here as if he were an angry divinity whose wrath must be propitiated with an offering in order to win his homecoming. Such a "drink offering" (λοιβή) is normally offered only to a god.[21] At *Il.* 9.500 a λοιβή is offered as part of the ritual of repentance and supplication that may placate divine wrath that arises on account of some transgression (personified in that passage as Ἀτή). In the present passage Odysseus is insincerely presenting himself as a wrongdoer, with the unstated understanding that he was led by Ἀτή into error. He further insinuates that, after accepting this propitiating drink offering, Polyphemos should relent from his wrath and no longer hold him back from returning home. He should instead grant him *pompē*. (Menelaos' successful propitiation of divine wrath in Egypt and his subsequent *pompē* home, as described above, provide an apt comparison of this ritual in its sincere, proper form.) All of this is deeply duplicitous, designed just to get Polyphemos to drink to excess. He follows the form of the ritual, including a ludicrous appeal to Polyphemos' "pity," knowing full well it will not work. Nor does Odysseus intend it to. But the success of his ruse rests, in part, on how well he can convince Polyphemos that he is sincerely following the protocol of the ritual. And in order to get him well and truly drunk, Odysseus gives him three drink offerings (*Od.* 9.360–1). In symptotic customs, such a triple libation has particular significance as an offering to Zeus, the other gods, and the heroes.[22] Odysseus is flattering Polyphemos by subtly suggesting that he can supplant all three groups.[23] This scheme works because Polyphemos, as he has rather blasphemously boasted, believes the Cyclopes to be god-like – or actually *mightier* (φέρτεροι) than Zeus and the other gods (275–6). In this way, Odysseus tries to effect his band's deliverance and homecoming, without any outside help. But his

---

[21] λοιβή appears only three other times in Homer (*Il.* 4.49, 9.500, 24.70), all denoting drink offerings made to gods (usually Zeus); the cognate verb λείβω, which can denote the same ritual action, has the same restricted usage, except when used in an extended sense of "pouring tears."

[22] An initial offering is made to Zeus and the Olympians, a second to the heroes, and a third to Zeus the savior. The evidence for this practice may be later than the *Odyssey*, but Odysseus is likely drawing on some antecedent ritual practice. See Cook 1995: 1123–5; Burkert 1985: 70–2.

[23] Stanford 1947: ad 9.349 ff. notes Odysseus' flattering offer of a λοιβή (though not the connection to the symptotic triple libation).

success is only partial. While Odysseus rescues his single ship's band (minus the six eaten) from immediate danger, their salvation is only temporary. All the remaining companions will perish on account of Poseidon's wrath. Odysseus might have succeeded completely, but he boasts and reveals his name, allowing Polyphemos to invoke Poseidon's wrath against him. Polyphemos prays that Poseidon will make it so that Odysseus comes home only after "losing all his companions" (534). The truth that Poseidon's anger over Odysseus' blinding of Polyphemos causes the deaths of all the remaining companions is confirmed by Teiresias (11.114). Poseidon's desire to give Odysseus a bad homecoming and keep him from Ithaca for an extended period of time (cf. 1.68–71) results in Odysseus losing his means of conveyance – his companions.

Rather than having the aid of a sender to give them *pompē* home from Polyphemos' cave, Odysseus and his companions encounter a further perversion of this theme. After they have blinded Polyphemos, escaped his cave, and Odysseus has revealed his name to him, the Cyclops tries to get Odysseus to return to him, holding out an offer of *pompē*:

> ἀλλ' ἄγε δεῦρ', Ὀδυσεῦ, ἵνα τοι πὰρ ξείνια θείω,
> **πομπήν** τ' ὀτρύνω δόμεναι κλυτὸν ἐννοσίγαιον·
> τοῦ γὰρ ἐγὼ πάϊς εἰμί, πατὴρ δ' ἐμὸς εὔχεται εἶναι.
> (*Od.* 9.517–19)

> But come here, Odysseus, in order that I may provide to you guest-gifts, and that I may rouse the famous earth-shaker to give conveyance. For I am his son, and he boasts to be my father.

Polyphemos' offer is just as insincere as Odysseus' earlier drink offering and Polyphemos' earlier offer of another "guest-gift." He means to trick Odysseus into understanding this as a genuine offer of conveyance. Odysseus rejects this false offer and further provokes Polyphemos by turning his offer of "sending" back upon Polyphemos: Odysseus mockingly says he wishes he could "send" (πέμψαι) Polyphemos to another home – "the house of Hades" (δόμον Ἄϊδος εἴσω, 524). Polyphemos then curses him, and the offer takes on an ironic significance: Polyphemos' promise of conveyance is, in a sense, fulfilled. Poseidon does "send" Odysseus on his way – only his divinely sanctioned journey is to be lengthy, arduous, and (at first) directed outward, away from home. Polyphemos underscores this ironic fulfillment of his promise by adapting his words from line 519, where he had referred to his divine parentage as grounds for Odysseus to believe that he could successfully prevail upon Poseidon to provide conveyance. The line is already remarkable as the only place in Homer where a character inverts the normal hierarchy of relations and says that a parent "boasts" in having the character as a son.[24] Only a few lines later he redeploys this language to authorize his prayer for Odysseus' disastrous return:

κλῦθι, Ποσείδαον γαιήοχε
εἰ ἐτεόν γε σός εἰμι, πατὴρ δ' ἐμὸς εὔχεαι εἶναι,
δὸς μὴ Ὀδυσσῆα πτολιπόρθιον οἴκαδ' ἱκέσθαι ...
(Od. 9.529–30)

...

ἀλλ' εἴ οἱ μοῖρ' ἐστὶ φίλους τ' ἰδέειν καὶ ἱκέσθαι
οἶκον ἐϋκτίμενον καὶ ἑὴν ἐς πατρίδα γαῖαν,
ὀψὲ κακῶς ἔλθοι ...
(Od. 9.532–4)

Listen, earth-embracing and dark-haired Poseidon,
If truly I am your son and you boast to be my father,
give that Odysseus the city-sacker not go homeward ...

...

But if it is fated for him to see his dear ones and reach
his well-built home and his own fatherland,
may he return late and in a poor state ...

Poseidon heeds this prayer and gives Odysseus and his crew a disastrous return – significantly, never called *pompē* – that substitutes for a proper, helpful conveyance home.[25] Polyphemos is, thus, as Egbert Bakker has put it, an "anti-donor," who gives difficulties in place of help at a structurally equivalent point in the narrative.[26] And the anti-*pompē* that Odysseus receives comes, at least in part, as a result of the poor way he treats his pseudo-host, Polyphemos. Odysseus wins his battle against the monstrous host but loses his easy path home. He declares his own identity (502–5) and seems recklessly indifferent to the threat posed by angering Poseidon. In his triumphant, independent self-assertion, he receives not help getting home but active opposition.

In their next adventure with Aiolos, Odysseus and his companions again receive unsuccessful *pompē* that ironically resonates with the later success on Scherie. There are numerous parallels between Aiolia and Scherie.[27] Both are remote, difficult-to-access islands, whose inhabitants are "dear to the gods" (φίλος/φίλοι ἀθανάτοισιν, 10.2/6.203). Both abut the sea with

---

[24] Muellner 1976: 72 observes one more parallel, with *Hom. Hymn. Herm.* 378. I add to Muellner's observations that in both cases the character is trying to use their true claim to divine parentage as grounds for the audience to believe their lying speeches.
[25] Reece 1993: 140.   [26] Bakker 2013: 22, 34.
[27] Here I extend the analysis of Clay 1985 and Alden 2017: 39–40.

unbroken cliffs where "smooth rock ran up" (λισσὴ δ' ἀναδέδρομε πέτρη, 10.4 [=5.412]); likewise, the island of the Aiolians and the palace of Alkinoös are encircled by bronze walls (10.3–4, 7.86).[28] The inhabitants of neither island are subject to the winds: Aiolos controls them at his will; the Phaiakians can ignore them and direct their ships by their will. In both episodes, descriptions of feasting, domestic arrangements, and entertainment of guests have particular emphasis.[29] On Aiolia Odysseus and his companions are kindly received and asked questions about the Trojan War and the returns of the Achaians (10.14–15). Odysseus "recount[s]" these adventures "all in proper order" (πάντα κατὰ μοῖραν κατέλεξα, 16), playing the part performed by Demodokos on Scherie, whom Odysseus bids in similar language to tell of the fall of Troy: "recount these things in proper order" (ταῦτα κατὰ μοῖραν καταλέξῃς, 8.496). In due time, Odysseus asks for conveyance:

> ἀλλ' ὅτε δὴ καὶ ἐγὼν ὁδὸν ᾔτεον ἠδ' ἐκέλευον
> **πεμπέμεν**, οὐδέ τι κεῖνος ἀνήνατο, τεῦχε δὲ **πομπήν**.
> (*Od.* 10.17–18)
>
> But when I myself then was asking for a way and was bidding him
> to send me, that man denied nothing, but made conveyance.

In this case, *pompē* consists of directing the winds to give Odysseus and his companions aid in sailing home.[30] Aiolos does this by binding all the winds in his famous "bag" (ἀσκός – properly a wineskin) and releasing only Zephyros, the west wind that would guide their ships home. Aiolos ties off the bag inside Odysseus' ship with a "bright, silver cord" (μέρμιθι φαεινῇ ἀργυρέῃ, 23–4). This bag serves doubly as an instrument of *pompē* and a parting guest-gift, which Aiolos "gave" (δῶκε, 19) Odysseus. As a gift, it resembles the chest that the Phaiakian queen Arete gives Odysseus, in which she stows gifts of clothing and gold (8.438–48).[31] A telling point

---

[28] The miraculous "unbroken bronze wall" (τεῖχος χάλκεον ἄρρηκτον, 10.3–4) that encircles Aiolia has a further parallel in the great encircling mountain threatened to fall upon the Phaiakians (13.152, 158).

[29] As Reinhardt 1960: 74–5 points out, we might have expected an extended description of the marvels of the fantastical, floating island of Aiolia. Instead, a good portion of this rather succinct episode (totaling only seventy-nine lines) is taken up with descriptions that parallel the focus of the Phaiakian episode.

[30] Cf. how Menelaos was kept by the gods from returning for lack of wind (4.360–2) or how Athena helped Telemachos with favorable winds (2.420–1, 15.292–4). On the importance of wind in general for *nostoi* in the *Odyssey*, see Purves 2010b: 332–44.

[31] It also may allude to the magical, potent wine that the Kikonian priest Maron gave Odysseus, which Odysseus took with him and used to trick Polyphemos. Odysseus brought this wine to the Cyclops' cave in a similar "great bag" (ἀσκὸν μέγαν, 9.196, 212). However, Odysseus does not say in what

of comparison is how, upon Arete's advice, he secures a lid on it with an "intricate bond" (δεσμὸν ... ποικίλον, 8.447–8) – evidently a cord with a knot.[32] He fears that the chest would be opened and its contents pilfered by thieves when he is asleep on the ship on his way home. In the case of the journey from Aiolia, the companions end up playing just such a role, thinking that the bag encloses treasures. In their foolishness, the companions open the bag while Odysseus sleeps, release the winds, and lose their *pompē* just off the coast of Ithaca.

It is noteworthy that, when released, the pent-up winds do not simply stop the ships' progress, as if there were now a new equilibrium of forces directing their travel, nor do they create a storm and blow the ships off course at random. Rather, the flotilla is "borne ... back" (ἐφέροντο ... αὖτις, 10.54–5) to Aiolia. The logic would seem to be that the natural forces at work operate with a kind of time-delayed equilibrium.[33] The three other winds did not cease to have any force; rather, the force they would have expended was merely held back and finally released in a cumulatively equal and opposite extent to the force of Zephyros. Therefore, in order for Odysseus to make it home, a kind of "debt" had to be incurred. Odysseus tries once more to appeal to Aiolos for aid. But even though he cites his companions and sleep as the culprits in losing their conveyance home (68), Aiolos perceives a divine power at work that hates Odysseus and brings him ruin (64, 74–5). Not wanting to incur divine disfavor himself, he refuses to help Odysseus further. The episode concludes with Odysseus and his companions grieving for their lot, "since conveyance no longer appeared" (οὐκέτι φαίνετο **πομπή**, 79). Much of this, as we shall see, is a negative mirror to Odysseus' later success on Scherie.

The two goddesses who detain Odysseus for lengthy periods each eventually give him conveyance, though it is much delayed. The companions live comfortably with Kirke for a full year, until they urge Odysseus to remember his fatherland and to return home (10.472–4). Thus persuaded, Odysseus takes his request to Kirke and pleads that she "fulfill for me the promise that you promised, to send us home" (τέλεσόν μοι ὑπόσχεσιν, ἥν περ ὑπέστης, οἴκαδε **πεμψέμεναι**, 483–4). This is a bit of an interpretive problem, since there is no earlier reference to such a promise, only an oath not to harm Odysseus (342–6) and an offer of restorative feasting (460–3).

---

container Maron gave him this wine (9.197). It may have been in a two-handled jar, like the wine the companions took from the Cicones (9.164) – although this wine is different than the wine Odysseus was given.

[32] Hainsworth ad loc. in Heubeck et al. 1988–92.   [33] Cf. Anaximander Fr. 1.

It may be that she never made such a promise and Odysseus is only exaggerating, or that the promise is implied by her hospitality.[34] At least one ancient critic thought the passage implies that Odysseus had supplicated her on other, unrecounted occasions and received a promise.[35] Regardless, the effect of it here is to underscore that a host ought to "fulfill" (τέλεσον) an initial offer to give conveyance before the delay causes grief, as it has on Kirke's island (484–6). When Kalypso later grants Odysseus conveyance, it comes after an even longer delay – seven years. Odysseus' grief and longing for home is commensurately greater here as well. She offers to "send him away" (ἀποπέμψω, 5.161) on a raft. She "devised his conveyance" (μήδετο **πομπήν**, 233) by giving him the tools and materials to build the raft. This takes five days, after which she "sent him" (πέμπ', 263) on his way. But initially, on account of all the earlier cases of failed *pompē*, he mistrusts Kalypso's kindly meant and genuine offer: "You, goddess, are plotting some other thing in this and not at all my conveyance" (ἄλλο τι δὴ σύ, θεά, τόδε μήδεαι οὐδέ τι **πομπήν**, 173). And so he demands she swear an oath that she is not planning for him "another evil harm" (πῆμα κακὸν … ἄλλο, 179). Because of all the "harms" (πήματα) that Odysseus has suffered thus far, he seeks assurance that he will have a *pompē* free of harm. Kalypso swears the oath he asks (187), though her oath covers only what harms she would herself intend. (Hermes did not tell her of the πήματα that are still fated to come from Poseidon. As we shall see, this too forms an implicit contrast to the Phaiakians, from whom he asks for and receives a *pompē* free of all πήματα, intentional or otherwise.) Although neither case of conveyance from these goddesses results immediately in a "harmless" return to Ithaca, both are partially successful since they advance him farther toward his home. And in both cases, despite some initial mistrust, Odysseus has to rely on their help and to cooperate in his *pompē*: with Kirke, he hearkens to and follows her directions; with Kalypso, he uses the tools she provides and builds his own raft as his means of conveyance.

3.5 Successful *Pompē* from Alkinoös

The pivotal instance of *pompē* in the *Odyssey* is the Phaiakians' final conveyance of Odysseus back to Ithaca. From the programmatic

---

[34] Exaggeration: de Jong 2001: 268; implied: Heubeck ad loc. in Heubeck et al. 1988–92, following Eisenberger 1973: 160.
[35] See the scholia ad 10.483.

announcement in Book 5 that Odysseus will find his *pompē* on Scherie (5.32, 37) until he lands safely on Ithaca in Book 13, the topic is never far from the thoughts and actions of the characters. Upon first meeting Nausikaä, whom Athena had tricked to come down to the river where he lay, Odysseus tells her of his twenty-day, miserable journey on the sea to her island and asks to be shown the city (6.170–8). From this request and from Odysseus' poor condition, she discerns that he will seek conveyance home from the lord of the city. She tells him what he must do "in order to quickly obtain conveyance and homecoming from my father" (ὄφρα τάχιστα **πομπῆς** καὶ νόστοιο τύχῃς παρὰ πατρὸς ἐμοῖο, 6.289–90): he must pass by her father and appeal to her mother, Arete. Odysseus follows her guidance and first begs Arete to "grant conveyance to reach my fatherland speedily" (**πομπὴν** ὀτρύνετε πατρίδ' ἱκέσθαι θᾶσσον, 7.151–2). Arete does not respond to this, but rather an elder of the Phaiakians urges Alkinoös to receive him kindly. Alkinoös agrees, and then promises to consider Odysseus' conveyance on the following day:

ἠῶθεν δὲ γέροντας ἐπὶ πλέονας καλέσαντες
ξεῖνον ἐνὶ μεγάροις ξεινίσσομεν ἠδὲ θεοῖσι
ῥέξομεν ἱερὰ καλά, ἔπειτα δὲ καὶ περὶ **πομπῆς**
μνησόμεθ', ὥς χ' ὁ ξεῖνος ἄνευθε πόνου καὶ ἀνίης
πομπῇ ὑφ' ἡμετέρῃ ἣν πατρίδα γαῖαν ἵκηται
χαίρων καρπαλίμως, εἰ καὶ μάλα τηλόθεν ἐστί,
μηδέ τι μεσσηγύς γε κακὸν καὶ πῆμα πάθῃσι
πρίν γε τὸν ἧς γαίης ἐπιβήμεναι·
(*Od.* 7.189–96)

In the morning, having summoned more elders,
let us entertain the stranger in the palace and to the gods
make good sacred offerings. Then about his conveyance
we will remember, how that stranger, without toil and grief,
by our conveyance may reach his fatherland
with joy speedily, even if he is from far off,
and how, on his way, he may not suffer any evil or harm
before he steps upon his native land.

If we take the clause introduced by ὥς χ' on line 192 as an indirect question, it echoes the indirect question of 1.87 and 5.31 – "how he may return" (ὥς κε νέηται) – and thereby Alkinoös begins to reveal the manner of Odysseus' conveyance.[36] The poem's audience, though assured

---

[36] See Chantraine 1953: 295 on ὡς with κε and a subjunctive verb, citing this example. Grammatically, the clause ὥς κε νέηται at 1.87 and 5.31 can be taken either as an indirect

Pompē *in the* Odyssey

in the opening of Book 5 that Odysseus will make it home by the aid of the Phaiakians, does not yet know how the Phaiakians will help him to escape from the unresolved problem of Poseidon's wrath. But Alkinoös promises that his journey will be "without toil and grief." The assembled Phaiakians concur with the plan to send Odysseus home (7.226–7).

In private, Alkinoös reveals more details: "For your conveyance, I appoint a time" (**πομπὴν** δ' ἐς τόδ' ἐγὼ τεκμαίρομαι, 7.317). He explains how Odysseus will lie asleep in one of their ships as it carries him to his home, wherever that may be. (Odysseus has yet to reveal who he is and where he is from.) Here a detail emerges that begins to explain how the conveyance will be free of harm: the Phaiakians are able to sail anywhere in the space of a day.[37] The speed of the voyage, unlike his twenty-day trip from Ogygia, will allow Odysseus to escape the notice of Poseidon.

The next day Alkinoös convenes his assembly. He puts Odysseus' situation before the Phaiakians and announces his will. The Phaiakians are to prepare Odysseus' *pompē*:

ξεῖνος ὅδ', οὐκ οἶδ' ὅς τις, ἀλώμενος ἵκετ' ἐμὸν δῶ,
ἠὲ πρὸς ἠοίων ἢ ἑσπερίων ἀνθρώπων·
πομπὴν δ' ὀτρύνει καὶ λίσσεται ἔμπεδον εἶναι.
ἡμεῖς δ', ὡς τὸ πάρος περ, ἐποτρυνώμεθα **πομπήν**·
οὐδὲ γὰρ οὐδέ τις ἄλλος, ὅτις κ' ἐμὰ δώμαθ' ἵκηται,
ἐνθάδ' ὀδυρόμενος δηρὸν μένει εἵνεκα **πομπῆς**.
(*Od.* 8.28–33)

This stranger – whoever he is I do not know – has come, wandering,
  to my house,
from men either of the east or the west.
He urges he be granted conveyance and prays that it be secure.
And let us, as in the past, hasten his conveyance.
For no one else, whoever comes to my home,
here in sorrow, waits long for the sake of conveyance.

There are two new elements here. First, in line 30 Alkinoös echoes Odysseus' request from Book 7 that the Phaiakians "grant conveyance" (**πομπὴν** ὀτρύνετε, 7.151), and then adds that the conveyance be "secure, trustworthy" (ἔμπεδον). Odysseus had not asked for this new element, but

---

question, as I have done, as a purpose clause, "*in order that* he may return," or perhaps as an indirect statement of fact, "*that* he may return." In favor of my interpretation, cf. 1.204–5, the only other place that this clause appears.

[37] They once made it to Euboea, the farthest place from Scherie, and returned in a single day (7.321–6).

it may be that Alkinoös is inferring Odysseus' needs from his recounting of his hardships at sea after Kalypso "sent" (πέμπε, 7.264) him on from Ogygia (240–97). Odysseus has been previously granted *pompē*, but it turned out not to bring him home.[38] He needs a *pompē* neither like that given by Aiolos, which failed to bring him home and could be retracted once it was revealed that he faced divine disfavor, nor like that promised by Kirke (10.483–4), which could be forgotten and delayed for a year before being given. Alkinoös' offer ironically foreshadows the failures of these negative versions of *pompē* that will be revealed in Odysseus' *apologoi*.

The second new element to the Phaiakians' *pompē* that is revealed here is that they are characteristically conveyors of strangers. On previous occasions (7.321–6) they have granted *pompē*, and they have done so promptly, so that their guests, unlike a guest of Kalypso or Kirke, do not have to "wait long for the sake of conveyance."[39] Later that day Alkinoös recounts a prophecy by his father in which he describes the Phaiakians as conveyors of everyone:

> ἀλλὰ τόδ᾽ ὥς ποτε πατρὸς ἐγὼν εἰπόντος ἄκουσα
> Ναυσιθόου, ὃς ἔφασκε Ποσειδάων᾽ ἀγάσασθαι
> ἡμῖν, οὕνεκα **πομποὶ** ἀπήμονές εἰμεν ἁπάντων·
> φῆ ποτε Φαιήκων ἀνδρῶν περικαλλέα νῆα
> ἐκ **πομπῆς** ἀνιοῦσαν ἐν ἠεροειδέϊ πόντῳ
> ῥαισέμεναι, μέγα δ᾽ ἡμῖν ὄρος πόλει ἀμφικαλύψειν.
> ὣς ἀγόρευ᾽ ὁ γέρων· τὰ δέ κεν θεὸς ἢ τελέσειεν,
> ἤ κ᾽ ἀτέλεστ᾽ εἴη, ὥς οἱ φίλον ἔπλετο θυμῷ.
> (*Od.* 8.564–71)

> But this I thus once heard from my father when he spoke,
> Nausithoös, who used to say that Poseidon bore a grudge
> against us, because we are harmless conveyors for all.
> He said that someday a beautifully made ship of the Phaiakian men,
> when it was returning from a convoy on the misty sea,
> Poseidon would smash and that he would enclose our city with
>   a great mountain.
> So the old man spoke. And the god may fulfill these things
> or they may be unfulfilled, as is dear to his spirit.

The Phaiakians give *pompē* abundantly to all who come, and they are "harmless" conveyors. The meaning of the adjective ἀπήμων, "harmless,"

---

[38] It is worth noting that this is Odysseus' limited perspective: the *pompē* granted by Kalypso did not bring him to Ithaca, but it did begin the journey that would bring him there by way of Scherie – a part of Zeus' plan never revealed to Odysseus.
[39] On this comparison, see Most 1989: 29.

is ambiguous. It can be either objective – a person may be "unharmed" – or subjective – may "cause no harm."[40] Apart from in this prophecy (repeated in Book 13), the adjective, when modifying a person, never carries the subjective sense of producing no harm. In fact, the context of Alkinoös' remarks suggests that he may be thinking of it in the objective sense as well, since he seems to be thinking of how, normally, their supernatural ships are never "harmed" (πημανθῆναι, 563).[41] Of course, it seems obvious that if the ship and the sailors carrying someone remain "unharmed," it would bring the passenger to his destination "unharmed." But, unfortunately for the Phaiakians, the reverse need not be true.

It turns out to be this element of "harm" that most angers Poseidon. When Odysseus has made it to Ithaca, Poseidon is not angry over the simple fact that Odysseus has returned: he acknowledges that Zeus had settled this as the eventual outcome (13.132–3). Rather, it is because Odysseus was conveyed peacefully – "while sleeping" (εὕδοντ', 134) – and "unharmed" (ἀπήμων, 138), with even more wealth than if he had made it home without encountering the troubles Poseidon had sent (137–8). This clarifies that the important meaning of the adjective ἀπήμονες in Nausithoös' prophecy was the subjective one: in the present case of Odysseus' conveyance, Poseidon is angry that the Phaiakians returned their passenger home without him suffering harm. As a result, Poseidon, using the language of the prophecy, says he will destroy the ship "as it returns from its convoy" (ἐκ **πομπῆς** ἀνιοῦσαν, 150 [=8.568, 13.176]), so that the Phaiakians will "cease from giving conveyance" (ἀπολλήξωσι . . . **πομπῆς**, 13.151). After Poseidon, modifying his original plan, petrifies the ship, Alkinoös repeats his father's prophecy (173–7). This results in a moment of recognition (like Polyphemos' at 9.501–16) when a prophecy's true significance becomes clear. Alkinoös' earlier doubts about whether the prophecy would come true or not (8.570–1) become his certain recognition of its fulfillment (13.178).

---

[40] The two meanings are well illustrated at *Il.* 13.744 and 748, where Polydamas gives a "harmless speech" (μῦθος ἀπήμων, 748) that presents a course of action that would allow the Trojans to go "unharmed" (ἀπήμονες, 744). An object might be called ἀπήμων if it would seem or be expected to cause no harm, even though it may unexpectedly result in harm (e.g., *Il.* 14.164). In the *Od.* 4.487 illustrates the objective meaning: it describes Achaians returning "unharmed" from Troy (in unstated contrast to Odysseus). For the subjective, *Od.* 4.519 describes the *nostos* of Agamemnon (to be precise, only the final leg of it by sea): it causes no harm to Agamemnon or his companions. At *Od.* 5.40 (=*Od.* 13.138) and *Od.* 13.39 it describes Odysseus' journey home.
[41] Thus Hainsworth in Heubeck et al. 1988–92 ad 8.564–71. Note that the root of the verb πημανθῆναι is the noun πῆμα, "harm."

However, the prophecy poses something of problem. Why would the Phaiakians go ahead and bring Odysseus home when they had already been told that Poseidon would be angered by this activity? And even more pointedly, Alkinoös' first recounting of this prophecy is mere moments before Odysseus begins the narrative in which he reveals, with almost uncharacteristic artlessness, that he, in particular, is an object of Poseidon's wrath. The poem does not provide an unequivocal explanation for why they went ahead and gave Odysseus conveyance home. Some ancient critics cited Alkinoös' nobility as one who keeps his promises; others suggested that he distrusted the prophecy.[42] Regardless, the prophecy has the effect of underscoring their generosity. For the Phaiakians are cut off from the rest of the world: Alkinoös commands them to "cease from giving conveyance" (πομπῆς ... παύεσθε, 180) and Poseidon encloses their island in an encircling mountain.[43] As a result, they can never go forth again from Scherie and receive a counter guest-gift from Odysseus. Odysseus will never repay all the enormous wealth with which they provided him. And, in a further layer of generosity, they take onto themselves all the wrath of Poseidon while – as befits "harmless conveyers" – their passenger Odysseus escapes unharmed.

The *pompē* of the Phaiakians inverts many of the motifs of Aiolos' *pompē*, which illustrates, in part, why and how it succeeds when Aiolos' failed. As I already mentioned, they have contrasting attitudes toward divine anger: the Phaiakians offer conveyance both before and after they learn that Odysseus is hated by a god; Aiolos, while offering it at first, withdraws it after he realizes that Odysseus is an object of divine wrath. Aiolos gives no parting gifts apart from the bag of winds, which is only a means of aiding conveyance. However, because the companions believe him to be more generous than he is, and to have given Odysseus gold and silver, they open the bag and lose their conveyance. In contrast, the Phaiakians give Odysseus great wealth, and do so openly, which results in Poseidon's taking away their future journeying, but not Odysseus' *pompē*. The Phaiakians' conveyance is swift, taking only a day. Aiolos' takes ten days. Leaving Aiolia, in his eagerness to reach Ithaca, Odysseus steers his ship without rest until he falls asleep on the tenth day. Then, while asleep, he loses his *pompē*, because the companions mistrust him.

---

[42] See the scholia ad 8.564 and 567.
[43] There is a textual crux at line 13.158. Aristophanes of Byzantium has an alternative reading in which Zeus modifies Poseidon's threat such that he would not enclose their island but only petrify the ship. I have followed the transmitted text, but many scholars follow Aristophanes' emendation. On the controversy, see Marks 2008: 53–60, esp. 55 n. 21 for further bibliography.

Pompē in the Odyssey

(The mistrust is reciprocal, however: Odysseus not only declines to tell them what is in the bag, he also does not trust them to steer the ship.) The Phaiakians make it to Ithaca while Odysseus sleeps. Perhaps because of their speed, they evade the notice of Poseidon until they have deposited Odysseus on Ithaca. The contrast in trust is noteworthy. Unlike the distrust that Odysseus has for his companions on their conveyance from Aiolia, which ultimately dooms them, Odysseus has to trust the Phaiakians. He has to choose to become dependent upon them. His earlier assertions of self-will in his struggle against Polyphemos and in his failed attempt to remain awake and in control of his ship for ten days on its way from Aiolia resulted in being passively driven, by Poseidon or by winds, farther from home. But through his cooperation with the Phaiakians, he succeeds in making it home.

The scene in which the thematic significance of *pompē* is perhaps most apparent is the "intermezzo" (11.328–84). Roughly halfway through telling the Phaiakians of his adventures after leaving Troy, he abruptly breaks off. He has recounted several instances of poor *pompē*, and leaves it in the hands of his audience to bring about a proper conveyance home. He ends this part of his story rather suddenly in the middle of the catalog of the women he encountered in Hades. He stops with an appeal for conveyance:

> πάσας δ' οὐκ ἄν ἐγὼ μυθήσομαι οὐδ' ὀνομήνω,
> ὅσσας ἡρώων ἀλόχους ἴδον ἠδὲ θύγατρας·
> πρὶν γάρ κεν καὶ νὺξ φθῖτ' ἄμβροτος. ἀλλὰ καὶ ὥρη
> εὕδειν, ἢ ἐπὶ νῆα θοὴν ἐλθόντ' ἐς ἑταίρους
> ἢ αὐτοῦ· **πομπὴ** δὲ θεοῖσ' ὑμῖν τε μελήσει.
> ὣς ἔφαθ', οἱ δ' ἄρα πάντες ἀκὴν ἐγένοντο σιωπῇ,
> κηληθμῷ δ' ἔσχοντο κατὰ μέγαρα σκιόεντα.
> (*Od.* 11.328–34)

> But I could not tell nor name all
> wives and daughters of heroes I saw
> before even immortal night has passed away. No, it is indeed time
> to sleep, either having gone upon a swift ship among companions
> or here. But my conveyance will be a care to the gods and you.
> So he spoke, and then all were hushed in silence
> and held by a spell throughout the shadowy halls.

In a similar way, when Odysseus ends his story with his arrival at Ogygia at the end of Book 12, he breaks off even more abruptly, mid-line (12.450). He has already told Alkinoös of his time on Ogygia and journey from there to Scherie (7.240–97), but, more to the point, he cannot continue. The narrative of the past is merging with the present, and yet this story of return home, of Odysseus' *nostos*, is incomplete. Odysseus is dependent upon his audience to complete the last stage of his journey with a proper *pompē*. The Phaiakians can become actors in the story. Odysseus, as a masterful story-teller, has left his audience enraptured: he twice holds the Phaiakians by a spell, a κηληθμός (11.334; 13.2).[44] Odysseus has transfixed his audience – in effect, enchanting them, like Kirke and the Sirens, in order to elicit from them a desire to complete his *nostos* with *pompē*;[45] that is, he entices the Phaiakians with what Peter Brooks calls "narrative desire," the desire to see a narrative end.[46] The Phaiakians are so captivated by Odysseus' story that they feel compelled to help him and ignore the warning of Nausithoös. One might wonder why the need to press the point in the "intermezzo," since Alkinoös has already agreed to send Odysseus home (7.317). But Odysseus has seen – and now the Phaiakians have heard as well – of earlier cases where he was promised *pompē*, but it failed to bring him home (Aiolos, Kirke). He cannot be sure of it until he has made it at last to Ithaca. Just as Kirke is urged to "complete" (τέλεσον, 10.483) her promise to send Odysseus home, so must the Phaiakians complete theirs.[47] In addition, Odysseus can receive even more wealth from the Phaiakians and have an even better *pompē*, if he delays for another day (11.335–41, 354–61).

Alkinoös assures Odysseus that he will provide him with his promised *pompē*:

πομπὴ δ' ἄνδρεσσι μελήσει
πᾶσι, μάλιστα δ' ἐμοί· τοῦ γὰρ κράτος ἔστ' ἐνὶ δήμῳ.
(*Od.* 11.352–3)

His conveyance will be a care to all men,
most especially me. For mine is the power among the people.

Alkinoös has adapted Odysseus' request for *pompē* from a moment earlier (332) and made it into a statement of his resolve to fulfill his promise. Furthermore, Alkinoös' remark makes for an even more striking comparison

---

[44] The noun κηληθμός is a hapax, but it comes from the verb κηλέω, which means to enchant with words, especially song. Cf. Archil. fr. 253W; Heraclitus fr. 92; Eur. *Alc.* 359; Pl. *Ly.* 206b; Pl. *Prt.* 315a; Pl. *Phdr.* 267d. On the depiction of poetry as enchantment in the *Odyssey*, see Maehler 1963: 29–30.
[45] See Bierl 2008: 177. Odysseus' success is in part due to the general ability of song to bring pleasure: see Macleod 1983: 8.
[46] Brooks 1984: 37–61, esp. 52: "If the motor of narrative is desire, totalizing, building ever-larger units of meaning, the ultimate determinants of meaning lie *at the end*, and narrative desire is ultimately, inexorably, desire *for* the end."
[47] On the uncertainty of the Phaiakians' hospitality, see Rose 1969; Most 1989: 27–8.

with Odysseus' earlier proclamation of his name, when he revealed his identity to the Phaiakians at the beginning of his *apologoi*:

εἴμ' Ὀδυσεὺς Λαερτιάδης, ὅς πᾶσι δόλοισιν
ἀνθρώποισι μέλω, καί μευ κλέος οὐρανὸν ἵκει.
(*Od.* 9.19–20)
I am Odysseus, son of Laertes, I who am a care to all men
for my wiles, and my fame reaches heaven.[48]

It is as though Alkinoös is recalling the words Odysseus used at the outset of his mini-epic answer to Alkinoös' question of who he was. But now, Alkinoös replaces Odysseus with his *pompē*. Odysseus and his conveyance merge.

3.6 Conclusion

If Odysseus is identified with his *pompē*, it means, in part, that he has become an agent who occupies the middle ground between an independent, autonomous, self-asserting hero and a passive, suffering victim. He must collaborate with helpers and trust them (and they must trust him) in order to find his way home. This is the sort of hero he becomes among the Phaiakians, and it allows him finally to return to Ithaca. Odysseus' worst experiences come when he is occupying one of the poles of agency. On the one hand, when he boastfully taunts Polyphemos, revealing his name only for the purpose of augmenting his fame among humans, he brings both years of further wandering upon himself and also, over the course of those wanderings, death upon all his remaining crew.[49] On the other hand, on his way back from Troy, Odysseus several times encounters storms, contrary winds, and currents that propel him away from Ithaca despite his efforts to sail home.

Collaboration and trust of the sort that Odysseus must engage in with the Phaiakians is risky – both for the one offering conveyance and the one

---

[48] In both cases there is a clause consisting of two hemistichs extending from the end of one line over the beginning of the next where something is "a care to all men" (although at 9.19 it is also possible to take πᾶσι with δόλοισιν). This is not the only other place in which a variation on this formulaic phrase appears: cf. *Od.* 1.358, where μῦθος is the subject of concern. In this example, μῦθος means the epic song of the νόστοι of the Achaians that Phemios has just sung. The verb μέλω commonly implies epic poetry: see Danek 1998: 160, 256–7. Thus, the construction of *pompē* with μέλω may suggest conveyance as a subject of epic.

[49] Cf. also Odysseus' failed attempt to single-handedly fight off Skylla. As Hopman 2012: 13–16 has shown, "Odysseus' eagerness to fight culminates in a parodic duel" (16). She further notes that Odysseus' failure in this encounter shows to the Phaiakians his need for help, for conveyance (22).

being conveyed. Aiolos recognized the danger of helping someone hated by the gods; Alkinoös did not recognize it (or ignored it) and suffered for it. Odysseus had already entrusted himself to the help of Kirke and Kalypso, and the results of their conveyance were mixed at best. Therefore, an agent who would seek conveyance must be prudent. Prudence of this sort serves Odysseus well on Ithaca. He tests potential helpers such as Eumaios before trusting them. But he must entrust himself to their help. Though he is tempted to despair, he must trust in the promises of Athena as well. For he knows he cannot succeed alone against so great a foe as 108 suitors (see, e.g., 20.36–43). Ultimately, by narrating his misfortunes that arose from extreme self-assertion and passive suffering, Odysseus learns how to become the balanced hero he needs to be in order to reach home safely and restore his household to proper order. And this sort of virtuous balance between wholly active and passive modes of agency is the essential characteristic of successful *pompē*.

CHAPTER 4

"What Country, Friends, is This?" Geography and Exemplarity in Valerius Flaccus' Argonautica

Jessica Blum

Valerius Flaccus' *Argonautica* exists in a time warp. Written sometime between 70 and 90 CE, it looks back to the dawn of the heroic age, when the Argo's launch initiated a new era of human *labor* and competition for *imperium*. The doubling effect of the poem's imperial time frames – the mythological rise of Jupiter's rule, and the establishment of the Flavian regime in Rome – raises the question of how a particular moment in history leads to triumph or tragedy, and whether these new rulers will prove favorable or destructive for their subjects. Both mythological and historical protagonists hover at the starting point of an unknown future.

The concept of the "journey" is therefore inseparable from the Argo's voyage in two dimensions, reflecting its physical route from Greece to Colchis, and its historical journey across time. Valerius' geography not only maps out the paths across which *imperium* will be contested, but also calls into question the outcome of this process.[1] The Argonautic myth itself has a dual ending, leading as it does to the achievement of the protagonists' epic mission and to the tragedy that awaits them beyond the (probable) scope of the poem.[2] How, then, do Valerius' protagonists understand their own journey? What prompts them to set out into the unknown, and how might this reflect the experience of Valerius' contemporaries as they witness the re-start of the Roman Empire under Vespasian and his sons? In this chapter I argue that the interactions of different genres in the *Argonautica* illustrate the tension between a divine perspective that sees the Argo's voyage as part of the rise and fall of nations and a human perspective that seeks meaning without access to this broader

[1] Cf. Hdt. 1.2.
[2] See Montiglio, Chapter 5 in this volume, p. 93, on multiple endings in Apollonius' *Argonautica*. On the intended length of the Valerius' *Argonautica*, see Manuwald 2015: 4–7.

continuum. Knox describes how the Sophoclean hero "acts in a terrifying vacuum, a present that has no future to comfort and no past to guide."[3] It is precisely this type of dislocation that Valerius and his protagonists try to avoid by constructing a martial-epic narrative for their story, giving themselves a clear view of past and future.

First we must define "martial-epic." As many have argued, the Roman poets' manipulation of generic categories requires a hypothetical ideal for each genre, a point of orientation from which to enact their manipulations of and deviations from the putative generic rules.[4] For epic, as Hinds puts it, this ideal was "all male, all war, all the time," despite the fact that epic was always already interwoven with other themes.[5] In the eyes of Valerius' Argonauts, this (artificial) construct constitutes a mode of response to the people and places encountered on their route: at every turn they seek opportunities to showcase their martial *uirtus* with the expectation of winning glory by doing so. As we will see, they treat every interaction as a stage for their martial-epic performance.

The Argonauts' defining motive is the quest for glory through a successful homecoming: they seek to enter the epic tradition as *exempla* – normative ethical models – for the next generation through the display of *uirtus*.[6] Their voyage provides a performance space in which they can act out the heroic story that they want to tell about themselves, and enables their evaluation (favorably, they hope) against the rubric of their ancestral standards. The Argonauts' focus on homecoming as a means to this end reflects their prioritization of Homeric models, as they follow a particularly Odyssean path to fame.

The Argonauts' epic-focused reading, however, precludes their awareness that their story has the potential to follow other scripts.[7] True to Odysseus' own experience, the Argonauts discover that their *exempla* – the behavioral models they follow – do not necessarily remain valid as they move farther away from home. Just as Odysseus' desire for knowledge and

---

[3] Knox 1964: 5.   [4] Hinds 2000: 221–7; Barchiesi 2001: 156–7; Gale 2004: xii.
[5] Hinds 2000: 223 describes how some of epic's most recurrent features (female passion) are systematically treated as threatening the essence of the genre. See Keith 2000 on epic as a normative genre for Roman masculinity.
[6] The Argonauts' *nostos* is thus ethical as much as physical. For homecoming as the collective goal of Apollonius' Argonauts, see Ap. Rhod. 1.336–7. Zissos 2012: 98–9 argues that Valerius' reference to the Pacuvian *Medus* invokes a Colchian *nostos* as the end point of Medea's story.
[7] Roller 2009: 215 describes how exemplary discourse assumes that "the past occupies a space of experience continuous with or homologous to the present."

gifts leads him astray, so too does the Argonauts' adherence to a Homeric script prompt them to take the wrong action at the wrong place and time. The foreign landscapes that they reach represent changing contexts in which their literary–ancestral models fail them, as they repeatedly confront tragic and civil war scenarios along the voyage. The Argonauts' heroic journey is to some degree self-deceptive: they adhere to an outward-looking, martial-epic script in the face of the multigeneric landscape of their literary tradition.

There is a further problem with the Argonauts' focus on the past for inspiration. As the first generation of epic heroes, they chronologically antedate Homer's heroes, and indeed have among their crew Nestor and the fathers of Achilles and both Ajaxes. Their focus on exemplarity, therefore, is doubly anachronistic. The poem's interwoven time frames reveal that the Argonauts' desired triumph was already precluded by the inevitable progress of fate. At the same time, Valerius' translation of his Greek myth into a Roman interpretive framework integrates the epic tradition in its entirety into Roman history. The Argonauts cannot realize that the *nostos* they pursue will bring about the Roman *imperium* that Jupiter anticipates, historical progress rather than a return to the Homeric past. By his very subject, then, Valerius gives a powerful warning that the *exempla* of the past may bring a very different *telos* than that envisioned by his protagonists.[8]

So far, I have outlined several points of investigation: Valerius' introduction of a Roman exemplary discourse into his Greek myth; the time frames at work in the *Argonautica*; and the interaction of different genres in the poem as a reflection of the possible outcomes of these mythological or historical processes. To bring these together, I start by examining the confluence of Roman exemplarity and Odyssean *nostos* as the way that the Argonauts understand their mission. I then suggest that this focus on Homeric models determines their actions throughout the poem, arguing that the crew's "epic reading" constitutes a necessary fiction that motivates them on their journey. Finally, I examine several stops along the voyage to see how the various places the Argonauts reach are foreign in terms of genre as well as geography. In their journey through history, the Argonauts sail across a changing world.

---

[8] Bakker, Chapter 2 in this volume, suggests that the *Odyssey*'s characters perceive the Golden Age as attainable (p. 14).

4.1 Roman *Nostos*

Valerius' opening lines reflect the importance of visibility as an indicator of heroic preeminence. His subject, he tells us, is not merely the voyage of the Argo, but specifically of this journey *as a means to exemplary status*:[9]

> Prima deum magnis canimus freta peruia natis
> fatidicamque ratem, Scythici quae Phasidis oras
> ausa sequi mediosque inter iuga concita cursus
> rumpere flammifero tandem consedit Olympo.
> (V. Fl. 1.1–4)

> I sing of the straits first traversed by the great sons of the gods and of the fate-speaking ship, which, having dared to pursue the shores of Scythian Phasis and to break its course through the clashing rocks, finally settled on flame-bearing Olympus.

This represents a marked shift away from the themes given top billing in Apollonius' proem (Ap. Rhod. 1.1–2): Ἀρχόμενος σέο Φοῖβε παλαιγενέων κλέα φωτῶν/ μνήσομαι ("Beginning from you, Phoebus, I will recount the famous deeds of men of old").[10] Apollonius' headline is the famous deeds of the Argonauts, a retrospective account that, like the songs of Achilles and Demodocus in the *Iliad* and *Odyssey*, provide the *exempla* that embody the heroic code of behavior.[11] Valerius, meanwhile, plays with his story's doubled status as simultaneous forerunner and heir of the Homeric epics. Rather than taking the backward-looking stance of Apollonius' narrative, in which the deeds of the Argonauts are viewed at a temporal remove, his is a forward-looking project, exploring the process by which those deeds acquire their exemplary status for future generations.

Valerius' presentation of his myth supports this interest.[12] In keeping with the Latin tradition, he asserts the Argo's status as the first ship, in a sort of transferred *primus . . . ego* claim that stakes out a programmatic role for his poem vis-à-vis the epic tradition. The *klea andron* that Achilles and Demodocus will sing, and from which the Homeric generation will learn how to be heroes, are the very events that Valerius narrates. In this

---

[9] This echoes Catull. 64.1 and 4.1, both of which make a ship their protagonist; these intertexts suggest that generic mixing is built into the *Argonautica* from its proem. Zissos 2008: 71 notes Valerius' focus on a broader view of human history and the concurrent omission of the Golden Fleece as the Argonauts' short-term goal.
[10] Kleywegt 2005: 5 cites Verg. *G.* 1.1–4 and Luc. *BC*. 1.1.   [11] Cf. *Il.* 9.189, 524; *Od.* 8.73.
[12] Zissos 2008: 78 notes that the Argo's catasterism is also referred to at V. Fl. 4.692–3, 5.293–5. Cf. Manilius, *Astron.* 1.37.

he follows Eratosthenes, who describes the Argo as a παράδειγμα σαφέστατον.[13] By laying claim to this tradition, Valerius suggests that the goal of both the Argo and its crew is to become an *exemplum* of the civilizing movement from west to east entailed by Jupiter's new age of heroic *labor*.[14] Valerius' proem thus establishes the Argo's visual preeminence and his exemplary work as the primary mode of communication between the divine and human spheres. By offering such a guide, the Argo and its crew inspire future generations to a kind of emulative mimesis that will give rise to the epic tradition that follows.[15]

The need for such a medium becomes apparent as Book 1 continues. Looking down on the ship from Olympus, Jupiter contextualizes the *Argo*'s voyage in the broad sweep of history:

> Tum genitor: "uetera haec nobis et condita pergunt
> ordine cuncta suo rerumque a principe cursu
> fixa manent (neque enim terris tum sanguis in ullis
> noster erat cum fata darem iustique facultas
> hinc mihi, cum varios struerem per saecula reges) ...
> arbiter ipse locos terrenaque summa movendo
> experiar, quaenam populis longissima cunctis
> regna velim linquamque datas ubi certus habenas."
> (V. Fl. 1.531–5, 558–60)

> Then spoke the father: "These matters, long ago established by me, all proceed in due course and remain fixed in the original order of things; nor indeed was my bloodline present anywhere on earth at the time when I decreed the course of fate, and for this reason I had the capacity for justice when I set out a line of kings through the ages ... I myself as judge, by shifting the seat of earthly power, will test which kingdom I wish to hold the longest rule over all the lands and with which I will with certainty leave the reins once given."

Jupiter outlines a Herodotean framework of reciprocal warfare that allows him to test the *uirtus* of the different nations that aspire to supremacy.[16] His assertion of impartiality implicitly recognizes the suffering that this process entails: each nation must fall in order for its successor to rise, in a continual interchange of triumph and tragedy. How, then, is each generation induced

---

[13] Jackson 1997: 255 and Zissos 2008: 72 cite Eratosth. [*Cat.*] 35 as the earliest Greek source to name the Argo as the first ship.
[14] Wacht 1991a: 19–23.
[15] Compare Apollo's words to Ascanius at *Aen.* 9.641: *sic itur ad astra*. By invoking this passage, Valerius enacts the chain of *literary* exemplary transmission in tandem with heroic inheritance.
[16] Stover 2012: 43. Cf. Silius' Jupiter, who justifies the Second Punic War as a test and renewal of Rome's ancestral *uirtus* (*Pun.* 3.573–4).

to enter into the contest? The answer, Valerius suggests, lies in the competition for exemplary status, a necessary fiction of epic triumph that holds out the prize of heroic immortality to those who pursue it.

As Jupiter outlines his program of *translatio imperii*, he describes ancestral emulation as a key motive for the Argonauts' journey (V. Fl. 1.544–5): *inde meae quercus tripodesque animaeque parentum/ hanc pelago misere manum* ("then my oaks and the tripods and the souls of their ancestors have sent this band out upon the sea"). And Jupiter himself participates in this intergenerational dialogue, turning aside to address his three sons who join the crew:[17]

> tunc oculos Aegaea refert ad caerula robur
> Herculeum Ledaeque tuens genus atque ita fatur:
> "tendite in astra, uiri: me primum regia mundo
> Iapeti post bella trucis Phlegraeque labores
> imposuit: durum uobis iter et grave caeli
> institui. sic ecce meus, sic orbe peracto
> Liber et expertus remeauit Apollo."
> (V. Fl. 1.561–7)

> Then he turns his eyes to the blue Aegean, gazing at the mighty Hercules and Leda's children, and speaks thus: "Strive for the stars, men: then first did my kingdom give me power over the world, after the battles of fierce Iapetus and the labors of Phlegra; for you, too, I have decreed a hard and wearisome path to the sky. Thus, see, thus, with the world traversed, did my Bacchus and Apollo, once tested, return."

Jupiter's words place competition at the heart of his historical scheme. Exemplary status of the kind achieved by Bacchus and Hercules converges with epic *kleos* as the guiding principle for the Argonauts and the generations who will follow them.[18] Each hero achieves immortality through the ongoing reenactment of his achievements, while the inaugural journey of ship and crew provides the stage on which they perform their exemplary *virtus*.

But how is such *uirtus* to be assessed? In order for the exemplary discourse to work, it assumes that "the past occupies a space of experience continuous with or homologous to the present"; in other words, that the ethical guidelines of the past remain valid in the present.[19] Under this

---

[17] On Jupiter's tone, see Otte 1992: 55. Polleichtner 2005: 353 points out Jupiter's focus on *robur Herculeum*.
[18] As will be discussed below, Hercules provides a model in real time for the crew.
[19] Roller 2009: 215; cf. also Roller 2004: 3–4, 32, 34.

rubric, heroic deeds must be evaluated against a common set of *mores* in order to achieve their value. For the Argonauts, however, this poses a tricky problem. While they continually strive for a geographical *nostos*, in which they will return to a home community that shares their heroic ethos, such a homecoming is impossible in temporal terms: as the first generation of epic heroes, they simply have no tradition to which to return, and the epic world is forever changed by their voyage. In their eyes, however, home and family provide a fixed point of orientation for their outward journey, as the audience for whom the Argonauts will perform and by whom they will be assessed. The Argonauts' ethos depends on the belief that they can and will come back to an unchanged world and that, by doing so, they can create the exemplary self-image they desire.

4.2 Home and Homer

From the very start of the expedition, Valerius shows the Argonauts' conflation of *kleos* and *nostos* to be the primary motivation for embarking on their expedition. Although Jason recognizes that his mission – to retrieve the Golden Fleece from Colchis – is a ploy by his uncle Pelias to kill him off, he still succumbs to the temptation of winning an epic prize:[20]

> heu quid agat? populumne leuem ueterique tyranno
> infensum atque olim miserantes Aesona patres
> aduocet? an socia Iunone et Pallade fretus
> armisona speret magis et freta iussa capessat,
> siqua operis tanti domito consurgere ponto
> fama queat? tu sola animos mentesque peruris,
> Gloria; te uiridem uidet immunemque senectae
> Phasidis in ripa stantem iuuenesque uocantem.
> (V. Fl. 1.71–8)

> Alas, what should he do? Should he call on the populace, fickle and hostile to the old tyrant, and the *patres* who have long pitied Aeson, or, relying on Juno and Pallas sounding her armor, should he rather take hope and venture onto the seas as bidden, if any fame could come from such a great undertaking when once the sea is overcome? You alone, Glory, set heart and mind on fire, you, flourishing and immune to old age, he sees standing on the bank of the Phasis and summoning youths.

---

[20] Buckley 2014: 309 argues that the political background established in this passage creates the potential for a Senecan tragedy to take place.

The description of glory *uiridis et immunis senectae* indicates that Jason looks beyond the text to the kind of (literary) immortality won by an Odyssean *nostos*. Likewise, the arrival of his companions, eager to prove their heroic *uirtus*, emphasizes the primacy of *kleos* in his, and their, calculations:

> Omnis auet quae iam bellis spectataque fama
> turba ducum, primae seu quos in flore iuuentae
> temptamenta tenent necdum data copia rerum.
> (V. Fl. 1.100–2)

The whole crowd of captains already proven in war and of known fame are ready, and those whom, in the first flower of youth, trials entice and the as-yet-ungiven opportunity for action.

At least for the younger members of the crew, no opportunity has yet arisen for heroic activity (*necdum data copia rerum*), and they are eager to get started. With this detail, Valerius emphasizes the importance of this inaugural journey as an essential performance space for his would-be epic heroes. But this means to glory brings with it the proviso that the Argonauts actually make it back to their home community – otherwise, they will find themselves in the same quandary as Odysseus, who continually faces the threat of an inglorious death:

> τρὶς μάκαρες Δαναοὶ καὶ τετράκις, οἳ τότ᾽ ὄλοντο
> Τροίῃ ἐν εὐρείῃ, χάριν Ἀτρεΐδῃσι φέροντες.
> ὡς δὴ ἐγώ γ᾽ ὄφελον θανέειν καὶ πότμον ἐπισπεῖν
> ἤματι τῷ ὅτε μοι πλεῖστοι χαλκήρεα δοῦρα
> Τρῶες ἐπέρριψαν περὶ Πηλεΐωνι θανόντι.
> (*Od*. 5.306–10)

"Thrice, four times happy Danaäns who in the time gone by
fell on the plain of Troy to please the sons of Atreus!
Would I had died there too, and met my doom the day a multitude
of Trojans hurled bronze spears at me over the body of
    Peleus' sons!"

For Odysseus, an appreciative audience is the essential ingredient without which his heroic performance is rendered pointless. In this sense, Odysseus wishes for a temporal as well as (or instead of) a geographical homecoming, with the *Iliad* representing his ideal of martial-epic heroism. In their quest for glory, the Argonauts subscribe to a similar principle. They continually return to a singular *exemplum* of how to "do" epic, thereby limiting the way in which they respond to the situations they encounter along their journey. In order to show this dynamic at work, I will first demonstrate that the Argonauts self-select the terms in which they read their own story along generic lines, and next, how the model on which they base these terms is in fact far more complex than their martial-epic reading takes into account.

4.3 Genre and the Journey

Even before they set out, the Argonauts confront different ways of reading their own story. On the eve of the launch, their two prophets, Mopsus and Idmon, each give a prophecy that posits a different endpoint informed by a different generic lens:[21] Mopsus' frenzied words describe Jason and Medea's tragic – and (presumably) extra-narrative – downfall, while Idmon focuses on the crew's homecoming, echoing Jupiter's words to his sons.[22]

First, Mopsus presents the Argonauts' voyage as the violation of a divine *lex*, a voyage full of suffering and loss that culminates in a scene straight out of Euripides:

> "heu quaenam aspicio? . . .
> . . . per quot discrimina rerum
> expedior! subita cur pulcher harundine crines
> velat Hylas? unde urna umeris niveosque per artus
> caeruleae vestes? unde haec tibi uulnera, Pollux?
> quantus io tumidis taurorum e naribus ignis!
> tollunt se galeae sulcisque ex omnibus hastae
> et iam iamque umeri. quem circum uellera Martem
> aspicio? quaenam aligeris secat anguibus auras
> caede madens? quos ense ferit? miser eripe paruos
> Aesonide! cerno et thalamos ardere iugales."
> (V. Fl. 1.212–26)

---

[21] Cowan 2014: 247 argues that the most fruitful interpretive approach is to take both prophecies as equally valid. Manuwald 2013: 39 suggests that the contrast between the two shows Jupiter's restriction of human knowledge throughout the poem. Zissos 2004: 321 discusses the phenomenon of two fully developed and divergent prophecies. Feeney 1991: 317 argues that the two prophecies depict the competition between epic's near and distant perspectives. On the authorization of both Mopsus and Idmon through Apollo's inspiration, see Stover 2012: 161–4.

[22] Lovatt 2013: 53 observes that the prophecies of Mopsus and Idmon "set up a dialogue between tragic theatricality and epic reticence." Such attempts to read the future, she argues, represent the human tendency to apply narratives to the events that befall them, to create a cohesive narrative out of randomness (70).

"Alas what do I see? ... Through how many dangers do I make my way! Why does fair Hylas suddenly cover his hair with reeds? Whence the pitcher on his shoulders and the blue garments on his snowy limbs? Whence, Pollux, these wounds of yours? Ah, what great fire from the bulls' flaring nostrils! Helmets lift themselves and spears from every furrow and now, now the shoulders. What battles do I see around the fleece? Who, dripping with gore, cleaves the air with winged serpents? Whom does she strike with a sword? Wretched Aesonides, save the little ones! I see too the bridal chambers ablaze!"

Mopsus' prophecy looks beyond the poem's events, an extratextual view of the tragedy that awaits its protagonists. His speech has an almost visceral effect on his audience, reflecting both its spectacular nature and the *aporia* it induces (V. Fl. 1.227–8): *iamdudum <...> Minyas ambage ducemque / terrificat* ("for a long time now has the seer terrified the Minyae and their captain").[23] This storyline, furthermore, is an *ambages*, a diversion from the Argonauts' anticipated narrative and therefore unreadable to his epic-oriented audience.

In this moment of terror and confusion Idmon inserts an alternate way of reading the story. Although his prophecy does not, in fact, contradict Mopsus', Idmon's calm assurance provides Jason and the crew with the roadmap that they need to embark on their voyage:

> sed enim contra Phoebeius Idmon ...
> sic sociis Mopsoque canit: "quantum augur Apollo
> flammaque prima docet, praeduri plena laboris
> cerno equidem, patiens sed quae ratis omnia uincet.
> ingentes durate animae dulcesque parentum
> tendite ad amplexus!" lacrimae cecidere canenti
> quod sibi iam clusos inuenit in ignibus Argos.
> (V. Fl. 1.228–39)

But then in response Idmon, son of Phoebus ... thus prophesies to his companions and Mopsus: "As much as the augur Apollo and the first flame teach me, indeed I see a course full of grievous labor, all of which the steadfast ship will nevertheless overcome. Endure, great souls, and strive towards the sweet embrace of your parents!" Tears fell as he sang, since he saw in the flames that Argos was already closed to him.

Idmon's prophecy focuses on the Argonauts' eventual homecoming, a reassuring contrast to Mopsus' tragic vision.[24] Valerius suggests, however,

---

[23] Wacht 1991b: 104 suggests that the fear caused by Mopsus is the expedition's first crisis. On the lacuna, see Zissos 2008: 198.
[24] Buckley 2014: 312.

that Idmon is the less reliable of the two speakers. The final two lines indicate his ability and willingness to conceal information from his companions, albeit for their own good: he elides the Argonauts' future losses (including his own death) in order to achieve their launch.[25]

That this is the subtext of Idmon's speech is made clear by his (unconscious) echo of the *Georgics*: his promise *ratis omnia uincet* appropriates Vergil's characterization of the Jovian world (*G.* 1.145: *labor omnia uicit*, "labor conquers all"), reinforcing the programmatic nature of the Argo's voyage.[26] Like Jupiter's words to his sons, the ship suggests a model of Herculean *labor* for the Argonauts to follow, a model that, like the combined prophecies of Mopsus and Idmon, reflects the extremes of epic triumph and imminent tragedy.[27] Jupiter's plans require that his human agents keep the short-term, epic view in sight, and ignore the tragedy lurking in the – for now – distant future.

Idmon's prophecy serves this purpose, self-consciously speaking the language of epic.[28] His exhortation *ingentes durate animae* echoes Aeneas' speech on the shore at Carthage (*Aen.* 1.207: *durate, et uosmet rebus seruate secundis*, "endure, and bear up for better days"), offering a model of perseverance from Valerius' epic *exempla*. Furthermore, with *durate* he looks to ancestral tradition, incorporating the phrasing of Vergil's Apolline oracle:

> "Dardanidae duri, quae uos a stirpe parentum
> prima tulit tellus, eadem uos ubere laeto
> accipiet reduces. antiquam exquirite matrem."
> (*Aen.* 3.94–6)

> "Long-suffering sons of Dardanus, the land which bore you first from your parent stock shall welcome you back to her fruitful bosom. Seek out your ancient mother."

Idmon fills in the gap that Aeneas cannot, replacing the Trojan goal of "finding their ancient mother" with the embraces of the Argonauts' parents: *dulcesque ... ad amplexus*.[29] The son of Apollo, he appropriates his father's Vergilian prediction, and, at the same time, anticipates Jupiter's

---

[25] Cf. Ap. Rhod. 1.440–7 on the Apollonian Argonauts' knowledge of Idmon's death.
[26] Feeney 1991: 330; Stover 2012: 53. Cf. Manilius, *Astron.* 4.932: *ratio omnia uincit*. Thomas 2004–5: 122 cites the prioritization of *labor* as the premise of the *Georgics* (*G.* 1.121–35). Buckley 2014: 312 describes how Idmon's prophecy aligns *labor* and *uirtus*.
[27] Hercules' apotheosis is overlaid with tragedy through Senecan echoes: cf. *Herc. Fur.* 66–8, 74, 958–9. Ganiban 2014: 265–7 discusses the restriction of apotheosis to Jupiter's sons.
[28] His self-editing process, however, indicates an even greater tragedy in the offing through its invocation of Lucan's Pythia (*BC* 5.200–3); this epic launch must ignore its tragic end.
[29] Perhaps an ironic (and tragic) reference to Jason and Medea's children.

advice to his own sons (*tendite in astra*).[30] The goals of *nostos* and *kleos* are brought together in a language authorized by familial–generic tradition, offering the Argonauts a tangible endpoint with clear *exempla* showing them the way.

Mopsus' and Idmon's very different – but equally accurate – prophecies effectively set up a choice for the internal audience of which reading to follow. In the absence of any direct knowledge of divine plans, the crew chooses the storyline that most closely aligns with their own heroic self-construction.[31] Jason himself is fundamentally uncertain as to where his mission will lead.[32] Despite this lack of perspective, however, he follows Idmon's example and chooses an epic storyline, suppressing his own doubts:[33]

> uix ea fatus erat iungit cum talia ductor
> Aesonius: "superum quando consulta uidetis,
> o socii quantisque datur spes maxima coeptis,
> uos quoque nunc uires animosque adferte paternos.
> non mihi Thessalici pietas culpanda tyranni
> suspectiue doli: deus haec, deus omine dextro
> imperat; ipse suo uoluit commercia mundo
> Iuppiter et tantos hominum miscere labores.
> ite, uiri, mecum dubiisque evincite rebus
> quae meminisse iuuet nostrisque nepotibus instent."
> (V. Fl. 1.240–9)

Scarcely had he spoken, when the Aesonian captain continued: "Since you see the purpose of the gods, companions, and to what great undertakings the highest hope is given, you, too, now bring to bear the strength and spirit of your fathers. It is not for me to blame the piety of the Thessalian tyrant, nor suspect deceit: the god, the god, with favorable omen issues these orders; Jupiter himself desires exchange for his world and to join the great labors of men. Come with me, men, and overcome doubtful circumstances, which it will be a delight to remember and which will inspire our grandsons."

---

[30] Ripoll 1998: 99–100 observes that Jupiter's apostrophe establishes astral immortality as the voyage's goal.
[31] Manuwald 2009: 589 argues that the clear knowledge gap in the *Argonautica* leads humans to formulate their own ideas about and motives for the voyage.
[32] Jason focuses on the separation from home and family (V. Fl.1.150). Ferenczi 2014: 146 argues that Jason's ignorance has a motivating function. Wacht 1991b: 116–17 points out Jason's increasing distrust in prophecy; cf. V. Fl. 4.538–46. Manuwald 2009: 591 infers that Jason "seems to believe in benign gods." While I agree that this is the initial impression given by his speech, his doubt suggests his conscious manipulation of the rhetoric of divine sponsorship.
[33] Wacht 1991b: 106 notes that Jason leaves no room for more doubts to be expressed.

Like Idmon, Jason, too, professes a confidence that he does not necessarily feel to give his companions a vision of the future that inspires them in the present. His speech echoes that of Aeneas after his fleet has washed up on the shore of Carthage in *Aeneid* 1:

> "O socii (neque enim ignari sumus ante malorum),
> o passi grauiora, dabit deus his quoque finem.
> uos et Scyllaeam rabiem penitusque sonantis
> accestis scopulos, uos et Cyclopia saxa
> experti: reuocate animos maestumque timorem
> mittite; forsan et haec olim meminisse iuuabit.
> per uarios casus, per tot discrimina rerum
> tendimus in Latium, sedes ubi fata quietas
> ostendunt; illic fas regna resurgere Troiae.
> durate, et uosmet rebus seruate secundis."
>
> (*Aen.* 1.198–207)

> "O comrades – indeed we have not been ignorant of misfortune before – you who have suffered worse, to this too the god will bring an end. You ventured near Scylla's fury and her resounding crags; recall your spirits and banish gloomy fear; perhaps it will some day be pleasing to recall even these misfortunes. Through varied obstacles, through countless hazards, we journey towards Latium, where fate promises a peaceful home. There it is granted that Troy's realm shall rise again; endure, and live for a happier day."

The scenes are structurally and rhetorically similar, taking place on a beach in the first books of their respective epics. The *Aeneid*, however, begins *in medias res*, giving Aeneas a very different perspective from which to speak. While Jason refers to the as-yet-unknown challenges of the sea, Aeneas' statement *neque enim ignari sumus ante malorum* represents a long history of obstacles overcome. He recognizes that tragedy is a part of his story, while Jason's response demonstrates that he limits his own perspective to the epic lens through which he would like his story told.

Aeneas gives his men a concrete goal: Latium, peaceful homes, and the rebirth of Troy. Jason's view of the future is necessarily much sketchier. Where Aeneas dwells on the rest that the Trojans will find in Latium and adds on the qualified suggestion *forsan et haec olim meminisse iuuabit*, Jason focuses on the reception of the Argonauts' deeds on their return: *dubiisque euincite rebus/ quae meminisse iuuet nostrisque nepotibus instent*. His proleptic *meminisse* represents an active construction of the crew's legacy, the reception that is a function both of their physical home and of their generic home in the epic tradition.

But the juxtaposition of prophecies in Book 1 shows that there *are* alternate versions of the story, that it can be (and had been) interpreted in tragic form. The exclusively epic lens that enables the Argonauts to set out on their voyage continually lands them in hot water, in situations that directly threaten their desire for *nostos* and the heroic fame that comes with it. As the Argo embarks on its journey, and the crew on its epic project, the unknown lands they reach are generically and geographically foreign, representations of the different strands running through the Argonautic tradition. As such, the Argonauts, like Odysseus, continually confront the possibility that they will be immortalized in a generic framework other than the type of epic storyline they envision.

4.4 Into the Wild: Genre and Geography

As the first generation to set sail, the Argonauts are operating in something of an exemplary vacuum. The Argo carries with it, however, a hero already well launched on his glorious career: Hercules. From the very beginning, Jupiter singles Hercules out among the crew (V. Fl. 1.561–2: *tunc oculos Aegaea refert ad caerula robur / Herculeum*), as one of the standard-bearers of his new regime. Embodying the promise of apotheosis won through *labor*, Hercules plays an active role in maintaining the voyage's forward progress.[34] The fact that he is himself at times unable to deal with the obstacles the Argonauts encounter hints, therefore, at the possible failure of the heroic storyline he represents.

In contrast to the rest of the crew, the majority of whom are eager to prove their as-yet-untested *uirtus*, Hercules is already well embarked on his Labors and provides an immediate *exemplum* of heroic achievement for his crewmates:

> molli iuuenes funduntur in alga
> conspicuusque toris Tirynthius.
>   (V. Fl. 1.252–3)
>
> the youths recline on the soft seaweed, and
> the Tirynthian lies conspicuous on his couch.

conspicuus from the get-go, Hercules functions as *exemplum* both for the crew and for the narrative as a whole. As both the ur-hero of epic and a tragic protagonist, he, like Mopsus and Idmon, offers the external audience

---

[34] On Hercules and Stoic thought in the Flavian period, see Tipping 2010 and Ferenczi 2014.

"What Country, Friends, is This?"

multiple lenses through which to read his story, a hypostatization of the diverse genres that intertwine in the Argonautic tradition that Valerius inherits. He is almost too big to fit comfortably into any one genre.[35] In taking him as the paradigm for their epic performance, then, the Argonauts unwittingly find themselves following a generically protean model.[36]

Hercules' transition from crewmember to extratextual *exemplum* takes place over the first three books of the poem. As the crew's primary model of behavior, he initially plays an integral role in perpetuating their chosen epic script and saving his companions from the trap of other genres. And here the structure of the Argonauts' journey comes into play, as they encounter people and places that are foreign ethically as well as geographically. The Argonauts follow a little too closely on Odysseus' heels: just as he makes a fatal mistake in assuming that individuals like Polyphemus will share his respect for the gods and the principles of *xenia*, so too do the Argonauts err in thinking that a Herculean model will suffice in the new worlds they encounter on this inaugural voyage.

Almost as soon as they set sail, the Argonauts and their audience see a hint of the limitations of this paradigm. To combat the Argo's intrusive voyage, Boreas rouses a storm against what he perceives as a *nefas* – a violation of the world's natural boundaries. The Argonauts, thinking that this is simply the nature of the sea, immediately panic:

> qui tum Minyis trepidantibus horror
> cum picei fulsere poli pauidamque coruscae
> ante ratem cecidere faces antemnaque laeuo
> prona dehiscentem cornu cum sustulit undam.
> non hiemem missosque putant consurgere uentos
> ignari sed tale fretum ...
> magnanimus spectat pharetras et inutile robur
> Amphitryoniades.
> (V. Fl. 1.621–6, 634–5)

What horror then seized the trembling Minyae when the pitchy skies flashed and blazing lightning fell before the fearful ship, and the sail-yard, leaning to port, raised a gaping wave on its point. Ignorant, they do not think that storm and winds rise because sent, but that such is the sea ... The great-souled son of Amphitryon gazes at his arrows and useless club ...

---

[35] Clauss 1993: 196–7 describes Hercules as an uneasy fit in the Argonauts' group endeavor.
[36] Hinds 2000: 223.

The epithet *magnanimus* reinforces Hercules' role as the archetypal epic hero, the predecessor of Homer's and Vergil's protagonists.[37] But the value of his sheer physical strength – the *robur Herculeum* that represents the material of martial epic – is immediately undermined by the realities of the voyage: the epithet *Amphitryoniades* emphasizes Hercules' mortal rather than divine parentage, suggesting that, in this episode at least, he shares his companions' human limitations. Off-shore, Hercules' physical prowess is rendered *inutile*, and he seems a bit of a throwback hero, a relic of Jupiter's rise to power and the mythological "old world." As a result, he does not readily adapt to the new challenges posed by the sea.[38] We can perhaps extend this predicament to poet as well as actor: the *robur* with which Hercules attempts to write his heroic legacy figures the shaky *robora* of his author's epic ship.[39] This narrative material, it seems, may not be a sound epic vehicle. Hercules will himself shortly progress beyond the realm of human achievement.[40] As an *exemplum* for the Argonauts, therefore, he succeeds in inspiring the crew to set out, but is unable to bridge the gap into their new heroic age.

The Lemnian episode – the first stop on the Argonauts' voyage – illustrates Hercules' normative role, enacting the contest between the crew's martial-epic mission and the allure of other generic possibilities. After reaching the island of Lemnos and being kept there by adverse winds, the Argonauts quickly learn to enjoy their enforced *otium*, taking the place of the husbands whom the Lemnian women have murdered:

> usque nouos diuae melioris ad ignis
> urbe sedent laeti Minyae uiduisque uacantes
> indulgent thalamis nimbosque educere luxu
> nec iam uelle uias, zephyrosque audire uocantes
> dissimulant ...
> (V. Fl. 2.369–73)

---

[37] See Hollis 2007: 208 on the Ennian overtones of compound epithets.
[38] On this passage, see Polleichtner 2005. Manuwald 1999: 253 observes that the storm shows Hercules' inefficacy in changing circumstances. The idea that Hercules is too much for the group mission is a consistent theme of the Argonautic myth: Apollonius twice refers to the earlier tradition that the Argo refused to carry Hercules' great weight (Ap. Rhod. 1.532 ff., 1168–71); Feeney 1986: 54 interprets this as an indication that Hercules does not truly belong in the group. Cf. Zissos 2006 on Valerius' storm; Bernstein 2013: 148–9 on the sea-storm *topos* in Flavian epic.
[39] *Robora* describes both Catullus' Argonautic crew (Catull. 64.4) and Aeneas' fleet (*Aen.* 4.398–400).
[40] Ganiban 2014: 262 and Buckley 2014: 324 describe how Hercules moves beyond the scope of the rest of the crew.

> Ever awaiting the new fires of a more favorable goddess, the happy Minyae rest in the city and, at leisure, indulge themselves in the widowed beds and while away the storms in luxury, nor do they now wish for travel and they pretend not to hear the calling winds ...

The Lemnian women are a type of challenge for which the crew is not prepared.[41] As in Homer and Vergil, Valerius' heroes are susceptible to elegiac temptation and easily diverted from their goal – ensnared in a world of Eastern *luxuria*, the Argonauts temporarily forget to continue their voyage. They exchange *amor rerum* for elegiac *amor*, choosing to play the sighing lover rather than the epic hero.

This episode, however, also shows the importance of the Herculean *exemplum* as the Argonauts' guide on their journey. While the others enjoy themselves, Hercules stays at his post, guarding the ship:

> donec resides Tirynthius heros
> non tulit, ipse rati inuigilans adque integer urbis:
> inuidisse deos tantum maris aequor adortis
> desertasque domos fraudataque tempore segni
> uota patrum; quid et ipse uiris cunctantibus adsit?
> (V. Fl. 2.373–7)

> Until the Tirynthian hero, himself, watching over the ship and untouched by the city, can bear their laziness no longer: the gods resent their assault on the sea, their homes are deserted and the prayers of their fathers betrayed by the time of inaction; and why does he himself attend on men who delay?

Unlike his companions, this Hercules is able to resist the temptations of wine and women that are his traditional weak points.[42] In contrast, the rest of the crew have abandoned themselves to *luxuria*, a term that evokes the Roman rhetoric of moral corruption through geographical expansion.[43] Their *nostos* narrative has been diverted in this foreign, amatory landscape; an implicit warning that Jupiter's program of expansion could lead in dangerous directions.

But in this instance, Herculean *labor* offers a way out. The adjective *integer* suggests that he, alone of the crew, remains uncontaminated by

---

[41] Buckley 2014: 315–16 shows their ties to Senecan tragedy; Feeney 1991: 322. Cf. Gildenhard and Zissos 2013: 174 on Juno as "stage-director" in the *Metamorphoses*.
[42] Feeney 1986: 55 notes Hercules' strikingly Stoic portrayal in this episode.
[43] On *luxuria*, cf. the introduction to Edwards 1993. Benton 2003: 271, 283 examines how Medea's myth allows Seneca to explore deep-seated Roman concerns about losing their identity through encounters with others.

the morally corrupt city and faithful to the epic ethos with which the crew set out.[44] And his is the voice that recalls the Argonauts to their journey:[45]

> "o miseri quicumque tuis accessimus actis!
> Phasin et Aeeten Scythicique pericula ponti
> redde," ait, "Aesonide: me tecum solus in aequor
> rerum traxit amor, dum spes mihi sistere montes
> Cyaneos uigilemque alium spoliare draconem.
> si sedet Aegaei scopulos habitare profundi,
> hoc mecum Telamon peraget meus."
> (V. Fl. 2.378–84)

"Oh wretched are we who joined your enterprise! Give Phasis and Aeetes and the dangers of the Scythian sea back to me, Jason," he says, "love of deeds alone dragged me into the sea with you, so long as I hoped to bring the Cyanean rocks to a halt and kill off another wakeful dragon. If you are resolved to settle among the rocks of the Aegean deep, my Telamon will persevere with me."

Hercules acts as a sort of collective conscience for the crew. He focuses on the duty owed to home and family: the Argonauts, he says, are neglecting their paternal inheritance. Hercules plays on his own exemplary status to illustrate proper heroic behavior (*me tecum solus in aequor / rerum traxit amor*). His request *Phasin et Aeeten Scythicique pericula ponti redde* makes Hercules into a stand-in for the Argonauts' home communities, the audience to whom achievements are owed.

The force of his *exemplum* is immediately felt. Shown the proper course, Jason regains his desire for glory:

> haec ubi dicta
> haud secus Aesonides monitis accensus amaris
> quam bellator equus, longa quem frigida pace
> terra iuuat quique in laeuos piger angitur orbes,
> frena tamen dominumque uelit si Martius aures
> clamor et obliti rursus fragor impleat aeris.
> tunc Argum Tiphynque uocat pelago<que> parari
> praecipitat; petit ingenti clamore magister
> arma uiros pariter sparsosque in litore remos.
> (V. Fl. 2.384–92)

---

[44] As a *comparandum*, Billerbeck 1986: 345–6 cites Scipio's choice between *Virtus* and *Voluptas* in *Pun.* 15 as an adaptation of Stoic doctrine in Flavian epic.

[45] Wacht 1991b: 120 notes the contrast between Vergil's Mercury and Valerius' Hercules: Hercules' speech clarifies that glory, rather than familial *pietas*, motivates the Argonauts.

When these words were spoken, the son of Aeson was roused by the bitter reproach, not otherwise than a war-horse, who enjoys a land numb with long peace – confined to the sloth of a short tether – nevertheless desires reins and master if the battle cry and the clash of forgotten bronze fills his ears. Then he calls to Argus and Tiphys and hastens to prepare for the sea. The helmsman with a great shout seeks at once the equipment, men, and oars strewn about the beach.

Valerius describes Jason's eagerness in a simile that echoes the *Georgics*: *tantus amor laudum, tantae est uictoria curae* (*G.* 3.112).[46] This allusion suggests Hercules' didactic role vis-à-vis his companions: he is the trainer, and Jason the warhorse whose spirits he reawakens. Furthermore, it reveals the generic implications of the Argonauts' departure from Lemnos: by following Hercules' lead Jason returns to the wider world of Jovian *labor* from the *laeui orbes* of the elegiac script he has temporarily been following. The sense of generic interplay is further developed by the description of *arma uiros pariter sparsosque in litore remos*.[47] What Hercules has achieved is no less than the re-launch of Valerius' poem, a reassembly of the arms and men that make up epic material.[48] This guidance, however, is ultimately misleading: in the event, it is through the blind pursuit of Hercules' example – his unwavering commitment to deeds of *uirtus* – that the Argonauts find themselves embroiled in tragedy at the following stop on their journey.

The next major threat to the voyage comes with the Argonauts' visit to Cyzicus. Where Lemnos temporarily succeeded in turning them into elegiac lovers (with the underlying possibility of family tragedy), the events that take place in Cyzicus show the potential for the Argonauts' martial *virtus* to be displaced into the world of implosive Lucanian epic instead of the outward-looking project on which they are embarked. As Stover has well shown, Valerius in many respects constructs his epic in contrast to the *Bellum Civile*, in which *virtus* is equated with crime.[49] As such, the Cyzicus episode diverts the Argonauts' quest for epic glory into tragedy and civil war, a type of epic that entails the destruction of home rather than a return to it.

Arriving in Cyzicus for the first time, the crew is warmly welcomed by its eponymous king:

"o terris nunc primum cognita nostris
Emathiae manus et fama mihi maior imago,

---

[46] Cf. *G.* 3.95–112.
[47] Oliensis 2004: 31 discusses Vergil's intratextual usage of *arma uirumque* at *Aen.* 1.119 to show the potential dismemberment of his epic by Juno's storm. Cf. Landrey 2014.
[48] Spaltenstein 2004: 205 notes the repetition of this formula at V. Fl. 2.392.
[49] Stover 2014: 301.

> non tamen haec adeo semota neque ardua tellus
> regnaque iam populis imperuia lucis eoae,
> cum tales intrasse duces, tot robora cerno.
> nam licet hinc saeuas tellus alat horrida gentes
> meque fremens tumido circumfluat ore Propontis,
> uestra fides ritus<que> pares et mitia cultu
> his etiam mihi corda locis . . ."
>
> (V. Fl. 2.639–47)

"O band of Emathia, now first known to our lands, and, I believe, a sight even greater than your fame, this land is not yet so removed nor hard to reach, nor the distant lands of the eastern sun so unattainable, when such captains enter, when I see such strength. For although on one side a barbarous land nurtures fierce peoples and the roaring Propontis flows about me with swollen outlet, here I find loyalty like yours and equal worship, and hearts gentle with culture."

Cyzicus' welcome suggests that he and his subjects share the same value system as their guests (*uestra fides ritusque pares et mitia cultu . . . corda*), despite the physical distance between their homelands. The Argonauts seemingly find themselves back in familiar territory, a space in which their performance of *uirtus* may be evaluated on its intended terms. The similarity between the two groups, however, makes their future enmity all the more unnatural. The descriptor *Emathiae*, used only here in the *Argonautica*, hints at the Lucanian conflict to come.[50]

While Hercules' exemplary authority saves the Argonauts in Lemnos, this same type of response proves misleading in Cyzicus. During a banquet in the Argonauts' honor, the king shows his guests a cup engraved with the scene of a night battle, in which the Cyzicans successfully rout an attack by the neighboring Pelasgians.[51] Seeing it, Jason wishes for another such battle, so that he and his companions might prove their loyalty to their new friends:

> subicit Aesonides: "utinam nunc ira Pelasgos
> adferat et solitis temptet concurrere furtis
> cunctaque se ratibus fundat manus; arma uidebis
> hospita nec post hanc ultra tibi proelia noctem."
>
> (V. Fl. 2.659–62)

The son of Aeson replied: "Oh if only rage might now bring the Pelasgians here and provoke them to their usual tricks, and their whole troop pour out of their ships; then you would see our weapons taken up in alliance, nor would you see any more battles after this night!"

---

[50] Stover 2012: 125.
[51] Spaltenstein 2002: 488–9 suggests that this narrative is modeled on Evander's description of Rome (*Aen.* 8.313 ff.).

Jason continues his one-sided focus on martial *uirtus*, believing the scene to offer him a correct heroic template to follow.[52] This mini-ecphrasis reemphasizes the central importance of visual *exempla* to the Argonauts' behavior. Battle provides a performance space for *uirtus*, which in turn creates *kleos* perpetuated by visual monument and epic narrative.[53]

Jason's misreading of both story and setting again derails his quest for glory. Having spent a few days enjoying the Cyzicans' hospitality, the crew sails off, only to be blown back to the same shore when their navigator Tiphys falls asleep in the night. Mistaking the Argonauts for the Pelasgians, the Cyzicans attack, causing panic among their erstwhile guests (V. Fl. 3.74–5): *Minyas anceps fixit pauor; aegra uirorum / corda labant, nec quae regio aut discrimina cernunt* ... ("doubtful fear holds the Minyae fast; the men's anxious hearts waver, nor can they tell what place it is and what perils ..."). Leaning on his *exempla*, however, Jason reinterprets the battle as the type of epic *labor* they seek, echoing his response to the two prophecies in Book 1:

> princeps galeam constringit Iason
> uociferans: "primam hanc nati, pater, accipe pugnam
> uosque, uiri, optatos huc adfore credite Colchos."
> (V. Fl. 3.80–2)

> Jason first fastens on his helmet, shouting aloud, "Father, accept this as your son's first battle and you, men, believe that here are the longed-for Colchians."

Jason recreates the unknown landscape as an arena for heroic display, the long-awaited chance to prove their martial valor. This performance, however, takes place in a type of civil war, the product both of the Cyzicans' and Argonauts' shared martial ethos and their cultural consonance. The depth of this effect is evident in a near miss between the brothers Castor and Pollux, who mistakenly attack each other in the darkness:

> Accessere (nefas) tenebris fallacibus acti
> Tyndaridae in sese: Castor prius ibat in ictus
> nescius; ast illos noua lux subitusque diremit
> frontis apex.
> (V. Fl. 3.186–9)

---

[52] Mitousi 2014: 166 reads Jason's eagerness as evidence of his "heroic unselfishness."
[53] Castelletti 2014: 179 notes that Jason's reaction shows his desire to present himself as a Homeric martial hero, and an indication of Jason's *pietas* toward his friends as well as the gods.

Driven together in the deceptive shadows the two sons of Tyndareus (monstrous crime) advance on each other. Castor, unknowing, was about to strike first, but a strange light and sudden beacon on their brows separated them.

Castor and Pollux represent an extreme version of the joined hands and houses of the two sides: their twin *aristeiai* reflect the mutual blindness of the battle through the pairing *nefas* ... *nescius*.[54] And although Jupiter saves his two sons from each other, the Argonauts kill Cyzicus along with many of his men. Overwhelmed by guilt, they find themselves in a shadowy tragic scene:

> illi autem neque adhuc gemitus neque conscia facti
> ora leuant; tenet exsangues rigor horridus artus,
> ceu pauet ad crines et tristia Pentheos ora
> Thyias, ubi inpulsae iam se deus agmine matris
> abstulit et caesi uanescunt cornua tauri.
> (V. Fl. 3.262–6)

But not yet can they utter groans or lift faces conscious of their crime. Terrible numbness grips their bloodless limbs, just as the Thyiad shudders at the hair and grim face of Pentheus, when the god has now withdrawn from the band of the maddened mother and the horns of the slaughtered bull vanish.

In hot pursuit of their prize, the Argonauts reach the lowest point of their outward journey. Their moment of glory is not the material of epic song, but very nearly an unspeakable deed, and the realization of what they have done shows the Argonauts their fatal misreading of place and script. Their collective desire for epic action causes them to violate an equally important aspect of the heroic code, the ties of guest-friendship. Their guilt and grief once again divert their quest:

> At non inde dies nec quae magis aspera curis
> nox Minyas tanta caesorum ab imagine soluit.
> bis Zephyri iam uela uocant: fiducia maestis
> nulla uiris, aegra adsiduo mens carpitur aestu
> necdum omnes lacrimas atque omnia reddita caesis
> iusta putant; patria ex oculis acerque laborum
> pulsus amor segnique iuuat frigescere luctu.
> (V. Fl. 3.362–8)

But thereafter neither day nor night, even more cruel with grief, frees the Minyae from such a vision of the slaughtered. Twice now have the winds called

---

[54] Spaltenstein 2004: 63–4 compares *Aen.* 2.682 ff. The scene follows Jupiter's *fax* at V. Fl. 1.568–73.

the sails. There is no assurance in the grieving men, their afflicted minds are consumed by unceasing turmoil, and not yet do they think that all tears and all dues have been paid to the dead; their homeland falls from view and their keen love of deeds is pushed aside, and it pleases to grow cold in slow grief.

The initial failure in navigation becomes a failure of the epic models that govern the Argonauts' mission. Their martial *uirtus* is displaced into the wrong circumstances, an echo of Hercules' *inutile robur* with far worse consequences. As Jason himself recognizes, their grief is characterized by the loss of desire both for home and deeds, echoing Hercules' words in Lemnos (V. Fl. 3.375–6): *cur immemores famaeque larisque / angimur?* ("why do we suffer, forgetful of our glory and our household gods?"). The Argonauts' orientation toward past epic models diverts their journey of forward-looking *labor*.

As the Cyzicus episode illustrates, it may be the Argonauts' focus on these very *exempla* that fails to equip them for their journey. And it is their primary model, Hercules, who most vividly enacts the potential to be diverted permanently from the world of epic into an altogether different storyline.[55] After the Argonauts have reached Mysia, the next stop on their journey, Juno seizes the opportunity to get rid of Hercules (V. Fl. 3.488: *tempus rata diua nocendi*, "the goddess reckoned it an opportunity to work harm"), by orchestrating his lover Hylas' rape by the nymph Dryope. Hylas, like his companions, is eager to prove himself on the voyage, and, like the others, focuses on a Herculean model in order to do so:

> sic ait et celerem frondosa per auia ceruum
> suscitat ac iuueni sublimem cornibus offert.
> ille animos tardusque fugae longumque resistens
> sollicitat suadetque pari contendere cursu.
> credit Hylas praedaeque ferox ardore propinquae
> insequitur; simul Alcides hortatibus urget
> prospiciens.
> (V. Fl. 3.545–51)

So she speaks, and among the trackless thickets she rouses a swift stag, and presents it, conspicuous, to the youth. Slow in flight and long hesitating, it rouses his spirits and provokes him to strive in equal course. Hylas falls for it, and wild for prey close to hand he follows, while Hercules, looking on, urges him forward.

---

[55] Buckley 2014: 311–12 shows how the interaction of Hercules and Juno in *Argonautica* 1 hints that tragic *ira* rather than Jovian *fatum* underpins the entire poem; this coincides with the two options presented by Mopsus and Idmon.

Hylas is all too eager to capture the trophy before him, echoing Iulus' similarly disastrous pursuit of a stag in *Aeneid* 7 (*Aen.* 7.496: *eximiae laudis succensus amore*, "aflame with desire for outstanding praise"); both are youths on the brink of manhood, who look to their father(-figure) as an *exemplum*.[56] Furthermore, the verb *credit* underscores Hylas' similarity to Jason's actions in Cyzicus (V. Fl. 3.82: *optatos huc adfore credite Colchos*). He, too, is beguiled by the promise of a false prize to be won. Where Jason had called his absent father to witness, Hylas performs for the ultimate epic audience, seeking to demonstrate his *uirtus* in front of Hercules. Juno's stag, however, leads him too far along this path, straight to the pool of the nymph Dryope where, dazzled by his own reflection, Hylas fails to recognize the threat lurking behind the glittering surface (V. Fl. 3.551–61).

He thereby enacts the dangers of the Argonauts' single-minded pursuit of a martial-epic storyline: the desire to construct their own reception blinds them to the possibility of forfeiting their *nostos* and becoming *exempla* of a very different generic path.

Hercules himself, far from a straightforward *exemplum* of glory won through physical prowess, performs exactly this type of generic displacement. Immediately after Juno has caused Hylas to disappear and Hercules to abandon the expedition to search for him, Jupiter reproaches her both for her cruelty to his son and the disservice she has just done the Argonauts:

> haeret inops solisque furit Tirynthius oris,
> at comite immemores Minyae facilesque relicto
> alta tenent. sic Iuno ducem fouet anxia curis
> Aesonium, sic arma uiro sociosque ministrat.
>   (V. Fl. 4.5–8)

> The Tirynthian is stuck helpless and rages on the deserted shores, but, forgetful of their comrade and content to leave him behind, the Minyae take to the seas. Thus anxious Juno cares for her Aesonian leader, thus she provides arms and companions to the man!

In effect, Jupiter interrogates Juno about how she is managing this storyline, mocking her version of *arma uirumque*.[57] The Argonauts have lost their guide, while Hercules himself looks surprisingly like an elegiac heroine deserted on the shore. The *immemores ... facilesque* crew plays Theseus to his Ariadne. Juno, Jupiter implies, has turned this epic in a (very inappropriate) elegiac direction.

---

[56] *Aen.* 7.475–510.   [57] On Juno in the *Argonautica*, see Monaghan 2005.

Hercules' disappearance illustrates the possibility that the voyage, too, will lose its epic bearings and fail to achieve heroic *nostos*. Both he and Hylas are (generically) transformed, swept off into the landscapes of elegy, epyllion, and tragedy: as Heerink and Buckley have shown, Valerius constructs the Hylas episode through dense allusion to Apollonius, Theocritus, Propertius, Ovid, and Seneca, offering a smorgasbord of non-epic points of orientation.[58] While Hylas himself is diverted by the very epic aspirations that the Argonauts also profess, Hercules succumbs to the Senecan *furor* hinted at from the very beginning of the poem:

> tum uero et pallor et amens
> cum piceo sudore rigor. ceu pectora nautis
> congelat hiberni uultus Iouis agricolisue,
> cum coit umbra minax, comitis sic adficit error
> Alciden saeuaeque monet meminisse nouercae.
> continuo, uolucri ceu pectora tactus asilo
> emicuit Calabris taurus per confraga saeptis
> obuia quaeque ruens, tali se concitat ardens
> in iuga senta fuga.
> (V. Fl. 3.577–84)

Then indeed comes pallor and frenzied numbness together with black sweat. Just as when Jupiter's wintry countenance chills the heart of sailor or farmer, when a threatening cloud gathers, so does his friend's absence afflict Alcides, and cause him to think of his cruel stepmother. Straightaway, as a bull pricked on its chest by the swift gadfly bursts out of the Calabrian thickets through all barriers, in such a rush he hurls himself, burning, into the rugged hills.

Hercules' violent reaction shows the potential dangers of his outsize strength: when channeled in the wrong direction his particular type of *uirtus* poses a threat both physical and generic, with a self-destructive effect similar to the Argonauts' martial fervor in Cyzicus. In both instances the desire to act out a martial model directly threatens the Argonauts' desire for *nostos*. Even as they seek to follow – as closely as possible – the script of Herculean heroism, they do so on the wrong generic stage, and thus confront the possibility that the reception of their deeds will take place on other terms than they themselves would wish. The Argonauts' journey leads them ever farther away from the home community that would guarantee continuity of evaluation.

---

[58] Buckley 2014: 319–24; Heerink 2015 *passim*.

4.5 In Hercules' Wake

Following Hercules' loss, the Argonauts, as in Cyzicus, lapse into temporary *aporia*, unsure whether and how to continue on their journey:

> ipse uel excelsi cum densa silentia montis
> strata uel oblatis ductor uidet aequora uentis,
> stat lacrimans magnoque uiri cunctatur amore.
> illius incessus habilemque ad terga pharetram,
> illum inter proceres maestaeque silentia mensae
> quaerit inops quondam ingenti conprensa trahentem
> uina manu et durae referentem monstra nouercae.
> (V. Fl. 3.604–10)

> The captain himself, as he sees the unbroken silence of the lofty mountain or the seas smoothed by ready winds, stands crying and hesitates out of his great love for the man. In vain he seeks his step, and the quiver ready at his back, and the man himself among the leaders and the silence of the mournful table, drinking the wine grasped by his great hand, and recounting the monsters sent by his stepmother.

Hercules' disappearance deprives the Argonauts of their most able hero, marked by a visual gap among the crew.[59] Jason's vivid memory of Hercules recounting his own heroic narrative (*durae referentem monstra nouercae*) pinpoints the exemplary function that Hercules had fulfilled for his companions, providing them with a model of how to perform the martial epic that they desire.[60]

In the Argonauts' attempt to deal with Hercules' disappearance, however, the pitfalls of this model continually emerge. As the group debates whether to continue with the voyage, loyalty to their friend contends with the *amor rerum* that he himself embodied. For the most part, the crew is impatient to set out, an eagerness given a decidedly negative cast by Valerius:

> at studiis iamdudum freta iuuentus
> orat inire uias: unum tanto afore coetu
> nec minus in sese generis dextrasque potentes
> esse ferunt. tali mentem pars maxima flatu
> erigit et uana gliscunt praecordia lingua.
> (V. Fl. 3.628–32)

---

[59] Wright 1998: 21 shows how both passage and crew focus on Hercules' iconic images.
[60] Spaltenstein 2004: 172–3 notes the contrast with Ap. Rhod. 1.1273, where the Argonauts forget Hercules and sail away.

> But the crew, trusting in their zeal, long since beseeches [Jason] to set sail: they say that only one will be missing in so great a troop, that they themselves are no less noble in lineage nor less strong in hand. With such boastfulness the majority raises its spirits and their hearts swell with empty vaunting.

The crew's indirect speech creates the impression of false courage and misplaced bravado.[61] The Argonauts' assertion of their prowess and *studium* for their task show their adherence to Hercules' model, but in the absence of Hercules himself, this is revealed to be *uana lingua*.

Telamon, first, anticipates that they will miss Hercules and his superhuman strength as they encounter further challenges along their journey:

> "saepe metu, saepe in tenui discrimine rerum
> Herculeas iam serus opes spretique uocabis
> arma uiri nec nos tumida haec tum dicta iuuabunt."
>   (V. Fl. 3.712–14)

> "Often in fear, often at the critical moment will you call, now too late, on Hercules' help and the arms of the abandoned hero, nor then will these overweening words please us."

His words indicate that as for Jupiter, so for the crew: Hercules functions as the representative of *arma uirumque*. Telamon's reaction suggests that the Argonauts may not have the *robur* to make up for his loss, that they may not have the raw material for his kind of epic.

Meleager, on the other hand, makes the case for leaving Hercules behind. He invokes the rhetoric used by Hercules himself in Lemnos, urging Jason to remember his *amor rerum* and set out again:

> "non datur haec magni proles Iouis; at tibi Pollux
> stirpe pares Castorque manent, at cetera diuum
> progenies nec parua mihi fiducia gentis.
> en egomet quocumque uocas sequar agmina ferro
> plura metam; tibi dicta manus, tibi quicquid in ipso
> sanguine erit, iamque hinc operum quae maxima posco . . .
> uos, quibus et uirtus et spes in limine primo,
> tendite, dum rerum patiens calor et rude membris
> robur inest."
>   (V. Fl. 3.667–81)

---

[61] Spaltenstein 2004: 179 suggests that *flatu* and *uana* give a moral tone to the narrative; cf. *Aen.* 7.234, 11.346, 12.9.

"This child of great Jupiter is not granted to us, but yet, see, Pollux and Castor, equal in birth, remain to you, and the other offspring of the gods, and I have no little confidence in my lineage. See, I for my part will follow wherever you call, I will cut down more ranks with iron, my hand is promised to you, to you whatever benefit in my very blood and now from this point I demand whatever task is the greatest ... You, who have both courage and hope in the flower of your youth, hasten onward, while your spirit endures labors and raw strength is in your limbs."

Meleager's imperative *tendite* echoes Jupiter's exhortation to his sons – *tendite in astra* – a speech that singled out Hercules and the Tyndaridae.[62] By addressing his fellow Argonauts in this way, Meleager thus implies their equal footing with the sons of Jupiter, and their ability to step into heroic shoes that are, perhaps, too big for them. He claims *Herculeum robur* for the group as a whole, as a sort of mandate to continue without Hercules himself.[63] However, as the sea-storm suggested in Book 1, *robur* is not necessarily the right tool to combat the challenges along the Argonauts' route. In claiming it, therefore, Meleager hubristically subscribes to the same heroic ethos that has already got the crew into trouble.

Meleager's claim to Herculean *robur* raises the question of whether he and the crew can match the standards set by Hercules, and, furthermore, whether the pursuit of such an excessive standard will lead them away from the narrative they envision. Meleager, for one, asserts that he is ready to follow wherever Jason may lead, to take on any task that may be required, and his oath sounds ominously close to that of Caesar's tribune in the first book of the *Bellum Civile*:

"per signa decem felicia castris
perque tuos iuro quocumque ex hoste triumphos,
pectore si fratris gladium iuguloque parentis
condere me iubeas plenaeque in uiscera partu
coniugis, inuita peragam tamen omnia dextra."
(Luc. *BC* 1.374–8)

"By the standards victorious in ten campaigns and your triumphs over any enemy, I swear, if you should bid me plant my sword in the breast of my brother or the throat of my father, or into the entrails of my wife, swollen with child, even as my right hand resists, nevertheless, I will do all."

This echo is especially problematic in the wake of the Cyzicus episode, in which the Argonauts demonstrated their potential to lapse into precisely

---

[62] Stover 2012: 184 reads this as a reminder of *uirtus* as a feature of Jupiter's rule, associated with Hercules.
[63] Stover 2012: 185 suggests the implication that the crew is collectively equal to Hercules.

the kind of Lucanian epic that would translate their *uirtus* into *nefas*. In this view, the Argonauts' competitive impulse threatens to become self-destructive.

Just as Hercules provided a focal point for the crew at the start of their voyage, so too does his absence make itself felt in visual terms. Setting sail from Mysia, the Argonauts gaze mournfully at the empty seat left behind by their lost companion:

> hic uero ingenti repetuntur pectora luctu,
> ut socii sedere locis nullaeque leonis
> exuuiae tantique uacant uestigia transtri.
> (V. Fl. 3.719–21)
>
> Now indeed their hearts are afflicted once more with deep grief, as his companions take their seats and see no lion's trophies, but the place lies empty on the mighty bench.

Even after his departure Hercules functions as the iconic image of the martial-epic narrative that the Argonauts unwillingly leave behind in their wake. Hercules' *exuuiae* – his trophies – disappear along with him, as this model of heroism diverges from the Argonauts' storyline and he himself embarks on a different path, traveling an unseen route to the Caucasus in order to liberate Prometheus from his mountain prison. This final *labor* – the deed that represents Hercules' last step toward achieving the immortality for which he and his companions strive – is invisible to the Argonauts:

> contra autem ignari – quis enim nunc credat in illis
> montibus Alciden dimissave uota retemptet? –
> pergere iter socii.
> (V. Fl. 5.171–3)
>
> Meanwhile in their ignorance (for indeed who would believe that Alcides was in those mountains and attempting anew his abandoned hopes?), his companions continue on their journey.

The Argonauts sail off, looking away from their chosen *exemplum* as their journey takes them not to Olympus, but to the tragedy that awaits them in Colchis.

4.6 Conclusion

Throughout their voyage Jason and Argonauts strive for the opportunity to prove their *virtus* against the standard set by Hercules. What they do not realize, however, is that this paradigm brings with it much more than the martial-epic script they try so hard to follow, and that, by adhering to this mode of behavior, they find themselves mired in a shifting landscape that destabilizes the value of their chosen *exempla*. The sites along their journey suggest that the *nostos* they seek – a successful return that would guarantee them recognition on the same terms under which they set out – is no longer possible in Jupiter's new age of *labor*.

PART II

Gendered Maps

Introduction

Part II explores the impact of gender on the epic journey, both through the presence of female travelers and through gendered perceptions of the journey. Together, the contributions ask several overarching questions: do the concepts or significance of "home" and "away" change when considered through the lens of gender? How does the journey establish (or subvert) the female traveler as a protagonist? And in the male-oriented world of epic, does the female traveler, by asserting her autonomy of movement, gender her journey, or is her own gender (or our perception of it) somehow altered?

Silvia Montiglio's chapter explores the parallels and contrasts between the journeys of two sets of lovers in Apollonius Rhodius' *Argonautica* and Heliodorus' *Aethiopica*. Through these couples' stories she calls into question the definition of "home," suggesting that, for the protagonists of the *Aethiopica*, "home" is embodied in the romantic partner: Chariclea and Theagenes' joint travels to Chariclea's homeland are the substance as well as the product of their relationship. Marriage, for them, is a mutual *nostos*. Apollonius' protagonists present a stark contrast. Jason and Medea diverge in how they conceive of their journey(s): Jason envisions an Odyssean return to home and family, while Medea can never return to her native land. Her only possible home is with Jason, and her *nostos* depends on his affections. As a woman, her social status is always contingent: her gendered model of the epic journey takes a person, rather than a place, as its reference point and ultimate goal. Montiglio's contribution, therefore, explores the many possible conceptions of "home," and the redefinitions of the journey that these entail.

Emily Baragwanath continues the conversation about the traveler's construction of "home" in the course of a journey. She examines Xenophon's depiction of his return to Greece in the *Anabasis*, exploring his representation of himself and his journey in Odyssean terms. Like Montiglio, Baragwanath nuances the definition of the *nostos* that Xenophon and his followers seek by focusing on the restoration of a harmonious relationship between men and women that symbolizes the ideal "home." Along the route, the women who travel with Xenophon's troops embody the *telos* of the expedition; as with Penelope and the heroines of the *Argonautica* and the *Aethiopica*, they suggest that a person, as much as a place, may represent *nostos* to the traveler far from home. Both Montiglio and Baragwanath trace the interaction between gender and travel, exploring how protagonists who seek to authorize their journeys through a shared Homeric paradigm manipulate the template of Odysseus' homeward journey.

Alison Keith's chapter brings female travelers to center stage, examining Vergil's heroines as the representations of narrative roads-not-taken. Focusing on the characters of Dido, Andromache, and the Trojan women who travel with Aeneas, Keith shows how Vergil enacts the gendered exclusivity of Classical epic by first raising, and then withdrawing from, the possibility of female travel in the *Aeneid*. Vergil constructs his heroines as potential divergences, which by their exclusion illustrate the epic genre's ultimately masculine orientation. As in the two preceding chapters, Keith's discussion shows the impact of the female traveler on the epic journey: by dismissing the possibility of a female-centric journey, Vergil actively shapes the tradition through his choice to adhere to a certain narrative paradigm.

In their treatment of the epic journey and the deeply embedded concept of "home," this trio of chapters offers a rich exploration of the impact of gender on genre, and vice versa. Together, they explore the different types of journeys undertaken by female protagonists, and in particular the way in which those protagonists reorient the journey to new destinations and new constructions of "home." In this way, Montiglio, Baragwanath, and Keith examine the narrative and generic implications of the relationships between genders (and their cultural constructions), individuals, and different models of the homeward journey. They show how gender functions as a *locus* for the interaction between multiple definitions of the epic journey, a vehicle through which writers illustrate their authorial process. Female protagonists, no matter in which direction they head, shape the epic journey.

CHAPTER 5

Wandering, Love, and Home in Apollonius of Rhodes' Argonautica *and* Heliodorus' Aethiopica

Silvia Montiglio

Narratives of return fulfill essential psychological needs: they turn chaos into order and are joyful, optimistic, promoting as they do the restoration of rightful power, the demise of wrongdoers, the renewal of society and even of life.[1] In Greek literature the production of plots centered on a return journey spans over a millennium, starting with the *Odyssey* and the other epic *nostoi*, continuing with Apollonius of Rhodes' *Argonautica*, and later with the novelistic tradition, especially with Heliodorus' *Aethiopica*.

The protagonist of the typical Greek narrative of return is eager to reach his destination. He might get lost along the way, or not make it home at all (like Philoctetes, according to Apollod. *Epit*. 6.15b), but he is unerringly directed there.[2] It might happen, though, that the homeward-bound travelers are not alone but are accompanied by someone who has followed them from abroad, for love. This is the case in Apollonius' *Argonautica* and Heliodorus' *Aethiopica*. The protagonists of the two narratives, Jason and Chariclea, travel to their own homes with their foreign betrotheds, who have chosen the beloved over fatherland and family. In this chapter I will discuss how the different degrees of importance attached to home and love respectively by the homeward-bound characters in the two narratives determine, in turn, the sense of belonging or — vice versa — of homelessness experienced by the character who has left everything behind. The different levels of commitment between the members of the two couples also shape

---

My gratitude goes to two anonymous readers, to the faculty and the graduate students at Yale University and especially to Thomas Biggs and Jessica Blum, for their generosity with their time and for their efficiency in organizing the conference "Home and Away: the Epic Journey" (Yale University, April 2014) from which this chapter stems; for their sharp comments, painstaking editorial work, and patient navigation through the publishing process.
[1] See Whitmarsh 2011: 14–15, 254, and *passim*.
[2] A lack of determination to return to one's native land is characteristic of travelers who fail in their mission: see Montiglio 2005: 228–9.

the movement of the journey, its purpose for the returning traveler, and the meaning of wandering abroad for both travelers.

Jason does not demonstrate the same passionate longing for home as does Odysseus. While the Homeric hero every day "wants and is eager," ἐθέλω καὶ ἐέλδομαι, to see the day of his *nostos* (*Od.* 5.219–20), Jason speaks about his need and hope to reach Iolcos but expresses no nostalgia: he says "when we return," "if we return," not "every day I want and am eager to go home."[3] His strongest manifestation of attachment to Iolcos occurs when the Argo first leaves the shore and he "tearfully (δακρυόεις) turns his eyes away from his native land" (Ap. Rhod. 1.535), as Odysseus cries (οὐδέ ποτ' ὄσσε/ δακρυόφιν τέρσοντο) looking at the sea day in day out from Calypso's island (*Od.* 5.151–2). Except in this one instance, Jason does not shed a tear for his fatherland.

One possible reason for such undemonstrative behavior is Jason's status as an unattached youth. If he does not yearn for Iolcos as Odysseus does for Ithaca, it may be because, unlike his Homeric counterpart, he has no loving wife waiting for him at home.[4] In this respect, as in many others, he rather resembles Telemachus, another unmarried youth, for whom "Home" means fatherland and *oikos* (*Od.* 15.65–6), whereas his father's notion of "Home" includes Penelope as a vital component.[5] Odysseus is of course reticent in this regard: it would be impolitic to mention Penelope to Alcinous, who offers him his daughter in marriage, and he tries his best to minimize his affection for his faraway wife when Calypso challenges him with these words: "you could be immortal, but you long to see your wife and desire her day after day (ἐέλδεαι ἤματα πάντα)" (*Od.* 5.209–10). As the scholiasts already noticed, in his reply to Calypso he changes the object of his longing: "but even so I want and desire day after day (ἐέλδεομαι ἤματα πάντα) to go home and see the day of my return" (*Od.* 5.219–20).[6] Odysseus repeats Calypso's phrase ἐέλδεαι ἤματα πάντα but replaces

---

[3] Ap. Rhod. 1.416–17, 2.414–15, 4.98. Jason thinking of his return: see also, e.g., 1.336, 3.175, 4.202–4, 4.1275–6, 4.1333–4, 4.1600.
[4] I wish to thank Emily Greenwood for suggesting this line of thought to me.
[5] See Baragwanath, Chapter 6 in this volume. Jason does not seem to miss his mother, while she, at his departure, imagines that she will desperately long for him (1.286: σεῖο πόθῳ μινύθουσα). Telemachus' mother likewise longs for him during his absence (*Od.* 2.375 and 4.748: ποθέσαι) while he at least once feels that his resolve to return to Ithaca is faltering (*Od.* 4.594–7). Both young men are objects more than subjects of longing.
[6] See schol. H.P.Q. 5.220: οἴκαδέ τ' ἐλθέμεναι] ἐπ' ἄλλα τρέπει τὸν πόθον. ἡ μὲν γὰρ ἔφη, ἱμειρόμενός περ ἰδέσθαι σὴν ἄλοχον, ὁ δὲ ὁμολογῶν τὴν ἐπιθυμίαν, οὐκ ἐπὶ τὴν Πηνελόπην πεποίηται τὴν ἀπόστασιν, ἀλλ' ἐπὶ τὰ οἶκοι. ("'To go home': he turns his longing toward other things. For she said, 'desiring to see your wife,' and he admits to his desire, but says that his desertion of her is not in order to go to Penelope but to his home").

Penelope with Ithaca, drawing attention to the replacement by means of the repetition, which sets it off. His is a tactful move: but is he also truthful?[7] An ancient reader does not hesitate to call Penelope "the cause of the *Odyssey*"; another claims that Odysseus rejected luxury and marriage with goddesses, choosing instead to wander so that he could go back to Penelope and have a pleasant tale for her; and yet another attributes Odysseus' tearful looking at the sea from the shore of Calypso's island to his longing for his wife.[8]

In addition to the absence of a romantic attachment, Jason's failure to wax nostalgic for Iolcos fits at least three narratological features of Apollonius' epic. First, the climax of the *Argonautica* is the capture of the Golden Fleece, which takes up more than a book, while the landing at Iolcos happens in a hurry and is only summarily mentioned.[9] It might be relevant in this respect that the same verb Odysseus uses to express his longing for Ithaca, ἐέλδομαι, describes the Argonauts' eagerness to touch the Fleece when Jason at last brings it to the ship (ἐελδόμενος, Ap. Rhod. 4.186). Later the Fleece, the couple's marital couch, inspires the nymphs who partake in the wedding ceremony with a "sweet longing" (γλυκερὸν πόθον) to touch it (Ap. Rhod. 4.1147). Apollonius' epic, unlike the *Odyssey*, is not only a narrative of return, but it recounts a journey out and back. Characters and readers look onward first and foremost, to Jason's contest and his conquest of the Fleece.

Jason's relative detachment from his native land might also be an implicit foreshadowing of troubles to come – one of the many such intimations of the future that are scattered throughout Apollonius' poem – namely of the calamities that will hit him at home beyond the span of the epic, and which will cause his exile. For the readers who know the sequel to the *Argonautica*, his words "it is enough, Pelias willing, for me to live in my fatherland" (Ap. Rhod. 1.902–3), with which he declines Hypsipyle's offer of settling down in Lemnos with her and ruling as king, ring ominous. And for those same readers, his lack of nostalgia is an unwitting anticipation, as it were, of the un-homelike reception he will be given in Iolcos, and of its dire consequences.

---

[7] See Eust. *Od.* 1.209.3–5: Σημείωσαι δὲ καὶ ὡς ἐπὶ πλέον θεραπεύων τὴν Καλυψώ, οὐδὲ λέγει ὡς ἐθέλω καὶ ἐέλδομαι εἰς τὴν γυναῖκα ἐλθεῖν, ἀλλ' οἴκαδε ἁπλῶς νοστῆσαι. ("Mark how much he flatters Calypso: he does not say, 'I want and desire to go to my wife,' but simply 'to return home.'").

[8] Palladas (*AP* 9.166.6), Julian (*Or.* 3. 112d–114a), and Epictetus (in Arr. *Epict. diss.* 3.24.18–21) respectively. The trend of romanticizing the goal of Odysseus' journey is traceable already in Xenophon's *Anabasis*: see Baragwanath, Chapter 6 in this volume.

[9] The last stretch of the journey is swift (4.1766) and emphatically uneventful (4.1776–*fin*.).

Yet another, and more important, narratological reason for Jason's disposition is that the hero's native land is not the gravitational focus of Apollonius' epic, as it is of Homer's. As has been noted, the *Argonautica* seemingly does not have "a center or locality against which to position the wandering of the main characters," who "are from but not visibly attached to any place."[10] Their detachment might be an indication that the epic's center is Ptolemaic Alexandria, which of course is not on the Argo's itinerary but is nonetheless the dedicatee of the multiple aetiological and geographical digressions that attempt to provide a "cultural mnemonic" for the relatively young city.[11] The failure of Iolcos to fill Jason's heart with longing is consistent with this poetic project.

Although Jason does not express Odysseus-like nostalgia, he is, like Odysseus, still firmly determined to return to his native country after his victory. The purpose of his journey is to make it back home and ruin Pelias' scheme, which was to "destroy Jason's return" (Ap. Rhod. 1.17). In the words of one critic, "[his] main object ... is always a safe return home."[12] There is not even one willing detour from the homeward-bound journey, such as the one Odysseus and his comrades, all excited, take when they embark on an exploration of the island facing the Cyclopes, then set out for the Cyclopes' own.[13] In the *Argonautica* wandering is always a forced condition. The main enrichment it provides is literary, allowing the poet to digress from the main narrative and season it with erudite forays into geography, myths, and cults. But the Argonauts themselves do not exhibit Odysseus' inquisitiveness: they generally do not wonder or even look with interest at the landscapes that meet their eye.[14] One exception is Aeetes' palace, before which they stand marveling (τεθηπότες, Ap. Rhod. 3.215), just as Odysseus drinks in all the beauties of Alcinous' palace in a parallel episode: "There he stood marveling (θηεῖτο) ... But when he had marveled at everything (πάντα ... θηήσατο) in his heart ..." (*Od.* 7.133–4). As is typical of his style, Apollonius compresses Odysseus' prolonged and emphasized amazement into one economical participle,

---

[10] Stephens 2008: 95.   [11] Stephens 2008: 97.
[12] Klooster 2012: 64, with references. This scholar, however, in my view exaggerates in calling the Argonauts "home-sick heroes" (75). They are not happy travelers, especially not on the way back, but, as we have seen, they do not suffer from nostalgia. On *nostos* as their objective, see also Montiglio 2005: 231.
[13] On Odysseus' exploration of the Cyclopes' island, see Bakker, Chapter 2 in this volume.
[14] On the Argonauts' lack of interest in the places they visit, see Klooster 2012. On geography in the *Argonautica*, see esp. Meyer 2012, with further references.

but the central idea remains. The normal Apollonian wanderer, however, is an outcast:

> Just as when someone, wandering away from his native land, as indeed we wretched mortals often wander, darts quickly with his thoughts, here and there, and no land seems far, but all the cities are visible, and he recognizes his house, and at once every path of the sea and on the dry land appears before his eyes ... (Ap. Rhod. 2.541–6)

This wanderer's only desire is to go back home. Though his mind, equipped with a bird's-eye view, is thrilled at seeing all the paths laid out over land and sea, and keenly shifts its attention from one to the other, his excitement is not caused by an eagerness to discover new places, but by the impression that his native land is near: the paths that unfold before his mind are the routes that would take him home.[15] This figure encapsulates the negativity of wandering for Apollonius' travelers and the homeward-bound focus of their minds.

But Jason's own homecoming has an added goal: marriage with Medea. As he stresses at the beginning of his journey from Colchis, "Her, as is her wish, I will bring home to be my wedded wife" (Ap. Rhod. 4.194–5). This wife-to-be, however, soon feels that she is not headed to a new home but is doomed to remain a wanderer, because Jason cannot provide her with the sense of belonging – his love – that would make up for her loss of her own home and family. While he is traveling to reach his native land, she sees her journey as a movement farther and farther away from hers. She is traveling *from* Colchis rather than *to* Iolcos, she is losing never gaining, and in this fundamental sense she is a wanderer.[16] She increasingly feels that her journey is a plunge into homelessness, and this separates her destiny from that of the Argonauts more and more dramatically along the way: while they will return home with the Fleece and see their parents again, she has not found anything to replace her home and parents.[17]

Already on the point of leaving, Medea experiences her departure as a flight caused by fear (Ap. Rhod. 4.11 and 22: Hera puts both fear and the thought of fleeing into her mind). She regrets her decision, and is already assailed by nostalgia – but a tragic nostalgia, with no going back, as the scene in her bedroom at the beginning of Book 4 demonstrates with its

---

[15] See Klooster 2012: 65. [16] On wandering as "traveling from," see Montiglio 2005: 30–4.
[17] Vergil's Dido summarizes Medea's predicament, which Apollonius' successor knows is hers from the outset of the journey, and which his own heroine decides to avoid: "Shall I accompany the exulting sailors, *lonely in my exile* (*sola fuga*)" (*Aen.* 4.543). On this passage see now Keith, Chapter 7 in this volume (I cite her translation).

tragic resonances. She pulls out her hair and cuts it (18–19, 27–8), she kisses her bed (26) and says farewell to her dear ones (30–2), all gestures typical of tragic heroines about to commit suicide. Medea, too, first thinks of suicide (20–1) but instead leaves. The departure is configured not as a passionate elopement to follow the man she loves, but as the alternative to death, and to be with a man who has disrupted her heart and life so irreparably that she wishes he had been "dashed into pieces" by the sea on his journey to Colchis (Ap. Rhod. 4.32–3).

The simile that follows this wish equates the fleeing Medea with a bondmaid, stealing away from a rich home. Fate has just severed her from her native land, and she has not yet made trial of grievous toil, but still unaccustomed to misery and shrinking in terror from slavish work, she goes about under the harsh hands of a mistress (Ap. Rhod. 4.35–9). Terror is the dominant note, Medea's terror of her father, the "mistress" of the simile, which also suggests that the girl has lost her home even before fleeing, that her betrayal ("fate") has caused her to be "severed from her native land" and robbed her of her home – in her own house. She lives in a "rich home," her father's, but now she would be a slave in it. Her kingly palace has no longer been her home since she helped Jason, but has become a prison from which she now escapes.

In the early stretch of the journey, however, Medea seems to entertain a faint hope that she will find in Jason her harbor. In the supplication she addresses to him the first time she is threatened by the Colchians, she gives voice not only to her sentiment of homelessness but also to her expectation that he will fill the void. She says: "I am severed from my fatherland and the glories of my home and even my parents, things that were dearest to me, and I am borne all alone far over the sea with the mournful halcyons" (Ap. Rhod. 4.361–3). But she adds: because of all I have done for you, "I say that I follow you to Greece as your daughter, bride, and sister" (Ap. Rhod. 4.368–9). Echoing Andromache's expression of all-encompassing affection for Hector and total dependency on him, as husband, father, mother, brother (*Il.* 6.429–30), Medea puts the prospect of being "everything" for Jason upfront as a driving force for journeying with him to Hellas. At this point she feels she can remind him that she has left for love of him and with the intention of marrying him at the end of the journey.

Not so by the time they arrive on Drepane, the island of Alcinous. Medea's feeling of homelessness reaches its peak in Phaeacian territory, where by contrast Odysseus becomes hopeful that he will see his home again and talks about Ithaca as lovingly and expansively as never before, anticipating the joy of his return (*Od.* 9.21–36). Apollonius twists the Homeric episode in many ways. He suggests that Phaeacia is closer to the Argonauts' home than it is to Odysseus' – in fact, that it "is" their home, for they are welcomed by the locals as if they were their very children back from a journey, and they themselves behave like homecomers: "The whole city was making merry around them. You would have said that they were rejoicing over their sons. And the heroes themselves went gladly among the crowd, as if they had set foot at the center of Haemonia" (Ap. Rhod. 4.996–1000).[18] This "home," though, does not bring the Argonauts security, as Phaeacia does Odysseus, but renewed dangers, for the Colchians pursue Medea again.[19] Her response to their threat is an anguished expression of homelessness, which builds a sharp and poignant contrast with the treatment of the Argonauts' arrival on Drepane as a homecoming:

> She addressed these words to each of the men in turn: "Because of you, by far the greatest heroes, because of the tasks you had to perform, now I am distraught with fear. It was by my will that you yoked the bulls and reaped the dreadful harvest of the earthborn men, and it is thanks to me that you travel home with the Golden Fleece. I have lost my fatherland, my parents, my home, and all the joy of life, but I have made it possible for you to dwell again in your fatherland and homes, and again you will see your parents, the sweetest sight. But a harsh god has taken from me all the splendors, and wretched I wander with strangers." (Ap. Rhod. 4.1030–41)

Medea risks being taken back to a home that cannot be a home to her, but one to which there is no comforting alternative. Following Jason apparently has not given her any sense of belonging, or even security, for the thought of Greece, where the journey is taking her, and of the man she will marry there has disappeared. She does not even supplicate her betrothed, as she did the first time around, but instead she tries to mollify his companions (Ap. Rhod. 4.1011–12), before pleading with the Phaeacian queen (Ap. Rhod. 4.1012–29), and finally with each of Jason's men, ἄνδρα ἕκαστον (Ap. Rhod. 4.1030): she counts on them more than on their leader. In this second supplication she stresses only her severance from her home and "all the joy of life," and contrasts her predicament – to be a wanderer in every land, wherever she is taken – with the Argonauts' happy prospect of recovering their homes and parents, because she has lost

---

[18] On the Phaeacian episode as a substitute for the Argonauts' homecoming, which is only summarily narrated, see Knight 1995: 248–9.
[19] This treatment of Phaeacia contrasts with the Odyssean section of the Argonauts' journey that ends with their arrival there, for Jason, unlike Odysseus, enjoys divine protection on that stretch and is saved from danger. See Knight 1995: 159, 216–19; Clare 2002: 139–43.

hers. The contrast is audibly pointed up by the identical rhythm of two of the verses with which, in close succession, she describes their diverging destinies: ἤνυσα, καὶ γλυκεροῖσιν ἔτ' εἰσόψεσθε τοκῆας (1039) and ἀγλαΐας, στυγερὴ δὲ σὺν ὀθνείοις ἀλάλημαι (1041). Both are strings of dactyls interrupted by a spondee in the fourth foot, but one line ends with "[your] parents," the other with "I wander."

Medea's feelings of homelessness look forward in her mythic biography and backward in literary history, to the heroine of Euripides. The tragic Medea has been a permanent exile since her departure from Colchis, "lonely, city-less" (*Med.* 255), and Jason's abandonment together with Creon's verdict turn her into a homeless wanderer for life (434–7, 511–15, 798–9). The ultimate reason the epic Medea feels homeless while she is traveling with Jason to his home is that the *Argonautica* presupposes Euripides' play and foreshadows it with numerous disturbing prolepses, of which a major one is the heroine's experience of her journey as a loss with neither love nor the prospect of a new home to make up for it.[20] To the epic Medea's lament, "I was severed from my fatherland ... and my parents" (Ap. Rhod. 4.361–2) responds her tragic counterpart's "father, city, from which I removed myself" (*Med.* 166). While Euripides' character recalls Jason's loving gestures with pain ("Ah, this right hand, which you used to take so often!" *Med.* 496), Apollonius' heroine anticipates with pain Jason's abandonment of her by coloring her experience of the journey with a growing sentiment of homelessness.

To recapitulate: Jason is all set to travel back home, like Odysseus, but he takes along a bride-to-be who instantly regrets having left her own home; these regrets grow stronger as her betrothed fails to replace her native land. Wandering for Jason is, even more than for Odysseus, an undesirable disruption of the homeward-bound journey, though, I should add, in Jason's case, contrary to Odysseus', the main episode of disorientating wandering occurs after the stay among the Phaeacians, when a fierce storm drives the Argo to the unknown shores of Libya (Ap. Rhod. 4.1280–9). More such disruptions trouble the last stretches of the journey (Ap. Rhod. 1539–47, 1696–1701).[21] For Medea, wandering is her very condition since she leaves Colchis behind like a fugitive slave, and her sentiment of lacking a home to go to intensifies during the journey. She,

---

[20] For other prolepses, see, e.g., Fantuzzi 1988: 145; Hurst 2012: 90. See also Hunter 1989: 19. On tragic foreshadowing in the *Argonautica*, see also Blum, Chapter 4 in this volume.

[21] See Montiglio 2005: 231–2. The placement of the most damaging storm after the Argonauts' stay in Phaeacia is yet another rewriting of Odysseus' journey.

a woman, involves herself in an epic journey, but sets the wrong goal for it: a loved person rather than a mission or even a place.[22] When she feels she has lost Jason, her "destination," she also feels that she is adrift, regardless of where she is or how she travels, whether on smooth or troubled waters (when stranded in Libya, she laments her fate with her maids, but shows no more despair than the Argonauts: Ap. Rhod. 4.1290–7). Jason has turned out to be one of the strangers with whom she wanders.

No hero or heroine of a Greek novel would ever call the loved one a stranger.[23] All the novels except *Daphnis and Chloe* narrate adventurous journeys in the mold of the *Odyssey*, but there are variations in the journeys' structure and movement. Either the protagonists meet in their common native land, marry there, leave and travel, mostly apart, until they reunite toward the end of their travels and return home – so in Chariton's *Callirhoe* and Xenophon of Ephesus' *Ephesiaca*; or the two meet in the hero's native land, leave and travel, most of the time together, reunite toward the end of their travels, and marry in the heroine's native land – so in Achilles Tatius' *Leucippe and Clitophon*; or again, the protagonists meet in the native land of neither one, travel, mostly together, to reach that of the heroine, and marry there. This is the skeleton of Heliodorus' *Aethiopica*, which the movement of the journey and its purpose bring close to Apollonius' epic.[24]

How? In both texts the journey is a *nostos* only for one of the characters (Jason, Chariclea), while the other (Medea, Theagenes) forsakes her or his native land; in both, the journey begins with a concerted elopement at night (just as Medea flees knowing, or at least strongly hoping, that Jason will agree to take her along [Ap. Rhod. 3.1120–30], Theagenes kidnaps Chariclea from her Delphic home with her agreement [*Aeth*. 4.17.2–4]);[25] the elopers in each narrative are immediately chased by armed pursuers (Jason and Medea by her brother and his people, Theagenes and Chariclea by the whole city of Delphi, women, children, and old men included [Ap. Rhod. 4.21.2–3]); in both, the couple travel together (in Heliodorus most

---

[22] Vergil's heroines who dare undertake epic journeys fail in other ways, for instance by not being granted a full narrative of their journeys: see Keith, Chapter 7 in this volume.
[23] In three novels out of five the two protagonists have the same birthplace, but this is less important for their feeling of togetherness than the power of their perfectly mutual love.
[24] The novels' debts to the *Odyssey* are numerous and often explicit, whereas the only certain reference to Apollonius' epic is in Chariton: see Ap. Rhod. 1.774 and *Callirhoe* 1.1.5, with Bowie 2000. The lack of citations, however, does not prove that the novelists, Heliodorus included, did not use Apollonius.
[25] An important difference, though, is that Medea leaves her native land whereas Chariclea leaves to return to hers.

of the time);[26] and the two journeys have two aims: the recovery of one's home and assets for the returning traveler and marriage for both travelers. These numerous thematic and structural parallels, however, underscore important differences in the travelers' priorities and goals.

Heliodorus grafts the adventurous wanderings of the *Odyssey* onto his protagonists' journey by linking it explicitly to Odysseus' travels. While the couple and their fatherly protector Calasiris are stationed on Zacynthos, their first stop after their flight from Delphi, the ghost of the Homeric hero appears to Calasiris in a dream and vents his anger for not having been honored as his heroic status requires: though nearby, Calasiris did not pay him a visit of worship. The punishment for this neglect will be a troubled journey, like Odysseus' own: "You will experience the same sufferings I did. Sea and land will be your enemies" (*Aeth.* 5.22.3). Odysseus' prediction comes true shortly after Calasiris and his wards depart, for they encounter two life-threatening storms (*Aeth.* 5.22.7, 5.27).

As a good Greek novelist, Heliodorus cannot pass over proper storms.[27] His, however, are minor disruptions compared to the deadly tempests that hit Odysseus, or even those endured by sailors in other novels. In Achilles Tatius the waves take numerous victims (3.1–5); in Xenophon the lull of the midday hour invites an attack on the ship and, in consequence, many passengers to throw themselves into the sea (1.13.5); and in the anonymous Latin novel *Historia Apollonii Regis Tyri* (11–12) a storm kills everyone except the hero. In Heliodorus, by contrast, everyone survives both storms, and the two episodes are unglamorous. The first warrants only a brief account, while the second, though decked with more literary frills (suddenness, thunderous winds, broken ropes), contains the specification that to put the travelers in danger was the incompetence of the helmsman more than the waves, which were not at their peak (*Aeth.* 5.27.4). This added detail drives home the point that this storm is not to be read as a cataclysm of epic proportions but as a much more mundane accident. The fiercest tempest in this novel, lasting "seven days and seven nights," is a lie, made up by the heroine in the deceptive autobiography that she weaves to her suitor Thyamis (*Aeth.* 1.22.4).

---

[26] This is true also of Achilles Tatius' novel, but its protagonists are forced to stay apart for a long narrative time (from Book 5 to Book 8) even when they are in the same city (Ephesus) and on the same estate. Morgan 2003: 440 finds the togetherness of Heliodorus' protagonists in their travels notable, and connects it to the novelist's choice to substitute the traditional novelistic pattern of separation and reunion with one of return: that is, a pattern closer to that of Apollonius' epic.

[27] Even Longus' protagonists, who stay on Lesbos, experience maritime misadventures.

Given that Odysseus identifies Calasiris' upcoming sufferings with his own, and his prediction functions as a frame and a template for the novelistic journey,[28] readers will mark the relative effortlessness and directedness with which Chariclea's *nostos*, compared with Odysseus', is accomplished. For, all in all, the crossing from Delphi to Ethiopia is fairly uneventful, as far as the itinerary goes. The travelers do not get lost and are not driven off course as they progress toward Chariclea's native land. After leaving Delphi they sail to the Ionian Islands with no unpredictable complication – they meet with a rough sea once, but in a place where the sea is always rough (*Aeth.* 5.17.1–3). They are the victims of only those two storms at the beginning of their journey, around Crete, and, regardless, they end up in Egypt, where after all they were directed (*Aeth.* 5.20.1).[29] This concentration of storms in the stretch of the journey, from Zacynthos to Egypt, that immediately follows Odysseus' curse, pays honor to the hero's power by making his threat instantly real. But after reaching Egypt the travelers continue to Memphis and further south to Meroe with no major detour. Though they often feel disoriented, their trajectory, in fact, is unwavering, north to south.[30]

The ease with which the *nostos* is accomplished constitutes an important difference also between Heliodorus' novel and Apollonius' epic, where the return journey meets with much more catastrophic disruptions than the journey out. Instead of major detours, Chariclea will face major opponents. "Sea and land will be your enemies," as Odysseus had warned Calasiris, not so much as natural elements as because they are filled with human enemies. The nature of the hurdles is consistent with the travelers' main concerns, which are different from Jason's. In his case, the disruptive detours with which he meets act as obstacles to counter his most important goal: to go back home. It may not be by chance in this respect that the most serious disruptions in his journey occur toward the end, when he should be close to reaching Iolcos. Chariclea, in contrast, is not so much set on going home as on protecting her relationship with Theagenes until they reach her home. Hence the obstacles they face are not unwanted detours but unwanted encounters, which threaten the couple's togetherness.[31]

---

[28] On Odysseus' prediction as a signal that we should read the novelistic travels against those in the *Odyssey*, see Whitmarsh 2011: 113.
[29] To be sure, they land where they do "without wanting to" (5.27.8), but Egypt was their destination.
[30] See Whitmarsh 2011: 115.
[31] Calasiris unwittingly points to this truth by wishing they had been drowned instead of being saved for the only purpose of enduring a more fearful destiny from the brigands who captured them (5.27.8).

Chariclea is an exceptional woman in Greek literature because she successfully accomplishes an epic journey, and does so as its main protagonist.[32] Her crossing could be labeled "epic" for several reasons: it covers a great distance (from Delphi to Ethiopia); it is a *nostos* like Odysseus' and, like his, it has the added goal of restoring the traveler to her birthrights; and, especially, it is under the declared aegis (or rather the curse) of the Homeric hero. Chariclea enjoys a freedom to travel that is remarkable even among the female protagonists of the Greek novels, who otherwise can make important autonomous decisions such as whom to marry and whether to raise a child or to abort. No other novelistic heroine sets out on a journey of her own accord, but they are all taken from place to place by adverse circumstances and against their will.[33] The greater latitude of movement displayed by Heliodorus' protagonist might also reflect women's increased freedom to undertake journeys in the real world, in addition to casting her as an Odysseus-like figure.[34]

Yet Chariclea is an epic traveler in a novel – that is, the main goal of her epic venture is romantic. Her quest for her native land is spurred not so much by her discovery of her origins or a desire to recover her family and princely status as by her passion for Theagenes, whom she can hope to marry *only* if she leaves her adoptive father.[35] Compared to the returning traveler in Apollonius, the priorities are reversed: Jason will marry Medea because her love will have made it possible for him to come back home with the Fleece (the fact that they are forced to consummate their marriage along the way is irrelevant),[36] but Chariclea will reach her home in order to be Theagenes' wife. This major shift in the purpose of traveling also corresponds with a major shift in the meaning of wandering for the homeward-bound traveler: not, as in Apollonius, losing one's way

---

[32] I can think only of the Amazon Penthesilea as another specimen (see Keith, Chapter 7 in this volume), though she is a defeminized woman.

[33] A partial exception is Leucippe at the beginning of her journey, when she chooses to elope for fear of her mother. But her departure has no positive goal.

[34] If the *Peregrinatio Aetheriae*, which records the travels of a wealthy woman to the Holy Land, dates to the second half of the fourth century CE, it is not distant in time from the *Aethiopica*. Chariclea's freedom to wander could also be part of the novel's Platonic underpinning: see below.

[35] Chariclea is proud to learn that she is a queen's daughter (4.12.1), but she also says, "either Theagenes will take me or my fate will" (ἐμὲ γὰρ ἢ Θεαγένης ἄξεται ἢ τὸ τῆς εἱμαρμένης διαδέξεται, 4.11.3). Calasiris knows her priority: in trying to persuade her to leave Delphi, the first reason he gives is the threat of marriage with a man she does not love; the second is the recovery of fatherland, parents, and status; and the third is marriage with Theagenes (4.13.2). The reasons of the heart receive twice as much emphasis. On Chariclea's motivation to leave I agree with de Temmerman 2014: 189. See also Montiglio 2013: 143–6.

[36] Clauss 1997: 167 speaks of a reversal of the familiar folktale motif, "hero must perform a contest to win a bride." Jason instead must win a bride before he engages in the contest!

unwillingly along the journey, but willingly embracing the risk of losing one's way, and even one's life, to search for the loved one.

Heliodorus' novel features a heroine who chooses to wander in order to gain something – or, rather, everything. To be sure, in this novel as in the others the journey begins as a violent displacement, a removal from home that, according to one critical approach, suggests the second phase in rites of passage, the experience of the margins.[37] The novels' protagonists are alone, strangers, homeless, because they have to go through a symbolic death. As Theagenes puts it, as soon as the pair and their protector leave Chariclea's adoptive father and home, the two lovers are "strangers and homeless, deprived of everything" (ξένους καὶ ἀπόλιδας ... πάντων ἀλλοτριωθέντας, *Aeth*. 4.18.2). Wandering is the alienating experience that the young man and woman have to undergo in order to be reintegrated and established in their society as adults.

But novelistic wandering is not only a privative condition, which bespeaks a temporary loss of status and cultural belonging; it can also be an active and willed movement to find the loved one. In Chariton, Chaereas is launched on a search for Callirhoe that causes him to travel all over Asia and to experience capture, slavery, and war. In Xenophon, Habrocomes likewise moves around the Mediterranean hoping to find his wife.[38] And in Heliodorus, Chariclea spiritedly sets out to search for her love and calls her search "wandering": "I and Calasiris will fight whatever happens until we reach the end of our wandering (τέλος τῆς πλάνης)" (*Aeth*. 6.7.9).

The phrase "τέλος of wandering" suggests the very end of the novel, harking back as it does to the vague τέλος δεξιόν, or "happy ending," which Odysseus predicts for Chariclea as reward for her chastity (*Aeth*. 5.22.3). The readers, equipped with their knowledge of generic patterns, will take the "τέλος of wandering" to refer also to "the end of the journey to Ethiopia," the accomplishment of the *nostos* – that is, the adventures' τέλος δεξιόν. But this is not what Chariclea means: for her, wandering will stop with the recovery not of her home but of her loved one. The dead son of a sorceress whom she and Calasiris meet en route also underscores the romantic goal of Chariclea's wandering. Shaken out of his final rest by his mother's necromantic ritual, he calls Chariclea one who "wanders all over the earth, so to speak, to search for her loved one, with whom, after countless toils and countless dangers, she will live at the edges of the earth the splendid life of a queen" (*Aeth*. 6.15.4). Though the dead man

---

[37] See Lalanne 2006: 109–17.   [38] For references, see Montiglio 2013: 62.

prophesies that Chariclea will recover her home and estate, he knows that her energy is all spent in her wandering search. Her homeward-bound journey at this point is not on her mind.

Chariclea's wandering after love naturally conjures up the Platonic conception of love as a restless condition, caused by the soul's longing to see the beautiful one.[39] Platonic motifs indeed abound in this novel, among which the representation of wandering as a quest plays a major part.[40] Chariclea's determination to search for Theagenes finds a parallel in the behavior of another novelistic heroine whose trajectory follows a Platonic script: Psyche in Apuleius' *Golden Ass*, who wanders relentlessly after losing Cupid. I will not, however, deal with the possible allegorical meanings of wandering in such contexts (our interpretive choices will depend on how seriously we take each novelist's exploitation of Platonic motifs), but will focus on the consequences that Chariclea's choice to set out on her search have for the direction of her journey, which, unlike Psyche's, starts off as a *nostos*. A wandering search that has a goal different from one's physical home could enter into conflict with, and even replace, a *nostos*.

The goal of love overshadows home in the other Greek novels as well. Chaereas, after he thinks Callirhoe lost to him, does not consider going back to his native Syracuse but, spurred by suicidal fantasies, he enrolls in a war. Going home without his beloved is not an option for him. Habrocomes, desperate from not finding Anthia in his wanderings all over the Mediterranean, and thinking her dead, does plan to return to their native Ephesus, but only to build a tomb for her and then kill himself (*Ephesiaca* 5.10). Though in these two novels the fatherland is important for the identity of the lovers, who invoke it in moments of despair, it cannot make up for love lost.[41] Only once does this happen, and only faintly, in the case

---

[39] Pl. *Phdr.* 251e3–5. See also *Symp.* 209b4.
[40] The most striking Platonic motif in Heliodorus' novel is the representation of falling in love as the ignition of recollection (3.5.4–5). This has been noted by many: see, e.g., Feuillâtre 1966: 125–8; Sandy 1982; Winkler 1982: 125; Fusillo 1989: 199; Dowden 1996: 279, n. 35; Morgan 2003: 453; Hunter 2005: 135; Graverini 2010: 72–3; Montiglio 2013: 118.
[41] For an insightful discussion of the significance of home in *Callirhoe* and the *Ephesiaca*, see Whitmarsh 2011, who demonstrates that the native land has a greater power in defining the protagonists' identity in these two earlier novels than in the later ones. Though I largely agree with his analysis, I think that even in the early novels the protagonists' home, important as it is for integrating and endorsing their love, could not offer comfort if they should lose each other for good. Callirhoe does express her nostalgia for home and parents more vocally than her longing for Chaereas, but this is after she thinks him dead. Before, she unambiguously states that Chaereas is more important to her than home and parents (2.11.1). I think that every novelistic lover, if forced to choose between home and love, would choose the latter, like Aegialeus and Thelxinoe in Xenophon. Hippothous (in the same novel) is another case in point.

not of a protagonist but of Dionysius in Chariton's novel, who consoles himself for the definitive loss of Callirhoe with the prospect of the long journey back to Miletus, his fatherland, and "of his authority over many cities and the statues of Callirhoe in Miletus" (8.5.15). But this lover is unloved. His native land is a consolation prize, and even so it will warm his heart not so much as his native land as because it is filled with semblances of the loved woman.

Though the priority of love over home is a shared novelistic feature, Chariclea pursues her goal with a singlemindedness that is missing from the other two novelistic heroes, Chaereas and Habrocomes, who travel the world looking for their beloved. Habrocomes does search for Anthia, but erratically: especially toward the end, he moves from city to city almost mechanically, and looking for his wife is more an afterthought than a set goal.[42] Chaereas, to be sure, is so eager to leave in search of Callirhoe that he cannot even wait until the sailing season (*Callirhoe* 3.5.1). But he is captured almost instantly, and his search meets with more obstacles until he gives up the prospect of recovering her and despair turns him into a warrior, elated to risk his life. Of all the novelistic heroes and heroines, Chariclea is the only one engaged in a quest for her native land; and yet she alone goes so far as to contemplate living a homeless life with her beloved – and this from the outset, as soon as she starts on her *nostos*.

When, upon leaving Delphi, Chariclea requires Theagenes to swear to pre-marital chastity, she adds this proviso: should they not reach her home, "you will make me your wife only if I give my full consent, otherwise, not at all" (*Aeth.* 4.18.5). The spirited woman is telling her fiancé that she will not accept rape, but might accept a life *more uxorio* without her family's imprimatur. She shows a stronger inclination for this prospect when, after losing Theagenes, she is captured, and laments: "I was hoping to spend the rest of my life with my dearest one, a life of wandering in foreign land (ξένον καὶ ἀλήτην βίον), but the sweetest in his company" (*Aeth.* 5.2.7). The misadventures she has suffered along her journey up to this last episode of captivity seem to have caused her to lose confidence in a successful *nostos*, or even to forget that goal: but not her goal of spending a lifetime with Theagenes, no matter where. While Medea describes her predicament as "wandering with strangers," of whom Jason is one, Chariclea would be happy to wander with her "dearest one" (τῷ φιλτάτῳ) forever. Her journey, as it turns out, is more toward securing a life of love than even toward a proper marriage, let alone her royal home.

---

[42] See Montiglio 2013: 62.

In addition, the emphasis on love as "Home" in Heliodorus' novel reconfigures the relationship of the partner who abandons his or her physical home with that home. Though the heroine of Apollonius also prioritizes love, and even betrays her family for it, she instantly misses her home, and feels like a refugee even by Jason's side. In contrast, Theagenes hardly ever mentions his native country and his family, in spite of their distinguished history – he is from Hypate, "the noblest city of Thessaly" (*Aeth.* 2.34.2), and a member of the Enianes, "the noblest people of Thessaly" (*Aeth.* 2.34.2), and purportedly a descendant of Achilles (*Aeth.* 2.34.4). Theagenes is ready to follow Chariclea from the outset, wherever in the world she should decide to go (*Aeth.* 4.13.2), and he never looks back.

This difference between Theagenes' mindset and Medea's might be partly related to gender: displacement is a more dire predicament for a woman than for a man, who is also freer to move outside and away from his family and country. As an added advantage, Theagenes has the prospect of further raising his status at the end of the journey, since marriage with Chariclea will make him prince consort and eventually king. But he shows no interest in wearing a crown; he is only eager to be with his beloved where he can be with her forever. Her home is his home.[43] Or rather, for both novelistic lovers their existence as a couple is "Home," for if they miss a place, it is Delphi (*Aeth.* 2.11.5), where they met.[44] The very fact that they fall in love not in either of their homelands, but in the adopted residence of the heroine, who soon discovers that her fatherland is elsewhere, devalues the position of home in its relationship with love: it is love that defines Chariclea's identity more strongly than either of her homes.[45] After the pair leave Delphi they are, to be sure, "strangers and homeless, deprived of everything"; but this is "in order to win only each other" (*Aeth.* 4.18.2).[46]

To conclude: Jason, like Odysseus, is all set on going back home. His failure to express as strong a longing for his native land as the Homeric

---

[43] In J. Maillon's translation (Lumb and Rattenbury 1960), Chariclea identifies Theagenes' fatherland with her own when she laments the death of Calasiris, who was "celui qui devait nous ramener dans notre patrie et nous rendre à nos parents" (7.14.7). Though the Greek does not quite support this rendering (no possessive adjective appears), it hits the truth of the couple's feelings. Chariclea does not emphasize that the fatherland they are seeking is hers. Later Thyamis says that the two are trying to reach "the native land" (τὴν ἐνεγκοῦσαν) (8.3.7). Here the lack of possessive adjective is more telling, for Thyamis does not mean his own native land.

[44] Emily Baragwanath (see p. 111 in this volume) writes on *Anabasis*: "one's "Home" and identity may reside not in place but in the positive relationships and unity forged with others."
Twisted romantically, this phrase could apply to Heliodorus' protagonists.

[45] On Chariclea's complicated ethnic identity (she was born in Ethiopia but raised in Greece) I refer again to the excellent treatment of Whitmarsh 2011.

[46] See Montiglio 2005: 234.

hero can be accounted for mainly in narratological terms, for it fits Apollonius' "Alexandrian epic," where Iolcos becomes unimportant, and a narrative whose climax is a feat at the end of the outward journey (rather than the homecoming, as in the *Odyssey*); a narrative, moreover, which is scattered with premonitions of the post-narrative future, homeless again for Jason. While he is all set on going home, taking Medea with him is unavoidable but secondary. As for her, she has no other mission to accomplish but to cling to the man for whom she has sacrificed her home. Accordingly, when he drifts away from her she is filled with increasingly strong regrets for having left her birthplace, and feels that she has no home to go to.

In contrast to Jason, the heroine of Heliodorus' novel is first and foremost set on marrying her traveling companion, and she embarks on a truly epic journey with this novelistic, rather than epic, purpose. Returning to her native land is instrumental to her romantic wish, but becomes irrelevant when, along the way, she loses the man she loves. For both Chariclea and Theagenes, love is more important than home in defining their identity.

The contrasting priorities of the returning travelers are reflected in the nature of the obstacles they face: unwanted disruptions ("wandering"), *Odyssey*-like, in the case of Jason, and encounters that threaten the couple's togetherness in the case of Chariclea, whose *nostos*, in spite of being framed by the ghost of Odysseus himself, is comparatively uneventful as far as its trajectory goes. Wandering together is a relatively desirable option for the novelistic couple, while it is not for either Medea or Jason: for him it means not reaching his goal, and for her it is synonymous with homelessness and loneliness. Perhaps they have known a brief period of love (Jason is moved to loving Medea when he sees her in tears: Ap. Rhod. 3.1077–8), but for Medea her love is tragic from the outset. Though she has staked her life on being "everything" to Jason, does she believe she is and will be? In the early phase of her journey she might, but only faintly. For even then there is no hint of a romantic spur, not even the hint we can trace in the heroine of Valerius Flaccus, who tells her own Jason words that would fit in Heliodorus' novel far better than in Apollonius' epic: "With you I will endure the seas, with you I will endure all the ways we have to go" (V. Fl. 8.50–1: *tecum aequora, tecum / experiar quascumque vias*). Chariclea says something very similar: "nothing is so terrible that I could not endure it with him" (*Aeth.* 5.2.7). The homeless, unloved heroine of Apollonius has no such comfort in hardship.

CHAPTER 6

Heroes and Homemakers in Xenophon

Emily Baragwanath

Xenophon's *Anabasis* recounts his journey with the 10,000 Greek mercenaries from Asia Minor into the heart of the Persian Empire and their return. It describes, after the battle of Cunaxa near Babylon, the tortuous trek north through the unknown and unforgiving desert and mountainous territories of eastern Anatolia, to reach the Black Sea and ultimately the coast of Asia Minor.[1] The story evokes Odysseus' epic journey, to which the narrative twice explicitly refers. In the aftermath of the treacherous assassination of their leaders, in a speech rousing the men to fight on, the character Xenophon expresses his fear lest he and the men, "once [they] learn to live in idleness and luxury, and to consort with the big and beautiful women and maidens of these Medes and Persians ... may, like the Lotus-Eaters, forget [their] homeward way" (*An.* 3.2.25): a reminder, not only of the *Odyssey*'s Lotus-Eaters (*Od.* 9.94–104), but also of the series of treacherous females who delay Odysseus' return. And upon reaching the Black Sea one of the soldiers voices his longing "to be rid of these toils" and to sail the rest of the way stretched out on his back like Odysseus (*An.* 5.1.2) – which recalls Homer's account of Odysseus' cruise from Phaeacia back home to Ithaca (*Od.* 13.75–118).

Beyond these explicit recollections of the *Odyssey*, *Anabasis* numerous times invokes Homer implicitly;[2] and like the Homeric poems it, too, is

---

I would like to thank Luuk Huitink, Mathieu de Bakker, an anonymous reader, and those who heard earlier versions of this talk in Basel, Yale, Heidelberg, Hamburg, and the University of North Carolina at Chapel Hill for their valuable and illuminating suggestions. I thank the two volume editors for organizing a terrific conference. The chapter was written in the ideal environs of the Seminar für Klassische Philologie in Heidelberg, with the support of an Alexander von Humboldt research fellowship.

[1] The journey from Cunaxa (late November 401 BCE) to their arrival at Trapezus (early May 400 BCE) took approximately five months: Brennan 2012 ("Snow Lacuna").
[2] Tuplin 2003 offers a comprehensive review of possible Homeric references in *Anabasis*. The journey of the Ten Thousand recalls that of Odysseus (Lossau 1990), while the situation of a community of soldiers conducting war abroad and the accounts of tensions and negotiations among their leaders

preoccupied with future memory and securing *kleos*.[3] Consequently readers are sharply reminded of Homer in general and Odysseus' journey in particular. This intertextuality implicitly figures Xenophon, leader of the men after the generals' assassination, as a latter-day Odysseus. But Xenophon offers no explicit guidance as to the significance of the Homeric texture.[4] Christopher Tuplin has helpfully formulated some possibilities. Is the *Odyssey* there to remind us that Xenophon fails the heroic test by not resuming his life at home? Or, since the travelers are "the Greeks," that a *nostos* is achieved once they have "reached Greece"? Or both these things: that Xenophon survives but fails to return home, but his companions get home, in which case he achieves the aim in *Od.* 1.5, thus surpassing Odysseus?[5]

Scholarship since Tuplin has emphasized the journey as failure. For John Ma the *Anabasis* is thus "structured around the difficulty or impossibility of return ... the protracted activity of 'going home' solves nothing; resolution and return are constantly deferred."[6] In similar vein Jonas Grethlein reads the Odyssean references as foregrounding the goal (*telos*) of *nostos*, only for the work to "pursue a strategy that ... denies the march a *telos* and the narrative a closure."[7]

My aim in this chapter is to suggest that in some key respects Xenophon depicts the journey as success: as achieving "Home." I do not wish to supplant the negative readings, but to complement them: for Xenophon's oeuvre is poised between poles of optimism and pessimism. At the end of the *Hellenica*, for example, the total confusion that reigns from the human perspective is tempered by the specter of a governing deity: a divine agent putting the world in order (*Hell.* 7.5.26). In *Anabasis* we may turn to an episode often felt to suggest the wider story: the dream that prompts Xenophon, after the seizure of the generals, to step forward, take

---

brings to mind the Greek camp at Troy in the *Iliad*. See Gautier 1911: 103–4; Rinner 1978; Dalby 1992: 21; Tsagalis 2002; Grethlein 2013: 76–7, 79. Cf. *An.* 3.1.37 ~ *Il.* 12.310; *An.* 4.8.14.

[3] E.g. Clearchus to Phalinus, envisaging the expedition's future fame: 2.1.17; cf. Rood 2006: 52; Xenophon encouraging his men: "it will surely be sweet, through some manly and noble thing which one may say or do today, to furnish memory (μνήμην) in those whom he wishes to remember him" (6.5.24); cf. 7.6.32: keeping safe "any fine thing" (τι καλόν) done against the barbarians of Asia, they have gained "other glory" (ἄλλην εὔκλειαν) vanquishing Thracians in Europe – thus implying that the process of their future memory has already begun. See Flower 2012: 34–8.

[4] The refusal to supply authorial direction is itself reminiscent of Homeric technique.

[5] Tuplin 2003: 140.   [6] Ma 2004: 333–4.

[7] Grethlein 2013: 75–6. See also Ma 2004: 333–4 (*An.* is about the impossibility of returning home); Bradley 2010: 539–49 (*An.* builds up impossible expectations); Purves 2010a: 159–95 (evocation and deferral of the notion of homeland); Flower 2012: 46. Return and (lack of) narrative closure, with reference to the *Odyssey*: Purves 2010a: 163 ff.; Flower 2012: 44–7, 111.

command, and encourage the men to embark upon the journey that leads them homewards:

> ἔδοξεν αὐτῷ βροντῆς γενομένης σκηπτὸς πεσεῖν <u>εἰς τὴν πατρῴαν οἰκίαν</u>, καὶ ἐκ τούτου λάμπεσθαι πᾶσα. περίφοβος δ' εὐθὺς ἀνηγέρθη, καὶ τὸ ὄναρ **τῇ μὲν** ἔκρινεν ἀγαθόν, ὅτι ἐν πόνοις ὢν καὶ κινδύνοις **φῶς μέγα ἐκ Διὸς** ἰδεῖν ἔδοξε· **τῇ δὲ καὶ** ἐφοβεῖτο, ὅτι ἀπὸ Διὸς μὲν βασιλέως τὸ ὄναρ ἐδόκει αὐτῷ εἶναι, κύκλῳ δὲ ἐδόκει λάμπεσθαι τὸ πῦρ, μὴ οὐ δύναιτο **ἐκ τῆς χώρας ἐξελθεῖν τῆς βασιλέως**, ἀλλ' εἴργοιτο πάντοθεν **ὑπό τινων ἀποριῶν**. ὁποῖόν τι μὲν δὴ ἐστὶ τὸ τοιοῦτον ὄναρ ἰδεῖν **ἔξεστι σκοπεῖν ἐκ τῶν συμβάντων μετὰ τὸ ὄναρ**. γίγνεται γὰρ τάδε. (*An.* 3.1.11–13)
>
> It seemed to him that there was a clap of thunder and a bolt fell <u>on his father's house</u>, and from this all was lit up. He awoke at once in great fear, and judged the dream **in one way** auspicious, because in the middle of labours and dangers he seemed to see a great light from Zeus; but **in another way** he was fearful, since the dream seemed to him to come from Zeus the King, and the fire seemed to blaze in a circle, lest he not be able **to escape out of the King's country**, but be shut in on all sides **by various difficulties**. What it means to have such a dream **it is possible to contemplate from the events that happen after it** – and they were these.[8]

After describing the dream Xenophon observes that "what it means to have such a dream it is possible to learn from the events that happen after it (μετὰ τὸ ὄναρ)" (*An.* 3.1.13) – a phrase that potentially embraces the whole of the remaining narrative.[9]

Those highlighting negative readings have interpreted the dream narrative accordingly; but its presentation may equally be programmatic in emphatically *combining* positive and negative possibilities (see the emboldened text in the quotation above), which might invite readers to adopt an interpretative middle way.[10] Working against the prediction of difficulties, the light from Zeus (φῶς μέγα ἐκ Διός, cf. λάμπεσθαι) thus suggests escape, survival, *life*; Tarrant has observed that in Homer "the noun φάος has one distinctive figurative sense, that of salvation or help."[11] In the event, after surmounting great difficulties most of the mercenaries will indeed escape the king's territory (cf. ἐκ τῆς χώρας … τῆς βασιλέως), in a narrative marked by the

---

[8] Translation after Brownson 1992.
[9] On the ambiguity of this expression see Flower 2012: 127; Dillery 1995: 73.
[10] Ma 2004: 336: "once he achieves his escape, Xenophon will find himself in exile – the paternal house is destroyed by fire, there is no going home"; Grethlein 2013: 83: the ring of fire mirrors the ring of narrative that evades closure.
[11] Tarrant 1960: 182. The Homeric texture perhaps makes Xenophon's interpretation less "strained and unexplained" (Flower 2012: 126).

pattern of Xenophon as one who enables the overcoming of *aporiai* – a pattern that again finds a seed in the dream sequence (see bold).[12] Stimulated by the final part of Tuplin's question (the possibility that the character Xenophon "achieves the aim of *Odyssey* 1.5") and by Xenophon's concept of "Home" as it appears elsewhere across his literary oeuvre, I wish to trace two further elements in *Anabasis*' depiction of an epic journey, elements that challenge the more negative theme. Thus I shall read the work as a tale of achieving *nostos* by securing *survival and salvation*, and (connected with that) as a tale of finding "Home" by forging relationships and generating a productive unity and harmony of all parties, including especially women: a tale that reveals the possibility – and necessity – of making "Home" even in the course of a voyage away. "Home" is indeed foregrounded by the dream narrative, with its reference to Xenophon's ancestral *oikos* (τὴν πατρῴαν οἰκίαν, *An.* 3.1.11).

Each of these themes is heralded in the opening stanzas of the *Odyssey*, where they stand in close connection to the idea of Odysseus' journey as a tale of *nostos* and failed *nostos* (see underlined):

Ἄνδρα μοι ἔννεπε, Μοῦσα, πολύτροπον, ὃς μάλα πολλὰ
πλάγχθη, ἐπεὶ Τροίης ἱερὸν πτολίεθρον ἔπερσε·
πολλῶν δ' ἀνθρώπων ἴδεν ἄστεα καὶ νόον ἔγνω,
πολλὰ δ' ὅ γ' ἐν πόντῳ πάθεν ἄλγεα ὃν κατὰ θυμόν,
ἀρνύμενος ἥν τε ψυχὴν καὶ <u>νόστον ἑταίρων</u>.
ἀλλ' **οὐδ'** ὣς ἑτάρους **ἐρρύσατο**, ἱέμενός περ·
αὐτῶν γὰρ σφετέρῃσιν ἀτασθαλίῃσιν **ὄλοντο**,
νήπιοι, οἳ κατὰ βοῦς Ὑπερίονος Ἠελίοιο
ἤσθιον· αὐτὰρ ὁ τοῖσιν ἀφείλετο <u>νόστιμον ἦμαρ</u>.
τῶν ἁμόθεν γε, θεά, θύγατερ Διός, εἰπὲ καὶ ἡμῖν.
**Ἔνθ' ἄλλοι μὲν πάντες, ὅσοι φύγον αἰπὺν ὄλεθρον,
οἴκοι ἔσαν**, πόλεμόν τε πεφευγότες ἠδὲ θάλασσαν·
τὸν δ' οἶον, <u>νόστου κεχρημένον</u> **ἠδὲ γυναικός**,
νύμφη πότνι' ἔρυκε Καλυψώ, δῖα θεάων,
ἐν σπέσσι γλαφυροῖσι, λιλαιομένη πόσιν εἶναι.
ἀλλ' ὅτε δὴ ἔτος ἦλθε περιπλομένων ἐνιαυτῶν,
τῷ οἱ ἐπεκλώσαντο θεοὶ **οἶκόνδε νέεσθαι
εἰς Ἰθάκην**, οὐδ' ἔνθα πεφυγμένος ἦεν ἀέθλων,
καὶ μετὰ οἷσι φίλοισι. θεοὶ δ' ἐλέαιρον ἅπαντες
νόσφι Ποσειδάωνος· ὁ δ' ἀσπερχὲς μενέαινεν
ἀντιθέῳ Ὀδυσῆϊ πάρος ἣν γαῖαν ἱκέσθαι.

(*Od.* 1.1–21)

---

[12] Vocabulary and theme of *aporia* in *Anabasis*: see esp. Purves 2010a: 177–9.

> Tell me, O Muse, of the man of many devices, who wandered full many ways after he had sacked the sacred citadel of Troy. Many were the men whose cities he saw and whose minds he learned, aye, and many the woes he suffered in his heart upon the sea, **seeking to win his own life** and the return of his comrades. Yet even so **he saved not** his comrades, though he desired it sore, for through their own blind folly **they perished** – fools, who devoured the kine of Helios Hyperion; but he took from them the day of their returning. Of these things, goddess, daughter of Zeus, beginning where thou wilt, tell thou even unto us.
>
> **Now all the rest, as many as had escaped sheer destruction, were at home**, safe from both war and sea, but Odysseus alone, filled with longing for his return **and for his wife**, did the queenly nymph Calypso, that bright goddess, keep back in her hollow caves, yearning that he should be her husband. But when, as the seasons revolved, the year came in which the gods had ordained **that he should return home to Ithaca**, not even there was he free from toils, even among his own folk. And all the gods pitied him save Poseidon; but he continued to rage unceasingly against godlike Odysseus until at length he reached his own land.[13]

Thus in the emboldened text we see the epic journey as a story of *survival* (*and of failure to survive*); and as a tale of return *to one's wife and* oikos.[14] Our positive reading will reveal Xenophon's use of Homer to authorize important aspects of his wider approach.

6.1 Xenophon's Conception of Home

But let us begin with a brief review of "Home" as understood by Xenophon. "Home" is a concept and reality that he engages with as closely as any Classical author. Over the course of his depictions, for example, of Ischomachus and Aristarchus' fifth-century Athenian aristocratic homes (in *Oeconomicus* and *Mem.* 2.7); the Persian Paradeisoi of Cyrus the Elder and Pharnabazus (in *Oeconomicus* and *Hellenica*); the plush household of a Sicilian tyrant's residence (*Hiero*); the exotic subterranean or wooden tower-top homes of foreigners encountered on the *Anabasis*, not only does Xenophon sketch these homes' physical reality, he also explores their symbolic capital and their potential as a site for the negotiation and expression of relationships, identities, and values.

A distinct conception of the ideal "Home" surfaces. It is a place supportive of human life: a place of shelter and supplies, of safety and

---

[13] Translation after Murray 1919. Text OCT (Allen).
[14] See Montiglio, Chapter 5 in this volume, p. 93 n. 8, for ancient readers regarding Penelope as Odysseus' primary goal.

security. Beyond its provisioning of basic needs, it is a place of unity and harmony: of close, harmonious, and enduring relationships marked by loyalty, trust, and friendship, especially between husbands and wives (an aspect to which I will return in a moment). The attainment of harmony and unity is not automatic, but involves an educational journey (like that on which the perfect gentleman Ischomachus leads his wife, or Simonides leads the tyrant Hiero): thus one does not simply acquire a home, one must purposefully *make* it, above all by establishing beneficial relationships. It is a place that affords relaxation and comfort, aesthetic enjoyment, and positive emotions (e.g. that of Pharnabazus in *Hell.* 4.1.33).[15]

What "Home" means becomes especially clear when a home is under threat or has been destroyed, or is not what it ought to be. As in the *Odyssey* – where Odysseus' home is in a state of disorder, being literally consumed by the suitors – so in Xenophon "Home" is a concept mostly honored in the breach.[16] The poet Simonides conjures up the ideal home when his tyrant interlocutor is suffering under its absence (*Hiero*). Pharnabazus describes his home to Agesilaus to bemoan its devastation (*Hell.* 4.1.33). Socrates' account of his conversation with Ischomachus about the latter's ideal household is motivated by the failure of Critobulus'; and even this ideal *oikos* is described against the backdrop of extratextual knowledge that it would later be torn apart by scandal (cf. Andoc. 1).[17]

That war is anathema to Xenophon's conception of home comes out vividly in *Hiero*, where the tyrant's house is not a home since he is in a constant state of war (3.8; cf. 2.8, 2.9). In the absence of *philia* his home has become a locale of fear and psychological imprisonment. War overseas is the condition of *Anabasis*, and Xenophon brings out starkly an age-old irony: the painful absence of home felt by the men on the march, but also the fact that these same men are destroyers of the homes of others. The soldiers pine for home and family (e.g. 3.1.3, 6.4.8; cf. 3.4.46), and grasp

---

[15] Safety, harmony: *Hier.* 2.8, 2.9, 3.7–8, cf. *Hiero* 6.11; *Cyr.* 7.5.60. Beauty, comfort, positive emotions: e.g. *Oec.* 4.13 ff.; *Hell.* 4.1.33; *An.* 4.2.23; *Mem.* 2.7.23.
[16] The *Odyssey* as the tale of a disordered *oikos*: Redfield 2009 [1983]. Despite its current devastation Penelope envisages her and Odysseus' *oikos* in all its former splendor (19.577–81 and 21.75–9), cf. Mueller 2007: 347: "the house that Penelope will remember is described as exceptionally beautiful (μάλα καλόν) and full of livelihood (ἐνίπλειον βιότοιο). Yet on numerous occasions we are told that the suitors are literally eating it … In her memory … the house of Odysseus is full of wealth and beauty. She memorializes the house in its prime." Cf. in *Iliad* 6 how the glimpses within Priam's palace, over which looms the reality that it is soon to be shattered, and the Iliadic similes of civilian life, bring into the poem a world that contrasts starkly with that of the fighting at Troy.
[17] Cf. Socrates' conversation with Aristarchus about his disordered *oikos* (*Mem.* 2.7).

at a sense of home, with its provisions and comforts, only for it to prove elusive, as in the following passage:

> **At the time, then,** they went into their quarters **very happily,** for they had provisions and likewise many recollections of the hardships that were now past (**τότε μὲν οὖν** ηὐλίσθησαν **μάλα ἡδέως** καὶ τἀπιτήδεια ἔχοντες καὶ πολλὰ τῶν παρεληλυθότων πόνων μνημονεύοντες). For during all the seven days of their march through the land of the Carduchians they were continually fighting, and they suffered more evils than all which they had suffered taken together at the hands of the king and Tissaphernes. In the feeling, therefore, that they were **rid of these troubles they lay down happily to rest** (ὡς οὖν ἀπηλλαγμένοι τούτων ἡδέως ἐκοιμήθησαν). **At daybreak, however** (Ἅμα δὲ τῇ ἡμέρᾳ), they caught sight of horsemen at a place across the river, fully armed and ready to prevent their passage. (*An.* 4.3.2–3)

Here, several key elements of "Home" are depicted – shelter, provisions, comfort, a sense of security, and distance from *ponoi* – only for troubles to resurface immediately, as is strongly felt in the contrast of *men—de* (*An.* 4.3.3).[18]

The several glimpses in *Anabasis* of the sweetness, pleasure, order, and positive relationships of home come in the jarring context of the mercenary army as home invaders and home destroyers. Thus Xenophon describes what "the Greeks found in their thorough plundering" (*An.* 5.4.27), as the foreign mercenaries tour through the stores of the forcibly abandoned homes of the local Mossynoecians, viewing and even tasting, guided by participants on one side in a civil war whom the Greeks have empowered at the expense of their enemies.[19] The Greeks' use of and "pleasure" in everyday items of home produces a disquieting and intimate perspective on war as a destroyer of homes and of the relationships that lie at their center.[20] The poignant account of a father who refuses to disclose an alternative route because his daughter lives in that area with her husband, with the upshot that the Greeks slit his throat (*An.* 4.1.23–4), conjures up the relationships and emotions that are key to "Home": the strength of the bond between father and daughter, the pathos of two homes destroyed

---

[18] Compare 4.4.9.
[19] "In plundering the strongholds the Greeks found in the houses ancestral stores, as the Mossynoecians described them ... [of loaves, grain, dolphin, dolphin blubber, nuts]. The Greeks also found wine, which by reason of its harshness appeared to be sharp when taken unmixed, but mixed with water was fragrant and delicious. When they had breakfasted there, the Greeks took up their onward march" (5.4.27–30).
[20] Cf. 5.4.29: when mixed the wine proves "fragrant and delicious" (εὐώδης τε καὶ ἡδύς) (above, n. 19).

(that of the father and of the couple), the sheer terror felt by locals vis-à-vis the mercenary army and the pillage, rape, and destruction it brings in its wake.[21] Later on we are given a glimpse of Greek mercenaries gratuitously burning local houses – "All those who on leaving the houses previously had burned them out of recklessness (ὑπὸ ἀτασθαλίας) paid the penalty by getting bad quarters" (*An*. 4.4.14) – with *atasthalia* recalling the *Odyssey*'s suitors, and signaling the morally reprehensible character of treating badly a home that has supported you.

A glimpse of the enduring relationships that characterize "Home" is found in the story of a local boy, son of a guide who ran away: the soldier Pleisthenes "fell in love with the boy, and when he got back home with him found him very loyal (οἴκαδε κομίσας πιστοτάτῳ ἐχρῆτο)" (*An*. 4.6.3). Here with utmost brevity Xenophon alludes to a future of safety at the end of the long march and (in the superlative, πιστοτάτῳ) a relationship of enduring faithfulness.

Spotlighting human relations as much as the physical dimensions of the *oikos*, Xenophon's treatment of "Home" invites us to step aside from the framework of Tuplin's question and contemplate the possibility of defining "Home" and "Return Home" in *Anabasis* not only in physical and geographical, but also in ethical and social terms.

6.2 Home as Survival

And so, to our first theme, "Home" as survival. We have noted that survival is a basic component of Xenophon's conception of "Home," and is highlighted in the *Odyssey*'s opening lines.[22] Anna Bonifazi has identified as the core meaning of *nostos* in Homer "surviving lethal dangers." She shows that in Homer as well as later poetry the term *nostos* may imply

---

[21] "They brought up the two men at once and questioned them separately as to whether they knew any other road besides the one that was in plain sight. The first man said he did not, despite all the numerous threats that were made to him; and since he would give no information, he was slaughtered before the eyes of the second one. The latter now said that the reason why this first man had maintained that he did not know any other road was because **he chanced to have a daughter living in that neighborhood with a husband to whom he had given her** (ὁ δὲ λοιπὸς ἔλεξεν ὅτι οὗτος μὲν οὐ φαίη διὰ ταῦτα εἰδέναι, ὅτι **αὐτῷ ἐτύγχανε θυγάτηρ ἐκεῖ παρ' ἀνδρὶ ἐκδεδομένη**)" (*An*. 4.1.23–4).

[22] Ideas of survival and of *nostos* may be closely intertwined; Dillery 1995: 70 thus remarks that *soteria* in Xenophon's *Anabasis* as well as Greek thought more generally can denote "return to Greece." And yet the explicit inclusion of "to Greece" at 6.4.8 – the mercenaries ἐπόθουν εἰς τὴν Ἑλλάδα σῴζεσθαι, "longed to return in safety to Greece" – implies that the two ideas are separable, each needing to be articulated.

direction toward home or elsewhere, but it need not imply any geographical movement at all:

> The basic concept underlying the uses and the meanings of *nostos* and its cognates in Homer as well as in later poetry is the idea of escaping death and saving oneself. This connects to the IE root whence all the terms at issue come, that is, the IE root *nes-. "**Saving oneself from any lethal danger, surviving**" is what I call the root of the meaning ... In a word, *nostos* conveys multidirectionality. The broader range of meanings of the words analyzed here sweeps away modern unidirectional interpretations and conceptualizations. Coming is also going, **returning home is also heading for somewhere other than home, homecoming is also having survived death.**[23]

Nostos thus contains multiple meanings; and I shall first read the *Anabasis* in terms of "homecoming [as] . . . having survived death," arguing that the Homeric texture underscores the fact that Xenophon, in the footsteps of Odysseus, achieves homecoming in the sense of salvation.

Survival for himself and his men is Xenophon's key objective. Consulting Apollo at Delphi before his trip he asks which gods to sacrifice to in order to survive (σωθείη, *An.* 3.1.6); the goal of survival is repeatedly mentioned through Books 3 to 5, until the point at which the men arrive at the Black Sea.[24] Here Xenophon takes stock, pausing to describe the review of survivors: "A review under arms and a counting occurred, and there were 8,600 men. **These were saved (οὗτοι ἐσώθησαν). The rest had perished (οἱ δὲ ἄλλοι ἀπώλοντο)** at the hands of enemy and snow and some by disease" (*An.* 5.3.3): and ἐσώθησαν here answers σωθείη in Xenophon's question at Delphi (*An.* 3.1.6). The prolepsis describing his offering of thanks to Apollo – and the stunning plot of ground near Olympia (*An.* 3.7–10) that he would purchase for Artemis – memorializes his survival and return, with Xenophon standing as a paradigm for the others who survived; and the description of the land in fact memorializes the success of the journey right back to mainland Greece.[25] Again, the sacrifice at Trapezus (*An.* 4.8.25–8) fulfills his earlier vow to Zeus Soter (the Savior); later his former seer congratulates him on his survival (ὅτι

---

[23] Bonifazi 2009: 506, my emphasis.
[24] This is expressed through the repeated use of the σῴζω- root rather than epic ἐρύω (cf. *Od.* 1.6), which occurs only once in Attic prose; and through the noun σωτηρία, "safety, survival." See Dillery 1995: 69–70 on safety (*soteria*) as the Cyreans' primary goal in "stage two" (after the loss of the generals).
[25] Artemis' share of the tithe he left behind with Megabyzus with instructions that it should be returned to him if he survived (ἢν μὲν αὐτὸς σωθῇ, 5.3.6), a conditional immediately answered in the ensuing account of how he did indeed receive it back.

ἐσέσωστο) (An. 7.8.1); and the theme recurs finally in the *mise en abyme* or "mini-Anabasis" that concludes the work (An. 7.8.8–19), the plundering expedition against a Persian noble from which the men "came through in safety (διασῴζονται)" (An. 7.8.19).[26] In the case of the soldiers, some return to their *oikoi* (An. 7.2.3), but those who survive, either to "mix" with the local cities (An. 7.2.3, εἰς τὰς πόλεις κατεμείγνυντο) or to be incorporated within the Spartan army (An. 7.8.24), perhaps also achieve a Homeric-style *nostos*, if (in Bonifazi's words), "returning home is also heading for somewhere other than home."

A further aspect of the "survival" motif is relevant to our discussion. The first stages of the march exhibit motifs drawn from the Persian Wars, reinforced by echoes of Herodotus' account of them, as Tim Rood has seen.[27] This background might prompt readers to notice ways in which Xenophon is figured as a latter-day Themistocles, and thus as following in the footsteps of an earlier architect of Greek salvation in a conflict of Greeks and Persians.[28] Beyond the intriguing historical affinities in the careers of these two figures – both have turbulent relationships with their home city, Athens; are recognized and rewarded by Sparta; face a future of exile from their home *polis*; are depicted as concerned to secure a place of refuge with foreigners – we may note some points of comparison in their literary depictions. The narrative introduction of each is delayed until the moment of crisis (with even the professional oracle readers confounded by the enigmatic Wooden Walls oracle; the Greek mercenaries mired in despondency after their generals' assassination).[29] The individual who will

---

[26] Here the achieved goal of "survival" stands clearly apart from the issue of return to one's *oikos*: for in the preceding section we heard that Xenophon was preparing to go home (*oikade*) since the sentence of exile had not yet been passed against him at Athens (7.7.57; cf. 7.8.2, οἴκαδε). There is a further reminder of home in the seer's question as to whether Xenophon has continued to sacrifice to Zeus Meilichios "as at home (ὥσπερ οἴκοι) . . . where I used to sacrifice for you, and with whole victims" (7.8.4).

[27] The Herodotean texture: e.g. 2.4.25–6 (bastard brother of Cyrus and Artaxerxes amazed as he watches the Greek army pass; cf. Hellespontian observer of Xerxes' army: Hdt. 7.56), 3.2.11–13 (Persian Wars examples in Xenophon's speech). See Rood 2004: 310–11 on Herodotean motifs.

[28] Themistocles as the architect of Greek salvation: Athenians σωτῆρας . . . τῆς Ἑλλάδος (7.139.5), followed by a narrative that underscores Themistocles' key role: 7.140–4; Thuc. 1.14, 1.74.1 (Themistocles most responsible for fighting in narrows, ὅπερ σαφέστατα ἔσωσε τὰ πράγματα), cf. 1.138. Themistocles is a prominent presence in discourse of the fourth (and third) centuries BCE, a time when the Persian Wars were being enlarged to something of greater dimensions, as inscriptions on the Acropolis including the (forged) "Themistocles decree" attest. Elsewhere in Xenophon's oeuvre he receives wholly positive press, with none of the shadows that cross his depictions in Herodotus and Thucydides. Cf. the high praise of Themistocles in the fragmentary *Alcibiades* written by Xenophon's fellow Socratic, Aeschines of Sphettos.

[29] Xenophon with Seuthes: An. 7.6.34: ἀποστροφὴν . . . καταθήσεσθαι; Themistocles with Xerxes: Hdt. 8.109.5: ἀποθήκην μέλλων ποιήσασθαι.

solve the crisis is then introduced for the first time, followed by a flashback with background information about him.[30] In the ensuing account each employs his powers of rhetoric to draw the majority to share the same view and focus on a common objective, so as ultimately – his greatest achievement – to contrive a fragile unity that secures salvation.

Themistocles' defining characteristics are cunning intelligence and masterful rhetoric; Xenophon is a masterful rhetorician whose speeches dominate the second part of *Anabasis*, and he too at times employs craft.[31] Each is a wise and creative advisor, and forges unity by reshaping others' notions of "Home."[32] Persuading the majority of Athenians that the "wooden wall" that will supply salvation is not Athens' Acropolis but her ships, Themistocles indicates that the *polis* is not the physical city but the men themselves and their lives. His threat that the Athenians will found a colony in Italy persuades the Spartan admiral of the Athenians' readiness to make a "Home" elsewhere than in Athens (*An.* 8.62) – which finally spurs the allies to action (*An.* 8.63).[33] He guides the Greeks to find "Home" in their identity and unity as Greeks (rather than citizens of different *poleis*). Xenophon's Panhellenic rhetoric enables the disparate group to regard themselves as Greeks, and the land of Greece as their geographical home, rather than their particular *patris*; like Themistocles he dissolves the impulse to scatter into disparate groups. Both capitalize on divine signs (oracle/sneeze) to promote morale and agreement, and so enable common action.[34] In our final glimpse of Xenophon, in the

---

[30] "**There was a certain Athenian, who had recently risen to be among the first men, whose name was Themistocles,** son of Neocles (Ἦν δὲ τῶν τις Ἀθηναίων ἀνὴρ ἐς πρώτους νεωστὶ παριών, τῷ οὔνομα μὲν ἦν Θεμιστοκλέης, παῖς δὲ Νεοκλέος ἐκαλέετο) . . . The advice of Themistocles had prevailed on a previous occasion" (flashback) (Hdt. 7.142.3–144.1). "**There was a man in the army named Xenophon, an Athenian,** who was neither general nor captain nor private (Ἦν δέ τις ἐν τῇ στρατιᾷ Ξενοφῶν Ἀθηναῖος, ὃς οὔτε στρατηγὸς οὔτε λοχαγὸς οὔτε στρατιώτης ὢν συνηκολούθει), but had accompanied the expedition because Proxenus, an old friend of his, had sent him at his home an invitation to go with him" (flashback) (Xen. *An.* 3.1.3–4).
[31] Eschewing heroics/employing indirect approaches: e.g. *An.* 4.6.10–15. Deceptions: e.g. *An.* 6.3.29.
[32] Cf. Xenophon at *An.* 4.6.10.
[33] Pelling 2009: 482: "it is the readiness of others to believe that Athenian land-loving is only skin-deep, that they can become plausible migrants, that eventually saves that Athenian land."
[34] Men's thoughts at *An.* 3.1.3, longing for "native states, parents, wives, children": Xenophon: "believe that the contest is now for Greece, now for children and wives" (3.4.46). Themistocles as contriver of unity: Baragwanath 2008: 291–8. Xenophon as contriver of unity: e.g. *An.* 5.6.31: renounces colonization plan himself and asks his supporters to do likewise (as Themistocles renounces his plan of pursuing the Persians and, in a rousing speech, persuades the Athenians as well: Hdt. 8.109), *An.* 5.6.32–3: standing together the men have honour and provisions, whereas if they should scatter they will neither secure food nor come off unharmed. Upshot a unanimous response: all (except Silanos) raise their hands (ἀντέτειναν ἅπαντες), 5.6.33. Cf. Wooden Walls (Hdt. 7.139) ~ omen of sneeze (*An.* 3.2.9). See Dillery 1995: 70 on the link in "stage two" (after the

penultimate sentence of the work, he is the focus of the unity he has forged between Laconians, captains, other generals, and soldiers, all of whom "joined in arranging" (συνέπραττον) for him to be given the best pick of the booty. In the very last sentence the army is united with "the rest of the Greek force" under Spartan command, so that the looming threat of their becoming outcasts from the Greek world is at last dissolved.[35]

6.3 Home Makers

The resonances of Themistocles, who was himself nicknamed "Odysseus," contribute to a reading in terms of positive closure in salvation.[36] Unlike Odysseus, Xenophon and many of the men do *not* return home to *oikoi* at the end of the story, but we have seen that by surviving they do achieve a *nostos* in a sense. They survive in large part because Xenophon as leader forges a "Home" for them in the sense of an orderly and harmonious environment that is suitable for supplying security and provisions (and Xenophon's vocabulary intriguingly invites comparison between the journey out of the Persian Empire and the journey out of household disorder).[37] The Themistoclean subtext has introduced a further idea: the notion that one's "Home" and identity may reside not in place but in the positive relationships and unity forged with others. To return to Xenophon's programmatic dream, we might say that in *Anabasis* the physical home of Xenophon's childhood (*An.* 3.1.11) comes to be supplanted by "Home" in the sense of a network of beneficial relationships.[38] Elsewhere Xenophon highlights the key importance of relationships, and their potential to transform one's sense of one's physical environment and home. Proxenus for example regarded Cyrus as more important to him than his *patris* (*An.* 3.1.4).

Next I shall focus on one important dimension of this: the role of relationships forged with women in contributing to the sense of "Home" achieved. In the *Odyssey* the *oikos* is crucial (even to the strange sidelining

---

loss of the generals) between unity and survival – how the survival of the individual depends on that of the collective. This is of course also a Homeric theme: Greek success at Troy is threatened by the antagonism of Achilles and Agamemnon.
[35] The final sentence of the work: quoted at p. 126–7 below.
[36] Themistocles nicknamed "Odysseus": Plut. *Mor.* 869 f., and see also Fornara 1971: 72–3.
[37] Journey out of the Persian Empire - out of household disorder: language of ἀπορία and εὐπορία, e.g. *Oec.* 9.1: at Ischomachus' teaching his wife is as pleased "as if she had found some easy way out of resourcelessness" (ὥσπερ ἐξ ἀμηχανίας εὐπορίαν τινὰ ηὑρηκυῖα)." Aporia in *An.*: Purves 2010a: 178 ff.
[38] See above, p. 113.

of Ithacan politics). The work's opening stanzas highlight the objective of arriving home to one's *oikos* and wife (see underlined text in the quotation at p. 111 above). Odysseus' thoughts of home are frequently interlinked with thoughts of his wife.[39] The contrasted conceptions of "Home" of Agamemnon and Telemachus serve as foils to that of Odysseus – and this is bound up with how their ideas about women and women's roles also stand in strong contrast to those of Odysseus. Agamemnon's murder at the hands of Clytemnestra thus appears to have retrospectively transformed his way of conceptualizing "Home" (which he conceives of in terms of an *oikos* with children and servants, *not* his wife: *Od.* 11.430–2).[40] The young Telemachus on the other hand – for whom "Home" means his fatherland and *oikos* (*Od.* 15.65–6)[41] – is not yet married, and is dismissive of his mother's activity and authority.[42] But it is Odysseus, not these character foils, who arrives home safely and has a home to return to – and thanks in large part to the enduring positive relationship he has forged with his wife.

For beyond the emotional connection of women with the notion of "Home," in the *Odyssey* Penelope's presence is existential: without her efforts on the home front and her decision to remain faithful Odysseus' return would have no point, for there would be no home to return to.[43] He would risk replaying the return of Agamemnon, which the poem invokes several times. As well as following her husband's instructions in preserving his *oikos* as well as she can in practical ways, especially in eliciting gifts from the suitors, Penelope employs her powers of memory to preserve the memory and *kleos* of the *oikos* at its prime, as Melissa Mueller has argued.[44]

The marriage of Odysseus and Penelope is a mutual partnership in which she enjoys respect and authority within the home. Heading to Troy,

---

[39] As upon leaving Phaeacia, where he hopes to return home to his "peerless wife and his friends" (ἀμύμονα δ' οἴκοι ἄκοιτιν / νοστήσας εὕροιμι σὺν ἀρτεμέεσσι φίλοισιν, 13.42–3), cf. 18.265. Cf. 11.161–2 (Anticlea to Odysseus: home as Ithaca and wife), 13.333–4 (Athena to Odysseus: home as wife and children; thus Athena adapts her formulation to the person with whom she is talking).

[40] ἦ τοι ἔφην γε ἀσπάσιος παίδεσσιν ἰδὲ δμώεσσιν ἐμοῖσιν οἴκαδ' ἐλεύσεσθαι ("I thought I was going to be welcomed home by my children and my servants").

[41] Telemachus to Menelaus (shortly after Athena has advised him to head back home to Ithaca): ὄρχαμε λαῶν, / ἤδη νῦν μ' ἀπόπεμπε **φίλην ἐς πατρίδα γαῖαν**· / ἤδη γάρ μοι θυμὸς ἐέλδεται **οἴκαδ' ἱκέσθαι (15.64–6)** ("let me go back now to my own country, for I want to get home.") Athena again adapts her words to her listener: in speaking to Telemachus she conceives of return "home" for him exclusively in terms of fatherland: "Not much longer shall he be absent **from his dear native land (φίλης ἀπὸ πατρίδος)**, no, not though bonds of iron hold him. He will contrive a way to go, for he is a man of many devices" (1.204–5).

[42] See 1.345–59, 21.343–53, esp. the last part: τοῦ γὰρ κράτος ἔστ' ἐνὶ οἴκῳ, "for mine is the authority in the *oikos*"; cf. 17.45–57.

[43] See Foley 1995.   [44] See *Od.* 19.577–81, 21.75–9, with Mueller 2007.

aware that he might not survive, Odysseus gave his wife control of the *oikos* (*Od.* 18.265–6). Meeting her again upon his return, he likens her to a divine king (*Od.* 19.107–14). The parallel between her ordeals at home and her husband's abroad is powerfully felt in the simile whose subject shifts from shipwrecked sailor to the woman who has waited for him at home (*Od.* 23.233–40). Penelope's description of her trials at home balances Odysseus' account of his trials abroad (*Od.* 23.300–10) – a balance that mirrors the shape of the *Odyssey*, which sets in parallel Penelope and Odysseus' respective trials. Odysseus acknowledges the balance (*Od.* 23.350–60; and here we find the language of mutuality, ἀμφοτέρω *bis*) and elsewhere speaks to his wife of their *shared* trials, both future and past.[45] Odysseus' understanding of marriage is exposed in his parting words to Alcinous and the Phaeacians, wishing them the ability to "make glad their wives and children" (εὐφραίνοιτε γυναῖκας / κουριδίας καὶ τέκνα, *Od.* 13.44–5). Characterized by *homophrosyne*, their partnership lives up to the picture of marriage as *homophrosyne* between men and women that Odysseus described in his speech to Nausicaa (*Od.* 6.180–5).

Odysseus' survival and *nostos* depend also on Arete, whose household supplies another positive model of marital *homophrosyne* and female authority in judgment and speech that complements male responsibility for translating that judgment into action.[46] It is in similar fashion that Penelope is responsible for the poem's key moral decision – to remain faithful to her husband – but Odysseus' contribution is essential to its ultimate confirmation by his use of force.[47]

Xenophon devotes a long treatise to the *oikos*, highlighting its importance – for the *oikos* is a key *locus* either of improvement of one's situation or of destruction[48] – and the equal value and mutual dependence of female and male spheres, with female labors within the *oikos* complementing male labors outside of it.[49] The ideal household is a harmonious partnership of

---

[45] Shared trials: 23.248–9; in the future: 23.248–9 (ὦ γύναι, οὐ γάρ πω πάντων ἐπὶ πείρατ᾿ ἀέθλων ἤλθομεν, "Wife, **we** have not yet reached the end of our trials") and past: 23.350–1.
[46] *Pace* Wohl 1993. It is Arete who makes the decision; Alcinous who translates it into action.
[47] Unlike his father Telemachus does not (yet) understand the sort of authority due to a woman.
[48] (Socrates to Critobulus) "And I can show also that some treat their married wives (γυναιξὶ ταῖς γαμεταῖς) in such a way that they keep them as fellow workers (συνεργοὺς) towards the increasing of households (συναύξειν τοὺς οἴκους), but some are destroyed most of all in this (πλεῖστον λυμαίνονται)" (Xen. *Oec.* 3.10).
[49] Complementary spheres, wife the "saviour/preserver" in hers: *Oec.* 7.20–2, cf. 7.33, 7.40, 8.10, 9.17; cf. 3.13–14: he controls what goes in, she controls what goes out. *Ponoi* of woman within the *oikos*, e.g. *Oec.* 7.32. The importance of the domestic sphere is further underscored by the analogy of the equal importance of civilian and military spheres in the Persian Empire (on which see Pomeroy 1994: 247).

men and women, each active in their complementary spheres, each with authority, working toward shared goals. Together they create a successful *oikos* that capitalizes on the strengths of all its members and forges a productive unity. Inside and outside are each as important as the other: activities within the home, as much as those outside of it, contribute to the safety and survival that home represents; and this order is divinely ordained.[50] The hierarchy in the relationship is one of merit: the wife may prove better than her husband and may become his judge.[51] She has powers of intellect, judgment, and memory.[52] Much of this, including the main idea that a vital aspect of "Home" is the presence of women, presents intriguing affinities with Homer's *Odyssey*. If Xenophon is reading the *Odyssey* as a love story, and as a story about a relationship between men and women that is characterized by mutuality, then he is not alone; some of the Greek novelists seem to be interpreting Homer similarly.[53] And this Odyssean connection doubtless helps explain further why *Anabasis* in its turn becomes an important intertext for Apollonius' *Argonautica*.[54]

6.4 Home in *Anabasis*

With this background in mind, let us now turn to "Home" on the march. In our first example, after a punishing march the army must contrive a fiercely contested crossing over the Centrites river:

> καὶ οἱ μὲν μάντεις ἐσφαγιάζοντο εἰς τὸν ποταμόν· οἱ δὲ πολέμιοι ἐτόξευον καὶ ἐσφενδόνων· ἀλλ' οὔπω ἐξικνοῦντο· ἐπεὶ δὲ καλὰ ἦν τὰ σφάγια, **ἐπαιάνιζον πάντες οἱ στρατιῶται καὶ ἀνηλάλαζον, συνωλόλυζον δὲ καὶ αἱ γυναῖκες ἅπασαι.** πολλαὶ γὰρ ἦσαν ἑταῖραι ἐν τῷ στρατεύματι. (*An.* 4.3.17–19)
>
> Meanwhile the soothsayers were offering sacrifice to the river, and the enemy were shooting arrows and discharging slings, but not yet reaching their mark; and when the sacrifices proved favourable, **all the soldiers struck up the paean and raised the war shout, while the women, every one of them, joined their cries with the shouting of the men** – for there were a large number of *hetairai* in the camp.[55]

---

[50] Partnership: *Oec.* 3.15, cf. *Oec.* 7.11, 28, 30, 42. Divinely ordained: see also 7.16, 18, 29, 31, 32.
[51] Wife as judge of husband, conscious if he lies or attempts to make the weaker argument the stronger: *Oec.* 11.25. Woman's authority: Queen bee analogy: 7.17, 32. Wife as νομοφύλαξ in household and distributing praise and honour like a βασίλισσα: 9.15.
[52] Woman's memory and concern: *Oec.* 7.26–7. Woman's involvement in deliberation/judgment: *Oec.* 7.12, cf. 7.33.
[53] See Montiglio, Chapter 5 in this volume (p. 102–3), on Heliodorus.
[54] *Anabasis* as an intertext of *Argonautica*: Clauss 2012.   [55] Translation after Brownson 1992.

Here the women of the army work in harmony with and in support of the men: when the sacrifices turn favorable, each joins her shout to the war shout of the soldiers. The women's shout of ritual support appears to be a context of all parties working together to a shared goal – seers, soldiers, and women – with equilibrium between men and women underscored lexically and syntactically (see the emboldened text). The upshot is the successful negotiation of a major physical obstacle. Some elements here might recall Homer, for example *Odyssey* 3, where the woman's cry of *ololuge* matches the men's conduct of sacrifice, and a further balance is felt, echoed in the verb forms, between the men's prayers and the women's ritual cry (οὐλοχύτας – ὀλόλυξαν, *Od.* 3.447–54); or *Iliad* 6, where the scene shifts from the Trojan men busy conducting the war and defending the city outside to the women performing ritual actions in defense of the city inside, honoring Athena with *ololuge* and petitioning her support.[56] In a more general way we might think of the picture of the women on the walls supporting the warriors on the shield of Achilles (*Il.* 18.478 ff.).

Xenophon's scene ends with the arresting explanatory statement that "there were many *hetairai* in the army": thus the ideal of reciprocity between the sexes shifts to the reality that these women are not wives but courtesans – a generalizing statement that reminds us of the presence and involvement of non-wife figures (who were important enablers and thwarters of Odysseus). Later in the Games put on at Trapezus, the courtesans again cheer on the soldiers, this time in sport:

> ἠγωνίζοντο δὲ παῖδες μὲν στάδιον τῶν αἰχμαλώτων οἱ πλεῖστοι, δόλιχον δὲ Κρῆτες πλείους ἢ ἑξήκοντα ἔθεον, πάλην δὲ καὶ πυγμὴν καὶ παγκράτιον †ἕτεροι†, καὶ καλὴ θέα ἐγένετο· πολλοὶ γὰρ κατέβησαν καὶ **ἅτε θεωμένων τῶν ἑταιρῶν πολλὴ φιλονικία ἐγίγνετο**. (*An.* 4.8.27)[57]
>
> The boys, most of them belonging to the captives, competed in a stadium race, more than sixty Cretans ran in a long race, others competed in wrestling, boxing, and the pancratium, and it made a fine spectacle; for many went down into the scene of contest, and **as much as the *hetairai* were looking on, there was a great deal of rivalry**.

The courtesans' presence and gaze ups the ante, generating rivalry on the part of the male contestants. Xenophon thus again underscores the productive

---

[56] Similar balance may be found in the poetic tradition more broadly: e.g. Bacchyl. 17.125–9 (maidens ὠλόλυξαν, young men παιάνιξαν).

[57] Reading "female companions," ἑταιρῶν, as conjectured by Brodaeus, rather than the version of the manuscript tradition, where the same word appears with a different accent (masculine ἑταίρων, "[male] companions").

harmony that exists between combatants and female non-combatants – however far from reality that might be. That adult women should here be watching sport is another way in which in the *Anabasis* traditional boundaries of mainland Greece are seen to be breaking down.

The women's contribution to both amusement and military effort is highlighted later on in the context of a symposium held in Paphlagonia (*An.* 6.1.4–14). At the locals' amazement at how the Greeks dance in armor, one of the men urges his comrade to bring in his dancing-girl. Light shield in hand, she performs the Pyrrhic elegantly and to rapturous applause. The startling spectacle of strength combined with beauty, and of male–female complementarity, prompts the foreign representatives to ask whether the Greeks' women also fought by their side (εἰ καὶ γυναῖκες συνεμάχοντο αὐτοῖς). The Greeks reply: "These were the women (αὗται) who had chased the Great King out of the camp!" Her performance is the climax of the evening, and Xenophon next notes that a treaty with the Paphlagonians followed the next day (*An.* 6.1.14). Not only has she provided high-quality entertainment and the pleasures of "Home," but she has helped them to convey an impression of martial strength.[58] We find a similar juxtaposition that suggests female agency in Xenophon's account of the assistance Epyaxa gives Cyrus (*An.* 1.2.12, 25).

Locals encountered on the march – men, but especially women – contribute to the mercenaries' safety. Thus upon arrival at a village in western Armenia the Greeks encounter women and girls fetching water outside. The women ask who the Greeks are, and then invite them within the wall to visit the chief:

> πορευομένων δὲ Χειρίσοφος μὲν ἀμφὶ κνέφας πρὸς κώμην ἀφικνεῖται, καὶ ὑδροφορούσας ἐκ τῆς κώμης πρὸς τῇ κρήνῃ γυναῖκας καὶ κόρας καταλαμ-βάνει **ἔμπροσθεν τοῦ ἐρύματος**. αὗται ἠρώτων αὐτοὺς τίνες εἶεν. ὁ δ' ἑρμηνεὺς εἶπε περσιστὶ ὅτι παρὰ βασιλέως πορεύονται πρὸς τὸν σατρά-πην. αἱ δὲ ἀπεκρίναντο ὅτι οὐκ ἐνταῦθα εἴη, ἀλλ' ἀπέχει ὅσον παρασάγ-γην. οἱ δ', ἐπεὶ ὀψὲ ἦν, πρὸς τὸν κώμαρχον συνεισέρχονται **εἰς τὸ ἔρυμα** σὺν ταῖς ὑδροφόροις. Χειρίσοφος μὲν οὖν καὶ ὅσοι ἐδυνήθησαν τοῦ στρα-τεύματος ἐνταῦθα ἐστρατοπεδεύσαντο, τῶν δ' ἄλλων στρατιωτῶν οἱ μὴ δυνάμενοι διατελέσαι τὴν ὁδὸν ἐνυκτέρευσαν **ἄσιτοι καὶ ἄνευ πυρός**· καὶ ἐνταῦθά **τινες ἀπώλοντο** τῶν στρατιωτῶν. (*An.* 4.5.9–10)

---

[58] The soldiers' identification of "these women" leaves the impression of women on the march as a group with a visible collective identity. By the end of the episode, the females are spoken of just as "women" (*gunaikes*), in a dissolution of rigid status differentiations that might again recall the world of Odysseus.

Heroes and Homemakers in Xenophon 125

As the army went on, Cheirisophus reached a village about dusk, and found at the spring **outside the wall** women and girls who had come from the village to fetch water. They asked the Greeks who they were, and the interpreter replied in Persian that they were on their way from the king to the satrap. The women answered that he was not there, but about a parasang away. Then, inasmuch as it was late, the Greeks accompanied the water-carriers **within the wall** to visit the village chief. So it was that Cheirisophus and all the troops who could muster strength enough to reach the village went into quarters there, but such of the others as were unable to complete the journey spent the night in the open **without food or fire**; and in this way **some** of the soldiers **perished**.

The women enable the move from outside to within, promoting the survival at this key juncture of those who reach the village; some of those left outside perish (*An.* 4.5.11). The motif of women as conduits to the men of power and the scenario at the spring might recall Homer.[59] In a more attenuated example, locals washing clothes at the river, seen by two young soldiers after one of Xenophon's divinely inspired dreams, this time unwittingly supply a means of safety by revealing a fordable point of the Centrites river:

καὶ ἀριστῶντι τῷ Ξενοφῶντι προσέτρεχον δύο νεανίσκω· ᾔδεσαν γὰρ πάντες ὅτι ἐξείη αὐτῷ καὶ ἀριστῶντι καὶ δειπνοῦντι προσελθεῖν καὶ εἰ καθεύδοι ἐπεγείραντα εἰπεῖν, εἴ τίς τι ἔχοι τῶν πρὸς τὸν πόλεμον. καὶ τότε ἔλεγον ὅτι τυγχάνοιεν φρύγανα συλλέγοντες ὡς ἐπὶ πῦρ, κἄπειτα κατίδοιεν ἐν τῷ πέραν ἐν πέτραις καθηκούσαις ἐπ' αὐτὸν τὸν ποταμὸν γέροντά τε καὶ γυναῖκα καὶ παιδίσκας ὥσπερ μαρσίπους ἱματίων κατατιθεμένους ἐν πέτρᾳ ἀντρώδει. ἰδοῦσι δὲ σφίσι δόξαι ἀσφαλὲς εἶναι διαβῆναι· οὐδὲ γὰρ τοῖς πολεμίοις ἱππεῦσι προσβατὸν εἶναι κατὰ τοῦτο. ἐκδύντες δ' ἔφασαν ἔχοντες τὰ ἐγχειρίδια γυμνοὶ ὡς νευσόμενοι διαβαίνειν· πορευόμενοι δὲ πρόσθεν διαβῆναι πρὶν βρέξαι τὰ αἰδοῖα· καὶ διαβάντες, λαβόντες τὰ ἱμάτια πάλιν ἥκειν. (*An.* 4.3.10–12)

While Xenophon was breakfasting, two young men came running up to him; for all knew that they might go to him whether he was breakfasting or dining, and that if he were asleep, they might awaken him and tell him whatever they might have to tell that concerned the war. In the present case the young men reported that they had happened to be gathering dry sticks for the purpose of making a fire, and that while so occupied they had descried across the river, among some rocks that reached down to the very edge of the river, an old man and a woman and some little girls putting away what looked like bags of clothes in a cavernous rock. When they saw

---

[59] Women as conduits to men of power: e.g. Nausicaa, Arete. But the pattern is also Xenophontic: Baragwanath 2002.

this proceeding, they said, they made up their minds that it was safe for them to cross, for this was a place that was not accessible to the enemy's cavalry. They accordingly stripped, keeping only their daggers, and started across naked, supposing that they would have to swim; but they went on and got across without wetting themselves up to the middle; once on the other side, they took the clothes and came back again.

The image of a family group treating the river in a domestic manner thus reveals a means of survival, and it is the positive relationship Xenophon has promoted ("for all knew that they might go to him . . .") that creates the opportunity. The episode perhaps recalls Odysseus' encounter with Nausicaa and the maidens.[60]

Finally, though Xenophon does not arrive home to a Penelope, upon reaching Pergamum he returns to "Greece" in the figure of Hellas – whose name thus perfectly combines ideas of both person and place. This influential female agent, wife, and mother (*An.* 7.8.8) welcomes him hospitably and effects his achievement of security, both material (for upon her direction he takes a great deal of plunder) and in terms of his relationships with his men:

> Ἐνταῦθα δὴ ξενοῦται Ξενοφῶν **Ἑλλάδι** τῇ Γογγύλου τοῦ Ἐρετριέως γυναικὶ καὶ Γοργίωνος καὶ Γογγύλου μητρί. αὕτη δ' αὐτῷ φράζει ὅτι Ἀσιδάτης ἐστὶν ἐν τῷ πεδίῳ ἀνὴρ Πέρσης· τοῦτον ἔφη αὐτόν, εἰ ἔλθοι τῆς νυκτὸς σὺν τριακοσίοις ἀνδράσι, λαβεῖν ἂν καὶ αὐτὸν καὶ γυναῖκα καὶ παῖδας καὶ τὰ χρήματα· εἶναι δὲ πολλά. ταῦτα δὲ καθηγησομένους ἔπεμψε τόν τε αὑτῆς ἀνεψιὸν καὶ Δαφναγόραν, **ὃν περὶ πλείστου ἐποιεῖτο**. ἔχων οὖν ὁ Ξενοφῶν τούτους παρ' ἑαυτῷ ἐθύετο. καὶ Βασίας ὁ Ἠλεῖος μάντις παρὼν εἶπεν ὅτι κάλλιστα εἴη τὰ ἱερὰ αὐτῷ καὶ ὁ ἀνὴρ ἁλώσιμος εἴη. δειπνήσας οὖν ἐπορεύετο τούς τε λοχαγοὺς τοὺς μάλιστα φίλους λαβὼν καὶ ἄλλους πιστοὺς γεγενημένους διὰ παντός, ὅπως εὖ ποιήσαι αὐτούς . . . ἐνταῦθα οἱ περὶ Ξενοφῶντα συντυγχάνουσιν αὐτῷ καὶ λαμβάνουσιν αὐτὸν καὶ γυναῖκα καὶ παῖδας καὶ τοὺς ἵππους καὶ πάντα τὰ ὄντα· καὶ οὕτω τὰ πρότερα ἱερὰ ἀπέβη. ἔπειτα πάλιν ἀφικνοῦνται εἰς Πέργαμον. ἐνταῦθα τὸν θεὸν ἠσπάσατο Ξενοφῶν· **συνέπραττον γὰρ καὶ οἱ Λάκωνες καὶ οἱ λοχαγοὶ καὶ οἱ ἄλλοι στρατηγοὶ καὶ οἱ στρατιῶται** ὥστ' ἐξαίρετα λαβεῖν καὶ ἵππους καὶ ζεύγη καὶ τἆλλα· **ὥστε ἱκανὸν εἶναι καὶ ἄλλον ἤδη εὖ ποιεῖν**. Ἐν τούτῳ Θίβρων παραγενόμενος παρέλαβε τὸ στράτευμα καὶ

---

[60] The young men are described as testing the river-crossing naked (γυμνοί), and they cross "without wetting their genitals" (τὰ αἰδοῖα); Odysseus in the Homeric poem emerges naked (γυμνός, 6.136), covering his genitals (μήδεα φωτός, "the genitals of a man," 6.130). Nor was this the only option available to Xenophon for expressing the idea: of men crossing the Euphrates he writes that they wet themselves "up to the navel," πρὸς τὸν ὀμφαλόν (4.5.2).

συμμείξας τῷ ἄλλῳ Ἑλληνικῷ ἐπολέμει πρὸς Τισσαφέρνην καὶ Φαρνάβαζον (*An.* 7.8.8–11, 22–4)

Here Xenophon was entertained by **Hellas**, the wife of Gongylus the Eretrian and mother of Gorgion and Gongylus. She told him that there was a Persian in the plain named Asidates, and said that if he should go by night with three hundred troops, <u>he could capture this man, along with his wife and children and property, of which he had a great deal</u>. And she sent as guides for this enterprise not only her own cousin, but also Daphnagoras, **whom she regarded very highly**. Xenophon, accordingly, proceeded to sacrifice, keeping these two by his side. And Basias, the Elean seer who was present, said that the omens were extremely favourable for him and that the man was easy to capture. So after dinner he set forth, taking with him the captains who were his closest friends and others who had proved themselves trustworthy throughout, in order that he might do them a good turn … There Xenophon and his men fell in with him, and <u>they captured him, his wife and children, his horses, and all that he had</u>; and thus the omens of the earlier sacrifice proved true. After that they came back again to Pergamum. And there Xenophon paid his greeting to the god; for the Laconians, the captains, the other generals, and the soldiers joined in arranging matters so that he got the pick of horses and teams of oxen and all the rest; the result was that he was now able even to do a kindness to another. Meanwhile Thibron arrived and took over the army, and uniting it with the rest of his Greek forces, proceeded to wage war upon Tissaphernes and Pharnabazus.

Fleetingly indicated also is his reliance on her judgment (cf. ὃν περὶ πλείστου ἐποιεῖτο). At this successful outcome the various groups under his leadership join together in presenting him with booty, "with the result that he was now able even to do a kindness to another" (*An.* 7.8.23). Hellas is thus the enabler who puts Xenophon in a position to inspire unity on the part of those he leads, and to reestablish a reciprocal, harmonious relationship with them. Her correct prophecy for Xenophon of future events (underlined) in fact – in this *mise en abyme* of the wider narrative – sits in parallel to Socrates' earlier premonitions (about how involvement in the expedition would affect Xenophon's relationship with the Athenians: *An.* 3.1.5). Thus emphasized again are the connections of women, the production of harmonious relationships, supplies, and safety. Hellas' key influence recalls the decisive female agency of Parysatis, an agent of the survival and arrival home of Cyrus the Younger, right at the beginning of the *Anabasis* (1.1–4). The especial emphasis on female agency at the beginning and end of the work might again hark back to Homer, shifting into the human realm the agency of goddesses that marks the beginning and end of the Homeric poems (Athena in the *Odyssey*, Thetis in the *Iliad*). It also takes us back to the framing of Herodotus' *Histories* through stories of influential females, Candaules' wife at the beginning and Xerxes' wife Amestris at the end: but that is another story.

Xenophon thus *makes* "Home" on the journey away by instilling order and harmony, inspiring all parties to work together in a shared objective, and in the creation of a symbolic "Home." The women on the march recall and symbolize this ideal, as well as contributing in a practical way to the men's survival. We encounter home in the sense of relationships rather than physical houses or places, or origins, with the implication that Xenophon as relationship-broker and "Homemaker" walking in the footsteps of Odysseus contributes crucially to the journey's success.

Why Odysseus? Himself an exile, with a troubled relationship with home, Xenophon likely embraced the illustrious tradition of complex and ambivalent heroes such as Odysseus and Themistocles. Odysseus is author of a famous ἀπόλογος (story/fable), the "apologetic" account (*apologoi*) that he recites to the Phaeacians (Books 9–12), and a natural forerunner perhaps for Xenophon's own apologetic *Anabasis*. Intriguingly in Plato's *Republic* (Book 10, 620c) Er reports on Odysseus' choice to reincarnate as a private citizen – thus, as Silvia Montiglio observes, choosing humanity and rejecting politics;[61] as Xenophon of course was compelled out from politics by his exile.

More importantly, in contrast to the Iliadic hero's demonstration of how one ought to die, "all Odysseus' life-experience" – to quote Margalit Finkelberg – "demonstrates how one ought to live."[62] Odysseus chose mortality rather than immortality: eschewing Calypso, he chose to live out his life as a mortal in the company of a mortal wife; and key among his achievements are those within the realm of interpersonal relations. Thus Odysseus was a useful figure for Xenophon's project of examining human relations in all their complexity, in exploring ethical achievement of individuals grappling with the complexities of human life, and his objective of presenting ideals of human association that are realistic and realizable (this by contrast with Plato's utopian schemes). The *Anabasis* may then be an "apology" in that it helps authorize Xenophon's remarkable interest, across his wider oeuvre, in home as well as the outside world and in relationships including those between men and women. Against the critical views of Odysseus that dominate Athenian discourse in the late fifth century BCE, and in the same spirit as the other Socratics' rehabilitation

---

[61] Montiglio 2011: 49.   [62] Finkelberg 1995: 10.

of Odysseus,[63] Xenophon thus implicitly promotes a positive image of the hero as the forger of an ideal home.

That the ideal "Home" is a highly fragile commodity does not compromise the ethical achievement represented by its creation; even as an impermanent condition, it deserves *kleos* (we can think again of Penelope remembering Odysseus' household at its prime). Its fragility perhaps even highlights the skill of the one responsible for maintaining it – as the dissolution of Cyrus the Elder's order in *Cyropaedia* underscored his skill as leader in forging and overseeing it.

The *Anabasis* is then as much a work about creating "Home" – creating unity, harmony, conditions for human survival and prosperity – as about the failure to find it and loss. And in this sense it contributes to the more general fourth-century examination of home (as in Lysias and Menander among others). Through the Odyssean intertextuality the picture Xenophon paints in *Anabasis* of survival as success and of "Home" as men and women working together, comes to be authorized by the great bard; and more broadly Xenophon's remarkable interest in home and the role of women finds a worthy pedigree as well. Conversely, Xenophon's reception of Homer in *Anabasis* offers a perspective that highlights the presence and value of positive relationships between the genders in the Homeric text.

---

[63] See Montiglio 2011.

CHAPTER 7

Women's Travels in the Aeneid

Alison Keith

From Homer to Claudian, Classical epic was a privileged site for negotiating issues of masculine identity. Individual instantiations of the genre conventionally submit the privileges and protocols of virility and military prowess to scrutiny from a variety of vantage points, both at home and on the road. The epic journey, therefore, is traditionally associated with "the man" – whether Odysseus, "the man of many ways, who was driven / far journeys, after he had sacked Troy's sacred citadel" (*Od.* 1.1–2: Ἄνδρα μοι ἔννεπε, Μοῦσα, πολύτροπον, ὃς μάλα πολλὰ / πλάγχθη, ἐπεὶ Τροίης ἱερὸν πτολίεθρον ἔπερσε·),[1] or Aeneas, "who first came to Italy and Lavinian shores, exiled by fate from the Trojan strand" (*Aen.* 1.1–3: *arma **uirumque** cano, Troiae qui primus ab oris / Italiam fato profugus Lauiniaque uenit / litora*); or even an ephebic collective, such as the Argonauts, "the heroes of old who sailed the good ship Argo up the Straits in the Black Sea and between the Cyanean Rocks in quest of the Golden Fleece" (Ap. Rhod. 1.2–4: παλαιγενέων κλέα **φωτῶν** / μνήσομαι οἳ Πόντοιο κατὰ στόμα καὶ διὰ πέτρας / Κυανέας βασιλῆος ἐφημοσύνῃ Πελίαο / χρύσειον μετὰ κῶας ἐύζυγον ἤλασαν Ἀργώ).[2] I have accordingly argued elsewhere – following feminist critical appropriations of theorists of folklore, narrative, and psychoanalysis – that Classical epic constitutes the female as the stay-at-home foil to the traveling male hero.[3] Teresa de Lauretis provides a succinct formulation of this gendered contrast, developed in her discussion of the Classical myths of Oedipus and Perseus, popularly theorized by Freud and Propp:

> the hero, the mythical subject, is constructed as human being and as male; he is the active principle of culture, the establisher of distinction,

---

My thanks to Tom Biggs and Jessica Blum for the invitation to deliver a paper at the original conference on "The Epic Journey," and to my fellow participants for their stimulating interventions. I am also grateful to my research assistant, Jen Oliver, for her help with bibliography, and to Sharon James and Amy Richlin for conversations about women's travels around the Mediterranean.
 Any errors or infelicities that remain are my own responsibility.
[1] Trans. Lattimore 1965. [2] Trans. Rieu 1959. [3] Keith 1999 and 2000: 36–64.

130

the creator of differences. Female is what is not susceptible to transformation, to life or death; she (it) is an element of plot-space, a topos, a resistance, matrix and matter.[4]

Such an analysis of the spatial articulation of classical epic is well illustrated by a passage at the opening of *Aeneid* 7, where Aeneas and the Trojans leave Port Caieta and sail along the coast of Latium toward the river Tiber:

> proxima Circaeae raduntur litora terrae,
> diues inaccessos ubi Solis filia lucos
> adsiduo resonat cantu, tectisque superbis
> urit odoratam nocturna in lumina cedrum
> arguto tenuis percurrens pectine telas.
> (*Aen.* 7.10–14)

> Next they sweep the shores of Circe's lands, where the wealthy daughter of the Sun constantly fills her remote groves with song, and burns scented cedar in her proud halls for light during the night, running through her slender web with the shrill shuttle.

The landscape in which she lives is inseparable from Circe, for she has given her name to it (*Circaeae ... terrae, Aen.* 7.10) and is identified only as "the Sun's wealthy daughter" (*diues ... Solis filia,* 7.11). Moreover, Vergil here multiplies descriptions of her home rather than of Circe herself: she lives in "remote groves" (*inaccessos ... lucos, Aen.* 7.11) and "proud halls" (*tectis ... superbis, Aen.* 7.12), which echo with the music of her singing and weaving. The poet's reference to the scent of cedar that pervades her halls is particularly choice, inasmuch as it imports the grove into her dwelling, thereby making the grove coextensive with her home. Of course, Vergil adds an undertone of menace to the sensual seductiveness of Circe's grove in the howls of rage uttered by the beasts, once men, who surround her home (*Aen.* 7.15–20). But at this juncture Vergil declines to measure Aeneas against Odysseus (or himself against Homer), by having Neptune speed the Trojans' ships past Circe's "dread shores" (*litora dira, Aen.* 7.22) as a reward for their piety:

> quae ne monstra pii paterentur talia Troes
> delati in portus neu litora dira subirent,
> Neptunus uentis impleuit uela secundis,
> atque fugam dedit et praeter uada feruida uexit.
> (*Aen.* 7.21–4)

---

[4] de Lauretis 1984: 119.

Lest the pious Trojans suffer such fates, carried down into her harbor, or lest they come up to her dread shores, Neptune filled their sails with favourable winds, granted them flight, and conveyed them beyond the seething shallows.

Circe's *inaccessos lucos* (*Aen.* 7.10), quite literally unbroached by the Trojans, confine Circe herself to the margins of Vergil's epic.

I remain committed to this analysis of the epic landscape in terms of the gendered contrast between mobile male hero and female ground of representation. But here I wish to explore a Vergilian innovation in this tradition: his representation of women who undertake epic journeys in the *Aeneid*. For it would be perverse to deny that Vergil innovates radically in the genre by including several female characters who negotiate extended journeys in the *Aeneid*. In my discussion I focus on Dido, Andromache, and the other Trojan women who travel extensively in the epic, in order to interrogate their journeys from the perspectives of gender, genre, and contemporary Roman conventions of travel.[5]

We may begin, like Vergil, with Dido, who is characterized throughout *Aeneid* 1 as an intrepid traveller – indeed, in Venus' words, as the leader of an epic expedition, *dux femina facti* (*Aen.* 1.364). In an unexpected epiphany to her son Aeneas, Venus supplies him (and Vergil's readers) with the backstory to Dido's extraordinary foundation of Carthage in Libyan territory (*Aen.* 1.338–68). The goddess identifies Aeneas' location in Africa as "the kingdom of Carthage, Agenor's city," inhabited by Tyrians (*Aen.* 1.338: *Punica regna uides, Tyrios et Agenoris urbem*) in "the territory of Libya" (*Aen.* 1.339: *sed fines Libyci*). The Libyans' ferocity makes them "unmanageable in war" (*Aen.* 1.339: *genus intractabile bello*), a trait that proleptically defines the Carthaginians as well. It is instructive to note not only the Carthaginian queen's association with her city and its territory, but also her experience of, and expertise in, the logistics of the epic voyage. Vergil implicates Dido in the ethnic stereotypes of her geographical history: she is a seafarer and savvy merchant, like the Phoenicians from whom she is descended (cf. *Aen.* 1.729–30) and from whose city she has sailed (*Aen.* 1.340: *imperium Dido Tyria regit urbe profecta*), leading a well-provisioned gathering of exiles (*Aen.* 1.361–3: *conueniunt quibus aut odium crudele tyranni / aut metus acer erat; nauis, quae forte paratae, / corripiunt onerantque auro. portantur auari*, "They came together

---

[5] Scholarship on travel in the ancient Mediterranean is overwhelmingly male focused: see, e.g., the standard studies of Casson 1959 and 1974; Graham 1964; von Martels 1994; and Malkin 1998. Dougherty 1993 and 2001, Dougherty and Kurke 2003, and Parker 2008 are welcome interventions in this androcentric tradition.

with her, those who felt either cruel hatred for the tyrant or keen fear; they snatched ships, which were by chance prepared, and loaded them with gold").[6] For her husband Sychaeus was the wealthiest Phoenician (*Aen.* 1.343: *huic coniunx Sychaeus erat, ditissimus auri*) and she left Tyre with his wealth (*Aen.* 1.358–9: *auxiliumque uiae ueteres tellure recludit / thesauros, ignotum argenti pondus et auri*, "And he disclosed old treasure in the earth, an aid for the journey, an unknown weight of silver and gold"). This wealth then enabled her to broker a sharp deal with the local North African king Iarbas, thereby securing the land on which to found her new city of Carthage:

> deuenere locos ubi nunc ingentia cernes
> moenia surgentemque nouae Karthaginis arcem,
> mercatique solum, facti de nomine Byrsam,
> taurino quantum possent circumdare tergo.
> (*Aen.* 1.365–8)

> They reached the place where you now see huge walls and the citadel of new Carthage rising, and they bought as much ground as they could surround with a bull's hide, and called it Byrsa from the name of the deed.

It is a critical commonplace to note that Venus' tale emplots Dido as the female counterpart of Vergil's epic hero, Aeneas: like him, she leads a people in exile (*Aen.* 1.341, 357) from their homeland over the sea (*Aen.* 1.364) to new territory where they successfully found a city (*Aen.* 1.364–8).[7] Indeed, it is often remarked that Dido is singularly more successful in her epic career than Aeneas is in his, at least at this point in the poem. It is also widely recognized that Vergil has modeled Aeneas on Homer's Odysseus, not least in terms of their epic voyages. But we should note as well Dido's especially close resemblance, as a sharp trader, to Odysseus – a resemblance that has not elicited much comment. Odysseus' Phoenician tales are an obvious point of resemblance, since Dido is herself originally Phoenician. While Aeneas' journey around the Mediterranean tracks that of Odysseus more closely than does Dido's abbreviated journey, the Carthaginian queen's mercantile dealings with Iarbas, and Phoenician interest in money, openly align her with the unscrupulous Odysseus, with his unaristocratic interest in profit and the unsavoury dealings it inspires[8] – far more so than *pius Aeneas*, whom Vergil carefully distinguishes from the

---

[6] Cf. Horsfall 1973–4.   [7] See Austin 1964 and 1971; Williams 1960, 1962, and 1972.
[8] On Homer's characterization of Odysseus in relation to the Phoenicians, see Dougherty 2001, with further bibliography.

duplicitous Greek in his personal piety and forthright dealings with the friends and strangers he meets on his travels.

Dido's abbreviated journey, however, stands in strong contrast to the long travels of Aeneas and Odysseus around the Mediterranean; certainly Venus mentions no other stops along the way, nor any digressions on Dido's voyage from Tyre to Libya. Nonetheless, the goddess characterizes Dido's history as itself a long and winding tale (*Aen.* 1.341–2: *longa est iniuria, longae / ambages; sed summa sequar fastigia rerum*, "the tale of her wrongs is long, and the windings long; but I shall follow the main points of the affair"). It is generally agreed that Venus' speech here resembles a tragic prologue, a fitting introduction to the tragic narrative Vergil gives Dido in *Aeneid* 4.[9] But at this juncture, in Book 1, Venus' words more naturally hint that she will tell the winding tale of a roundabout epic journey like that of Odysseus, in *Odyssey* 9–12, or of Aeneas, in *Aeneid* 2–3. Elsewhere in Latin epic, for example, Ovid uses the noun *ambages* of the windings of the Cretan labyrinth (*Met.* 8.161: *uariarum ambage uiarum*), alluding to Vergil's evocative description of the Minotaur's lair in *Aeneid* 6 (*Aen.* 6.29: *dolos tecti ambagesque resoluit*), while the elder Pliny employs the word in conjunction with *iter*, precisely in order to describe roundabout journeys, *itinerum ambages* (*HN* 36.13.19).[10] It is all the more striking, therefore, that Aeneas hears neither a circuitous journey nor an evasive tale from his mother. For the other arena in which the word is employed by Latin authors is, in metaphorical usage, of speech, especially in narrative and oracular contexts.[11] Venus' words *longa est iniuria, longae / ambages* (*Aen.* 1.341–2) imply that Dido has experienced an extended epic journey, replete with digressions and false trails, fully worthy of an epic narrative; but her brief, third-person account, neither obscure nor digressive, focuses instead on an internecine family feud (the stuff of Medean tragedy) rather than on a long and difficult voyage (the stuff of Odyssean epic). In this way Vergil respects the conventions of both gender and genre in his introduction of Dido, keeping her in the house rather than on the high seas, and sketching her story in tragic, rather than epic, terms.

Still, it is altogether surprising to learn that a woman had even acted as captain of the ship of epic. Is there precedent for Dido's leading role here? I would suggest that Vergil owes a debt not to Homeric epic but to the

---

[9] Harrison 1972–3 and 1989; Foster 1973–4; Muecke 1983; Moles 1984.
[10] L&S s.v. I (Lit.); cf. *OLD* s.v. 1a and 1b.
[11] For *ambages* in the sense of "circumlocution, evasion, digression," see L&S s.v. IIA; *OLD* 2. In the sense of "obscurity, ambiguity," especially of the language of oracles, see L&S s.v. IIB.

epic cycle in representing a woman as leader of an epic expedition. But for that we will need to move on to Aeneas' first glimpse of the queen, later in the book:

> ducit Amazonidum lunatis agmina peltis
> Penthesilea furens mediisque in milibus ardet,
> aurea subnectens exsertae cingula mammae
> bellatrix, audetque uiris concurrere uirgo.
> haec dum Dardanio Aeneae miranda uidentur,
> dum stupet obtutuque haeret defixus in uno,
> regina ad templum, forma pulcherrima Dido,
> incessit magna iuuenum stipante caterua.
> (*Aen.* 1.490–7)

> Penthesilea led the Amazons' ranks with their crescent-shields in fury and she blazed amidst thousands; binding a golden belt beneath her exposed breast, a warrior maiden, she dared to clash with men. While these wonderful sights are witnessed by Dardan Aeneas, while he stands amazed and hangs rapt in one gaze, the queen entered the temple, Dido, most beautiful of figure, accompanied by a great company of youths.

Vergil's juxtaposition of Dido with Penthesilea is significant on many levels, most obviously in its characterization of Dido as both Amazonian and a potential love-interest for the epic hero. But it also points to the opening of the *Aethiopis*, which followed immediately upon the last line of the *Iliad* (schol. ad. Hom. *Il.* 24.804: τινὲς γράφουσιν· "Ὣς οἵ γ' ἀμφίεπον τάφον Ἕκτορος. ἦλθε δ'Ἀμαζὼν / Ἄρηος θυγάτηρ μεγαλήτορος ἀνδροφόνοιο, "Some write: 'Thus they performed the burial of Hector. / Then came an Amazon, daughter of great-hearted Ares, the slayer of men'"). Vergil's use of material from the epic cycle is well documented for the episodes on display both in the frieze in Juno's temple in Carthage in *Aeneid* 1 and in Aeneas' narrative of the *Iliupersis* in *Aeneid* 2, and so need not detain us here.[12] What I would like to emphasize rather is Vergil's mobilization of Penthesilea as an epic precedent for Dido, right down to the detail of the Amazon queen's marshaling of an epic expedition: the verb *ducit* (1.490), which introduces Penthesilea, is important in this respect (cf. 1.364, quoted above, where Venus uses the verb of Dido), even if Penthesilea's journey to Troy was probably overland rather than aboard ship. The implied Penthesilea comparison aligns Dido, on the one hand, with the Trojans, since the Amazons came to their aid; and this

---

[12] See Austin 1964 and 1971 ad loc.; Williams 1960, 1962, and 1972 ad loc.

surely conforms to Aeneas' sympathetic reading of the frieze (cf. 1.459–63). On the other hand, the characterization of Penthesilea as a female warrior, who dares to clash with men on the battlefield, instantiates a conventional mythic "battle between the sexes" (e.g. Hercules and the Amazons, Perseus and Medusa) that hints at a gendered opposition between Dido and Aeneas, and would thereby align the Carthaginian queen with a long tradition of feminized epic losers (e.g. Paris in the *Iliad*, Penelope's suitors in the *Odyssey*, etc.). This implication is further buttressed by Penthesilea's fate, which was to die at Achilles' hands. Dido's epic pretensions are thus both confirmed and undone by the implied Penthesilea comparison in *Aeneid* 1.

Finally, we may recall that there was also contemporary historical precedent for Dido's leadership on a sea-voyage, and Vergil even includes that scandalous exemplar within the ambit of his epic:

> hinc ope barbarica uariisque Antonius armis,
> uictor ab Aurorae populis et litore rubro,
> Aegyptum uiresque Orientis et ultima secum
> Bactra uehit, sequiturque (nefas) Aegyptia coniunx.
> ...
> ipsa uidebatur uentis regina uocatis
> uela dare et laxos iam iamque immittere funis.
> illam inter caedes pallentem morte futura
> fecerat Ignipotens undis et Iapyge ferri,
> contra autem magno maerentem corpore Nilum
> pandentemque sinus et tota ueste uocantem
> caeruleum in gremium latebrosaque flumina uictos.
> (*Aen.* 8.685–713)

> On this side Antony, with barbarian wealth and varied arms, victor over the peoples of the East and the red sea, leads Egypt in his train, the forces of the Orient and Bactra at the end of the world, and his Egyptian wife (a crime!) follows ... The queen herself seemed to summon the winds and set sail, and now already to fling loose the slack sheets. In the midst of the slaughter, the fire-god had fashioned her pale with coming death, carried by the waves and Iapyx' breezes, but opposite was the grieving Nile, with his huge body, opening his folds and with his whole cloak welcoming the conquered into his blue lap and sheltering streams.

Cleopatra is not initially credited on Aeneas' shield with leading the Egyptian fleet at Actium – Vulcan (and Vergil) reserve that dubious distinction for Antony (*uehit*, 8.688), whom she follows into the sea-battle (*sequitur, Aen.* 8.688). The Egyptian queen does, however, lead the retreat, summoning the winds to take her home to the Nile (*Aen.* 8.707–8), as befits another feminized epic loser (cf. *uictos, Aen.* 8.713).[13] Her voyage too is direct, without divagation, and echoes Dido's by ending in ignominious death (*Aen.* 8.709; cf. *et pallida morte futura, Aen.* 4.644).

Dido herself contemplates another, final, sea-voyage, only to reject the idea as impractical:

> Iliacas igitur classis atque ultima Teucrum
> iussa sequar? quiane auxilio iuuat ante leuatos
> et bene apud memores ueteris stat gratia facti?
> quis me autem, fac uelle, sinet ratibusue superbis
> inuisam accipiet? nescis, heu, perdita, necdum
> Laomedonteae sentis periuria gentis?
> quid tum? sola fuga nautas comitabor ouantis?
> an Tyriis omnique manu stipata meorum
> inferar et, quos Sidonia uix urbe reuelli,
> rursus agam pelago et uentis dare uela iubebo?
> quin morere ut merita es, ferroque auerte dolorem.
> (*Aen.* 4.537–46)

> Should I therefore follow Ilion's fleet and the final commands of the Trojans? Since it pleased them before to be helped by my aid and gratitude remains among them, remembering my former good deed? But suppose I were willing, who would allow me and receive me, hated as I am, on their proud ships? Alas, don't you see? Ruined woman, do you still not recognize the lies of Laomedon's race? What then? Shall I accompany the exulting sailors, lonely in my exile? Or shall I be borne, accompanied by Tyrians and the whole band of my people, and, shall I lead them over the sea again, when I could scarcely pluck them from the Sidonian city, and shall I bid them set sail?

Her words offer interesting insight into the difficulty she faced as the leader of an epic sea-voyage. The ships she led lay ready in harbor (*Aen.* 1.362, quoted above), but equipping them with men was apparently not so easy (*Aen.* 4.545). Her difficulty was not elaborated in *Aeneid* 1 (cf. *Aen.* 1.360: *his commota fugam Dido sociosque parabat*) and stands in uneasy tension with the poet's notice of the hatred many felt for her tyrannical brother Pygmalion (*Aen.* 1.361–2, quoted above).

Vergil enriches his memorable portrait of Dido by endowing her with effective mastery of the daunting experience of epic travel. In this she is a figure reminiscent not only of the epic heroes Odysseus and Aeneas,

---

[13] Quint 1993.

but also of Achilles' epic opponent Penthesilea and Augustus' historical adversary Cleopatra. But she is far from being the only woman to embark on sea travel in the *Aeneid*, and it is to these other intrepid women that we may now turn.

Aeneas concludes his account of the sack of Troy with his astonishment at discovering a crowd of survivors assembled at the ancient temple of Ceres outside Troy, poised for exile and awaiting his leadership:

> atque hic ingentem comitum adfluxisse nouorum
> inuenio admirans numerum, matresque uirosque,
> collectam exsilio pubem, miserabile uolgus.
> undique conuenere animis opibusque parati
> in quascumque uelim pelage deducere terras.
> iamque iugis summae surgebat Lucifer Idae
> ducebatque diem, Danaique obsessa tenebant
> limina portarum, nec spes opis ulla dabatur.
> cessi et sublato montis genitore petiui.
> (*Aen.* 2.796–804)

And here I find, in amazement, a huge crowd of new comrades has streamed in, mothers and men, youth gathered for exile, a pitiable crowd. From every side they have come together, ready in heart and fortune, for me to lead them over the sea to whatever lands I want. And already the day star was rising above Ida's highest ridges, leading in the day, and the Danaans held in blockade the thresholds of the gates, nor was any hope of aid offered. I gave way and, having taken up my father on my shoulders, I made for the mountains.

The Trojan survivors' initiative in assembling under Aeneas' leadership offers an instructive contrast with the reluctance of Dido's Tyrians to travel despite their fear and hatred of the tyrant Pygmalion. Moreover, Aeneas explicitly specifies the inclusion of women (*matres*) in the group of overseas travelers, a fact that not only sharply distinguishes his followers from Odysseus' men (both his soldiers at Troy and the survivors who constitute his crew on the return to Ithaca) and Jason's comrades (the Argonauts), but also differentiates Aeneas himself from these two epic exemplars on the voyage: unlike either Odysseus or Jason, Aeneas leads a colony of displaced persons to settle them in a new home.[14] In this regard, of course, Dido is his closest comparator, though it is by no means clear how many women (besides Anna and Sychaeus' nurse Barce) accompany her on the voyage to Libya.

---

[14] Apollonius reports Jason's refusal to enlist Atalanta in the company of Argonauts "because he feared terrible conflicts for the sake of love" (Ap. Rhod. 1.773). In this way, he may allude to an alternate tradition that Atalanta had been a member of the company; for her participation on the voyage, see Diod. Sic. 4.48.5; Apollod. *Bibl.* 1.9.16.

The appeal to the surviving Trojan matrons of joining Aeneas' voyage emerges particularly clearly from the hero's report at Dido's banquet of his return to the sacked city to look for his missing wife, Creusa:

> et iam porticibus uacuis Iunonis asylo
> custodes lecti Phoenix et dirus Ulixes
> praedam adseruabant. huc undique Troia gaza
> incensis erepta adytis, mensaeque deorum
> crateresque auro solidi, captiuaque uestis
> congeritur. pueri et pauidae longo ordine matres
> stant circum.
> (*Aen.* 2.761–7)

> And now in the empty courtyard of Juno's sanctuary, Phoenix and dread Ulysses, chosen guards, were watching the booty. Here from every side Troy's treasure, snatched from blazing shrines – tables of the gods, bowls of solid gold, plundered vestments – are heaped up. Boys and trembling mothers stand around in long array.

There he sees the survivors of the sack, matrons and children who were unable to escape from the city, rounded up as captives, spoils of the long war. They are subject to another kind of sea-voyage, taken aboard the ships of the victorious Greeks and forcibly deported from the Troad as captives, bound for slavery in Greece. We can judge their unhappy lot from the report of Andromache of her experiences after the sack of Troy:

> "o felix una ante alias Priameia uirgo,
> hostilem ad tumulum Troiae sub moenibus altis
> iussa mori, quae sortitus non pertulit ullos
> nec uictoris heri tetigit captiua cubile!
> nos patria incensa diuersa per aequora uectae
> stirpis Achilleae fastus iuuenemque superbum,
> seruitio enixae tulimus ..."
> (*Aen.* 3.321–7)

> "Oh alone happy before the rest, virgin daughter of Priam, commanded to die beneath the high walls of Troy at the enemy's tomb, who neither suffered any allotment nor touched a victorious master's bed in captivity! After our fatherland was razed, we were borne over distant seas and endured the pride of Achilles' son, an arrogant youth, gave birth in slavery ..."

In a slave economy, such forced deportation and sea-travel, along with violent usage and sexual assault, must be expected. Indeed, Andromache's summary of her experiences after the fall of Troy allows for an unusually direct look at the sexual violence that was the experience of so many historical women who lost their homes and cities as a result of war in antiquity.[15] But I should hazard a guess that the historical women who experienced *andrapodizing* – the technical term for this treatment, as Kathy Gaca has shown in a series of important articles, preparatory studies for her forthcoming monograph on the subject – never enjoyed Andromache's "happy" outcome of remarriage to a compatriot ruling a newly founded city named for their lost city and populated by their fellow townsmen.

Despite their escape from *andrapodizing*, the Trojan matrons are represented as unenthusiastic travelers – not surprisingly, considering that their primary job on the trip is apparently to offer public witness to the destruction of Troy.[16] Thus at the opening of Book 3, after the Trojans have built and, quite literally, manned (3.5–8) a fleet, the exiles leave the Troad and put in, first, at Thrace, where Aeneas comes upon Polydorus' corpse beneath a mound of myrtle and cornel bushes. Agreeing that this is no place in which to establish an expatriate Trojan foundation, Aeneas buries Polydorus with all due funeral rites, including altars, bowls of warm milk, cups of victims' blood, and a choir of female mourners:

> ergo instauramus Polydoro funus, et ingens
> aggeritur tumulo tellus; stant Manibus arae,
> caeruleis maestae uittis atraque cupresso,
> **et circum Iliades crinem de more solutae**;
> inferimus tepido spumantia cymbia lacte
> sanguinis et sacri pateras, animamque sepulcro
> condimus et magna supremum uoce ciemus.
> (*Aen.* 3.62–8)

> Therefore we renew the funerary rites for Polydorus, and earth is heaped high on the mound; altars are set up to the dead, gloomy with dark fillets and black cypress, and the Ilian women stand around, with their hair released according to custom; we bring foaming bowls of warm milk and cups of sacred blood, we lay the spirit to rest in the tomb, and with loud voice we rouse the final call.

The Trojan women loose their hair in communal public lament for the last son of Priam, bearing mournful witness not only to the death of an individual but also to the permanent loss of their city.

---

[15] On sexual warfare against girls and women, see Gaca 2008, 2010, 2011, 2011–12, 2010–11, 2014, and forthcoming. McGinn 2004 collects the ample evidence that female slaves and sex workers were imported into Rome from the eastern empire.

[16] Cf. Keith 2016. On lament in the *Aeneid*, see Barchiesi 1978; Fantham 1999; Nugent 1992; and Perkell 1997.

The Trojans next attempt to reestablish on Crete a mini-Troy that Aeneas names Pergamum:

> fama uolat pulsum regnis cessisse paternis
> Idomenea ducem, desertaque litora Cretae,
> hoste uacare domum sedesque astare relictas.
> linquimus Ortygiae portus pelagoque uolamus
> bacchatamque iugis Naxon uiridemque Donusam,
> Olearon niueamque Paron sparsasque per aequor
> Cycladas, et crebris legimus freta consita terris.
> nauticus exoritur uario certamine clamor:
> hortantur **socii** Cretam proauosque petamus.
> prosequitur surgens a puppi uentus euntis,
> et tandem antiquis Curetum adlabimur oris.
> **ergo auidus muros optatae molior urbis**
> **Pergameamque uoco**, et letam cognomine gentem
> hortor amare focos arcemque attollere tectis.
> iamque fere sicco subductae litore puppes,
> **conubiis aruisque nouis operata iuuentus,**
> **iura domosque dabam.**
>
> (*Aen.* 3.121–37)
>
> A rumor goes round that the leader Idomeneus has left his paternal kingdom in exile, that Crete's shores have been abandoned, homes lie empty of the enemy and abandoned dwellings await. We leave Ortygia's harbour and fly over the sea, past Naxos, with its Bacchic rites on the mountain ridges, green Donysa, Olearos, snowy Paros, and the Cyclades sprinkled through the sea. Sailors' shouts rise in varied contest; comrades cheer "Let's seek Crete and our ancestors!" A rising wind follows from the stern; we go and at last we put in to the ancient shores of the Curetes. And so I greedily undertake the walls of our desired city and I call it Pergamum, and I urge my people, happy in the city's name, to love their hearths and raise a citadel with lofty roof. And now the ships were just drawn up on dry land, our youth were busy with marriages and new fields; I was giving laws and homes.

This passage, which uncannily anticipates Helenus' refoundation of Troy at Buthrotum (*Aen.* 3.294–7), is one of the few places in the poem where Vergil lingers over the details of the Trojans' travels. Even here, however, it is clear that Aeneas and his Trojan followers desire not the epic voyage but its goal, city foundation. The Trojans' enthusiasm for homes (*Aen.* 3.123, 137) and marriages (*Aen.* 3.136) underscores the demographic range of the community's membership – despite the reference to *socii* (*Aen.* 3.129), which implies a more narrowly conceived Trojan community, constituted by Aeneas' (male) crew alone.

The themes of female lament and the Trojan desire for city foundation come together in the final passage I wish to consider, the Trojan women's lament for Anchises in *Aeneid* 5.[17] While Aeneas, Ascanius, and the other Trojan men publicly celebrate the anniversary of Anchises' death with spectacular funeral games, the Trojan women mark the anniversary with private lamentation in isolation from their menfolk (*Aen.* 5.613–15: *at procul in sola secretae* **Troades** *acta / amissum Anchisen* **flebant**, *cunctaeque profundum / pontum aspectabant* **flentes**; "but removed far away, on the lonely promontory, the Trojan women wept for dead Anchises and weeping all looked out over the deep sea"). Collectively identified as *Troades* here, the Trojan women assume the role of mourners borne by their namesakes in the eponymous Euripidean tragedy, as Vergil underlines with his emphatic verbal repetition *flebant . . . flentes* (*Aen.* 5.614–15).[18] But the Trojan women collectively indulge in more than merely personal grief on this occasion, for their focus moves swiftly from Anchises to their desire for a city (*urbem orant*, *Aen.* 5.617). It is thus in communal lament for the sacked city of Troy that Juno's henchman Iris, disguised as the Trojan "Beroe," leads "the Dardanians' mothers" when she articulates their collective grief on the Sicilian strand:

> ac sic Dardanidum mediam se matribus infert.
> "o miserae, quas non manus" inquit "Achaica bello
> traxerit ad letum patriae sub moenibus! o gens
> infelix, cui te exitio Fortuna reseruat?
> septima post Troiae excidium iam uertitur aestas,
> cum freta, cum terras omnis, tot inhospita saxa
> sideraque emensae ferimur, dum per mare magnum
> Italiam sequimur fugientem et uoluimur undis."
> (*Aen.* 5.622–9)

And thus she inserts herself into the midst of the Dardanian mothers: "O wretched women," she said, "whom the Achaean band could not drag to death in war beneath the fatherland's walls! O unhappy people, for what end does Fortune preserve you? Already the seventh summer after the fall of Troy rolls by, and having measured out all the straits and lands, so many unwelcoming rocks and stars, we are carried over the great sea while we follow fleeing Italy and are tossed upon the waves."

---

[17] On the passage, see Nugent 1992. The convergence of the themes of city foundation and lament is striking evidence of Vergil's ktistic program in the *Aeneid* and its relationship to the Hellenistic tradition of foundation epics. By contrast, contemporary Roman elegy draws on a Greek elegiac tradition of lament that diverges significantly in its focus. On women's travels in Latin elegy, see Parker 2008; Keith forthcoming.

[18] On female lament in Greek tragedy, see Holst-Warhaft 2000; Foley 2001; Suter 2003; Dué 2006.

Anchises goes unmentioned in the speech of "Beroe," who focuses the Trojan women's lament on the passage of time since the city's fall and the hazards of their travels at sea instead.[19]

The close connection between the city the Trojan women desire and the fallen city of Troy emerges particularly clearly in the proposal of "Beroe" that the Trojans remain where they are in Sicily and reestablish "Troy" there:

> "hic Erycis fines fraterni atque hospes Acestes:
> quis prohibit muros iacere et dare ciuibus urbem?
> o patria et rapti nequiquam ex hoste penates,
> nullane iam Troiae dicentur moenia? nusquam
> Hectoreos amnis, Xanthum et Simoenta, uidebo?"
> (*Aen.* 5.630–4)

> "Here is the territory of fraternal Eryx and our host Acestes; who prevents us from laying walls and giving our citizens a city? O fatherland, Penates stolen in vain from the enemy, will there now be no walls named for Troy? Will I nowhere see Hector's rivers, Xanthus and Simois?"

Like Andromache with her "retrograde" fixation on the past in *Aeneid* 3,[20] the Trojan women in *Aeneid* 5 look for nothing beyond the renaissance of Troy; in particular, they are tired of the rigors of sea travel (cf. *Aen.* 3.626–9, quoted above). At the end of the book, therefore, after the Trojan women have disgraced themselves by setting fire to their own ships, the Trojan elder Nautes recommends to Aeneas that the women be left behind on Sicily and enrolled in the new city ruled by their kinsman Acestes:

> "nate dea, quo fata trahunt retrahuntque sequamur;
> quidquid erit, superanda omnis fortuna ferendo est.
> est tibi Dardanius diuinae stirpis Acestes:
> hunc cape consiliis socium et coniunge uolentem,
> huic trade amissis superant qui nauibus et quos
> pertaesum magni incepti rerumque tuarum est.
> **longaeuosque senes ac fessas aequore matres**
> **et quidquid tecum inualidum metuensque pericli est**
> delige, et his habeant terris sine moenia fessi;
> urbem appellabunt permisso nomine Acestam."
> (*Aen.* 5.709–18)

---

[19] On women's lament in the Greek tradition, especially in Greek epic, see Alexiou 1974; Loraux 1990; Easterling 1991; Holst-Warhaft 1992; Beissinger, Tylus, and Wofford 1999; Murnaghan 1999; Derderian 2001; Alexiou 2002; Dué 2002; Perkell 2008.

[20] Quint 1989: 22–5, reworked in Quint 1993: 58–61.

"Goddess-born, let us follow where destiny leads and releads us: whatever will happen, every fortune must be vanquished by bearing it. You have here the Dardanian Acestes, of divine stock; henceforth make him your ally in planning and make him a willing one; to him hand over those who, with their ships lost, remain and those who are weary of your great undertaking and affairs; choose out the aged old men and mothers tired of the sea, and whoever in your company who is weak or fearful of the danger, and let them, tired out, have walls in these lands; they will call the city Acestes, if the name is allowed."

When Aeneas accordingly enrolls the women in the new Sicilian city (*Aen.* 5.750: *transcribunt urbi matres*), he seems to respect the women's retrograde desire for a renascent Troy, for he names it Troy (*Aen.* 5.755–7: *interea Aeneas urbem designat aratro / sortiturque domos; hoc Ilium et haec loca Troiam / esse iubet*, "Meanwhile Aeneas marks out the city with a plough and allots homes: he bids this be Ilion and these places Troy"). As a result, the Trojan exiles who reach Italy are – with the infamous exception of Euryalus' mother[21] – not just male only, but fighting-age men at that.

The *Aeneid* repeatedly sounds out the possibility of female participation in the epic voyage, though the poem ultimately draws back from full-scale feminine participation in the epic project, whether conceived as journey, city foundation, or narrative. Dido's abbreviated epic voyage neither receives an independent first-person epic narrative nor offers poetological refraction of its author's literary project. For Vergil, both Dido and Cleopatra constitute narrative and historical dead-ends. Likewise, Andromache and the Trojan women, who enroll in the Sicilian city of Acesta, remain figures for narrative paths not taken, just as the city foundations of Buthrotum and Acesta represent narrative culs-de-sac as against the *Aeneid*'s stated goal of Lavinian shores, Latium, Alba, and the walls of high Rome (*Aen.* 1.2, 6–7). While not entirely subject to the rhetorical figure of *praeteritio*, women's travels in the *Aeneid* enact the displacement of all but the young elite Roman male from the path of Vergil's epic song.[22]

---

[21] On Euryalus' mother, see Nugent 1992; Perkell 2008; Sharrock 2011.
[22] In this regard, as in so many others, Vergil's epic successors elaborate themes broached but not finally contained by the Augustan master-poet: cf. Hardie 1993. Women's travel in epic emerges as a particular theme for reflection in imperial Latin epic, perhaps because of women's increased travel with their husbands on imperial service. On Medea's travels in *Metamorphoses* 7, see Newlands 1996; on Cornelia's stay on Lesbos and her travels after the battle of Pharsalia in Lucan, see Keith 2008 and Littlewood 2016; on Argia's flight from Argos to Thebes in Statius' *Thebaid*, in a trajectory that takes her from bedroom to battlefield and likens her to an epic hero, see Bessone 2015.

PART III

Rome's Journey: Constructions of Rome through Travel

Introduction

Part III turns to Roman journeys, focusing on Greek and Latin modes of thinking about movement, mobility, empire, and identity in the Roman world. With a timespan that includes the third century BCE and the Third Sophistic, "Rome's" journey is far from singular, shifting its gaze from comedic Carthaginians to Greek historians, and thence to Roman generals and emperors. Within these chapters the first journey in Roman history – Aeneas' exile and westward voyage to Italy – meets the eastward voyages of Germanicus, himself a figure of history whose head is perhaps stuck in the nostalgic clouds of the mythic past. In this part, the city of Rome emerges as a template for motion, a landscape of travel, of micro-journeys reflective of the new Augustan invitation to empire-wide movement. Travel, however, is not always an elective activity: Dido, Aeneas, and Polybius all journey because they have lost their homes, and in different ways it is Rome that serves as a reference point in the construction of their new identities.[1] Germanicus is a willing voyager, but one forced to take less desirable paths. His travels in particular allow for an exploration of the various media at stake in the study of the ancient journey; between history and historiography, textual and material evidence, lies the scholarly toolkit for approaching Germanicus' Roman voyage. Nevertheless, even this most documented of journeys is spun out to different ends, and it emerges from fragmentary glimpses that are nearly as precious and opaque as the textual remains of Naevius' *Bellum Punicum* and the histories of Timaeus.

In the first chapter Timothy O'Sullivan shows how the *Aeneid* has a lot riding on "acts of motion." Movement is key to the epic journey, and the Trojan exiles' migration is epic travel par excellence. Beyond the core transition from east to west, however, sits motion's ability to represent

---

[1] On Dido's journey, see Keith's discussion in Chapter 7 of this volume.

changes that were once far more abstract. In the *Aeneid*, real and metaphorical acts of motion occur on horizontal and vertical axes that express progress and its opposites. In fact, O'Sullivan suggests, a new mapping of movement was perhaps needed in the *Aeneid*, as the Augustan age ushered in nearly endless transformations – some disguised as restoration or preservation of the status quo, all tied to Augustus' role in the return of order in the face of chaos and civil conflict. Different types of motion do move the epic's plot forward, but some, chaotic and uncontrolled, are set in stark contrast to calm, orderly motion. Vertical movement occurs in a textual space stretching from the shades of the Underworld to the stars above: it includes both the fall of cities and the rise of new city walls. Among acts of horizontal movement, wandering figures prominently. The wandering of an epic voyage can result in *nostos* or the founding of a new home, reversing the apparent lack of direction behind such motion. Foundation and homecoming thus represent cessation of the journey, stationary goals that offer *telos* to the labor of movement but threaten the epic narrative with its *finis*.

The Trojans of the *Aeneid* journey from sacked city to proto-civil war, from a city in ruins to a Palatine made of pre-ruins, but, as O'Sullivan details, the journey as narrative in the *Aeneid* is also paralleled by the Augustan present. And in this present, movement through Rome is made possible by the reopening of the city's urban nodes to the flow of citizens, an image that offers a multiform representation of the *res publica restituta*. Since Vergil's conceptions of urban mobility inform much of his poetic city-lab, the mapping of spaces – past, present, and future – and the hero's movement through them in time and space are key to the chapter. O'Sullivan reminds us that the view from above is an integral part of the poet's construction of a vantage to take in all of this spatio-temporal movement and change, a narrative perspective that returns in Part IV, where Martin Devecka and Karen ní Mheallaigh both consider the view from above on a cosmic scale. The Augustan view from on high, however, was already cosmic – no trip to the moon was needed to take in the view of the *urbs* as *orbis*. The distance between viewer and place actually works to create connection not disjuncture, which is itself shaped less by the perspective of philosophical *somnium* than the experienced interstices of the city, the places designed for the *populus*. This chapter is concerned, therefore, with the ability to move within Rome and with the very invitation to do so, at home and even when away, out there in the distant reaches of the empire, which, as Cynthia Damon and Elizabeth Palazzolo remind us in Chapter 10, were quickly becoming R/home in their own ways.

Thomas Biggs' contribution explores the functions of *pietas* in the epic journeys of early Roman literature. In particular, he suggests that *pietas* can serve as the guiding principle for a reevaluation of Roman and Carthaginian perspectives in Naevius' *Bellum Punicum* and Plautus' *Poenulus*. Biggs first analyzes the relationships between Naevius' Aeneas and earlier depictions of Dido's journey in the Sicilian Greek historian Timaeus. The chapter then examines Justin's summary of Pompeius Trogus, since his account of Dido's voyage is the most extensive to survive from antiquity and may preserve relevant aspects derived from its earliest sources. After suggesting that Dido's journey, and its connections to piety, may predate and even influence the Trojans' epic voyage in the *Bellum Punicum*, Biggs treats Punic piety diachronically by focusing on Plautus' *Poenulus*. While *Punica fides* may have become a powerful stereotype, Biggs suggests that we should be attentive to the echoes of *Punica pietas* throughout a generally hostile and reductive Roman literary tradition. Scholars have shown that Plautus' *Poenulus* highlights the *pietas* of Hanno the Carthaginian – a surprising narrative move in the wake of the Second Punic War, within a play set in Aetolia during the age of Fulvius Nobilior's campaigns. While some have seen this characterization as insincere, a *pius* Carthaginian actually evokes a larger cultural tradition that has hitherto remained unexplored. Hence Biggs connects the *Poenulus'* attribution of Hanno's successful voyage to the power of *pietas* with the glimpses of the concept in Naevius' "Aeneid" and, more suggestively, in the pre-Naevian Dido legend. The presence of Aphrodite and the thematic importance of the preservation of female virginity in tales of epic journeying offer further potential links between these narratives. In the end, Biggs' comparative reading offers new insight into a key Roman quality's literary development and its ties to the epic journey and the concept of "home."

Cynthia Damon and Elizabeth Palazzolo address Roman conceptions of "home" and "away" by examining Tacitus' narrative of Germanicus' ill-fated mission to the eastern provinces in the *Annals* and his final, funereal "homecoming." What Germanicus ultimately discovers is that the edges of empire are still well within the reach of the Roman center, of home – an element of constriction ultimately attributable to the Augustan "opening up" of space that O'Sullivan explores. A member of the imperial family is always restricted by status – each movement outwards brings the *domi* further into the *militiae*. And in a Rome fraught with anxiety, ruled by a calculating elite, a prominent member of the imperial family can never truly leave home and return to the same status, or perhaps cannot even return safely.

Damon and Palazzolo begin by exploring such themes in Tacitus' account of Germanicus' eastern journeys. Through close reading and careful analysis of the text, the fickle baggage of imperial status is shown to weigh down Germanicus and render his journey no ordinary political trip. The stakes are higher, and all eyes – at home and away – are on him, especially those of Tiberius. After consideration of Tacitus' account, the chapter turns to the traces of Germanicus' journey found in the material record. Historical journeys often exist outside of texts, and it is a distinct merit of this chapter to show the approaches of varied media to recording imperial movement. Numismatic and epigraphic evidence takes center stage as Damon and Palazzolo provide a detailed account of the whereabouts of Germanicus, Agrippina, and their ever-growing brood as they make the rounds in the East. The comparison between the material and historiographical records shows how Tacitus actively shapes this section of his history, thereby offering insights into his composition as well as into fruitful methodologies for modern scholars working in the spaces between texts and objects. Literary concerns return to the fore in the last stretch of the chapter, where Tacitus is shown to connect Germanicus' journey with several famous predecessors and peers. Epic journeys are always modeled on earlier voyages – an Aeneas is always at least partially an Odysseus – yet Germanicus' models often spell disaster for his trip's return leg. Tiberius and Alexander the Great, Antony and Caesar: numerous models help characterize Germanicus as he moves through imperial space. His ultimate demise and unrealized *nostos* thus engage with a plotline found elsewhere in the exploits of the early empire as well as in ancient epic.

Andrew C. Johnston turns to Greek authors under Roman rule in this part's final chapter, devoting his attention to the roles of antiquity's most famous traveler, Odysseus. Johnston's gaze takes in authors ranging from Polybius to the emperor Julian. Odysseus, the ἀνήρ πολύτροπος, is an ever-adaptable figure, hence his vitality throughout the Classical world and his ability to move between and within Mediterranean cultures while wearing numerous and different masks. Johnston shows us how the Ithacan serves as a multifaceted actor himself and as a plastic intellectual subject, and that it is this malleability that keeps him relevant for Greek identity construction deep into the Roman world's twilight years.

Of many facets of the complex Odyssean personality, Johnston's interest in this chapter is in Homer's primary characterization of him as ὃς μάλα πολλὰ πλάγχθη ("the man who wandered far and wide"). It is "Odysseus the wanderer" that Johnston tracks throughout the writings of Greeks under Roman rule, from the late Republic through the Second and Third Sophistics. Many of the figures Johnston analyzes have received little to no attention in relation to their Odyssean identities, especially several geographers of the second and first centuries BCE and four significant intellectuals of the high empire: Dio of Prusa, Aelius Aristides, Lucian, and the emperor Julian. While earlier research into Odysseus' various incarnations in historiography and ancient geography sets the groundwork for the present chapter, Johnston himself is an explorer of uncharted territory. His core argument is a clarion call for scholars to take seriously what Greek authors are doing with Odysseus throughout the empire. Reference to the *aner polytropos* is often far more than learned allusion and elite poetic play: it is the invocation of a figure essential to the construction of identity, to the definition of new cultural landscapes, and to resistance to Roman domination, be it political, military, or cultural.

CHAPTER 8

Epic Journeys on an Urban Scale: Movement and Travel in Vergil's Aeneid

Timothy M. O'Sullivan

La révolution c'est le mouvement mais le mouvement ce n'est pas une révolution.
— Paul Virilio, *Vitesse et politique* (Paris, 1977: 27–8)

In his 1993 book *Epic and Empire*, David Quint demonstrates how Vergil's *Aeneid* established a model for subsequent explorations of imperial power in epic verse. The poem fixed epic as *the* genre of monarchical power and imperial drive, while also laying the groundwork for "anti-epics" that call into question the entire project that unites narrative and imperial progress:

> Virgil's poem attached political meaning to narrative form itself. To the victors belongs epic, with its linear teleology; to the losers belongs romance, with its random or circular wandering. Put another way, the victors experience history as a coherent, end-directed story told by their own power; the losers experience a contingency that they are powerless to shape to their own ends.[1]

For Quint, then, Aeneas' wanderings in *Aeneid* 3 are, in one sense, *not* an epic journey at all, but a romantic adventure that the poem explicitly rejects in favor of the martial, epic progress of the second, Italian, half of the poem. Quint is one of many scholars to point out the ways that Book 3 involves a high degree of missteps and empty repetition, resulting in a picaresque parody of the epic journey.[2] Yet Quint's formulation also draws

---

The ideas developed in this chapter were previously presented at Yale, Gothenburg, and Kansas; I would like to thank those audiences for their feedback, and Christina Kraus, Ida Östenberg, and Emma Scioli for the invitations. For comments on earlier drafts, I would like to thank Thomas Biggs, Jessica Blum, Leah Kronenberg, and the anonymous readers for the Press. Except where noted, all translations are my own.
[1] Quint 1993: 9.
[2] Cf. Hexter 1999: 66: "Book 3 is . . . a history of false starts and failed attempts to found a new Troy."

our attention to the distinction between different types of movement in the *Aeneid*, and their relation to larger ideological patterns.

This distinction, I shall argue, applies to movements of all kinds in the poem. As we shall see, Vergil is keenly attuned to the symbolic possibilities of acts of motion both in his poem and in his broader milieu. As many scholars have observed, the *Aeneid* is particularly interested in exploring the relationship between order and chaos in the social, political, and natural world: acts of movement thus become a physical representation of the tension between destructive and constructive forces that is a central concern of the poem.[3] In the *Aeneid*, then, we cannot understand the *topos* of the epic journey without examining the contrast the poem establishes between wayward motion and directed motion. The tension between destructive and constructive forces in the poem plays out in the epic journey on both a physical level – are the Trojans wandering lost or are they moving purposefully toward Italy? – and at a more metaphorical level – are the Trojans in control of their destiny, or are they buffeted against their will across the seas? It is therefore no surprise that Jupiter is the character who most frequently appeals to steady, forward motion, whether through space or through time.

But, as we shall see, the poem is not only concerned with different types of travel through space, but also with movements on a smaller scale, both on a horizontal and a vertical axis. I will in this chapter first consider patterns of horizontal movement in the *Aeneid* – including journeying, wandering, rushing, and coming to a halt. I will then consider movement along a vertical axis – movement up and down, collapse, and restoration. A particular point of emphasis in movement on the vertical axis are scenes where someone mounts a hill or other lofty space to enjoy an elevated point of view. In the final part of the chapter we will consider the ways that the *Aeneid*'s paradigms of chaotic and orderly movement through space accord with similar patterns in Augustan culture more broadly.

8.1 Horizontal Movement: Wandering, Rushing, and their Opposites

When we think of movement across space in the *Aeneid*, we inevitably think of Aeneas' journey from Troy to Italy. The journey of course has obvious parallels in other epic travels, most notably those of the *Odyssey* and the *Argonautica*. The ancient reader thus had available a number of archetypes,

---

[3] See esp. Hardie 1986; Bartsch 1998; Feeney 2014: 211–21.

both literary and historical, for understanding the Trojan journey in the first half of the poem. The Trojans are exiles – or, better yet, refugees; Dido clearly sees her own travails in Aeneas' experience, for instance. Yet their journey is also figured as a homecoming, of sorts, given Apollo's mysterious injunction to seek out their "ancient mother," the original homeland of their forefather Dardanus (3.96). Moreover, the journey of the Trojans also consciously evokes the act of colonization, as Horsfall has shown, and even acts as a harbinger of future imperial expansion.[4]

The Trojan journey across the Mediterranean in the first half of the poem for the most part takes on the character of involuntary wandering, which is clearly given a negative valence in the poem.[5] Significantly, the *Aeneid* shows little interest in traveling to acquire knowledge, despite the fact that Odysseus' adventures had already been recast as a model for intellectual inquiry as early as the fifth century.[6] Vergil in fact foregrounds the Trojans' wandering as the most difficult aspect of the effort to found Rome in the prologue: "... driven by the Fates to wander year after year round all the oceans of the world. So heavy was the cost of founding the Roman race" (1.31–3: *multosque per annos / errabant acti fatis maria omnia circum. / tantae molis erat Romanam condere gentem*).[7] Aeneas, too, in introducing himself to his mother in disguise, adopts the same focus: "we wander," he says, "ignorant of the inhabitants and the location, driven here by the wind or by vast waves" (1.332–3: *ignari hominumque locorumque / erramus uento huc uastis et fluctibus acti*). Or again some fifty lines later: "I am a helpless stranger, driven out of Europe and out of Asia, tramping the desert wastes of Libya" (1.384–5: *ipse ignotus, egens, Libyae deserta peragro, / Europa atque Asia pulsus*). The emphasis throughout Book 1, then, is on two closely related types of wayward horizontal motion: involuntary movement (summed up by *iactatus* in 1.3), and wandering movement. In both of these, Aeneas will find his counterpart in Dido, and Venus knows to foreground that part of the story in her effort to arrange a rapprochement between the two leaders, telling her son about the Tyrian queen's *longae ambages* (1.341–2). Vergil's readers, moreover, may have been familiar with the claim, first made by the early third-century historian Timaeus, that Dido's very name meant "the wanderer" in a local Libyan

---

[4] Colonization: Horsfall 1989; imperial expansion: Horsfall 1976: 76.
[5] On wandering as a *topos* in the poem, see Perkell 2013.
[6] Montiglio 2005: 123–9. One notable exception to this pattern is the urban tour, which we might consider wandering on a smaller scale; see further below.
[7] Trans. D. West 2003.

tongue.[8] For Dido and Aeneas, then, their *similis fortuna* (1.628) revolves around their shared experience of involuntary and wandering movement from a city in the East to unknown shores.[9]

Dido has of course now settled down, and the lure of this settlement is powerful for Aeneas: he knows he is supposed to settle down too, so why not here?[10] But in Book 4, as he briefly gives in to the temptation of finally stopping his wandering, it is *Dido* who resumes the wandering, this time as a symptom of her passion. In a sense, then, since this love comes in large part from the interference of Venus and Cupid, Dido resumes her involuntary, wandering movement from earlier in her story, this time in her own city. Again and again, Vergil calls attention to the way her confusion and passion manifests itself in compelled, wandering motion: like a wounded deer (4.68–73); like a Bacchant (4.300–3); chased by Aeneas in her dreams (4.465–6); wandering lost and alone on a road (4.466–8).[11] Aeneas, by contrast, is the oak buffeted by the winds (4.437–49), a simile designed to convey his mental stability as much as his physical constancy, and a telling contrast to his being buffeted by the storm in Book 1. His mental immobility is emphasized both leading into the simile: *nullis ille mouetur / fletibus* (4.438–9: he is moved by no laments); and coming out of the simile: *mens immota manet* (4.449: his mind remains immovable).[12]

Wandering and being buffeted are not the only versions of horizontal motion that the poem invests with a negative valence. The poem frequently draws our attention to violent, chaotic motion forward, whether in the storm of battle or in an actual storm. A particular *topos* is the act of rushing forward into battle, such as Aeneas' waking reaction to his dream visit from Hector:

> arma amens capio; nec sat rationis in armis,
> sed glomerare manum bello et concurrere in arcem

---

[8] *FGrH* 566 fr. 60, cited in Pease 1935: 22 n. 142; see Biggs, Chapter 9 in this volume, p. 179.

[9] For more on Dido's role as a leader of her own "extended epic journey," see Keith, Chapter 7 in this volume. For the pre-Vergilian history of Dido's wanderings, see Biggs, Chapter 9 in this volume.

[10] Notice how Dido summarizes her story as the act of coming to rest after a period of compelled movement: "A similar fortune has willed that I too, harassed through so many labors, finally settle in this land" (1.628–9: *me quoque per multos similis fortuna labores / iactatam hac demum uoluit consistere terra*).

[11] Vergil's depiction of lovesick Dido as a wanderer is also no doubt influenced by Apollonius' depiction of Medea, on which see Montiglio, Chapter 5 in this volume, eps. p. 96–99.

[12] Many commentators (e.g. Briggs 1980: 38; Dyson 2001: 211) have seen in the tree's vertical reach an allusion to Aeneas' own future travels to the Underworld and to heaven itself; if they are right, then the simile not only contrasts Aeneas' stability with Dido's wandering, but also his vertical trajectory with her wayward motion on the horizontal plane.

> cum sociis ardent animi; furor iraque mentem
> praecipitat, pulchrumque mori succurrit in armis.
> (*Aen.* 2.314–17)

> Out of my senses, I grab my weapons. And there is no real plan in taking the weapons, but my spirit burns to gather together a band of men for battle and to run into the city with my comrades. Madness and rage drive my mind forward and it occurs to me that it would be a beautiful thing to die in arms.

Notice here the way that physical and psychological speed are brought together: Aeneas' body rushes to go out to war because his mind is also in violent motion, spurred on by *furor* and *ira*. Throughout the poem, fury inspires people to violence and madness, and the physical manifestation of that violence is violent chaotic motion.

Think, too, of Allecto's work in Book 7: infected by Allecto's venom, Amata delivers an impassioned but ineffectual speech to her husband, whom she can clearly see stands opposed (7.374: *contra stare uidet*); the serpent then penetrates her more deeply and wanders all over her body (7.375: *totamque pererrat*), and Amata responds by raging throughout the city (7.377: *immensam sine more furit lymphata per urbem*). There follows the famous simile of the top driven by young boys, a simile which not only conveys her speed but her inability to control her own movements. The simile, along with the obvious similarities of Amata and Latinus in this book to Dido and Aeneas in Book 4, reminds us of another aspect of controlled versus chaotic motion in the *Aeneid*: the dichotomy often breaks down along the lines of gender. It is a clear point of contrast in Book 4, and a clear point of contrast between Jupiter and Juno on the celestial plain. In this simile, it is no accident that it is young *boys* who drive the top, through vast *atria* no less (7.379–80), no doubt surrounded by the waxen images of the male ancestors whom they will grow up to imitate in every way, including in their stately, controlled motion.[13] Continuing the gendered contrast, Amata emerges from the simile and heads for the woods (7.385–91), where she rages in a Bacchic frenzy that further unites her with Dido in Book 4. She is a physical and kinetic manifestation of Mercury's notorious dictum that "woman is an inconstant and changeable thing" (4.569–70: *uarium et mutabile semper / femina*).

In a way, this contrast between chaotic uncontrolled motion and calm control is set up not only by the top simile but indeed in the very first

---

[13] On gait as a marker of gender, see Gleason 1994: 60–2; Corbeill 2004: 117–23; Fowler 2007; O'Sullivan 2011: 16–28.

simile in the poem, when Neptune's calming of the stormy waters is compared to the soothing effect of a Roman statesman's appearance before an angry crowd (1.142–57). The simile has often been read as representative of the themes of the entire poem, most recently by Denis Feeney, who notes that the passage acts as "an emblem of restoration of order after chaos which generates a set of expectations for the rest of the poem."[14] The simile thus introduces the reader to the ideological impact of different types of movement in the poem. Above all, the power of Neptune and the Roman statesman is made manifest by their control over the restless movements of other entities. The comparison of the roiling crowd to the churning sea is as old as Homer, but, as Servius notes, it seems clear that Vergil is also referring to the particular political use of this metaphor that emerged in the chaotic days of the late Republic. Vergil, Servius tells us, "makes the motion of the populace the point of comparison for a storm, while Cicero makes the storm a point of comparison for the [Roman] people: in the *Pro Milone* 'indeed the other storms and tempests in the very swells of the *contiones*.'"[15] In fact, as Servius notes on the next line, again appealing to Cicero, sedition itself involves a kind of movement among the populace – a kind of ancient equivalent of the Paul Virilio quotation that is the epigraph to this chapter.[16]

All of these images come together to make the Augustan reading of the calmed waters quite obvious. It is not just the image of the calm aristocrat that puts us in mind of the late Republic, but the very comparison of a raging storm to a crowd of people. The moment is also appealing, however, for the contrast between the stillness of the orator and the churning of the crowd. His placid demeanor is, importantly, not some natural state of the great man, but a calm that is hard won. We see this most clearly not in the simile but in the figure of Neptune himself. When he spots the storm he is "gravely agitated" (1.126: *grauiter commotus*); Servius has a nice comment on how this observation makes perfect sense, since Neptune *is* the sea, and if the sea is agitated then he must be as well. But then we are able to witness him calming himself down first, in that famous aposiopesis (1.135), as a necessary prelude to the external calm

---

[14] Feeney 2014: 189.
[15] Serv. Auct. ad *Aen.* 1.148: ac ueluti magno in populo *iste tempestati populi motum comparat, Tullius populo tempestatem: pro Milone "equidem ceteras tempestates et procellas in illis dumtaxat fluctibus contionum."* The citation is from Cic. *Mil.* 5; cf. Cic. *Mur.* 35, Quint. *Inst.* 8.6.48. As Servius goes on to note, Homer famously makes the very same analogy at *Il.* 2.144.
[16] Serv. Auct. ad *Aen.* 1.149: seditio "seditio" est <dissensio ciuium>, sicut Cicero ait in de re publica "eaque dissensio civium, quod seorsum eunt alii ad alios, seditio dicitur."

that he is about to engineer. Self-rule is the important precursor to rule, and both of these actions involve stilling the motions – first within, then without. The overlap in meaning of Latin *motus* helps here – both internal turmoil (the emotions) and external turmoil (riots). In this context, we should not forget that Augustus himself refers to the turmoil of the late 40s BCE as *ciuilis motus* ("civilian movement") in the *Res Gestae* (10).

8.2 Vertical Movement: Collapse, Resurgence, and Hilltop Views

Thus far we have seen how, in the *Aeneid*, the motif of the epic journey is a subset of a larger group of different sorts of movement through and across space: on the negative side of the spectrum, the reader constantly encounters scenes of passive, uncontrolled movement, such as characters wandering lost, or rushing forward chaotically; on the positive side of the spectrum, there is the promise of a resting place, a *sedes*, a permanent home that promises both physical and emotional stability.[17] This paradigm, as we shall see, accords more or less with the broader ideology of the Augustan transformation, but before we consider those connections we must also examine the way that Vergil pairs this paradigm with a similar opposition of negative and positive movement along a *vertical* axis.[18] Just as Vergil explores the contrast between orderly and disorderly motion through space, the contrast between wandering and settling down, he also explores similar contrasts on a vertical axis: between collapse and restoration, between the violent disorder of Hell and the (mostly) benign celestial order, between falling into the abyss of the sea and climbing the heights, and ultimately reaching the stars, at least metaphorically.[19] Throughout the *Aeneid*, Vergil figures the Augustan transformation as a reversal of chaotic disorderly movement on both the horizontal and vertical

---

[17] Montiglio brings out a similar connection between emotional and physical stability or chaos in Apollonius' *Argonautica* and Heliodorus' *Aethiopica* (see Chapter 5 in this volume).

[18] On the establishment of a vertical hierarchy in the *Aeneid*, see Hardie 1986: 267–85, esp. 268: "Virgil exploits to the full the inescapable tendency of the human mind to ascribe value to the descriptive terms 'up' and 'down'; physical space is politicized and moralized, that is to say, peopled by sentient and intelligent forces whose characteristic it is to expand to fill the space available. On the human level this expansion is the historical growth of Rome, and is presented fairly realistically in terms of the horizontal axis; but it may also, more fantastically, be understood as expansion along the vertical axis."

[19] On the contrast between "Heaven and Hell" in the poem, see Hardie 1993: 73–6. On the *Aeneid* as the story of "a journey to the heavens or the stars," and its relation to similar themes in Lucretius, see Hardie 1986: 195–8. On the theme of catasterism in epic, see also Blum, Chapter 4 in this volume.

planes: from the collapse of Troy to the erection of walls and buildings in Italy; from the chaotic movements of war, of storm, of traveling lost, to the steady movement through a restored Augustan topography.

The poem's foregrounding of the verb *ruo/ruere* encapsulates Vergil's interest in disorderly movement, since it can refer to rushing movement on both a horizontal and a vertical plane. We have already seen how the poem thematizes the chaotic speedy motion of war and other undesirable moves, such as running through the woods. But *ruo* also of course is the root of *ruina*, and a key term for Vergil's attempt to unite physical collapse with chaotic speed. Hector's words to Aeneas are a good example:

> "heu fuge, nate dea, teque his" ait "eripe flammis.
> hostis habet muros; ruit alto a culmine Troia . . .
> sacra suosque tibi commendat Troia penatis;
> hos cape fatorum comites, his moenia quaere
> magna pererrato statues quae denique ponto."
> (*Aen.* 2.289–90, 293–5)

> "Ah, child of a goddess – flee!" he said. "Pull yourself out of these flames! The enemy holds the walls; Troy is collapsing from her high summit . . . Troy entrusts to you her rites and her gods. Take them as the companions of your destiny, and seek out for them great walls which you will erect at long last after you have wandered over the sea."

Hector sums up for Aeneas the entire arc of his future life as a series of horizontal and vertical movements: Troy is collapsing to the ground, so Aeneas and his followers must rush out of the city, wander across the seas, then come to a stop and erect walls in Italy: Aeneas' destiny is to find in Italy a place where he can reverse the disorderly motion that he experienced in Troy and on the Mediterranean.[20] Similarly, at the end of Book 1 Dido asks Aeneas to narrate his adventures thus far, calling them *casusque tuorum / erroresque tuos* (1.754–5: "the misfortunes of your people and your wanderings"). As Servius first noted (ad *Aen.* 1.755), the two noun phrases provide a précis of Books 2 (*casus*) and 3 (*errores*). But they also situate Aeneas' misadventures as acts of wayward movement on both a vertical (*casus*) and horizontal (*errores*) plane. The poem thus figures the foundation of a city in Latium as the physical inverse of what preceded it.

---

[20] Note how Vergil uses word play to reinforce the connection between Troy and its tumbling walls. In the sentence *ruit alto a culmine Troia*, the first five letters of *ruit alto* are a near-anagram of *Troia* at the end (particularly since the Romans themselves saw the exact anagram *Truia* as an alternative form of *Troia*) – as if Troy "contains" collapse, and as if by collapsing Troy fulfills its destiny.

Building walls is a common leitmotif in the poem, and a clear counterpart to the destruction of Troy, but I would argue that there are still other motifs that the poem also posits as the positive inverse of downward collapse.[21] One such motif is the journey up a hill to gain a vantage point on a scene below.[22] There are three key scenes in Book 1 where characters adopt a view from above. In the aftermath of the storm in Book 1, for example, Aeneas climbs up to the cliff's edge to survey the sea. Instead of the lost ships of his comrades, he sees three stags on the shore, with a herd behind them:

> Aeneas scopulum interea conscendit, et omnem
> prospectum late pelago petit, Anthea si quem
> iactatum uento uideat Phrygiasque biremis
> aut Capyn aut celsis in puppibus arma Caici.
> nauem in conspectu nullam, tris litore ceruos
> prospicit errantis; hos tota armenta sequuntur
> a tergo et longum per uallis pascitur agmen.
> constitit hic arcumque manu celerisque sagittas
> corripuit fidus quae tela gerebat Achates,
> ductoresque ipsos primum capita alta ferentis
> cornibus arboreis sternit, tum uulgus et omnem
> miscet agens telis nemora inter frondea turbam;
> nec prius absistit quam septem ingentia uictor
> corpora fundat humi et numerum cum nauibus aequet;
> hinc portum petit et socios partitur in omnis.
>
> (*Aen.* 1.180–94)

Meanwhile Aeneas climbed a rock to get a view over the whole breadth of the ocean and see if there was any trace of the storm-tossed Antheus or of the double-banked Trojan galleys, Capys perhaps, or Caicus' armour high on the poop. There was not a ship to be seen, but he did see three stags wandering about the shore with all their herd behind them grazing the low ground in a long line. He stopped in his tracks and snatched his bow and swift arrows from the trusty Achates. First he took down the three leaders with their high heads of branching antlers. The whole of the rest of the herd scattered into the leafy cover of the wood, but not before he succeeded in stretching seven huge carcasses on the ground, one for each of the ships. He then made for the harbour and gave them out to all his men.[23]

---

[21] On the motif of erecting walls in the *Aeneid*, see Morwood 1991.
[22] As Lovatt 2013 notes, the view from a higher vantage point is an epic *topos*, particularly associated with the divine perspective of Zeus/Jupiter (33–9), but also sometimes appropriated by the narrator (42–5), or by other characters in the poem (including Aeneas himself: 88–94).
[23] Trans. D. West 2003.

This scene signals in a number of ways the restoration of order after the disruption of the storm. Whereas on the sea Aeneas and his men were at the mercy of furious nature (and, by proxy, of the gods above), here Aeneas is restored to a position of literal and metaphorical superiority; whereas on the sea his only view down portended doom, as the severity of the storm had exposed the seabed below (1.106–7), here his view down offers hope and sustenance for his men. Unlike in the previous scene, the stags now wander (1.185: *errantis*) instead of Aeneas and his men, and the hero himself stands fast (1.187: *constitit*), safe in his hilltop vantage point; the stags take the place of the agitated sea and the agitated crowd in the first simile, hence the political language used to describe them (1.190: *uulgus*; 1.191: *turbam*). The stags are then laid low, just as many of Aeneas' ships had been in the previous scene; and, to drive the point home, Aeneas "matches the number [of slain stags] to the number of ships" (1.193: *numerum cum nauibus aequet*). Here on land, humans are restored, via the hunt and the act of sacrifice, to their normal spot atop the totem pole, a spot that is a welcome reversal of their situation – and their physical position – at sea.

Moreover, in the speech that follows (1.198–207) Aeneas takes a temporal "long view," just as he had adopted a "spatial" long view in his survey of sea and shore. He emphasizes that their destination is a settling point, an end to horizontal movement (1.199: *finem*; 1.205: *sedes . . . quietas*). Once they arrive in Latium, a safer form of vertical movement can commence, as the kingdom of Troy will rise again (1.206: *illic fas regna resurgere Troiae*). From that safe and distant vantage point, the future Romans may look down on their physical territory (cf. 1.7: *altae moenia Romae*) and look back on their past adventures, far off in time and space, with some pleasure.

In the scene that follows, Jupiter takes the same "long view," both spatially and temporally, that we have just seen Aeneas take in North Africa.[24] Jupiter, like Aeneas before him, first adopts a view from above, surveying sea and shore (Aeneas: *prospicit* 185; Jupiter: *despiciens* 224); he stands fast on the summit of heaven (225–6: *sic uertice caeli / constitit*), just as Aeneas had taken up his position on the cliff in the previous scene (187: *constitit hic*). Then, just as Aeneas had done before him, he gives a consoling speech that takes the temporal long view that is the counterpart

---

[24] On the connection Vergil draws between Jupiter's authority and his "vertical perspective" in this scene, see Lovatt 2013: 35–6. And see too p. 39: "The normative controlling gaze of the king of gods and men is a key ingredient of epic."

of the spatial long view that he had from his vantage point moments earlier. His speech to Venus begins:

> "parce metu, Cytherea, manent immota tuorum
> fata tibi; cernes urbem et promissa Lauini
> moenia, sublimemque feres ad sidera caeli
> magnanimum Aenean; neque me sententia uertit."
> (*Aen.* 1.257–60)

> "Spare yourself these fears, my lady from Cythera. You can be sure that the destiny of your descendants remains unchanged. You will see the city of Lavinium and its promised walls. You will take great-hearted Aeneas up to the stars of heaven. No argument changes my mind."[25]

Jupiter's words highlight the way in which the optimistic reading of Roman *imperium* can be understood in spatial terms, and on both a horizontal and vertical plane: stopping wayward movement, and raising the Romans to great heights. Jupiter is steady, unturnable, and therefore Roman destiny is as well; whether or not the poem in the end endorses this as true is a different question. Moreover, the physical rise of Rome's walls is not merely a vertical counterpart to the horizontal wanderings that precede it (and will enable it) in the poem, but also the inverse movement of the physical collapse of Troy's walls. This comes across most clearly in Venus' speech, where she balances, in her mental scales, the fall of Troy (1.238: *occasum Troiae tristisque ruinas*) with the (implied) rise of Rome. The effect of all this balancing on an Augustan reader is also at issue here: just as the "optimistic" reading of movement in the poem balances the fall of Troy and the destructive wanderings with new building in a settled location (1.437: *o fortunati, quorum iam moenia surgunt*), some Romans surely balanced the *ruina* of the Roman Republic with the rise of Augustan Rome, and Augustus himself (whose name, after all, basically means the "increaser").

After these two scenes of high vantage points – Aeneas on his cliff, and Jupiter from the heavens – we see Aeneas adopt yet another hilltop view, this time over the rising city of Carthage:

> Corripuere uiam interea, qua semita monstrat,
> iamque ascendebant collem, qui plurimus urbi
> imminet aduersasque aspectat desuper arces.
> miratur molem Aeneas, magalia quondam,

---

[25] Trans. D. West 2003.

miratur portas strepitumque et strata uiarum.
instant ardentes Tyrii: pars ducere muros
molirique arcem et manibus subuoluere saxa,
pars optare locum tecto et concludere sulco;
iura magistratusque legunt sanctumque senatum . . .
"o fortunati, quorum iam moenia surgunt!"
Aeneas ait et fastigia suspicit urbis.
(*Aen.* 1.418–26, 437–8)

> Meanwhile they hastened along where the path was guiding them, and then they were climbing a hill that looms high over the city and looks down on the citadels across the way. Aeneas marvels at the massive construction, where there were once small huts; he marvels at the gates and the din and the paving of roads. The Tyrians, on fire, work urgently: some of them build walls, erecting the citadel and rolling rocks by hand; others are choosing a spot for a dwelling and enclosing it with a trench. They select laws and magistrates and a sacred senate . . . "Fortunate are those whose walls are now rising!" Aeneas says, and looks up at the heights of the city.

The importance of Aeneas obtaining a view over the city, rather than seeing it from below, is such a point of emphasis for Vergil that he makes his protagonist climb a hill that somehow enables him to look down on the lofty *arces* across the way. As the poem makes clear, the scene of a city in the process of being built, rather than already completed, has obviously poignant appeal for a man who has just witnessed a city "move" in the opposite direction, and who longs to see his own city rise in compensation for his difficult history. That the rising Carthage is a positive inversion of the destruction of Troy as well is also conveyed by the Tyrians, who are burning in their diligent work (423) – a nice contrast to the fire that brought his city down. Aeneas is clearly aware of the contrast, and his famous cry reveals the implicit comparison that is on his mind.[26] Notice, too, that the passage introduces some confusion about the relative heights of Aeneas and the city. In the opening of the scene Aeneas looks down on the construction from a high vantage point, but by the end he looks up at the heights of the city. It is as if the walls have been raised while we look at the working Tyrians, so that at the end Aeneas must look up to see their *fastigia*.[27]

---

[26] Furthermore, as Leah Kronenberg points out to me, the Roman reader would be aware of further ironies: the *altae moenia Romae* that Aeneas' adventures will enable will one day lead to Carthage's walls coming down.

[27] A less optimistic reading of Aeneas' point of view in Book 1 might emphasize, as the anonymous reader of this volume notes, his *limited* mortal perspective: he is shrouded in mist, and misreads much of what he looks upon, most notoriously the images in Juno's temple.

The emphasis on the perspective attained by taking a view from a hill or, better yet, from Heaven itself is a reflex, I would argue, of the increased interest in geographic perspective that was a hallmark of the Augustan era, as Nicolet in particular has demonstrated.[28] While it is true that the view on action from a high spot is as old as the *teichoskopia* in *Iliad* 3, and equally true that the perspective-altering view from above becomes a staple of philosophical thought from Plato onward, there is also no doubt that the *topos* takes on added resonance in the Augustan age.[29] Part of this, of course, is the simple fact of Roman topography, and the importance of both the Palatine and the Capitoline hills.[30] There is also the increased importance of the tower retreat, as both the tower of Maecenas and Augustus' own "Syracuse" indicate.[31] But I would also connect Vergil's interest in the *topos* to the increased importance of what Lindheim (2010) has called the "mapping impulse" in the Augustan age. In this reading, the view from above gives the spectator a lie of the land akin to a map, and the power of topographical knowledge. In the *Aeneid* we see this most clearly, ironically enough, in Book 6, with the repeated overviews of the Underworld, and for this reason many scholars have wanted to see Vergil's Underworld as a reflection of the topography of Rome in particular, especially the Campus Martius.[32]

It is also telling that we see Augustus himself adopt the view from above twice on the shield in Book 8. In the battle of Actium scene, for example, Augustus sails in, "standing on the high stern, and his happy temples emit twin flames and his father's star appears over his head" (8.680–1: *stans celsa in puppi, geminas cui tempora flammas / laeta uomunt patriumque aperitur uertice sidus*). In a similar vein, Actian Apollo looks down (8.704–5: *cernens ... desuper*) from his promontory, while the heavily orientalized enemy turn their backs in fear below. Later, back in Rome, Augustus proceeds in stately fashion in his triumphal procession, then sits ensconced on the Palatine hill, on the threshold of Apollo's temple, receiving gifts from representatives of the conquered races below him. And in all this, art imitates reality, or the "reality" of the text, in that each of these scenes is

---

[28] In addition to Nicolet 1991, see Lindheim's summary of the "mapping impulse" in Augustan Rome (Lindheim 2010: 164–73).
[29] On the view from above, see Rutherford 1989: 155–61; Hadot 1995: 238–50; Williams 2012: 27–9 and 48. As a *topos* in epic in particular, see Purves 2010a: 35–6 and Lovatt 2013: 33–45 (on divine perspective) and 217–25 (on *teichoskopia*).
[30] Jenkyns 2013: 181–2 notes how the particulars of Roman topography made a nice pair with the philosophical *topos* of the view from above.
[31] On Augustus' Syracuse, see Gowers 2010; on the tower of Maecenas, see Colini 1979.
[32] See especially Kondratieff 2014: 167–79.

evoked in later moments in the epic: in Book 9, when Apollo looks down from his ethereal region (9.638–9: *aetheria ... plaga ... desuper*) and approves of Ascanius' first kill on the battlefield: "that's the way to the stars," he tells the young hero (9.641: *sic itur ad astra*).[33] And in Book 10 Aeneas will stand in the same position as Augustus on the shield (10.261: *stans celsa in puppi*), holding the shield no less: flame pours from Aeneas' head and from the golden shield, like comets or burning stars in the sky. Building high walls, or climbing a hill to look down below – these turn out to be waystations along the road to the ultimate destination for Aeneas, Augustus, *imperium Romanum*: heaven itself.

8.3 Conclusion: Augustan Movement

In some ways it is no great surprise that the *Aeneid* privileges up over down, and steady movement over disorderly movement. Vertical hierarchies, for example, are probably a cultural universal: many cultures build on hills (and not only for metaphorical reasons), many cultures literally elevate powerful individuals, and so on. Still, even within the world of the *Aeneid* itself we receive reminders that there are alternative models for the relationship of power and movement. The notorious description of Fama in Book 4 is a good example: she who "thrives on mobility and acquires strength by moving" (4.175: *mobilitate uiget uirisque adquirit eundo*). She moves fast and in every direction, with her head in the clouds and her feet on the ground simultaneously. In essence, the way in which her power is described confirms the more normal hierarchical power endorsed elsewhere in the poem. Hers is an alternative, chaotic, primordial sort of power, with a different paradigm of movement, less obviously hierarchical or ordered in terms of horizontal and vertical motion.[34] This is key: there is no reason, for instance, that the value paradigm in the poem couldn't privilege movement in every direction with all speed as *the* most powerful, most valued version of movement; by contrast, the controlled, directed movement up a hill or through a city might seem feeble by contrast. But it

---

[33] As one of the reviewers of this volume points out to me, Apollo's support of Ascanius does not prevent his errors in judgment (endorsing the expedition of Nisus and Euryalus, almost letting the Trojan camp be captured), perhaps an indication of his more limited mortal viewpoint. I shall have more to say about the way in which the *Aeneid* undercuts some of these vertical and horizontal hierarchies in the concluding section of this chapter.

[34] Cf. Hardie 1986: 273: "It is an essential feature of the personification of *Fama* that she expands to fill space. This expansion is presented on both the horizontal and the vertical axes." Note, too, that Fama's movement accords with the gendered contrast we examined earlier in the description of Amata's frenzy; on gendered movement, see Keith, Chapter 7 in this volume.

chooses not to, for the Augustan paradigm is different. Instead, something like Mercury's orderly approach down from Olympus, which immediately follows Fama's rage, is clearly the kind of movement invested with a positive value in the poem.[35] Famously the poem leaves unsettled the question of whether the hierarchical paradigm can actually withstand the violent forces that constantly threaten to upend it; but I will leave that particular thorny question aside for the moment.

Similarly, there are also other possible cultural models for dealing with chaos and disorder. There is little space for accommodating Bacchic revelry or dancing in the poem; being compared to a Bacchante dancing and raving in the woods is always an invidious comparison. Notice, too, how the poem treats the Phrygian origins of the cult of Magna Mater with such delicacy. The Augustan model for controlling movement is more about physical restraint, even confinement – think of Furor in chains in Book 1, for instance (an image which famously evoked a painting later housed in the Forum of Augustus).[36] Or think of the labyrinthine, but decidedly unchaotic, movements of the young Trojans performing the Lusus Troiae in Book 5: that is as positive a version of confused movement that the reader encounters in this poem, and the whole point of that ritual is the precision lurking beneath the "confusion." The Lusus Troiae represents the Trojan movement that Augustan Rome wants to resuscitate, not the chaotic dancing by self-castrating priests of the Magna Mater.[37]

On an individual scale, the manifestation of physical restraint is also advertised by the emperor's own body. As Fowler has shown (2007), the emperor's favorite maxim *festina lente* ("make haste slowly") is not a quaint aphorism, but an appeal for moderation at all levels: physical, ethical, and political. As such, a metaphor of movement serves to symbolize in physical terms the dominant ideology of the Augustan age.[38] Here again we should think of the role of movements chaotic and still, internal and external, in Neptune's calming of the waters in Book 1. But a similar emphasis on controlled movement is also notable in the visual iconography of the

---

[35] On the similarities and differences between Fama and Mercury in this scene, see Hardie 1986: 277–9. Hardie also notes that Fama is a counterpart to Jupiter (Hardie 2012: 94): "*Fama* is constantly on the move, a personification of uncontrollable metamorphosis, a chthonic thunderbolt rebellious against the proper wielder of the thunderbolt, Jupiter."
[36] On the relationship of art and confinement in the *Aeneid*, see Bartsch 1998.
[37] The "un-Roman" behavior of the *galli* is used to taunt the Trojans explicitly by Numanus Remulus (9.614–20) and implicitly by Iarbas (4.215: *semiuiro comitatu*) and Turnus (12.99: *semiviri Phrygis*). By contrast, Cybele is treated reverentially in the poem, and Wiseman goes so far as to argue that Vergil takes part in an "Augustan rehabilitation" of the goddess (Wiseman 1984: 127).
[38] On the importance of the motto to Augustus' image, see also Yavetz 1990: 34.

period, such as the Ara Pacis and the Prima Porta Augustus.[39] Augustan literature and art called attention to the conflation of physical and ethical propriety under the new regime, and the body of the leader and those of his family reflected and promoted the ideals of the age.

Many readers will by now have thought of ways in which the *Aeneid* also works hard to *disrupt* the vertical and horizontal hierarchies I've been discussing here, no more so than in the famously unsettling end of the poem. We might think of the ambiguities of the term *superbus* in the poem, for instance, and the fact that the man who looms above the humbled enemy at the end of the poem ends up aligned more with the forces of violent, disorderly motion than with Augustan self-control. Aeneas' deadly spear, for instance, flies like a black whirlwind (12.923) – like Amata-as-top, like the storm at the start of Book 1. Even the way Aeneas hesitates (12.940: *cunctantem*) suggests a kind of Augustan-level modest restraint that vanishes in a heat of rage in the last moment. Turnus' spirit flees, yes, and down below, but we know from Book 6 that the Underworld contains both Elysium and Tartarus; conversely, comparisons of Aeneas to figures such as Briareus (10.566) remind us that attempts at the stars can have hints of hubristic gigantomachy as well as triumphant victory.[40] To many readers, the poem's frequent attempts to align the imperial Augustan (or Roman) mission with the will of Jupiter comes across as a form of special pleading, as political claims about who has the right to claim power over the heavens.

The ideology of movement in the *Aeneid* is thus infused with the same tensions that countless scholars have raised about the poem and its relationship to its contemporary context. As a way out, we might read the ambiguities of movement at the end of the poem not as a particular stance on Augustan propaganda but as a symptom of the ambiguities of the revolution itself. Revolution, as the Paul Virilio quotation at the start of this chapter puts it, is all about movement: from the point of view of the revolutionaries it is about challenging authority through movement; from the perspective of the ruling party it is about controlling wayward motion. Yet the Augustan revolution was no ordinary revolution, and it generated

---

[39] The Tellus relief, like the first simile of the *Aeneid*, idealizes Augustan order by reference to a divinity in control of the wind and water. Compare, too, Zanker's reading of the acanthus vines on the Ara Pacis (1988: 180–1): "these symbols of the unrestrained growth of nature combine into a model of perfect order ... [which] reflects on the aesthetic level the almost fanatical preoccupation of the Augustan Age with law and order."

[40] For these points, and many other points in this paragraph, I am grateful to Leah Kronenberg.

much of its staying power, as it were, by emphasizing continuity as much as change. Emily Gowers puts the point well in a somewhat different context: "[The Augustan revolution] is a revolution characterized as a status quo, threatened only by the noise and ambitions of the disaffected."[41] The quotation draws our attention to the way in which terms such as "revolution" and "ambition" involve a kind of movement through space, or, in the case of status quo, the absence of movement – the still position of the body, and the body politic, restored to its proper place. Yet, as her quotation also emphasizes, the conservative aspect of the Augustan revolution emphasized the disorderly motion of the *losing* side; even a metaphor such as *res publica restituta* implies a restoration of something that has moved in a way it should not, setting the state back up as if it were a toppled statue or a ruined building. The precise meaning – or even existence – of that phrase has been controversial, but it is unquestionably true that Augustan ideology regularly appealed to metaphors of movement to justify the new arrangement.[42] Take, for example, the *aureus* issued by Cossus Cornelius Lentulus in 12 BCE, in which Augustus helps the personified Republic back onto her feet, so she can move forward again.[43]

Finally, the ideology of movement in the *Aeneid* sheds light, I would argue, on the experience of the space of Augustan Rome. If the *Aeneid* reflects contemporary ideology, whereby apologists of the Augustan Age claimed that the new *princeps* "replaced" disorderly movement with orderly movement, then walking through a peaceful city is the polar opposite of wandering lost at sea, or, as in Book 2, running scared through a besieged and falling city. Even in the descriptions of urban encounters within the *Aeneid* we see such a development: the confused and frightening encounters with Troy in Book 2 give way to Aeneas' tour of a pale imitation of the city in Book 3, which yields to Dido guiding Aeneas around a rising and independent Carthage in Book 4, which is itself "improved upon" by the tour of the future site of Rome in Book 8. Even on that site we have the older, chaotic experience of the city by Hercules and Cacus replaced by the future, calm experience of the city by Aeneas and Evander. If this is a paradigm of development over time, the Augustan reader knows how it will end (8.348: *aurea nunc, olim siluestribus horrida dumis*).

---

[41] Gowers 2012: 59.
[42] For the argument that the phrase was not in fact used by Augustan apologists, see Judge 1974.
[43] On the coin (*RIC* I² 413), see Zanker 1988: 91. Its authenticity, too, has been called into question: see Kuttner 1995: 249. For a recent defense, see Burnett and Oldman 2015: 92–5.

Strabo saw the point rather well: in his famous praise of the newly renovated Augustan city, the geographer captures the easy shift between physical and metaphorical in the new Augustan movement. Not only has Augustus restored order in the political realm, but his urban beautification has also freed the city up for easier transit by pedestrians and for athletic activities in the Campus Martius:

> καὶ γὰρ τὸ μέγεθος τοῦ πεδίου θαυμαστὸν ἅμα καὶ τὰς ἁρματοδρομίας καὶ τὴν ἄλλην ἱππασίαν ἀκώλυτον παρέχον τῷ τοσούτῳ πλήθει τῶν σφαίρᾳ καὶ κρίκῳ καὶ παλαίστρᾳ γυμναζομένων· καὶ τὰ περικείμενα ἔργα καὶ τὸ ἔδαφος ποάζον δι' ἔτους καὶ τῶν λόφων στεφάναι τῶν ὑπὲρ τοῦ ποταμοῦ μέχρι τοῦ ῥείθρου σκηνογραφικὴν ὄψιν ἐπιδεικνύμεναι δυσαπάλλακτον παρέχουσι τὴν θέαν. πλησίον δ' ἐστὶ τοῦ πεδίου τούτου καὶ ἄλλο πεδίον καὶ στοαὶ κύκλῳ παμπληθεῖς καὶ ἄλση καὶ θέατρα τρία καὶ ἀμφιθέατρον καὶ ναοὶ πολυτελεῖς καὶ συνεχεῖς ἀλλήλοις, ὡς πάρεργον ἂν δόξαιεν ἀποφαίνειν τὴν ἄλλην πόλιν. διόπερ ἱεροπρεπέστατον νομίσαντες τοῦτον τὸν τόπον καὶ τὰ τῶν ἐπιφανεστάτων μνήματα ἐνταῦθα κατεσκεύασαν ἀνδρῶν καὶ γυναικῶν. ἀξιολογώτατον δὲ τὸ Μαυσώλειον καλούμενον, ἐπὶ κρηπῖδος ὑψηλῆς λευκολίθου πρὸς τῷ ποταμῷ χῶμα μέγα, ἄχρι κορυφῆς τοῖς ἀειθαλέσι τῶν δένδρων συνηρεφές· ἐπ' ἄκρῳ μὲν οὖν εἰκών ἐστι χαλκῆ τοῦ Σεβαστοῦ Καίσαρος, ὑπὸ δὲ τῷ χώματι θῆκαί εἰσιν αὐτοῦ καὶ τῶν συγγενῶν καὶ οἰκείων, ὄπισθεν δὲ μέγα ἄλσος περιπάτους θαυμαστοὺς ἔχον. (Strabo 5.3.8)

> The size of the plain [sc. the Campus Martius] is marvellous, permitting chariot-races and other feats of horsemanship without impediment, and multitudes to exercise themselves at ball, in the circus and the palaestra. The structures which surround it, the turf covered with herbage all the year round, the summits of the hills beyond the Tiber, extending from its banks with panoramic effect, present a spectacle which the eye abandons with regret. Near to this plain is another surrounded with columns, sacred groves, three theatres, an amphitheatre, and superb temples in close contiguity to each other; and so magnificent, that it would seem idle to describe the rest of the city after it. For this cause the Romans, esteeming it as the most sacred place, have there erected funeral monuments to the most illustrious persons of either sex. The most remarkable of these is that designated as the Mausoleum, which consists of a mound of earth raised upon a high foundation of white marble, situated near the river, and covered to the top with evergreen shrubs. Upon the summit is a bronze statue of Augustus Caesar, and beneath the mound are the ashes of himself, his relatives, and friends. Behind is a large grove containing charming promenades.[44]

---

[44] Trans. Hamilton and Falconer 1854–7.

Elsewhere (5.3.7) Strabo even discusses the emperor's efforts to deal with the frequent collapse of dilapidated buildings, as if to give a physical analogy for Augustus' wholescale "shoring up" of the empire. Vergil's mythological paradigm simply provided the aetiology for Augustus' urban reforms. And notice, too, how Augustus wanted to be physically positioned for all time – at the top of his enormous mausoleum, watching the people walk below in "charming promenades." For all time, he looked down from above, not on the exoticized scurrying enemy he watched from the top of his ship at Actium, nor on the shackled prisoners he watched from the top of the Palatine in the aftermath of his triumph, but on Roman citizens taking a stroll – advertising, by their leisurely, controlled pace, the ideology of the *pax Augusta*.

CHAPTER 9

Roman and Carthaginian Journeys: Punic Pietas *in Naevius'* Bellum Punicum *and Plautus'* Poenulus

Thomas Biggs

Among the virtues that define Vergil's Aeneas, piety is the most significant. His *pietas*, consistently displayed toward his homes, both old and new, his family, and the gods, overcomes even the most difficult of journeys available to the epic hero, the voyage into the Underworld; as Anchises exclaims upon Aeneas' arrival in Dis, *uenisti tandem, tuaque expectata parenti / uicit iter durum pietas* (*Aen.* 6.687–8: "At last you have come, and your piety, awaited by your father, has conquered the harsh journey").[1] Yet Aeneas' journey to Italy also contains strong parallels to Dido's westward voyage to found a new home, as Keith discusses in this volume. Although Dido's characterization is marked by Vergil's well-noted ambivalence, her inherent opposition to Aeneas' Italian goals and her progressive adoption of positions that the poet characterizes as *impius* can easily lead a reader to see her actions as the inverse of Aenean *pietas*. From her founding of Carthage through the deceit of the cowhide to the fateful decision to abandon her steadfast celibacy after the death of Sychaeus, Dido's journey is one seemingly colored by *facta impia*.[2]

---

[1] Syson 2013: 88: "Aeneas' devoted remembrance of his father is powerful enough to flout the usual rules that govern life and death." Garrison 1992: 2: "This rhetorical question expresses the essential bond of the poem as a heroic virtue answerable to the demands of the voyage fiction: *pietas* conquers the journey." In *Fab.* 254, Hyginus includes Aeneas among *qui piissimi fuerunt*. Cf. Rogerson 2017: 3–4.

[2] Cf. e.g. *Aen.* 4.596: *infelix Dido, nunc te facta impia tangunt?* On the ambiguity and various possible readings of this phrase, see Casali 1999. Dido is, of course, pious when considered from different angles within the epic. It is important to clarify at the outset that refining or redefining our conception of *pietas* and its meaning in the *Aeneid*, as well as in the socio-cultural life of Rome at the end of the first century BCE, is not a goal of this chapter. For *pietas* generally, see Lee 1979: 17–19, 45; Monti 1981: *passim*; Garrison 1992; Galinsky 1996: 82, 86–8, 189, 204, 287; and, more recently, *VE* 3.1007–8. Syson 2013: 69: "Being really very good at *pietas*, as Aeneas and the Trojans are said to be, means being attentive to the acts, thoughts, and emotions that make people function fully as humans in society, according to Roman thought. It means remembering what one owes all the different people and gods to whom one is connected." Lee 1979: 17–18: "Virgil rightly called his hero the *pius* Aeneas, for *pietas*, at least from the generation before his own, had come to mean three-fold devotion to family, country, and gods."

In this chapter I will revisit the simplistic picture offered in the preceding paragraph and explore the curious fact that some of the central aspects of Vergil's *pius Aeneas* and his *pietas* were attributes of other Trojan and Carthaginian voyagers before the *Aeneid*. In a sense, this study is an archaeology of pre-Vergilian poetic *pietas*. The primary goal is to show how an essential virtue of Vergil's hero has a far more polyvalent and multicultural origin within Latin literary history. Additionally, in what follows I will construct some of the historical and cultural contexts that shaped the development of piety within the Trojans' epic journey during the Middle Republic. Methodologically, this chapter will compare several journeys in Roman texts and the ways they intersect in relation to *pietas* and the Trojan voyage, especially concerning Aphrodite, sacred sex, and the creation of new peoples. Not every connection will prove the result of direct influence, but the payoff of this comparative reading is substantial.

To conceive of travel's impact on characters and readers it is essential to consider how and why a journey is undertaken. In the shadow of the Punic Wars, *pietas* appeared in Roman literature as a cross-cultural quality that drove the epic journeys of Dido, Anchises, Aeneas, and Plautus' Carthaginian Hanno, even though these "pious" journeys ultimately led to or reflected trans-historical conflict between Carthage and Rome. Vergil's *Aeneid* helped enshrine the *pietas* of Aeneas as a collective Roman virtue, but how much of a role it played in Naevius' epic *Bellum Punicum* (late third century BCE) remains unexplored.[3] A significant fragment of the first Latin poem to depict the voyage of Aeneas connects Anchises and the Trojan journey directly with *pietas*.[4] Accordingly, in the first section of this chapter I analyze the relationship between Naevius' Trojans and earlier depictions of Dido's exilic journey in the Sicilian Greek historian Timaeus (*c.*345 BCE–*c.*250 BCE) and in Justin's epitome of the Augustan historian Pompeius Trogus (*c.* second–third centuries CE).[5] After showing that Dido's journey, along with its connections to *pietas*, may firmly predate and perhaps even underscore the contours of the Trojan and Roman journeys in the *Bellum Punicum*, the second section treats Punic piety diachronically by focusing on Plautus' *Poenulus*. While *Punica fides* (Carthaginian faith[lessness]) may have become a powerful stereotype, there are echoes of *Punica pietas* throughout a generally hostile and reductive Roman

---

[3] But see Barchiesi 1962. [4] *FPL* F 9.
[5] *BNJ* 566 F 82 (= Anonymi Paradoxographi, *De mulieribus* 6.215); Just. *Epit.* 18.4.1–6.8.

literary tradition.[6] The *Poenulus* highlights the *pietas* of Hanno the Carthaginian, a surprising ethical move in the wake of the Second Punic War. In fact, *pietas* guides Hanno's journey toward the (re)creation of home. I build on this aspect of the play to connect *pietas* and its role in Hanno's trans-Mediterranean journey in search of his lost daughters with the fragmentary glimpses of *pietas* in Naevius' "Aeneid" and in the pre-Vergilian treatments of the Dido legend. Through this analysis, I submit that Vergilian *pietas* is crafted from a complex tradition, wherein the virtue was not yet attributed solely (if at all) to Aeneas but was the hallmark of his father and, far more destabilizing, of the Romans' mythical and historical Carthaginian rivals.

Definitions of *pietas* vary widely, and the term's valence in Vergil is contested, but the texts brought to bear on its interpretation rarely stray outside of a small canon.[7] Nevertheless, the Dido of authors such as Timaeus is driven by a character-defining piety, one easily recognizable as the "Roman" virtue so essential to the identity of Vergil's later Aeneas. Carthaginian travelers such as Plautus' Hanno show that *pietas* enables voyages for the restoration of homeland and home among Dido's descendants. Thus, I argue, the underappreciated presence of *Punica pietas* in the various voyages of Carthaginian travelers adds further complexity to any reading of Vergil's depiction of the journeys underway in the *Aeneid*.

9.1 Naevius, Anchises, and the Pre-Vergilian *Pia Dido*

Gnaeus Naevius composed his epic *Bellum Punicum* soon after the First Punic War (264–241 BCE). Rome's first war with Carthage provided the subject matter for most of the epic, but at some point in the narrative a shift to the Trojan past occurred, and Aeneas' journey from Troy to Italy was recounted.[8] From the extant fragments it is possible to read of the

---

[6] On the stereotype, for which there is a massive bibliography, see e.g. Franko 1996; Palmer 1997; Starks 1999 and 2000; Prag 2006 and 2014. As Gildenhard notes after a brief discussion of pre-Vergilian Dido (Gildenhard 2012: 254), "some readers in antiquity resisted the allure of Virgil's poetry. And with a bit of sleuthing and rummaging around in the debris of literary history, we are still able to recover a Dido untainted by Virgil's lurid imagination."

[7] Lee 1979; Garrison 1992. Italian art and iconography suggest the presence of *pietas* in Aeneas' tale as early as the sixth–fifth centuries BCE, leading some to probe the precise point when the concept of *pius Aeneas* took its well-known Roman shape; see e.g. Galinsky 1969a. The standard passages for understanding pre-Vergilian *pietas* include Cat. 76; Lucr. 5.1198–1203; Cic. *Nat. D.* 1.41.115; Cic. *Planc.* 35.80; Cic. *Rep.* 6.15.15.

[8] On the structure of the epic, often thought to transition from "historic" to "mythic" time via an ekphrastic flashback, see discussion throughout the scholarship: e.g. Rowell 1947; Barchiesi 1962; Feeney 1991; Dufallo 2013. Rowell 1947 explores the idea of a "story within a story," a conception

Trojans' flight from the city, as well as their exploits along the way to Italy.[9] The traveling Trojans' interactions with humans will receive treatment later; for now it is their interactions with the divine that concern us. A substantial fragment preserves the earliest extant depiction of the role of *pietas* in the Trojan journey, potentially the earliest Latin literary use of *pietas* in any text:

> senex fretus pietati deum adlocutus
> summi deum regis fratrem Neptunum
> regnatorem marum
>
> (*FPL* F 9)
>
> The old man depending on *pietas* called upon the god,
> Neptune, the brother of the highest king of the gods,
> the ruler of the seas

What strikes a post-Vergilian reader is neither that *pietas* is present in the epic, nor that the need to call upon the god of the sea would receive such explicit treatment during a maritime voyage. The surprise is that it is a *senex* defined by his *pietas*, not Aeneas.[10] There is general agreement that this fragment depicts Anchises, who is known to have made it to Italy in several pre-Vergilian versions of the narrative.[11] With *pater Anchises* along for the entire ride and in possession of prophetic powers only hinted at in Vergil's epic,[12] it appears that Aeneas was himself not yet imbued with all of the characteristics we are conditioned to expect from later depictions. In fact, Anchises' early death in Vergil's telling may be the factor that allows

---

with wide acceptance, at least in a general form; its contours were questioned by Mariotti 1955 and Barchiesi 1962. See Clauss 2010 for a recent wide-ranging discussion and the treatment in Feeney 2016.

[9] Cf. e.g. *FPL* 5: *amborum uxores / noctu Troiad exibant capitibus opertis, / flentes ambae, abeuntes lacrimis cum multis* ("Both of their wives were departing from Troy at night with their heads covered, both crying, leaving with many tears"). *FPL* F 6: *eorum sectam sequuntur multi mortales / multi alii e Troia strenui viri / ubi foras cum auro illi<n>c exibant* ("Many mortals follow their path, many other vigorous men from Troy, when with gold they were departing out through the doors").

[10] In the *Aeneid*, *pius* is employed as a heroic epithet (or simply as an adjective) only for Aeneas, outside of 3.75, where it is applied to Apollo, who is there called *arquitenens*. It is perhaps worth noting that this compound adjective is rather rare and first appears in extant Latin in a description of Apollo from Naevius' *Bellum Punicum*: *Prima incedit Cereris Proserpina puer* (*FPL* F 22); *dein pollens sagittis inclutus arquitenens / sanctus Iove prognatus Putius Apollo* (*FPL* F 24). See Fratantuono's tabulation of *pietas* and discussion at *VE* 3.1007: "In Virgil, *pietas* is a characteristic virtue of Aeneas (A. 1.10, 1.220, 1.305, 1.545, 3.42, 3.480, 4.393, 5.26, 5.286, 5.418, 5.685, 6.9, 6.176, 6.232, 6.403, 6.405, 6.688, 6.769, 7.5, 8.84, 9.255, 10.591, 10.783, 11.170, 11.292, 12.175, 12.311), who twice asserts his own piety (A. 1.378, 10.826)."

[11] See Strzelecki 1964: 450 ff.; Horsfall 1990: 143. For explicit verbal engagement with Anchises' *pietas* in the *Aeneid*, see *Aen*. 2.690, 3.266.

[12] See *FPL* F 4.

for certain qualities to transfer to Aeneas as he becomes the *pater* of the expedition.[13] Aside from these largely obscure features, it is clear from the fragment that *pietas* is a quality that defines Anchises and assists in the Trojan journey. But how can we begin to understand the resonance and implications of *pietas* in the epic when it is the first time Aeneas' voyage appeared in Latin literature?

The opposite of *pietas* in early Latin epic can shed some light on the matter. In the *Odusia* of Livius Andronicus, Naevius' only Latin epic predecessor, the Cyclops Polyphemus is described as impious (*FPL* F 39): *cum socios nostros Ciclops impius mandisset* ("When the impious Cyclops had devoured my companions").[14] Polyphemus, the stereotypical breaker of the bonds of hospitality and famous example of the monstrous periphery of the human-centric world of the *nostoi*, is characterized by his embodiment of impiety, the opposite of Naevius' Anchises.[15] When these fragments are compared, the *pietas* of Anchises and the expedition of the Trojans can be understood in contrast to the *impietas* of a figure like Andronicus' Polyphemus. Although it is perhaps too tenuous to suggest that Anchises' prayer to Neptune in the fragment would evoke the baneful relationship between Poseidon and Odysseus instigated by the latter's blinding of his son Polyphemus, it is not beyond the interpretive possibilities allowed by these ever-so-scanty lines. Nor is it likely to be a coincidence that Vergil's Neptune, as he calms the seas, is compared to a Roman statesman who is similarly defined by his *pietas* and paternal role in quelling the masses (*Aen.* 1.54–6):[16] *tum,* **pietate grauem** *ac meritis si forte virum quem / conspexere, silent arrectisque auribus astant* ("then, if they have caught sight of some man who carries weight because of his public devotion and service, they stand silent, their ears ready to listen").[17]

---

[13] Horsfall 1990; Lee 1979.

[14] Due to the scansion of the line, many scholars do not think this exact fragment preserves Andronicus' poem. Cf. Wigodsky 1972: 17–18 for discussion of the proposal that this line is from a second-century BCE hexameter *Odusia*. Since the work will have played a role in the second-century receptions of these epic texts, I consider the line fair for interpretation, even if it may not reflect the diction of the Andronican original.

[15] On Polyphemus' Homeric characterization, see Bakker, Chapter 2 in this volume.

[16] See O'Sullivan's treatment of the simile in this volume (Chapter 8, p. 155–6, 160, 166 n. 39). Cf. Galinsky 1996: 20–1, 239. Consider Fratantuono at *VE* 1007: "Venus also complains to Neptune that Juno has no *pietas* that might restrain her from harassing the Trojans (*A*. 5.783)." We must also recall the ambiguity of Vergil's *pius Anchises*; often his *pietas* can be read as a factor that leads to misinterpretation and misdirection.

[17] Trans. Galinsky 1996: 21.

A brief genealogical fragment of Ennius' *Annales* further confirms that the *Bellum Punicum*'s *senex* was likely Anchises and that *pietas* was a defining characteristic:

> Assaraco natus Capys optimus isque pium ex se
> Anchisen generat
> (Sk. *Ann.* 28–9 = Serv. Dan. ad *G.* 3.35)
>
> Capys the best was the son of Assaracus, and he bore pious Anchises

Although very little information is conveyed here, the verses define Ennius' Anchises through his status as *pius*.[18] Aeneas may even speak these lines, containing, as Barchiesi puts it, "the credentials presented by the Ennian Aeneas to the king of Alba Longa."[19] If so, Aeneas is the one who refers to his father with the epithet *pius*, a rather curious matter. Skutsch is certainly too forceful in his influential condemnation of the idea that *pietas* may have primarily defined Anchises in the Latin tradition before Vergil: "The idea that Aeneas derives his standing attribute from his father cannot be entertained."[20] In the most basic terms, however, what we see in Naevius and Ennius is the marked significance of piety for Anchises and, so too, for the Trojans' journey to Italy.[21] Their relationships with the gods and their encounters with *impius* figures such as Polyphemus who dot the landscape of the epic journey are defined in early Roman epic by the presence of *pietas*.

In the *Bellum Punicum*, however, it is not only the Trojans who journey, but also the Romans and Carthaginians of the First Punic War who take to the sea in a cataclysmic conflict. Depictions of the proto-Roman Trojans at sea and reliant on *pietas* to achieve their *nostos* would easily color the reader's experience of Naevius' Roman marines as they leave Italy's shores behind for the first time.[22] To understand how

---

[18] Genealogy is a clear *locus* for variation in the Trojan legend. Cf. Serv. Dan. ad *Aen.* 1.273.
[19] Barchiesi 1997: 173 n. 55. He here follows suggestions found in Skutsch 1985.
[20] Skutsch 1985: ad 1.28.
[21] For the Trojans as pious in the *Aeneid*, cf. VE 3.1007: "Ilioneus asserts to Dido that the Trojan race is pious (*A.* 1.526), a sentiment the omniscient narrator shares (*A.* 7.21)."
[22] The battering of the Trojans upon the waves finds clear parallels in the Romans' own destructive losses on the main; cf. Leigh 2010; Dunsch 2015. For the Trojans and the storm in Naevius, see Macrob. *Sat.* 4.2.31 and Serv. ad *Aen.* 1.198. For Odysseus and the storm in Andronicus' *Odusia*, see *FPL* F 30: *igitur demum Ulixi cor frixit prae pavore* (cf. *Aen.* 1.92: *exemplo Aeneae solvuntur frigore membra*). Consider Leigh 2010: "[At this time] that Roman landsman had, in fact, taken to the sea, and had done so in quite unprecedented numbers. He now knew what it was to be an Odysseus, to be an Aeneas trapped in a storm" (p. 278:); "... for those who have seen the cruel sea at first hand, the epic storm is more than just a stock trope of the poets" (p. 276). "Maritime Moment" is Leigh's phrase.

pervasive and resonant the impact of this "Maritime Moment" would have been, one can consult the scale of Roman losses at sea during the war as reported later by Polybius (1.63.4–6). With the fate of so many at stake, the perspective of a novice Roman sailor (from ship to shore) was surely defined by an anxious wavering between home and away.[23] We can locate explicit evidence that Roman soldiers in the *Bellum Punicum* were connected with notions of maritime trauma and *nostos* in the fifth book of the epic:

> seseque ei perire mauolunt ibidem
> quam cum stupro **redire** ad suos popularis
> (*FPL* F 50)
>
> They prefer to die there and then
> rather than **to return home** to their people in shame
>
> sin illos deserant fortissumos uiros,
> magnum stuprum populo fieri **per gentis**
> (*FPL* F 51)
>
> If they should forsake the bravest men,
> there would be great shame for the people throughout the
>   nations of the world

This desire for an honorable return home in the face of adversity contains a glance back toward Italy, toward Rome and its cultural values while out on the waves and campaigning on Sicily. It is also construed in language and tone reminiscent of the Odyssean as defined by Andronicus' *Odusia*:[24]

> partim **errant**, nequinont Graeciam **redire**[25]
> (*FPL* F 11)
>
> some wander astray, they are unable to return home to Greece

Although it is Greeks who experience *errationes* and are unable to achieve their *nostos*, to return home to Greece, readers of Andronicus' epic would have been able to map these terms onto their own recent experience in the First Punic War. It is this type of allegorical connection that Naevius exploits in

---

[23] See Malkin 2011: 48.
[24] See the later Catullan engagement with a similar theme and its language (Cat. 101.1–2): "Conveyed through many nations (*multas per gentes*) and through many seas, I am come to these miserable funeral rites, my brother."
[25] Cf. e.g. Vitr. *De arch.* 7.5.2, where popular Homeric wall paintings are discussed, including Odysseus' *errationes per topia*. See also O'Sullivan, Chapter 8 in this volume (On *nostos* as "return to Greece," see Baragwanath, Chapter 6 in this volume (p. 109).

defining Roman experience as parallel to the *nostos* of Aeneas.[26] Their journey to Sicily, the land of the *impius Cyclops* and the Carthaginian foe, is a voyage analogous to that of the Trojans. To view Roman travel, suffering, and victory in the mythic light introduced by the narration of the Trojan tale is surely a feature of the epic that its unique, if elusive, structure works to enact.

What of Rome's enemies in the *Bellum Punicum*? Little of the epic's depiction of the Carthaginians survives,[27] but we are informed of one significant figure's presence: Dido. A direct reference to Dido is found in Servius (ad *Aen.* 4.9 FPL F17): *Anna Soror cuius filiae fuerint Anna et Dido, Naeuius dicit* "The sister Anna, whose daughters were Anna and Dido, as Naeuius states". Further evidence comes from Servius in relation to the sea-storm and Aeneas' famous speech at *Aen.* 1.198, but even this and Macrobius' similar *testimonium* only serve to suggest that a Libyan episode occurred in the epic. There is also a highly controversial fragment that may support Dido's role (*FPL* F 20): *blande et docte percontat, Aenea quo pacto / Troiam urbem liquerit*... ("Gently and learnedly she/he asks, how Aeneas left from the city of Troy..."). Many have identified Dido as the subject of *percontat*, whereby she performs the banquet scene Q&A well known from Homer's *Odyssey* and attested within the *Odusia* of Naevius' epic predecessor.[28] There are verbal parallels with the *Aeneid* that lend support to this reading, but, for example, Livy's depiction of Latinus' questioning of the newly arrived Trojans also contains similar connections.[29] In the end, this fragment only serves to confirm that Aeneas was questioned during the journey and may have engaged in speech. While any suggestions of Dido's exact role in the *Bellum Punicum* are based on slender evidence, the very fact that we can be certain she was mentioned in the poem still demands attention.[30] If the Trojans and their pious adventure

---

[26] Feeney 2016: 59: "Most strikingly, the disparate fates and homecomings of Homer's heroes are focalized through the imperial view of the Roman state, so that their longed-for destination becomes 'Greece,' a geopolitical concept that was not available to them or to their original poet."

[27] Ennius' *Annales* contains more preserved fragments in this regard, many focused on negative characterizations: see Biggs 2017: 358. See discussion and tabulation in Elliott 2014.

[28] *FPL* F 7: *tuque mihi narrato omnia disertim* ("and you relate everything to me clearly"); *FPL* F 17: *simul ac dacrimas de ore noegeo detersit* ("at once he wiped the tears from his face with his cloak"). The latter fragment likely comes from the Phaeacian banquet, where tales of Troy prompt Odysseus to grieve. Telemachus does the same at Hom. *Od.* 8.87–8, so this fragment of the *Odusia* could depict him.

[29] Cf. Horsfall 1990: 140–1. Livy 1.1.3: *alii, cum instructae acies constitissent, priusquam signa canerent processisse Latinum inter primores ducemque aduenarum euocasse ad conloquium;* **percontatum** *deinde qui mortales essent, unde aut* **quo casu** *profecti domo quidue quaerentes in agrum Laurentinum exissent.*

[30] See Feeney 1991: 109: "It is virtually impossible to accept that Naevius described a failed love-affair between Aeneas and Dido, for the universal testimony to Vergil's invention of the story is hardly to

color the Romans of the First Punic War, how do we read Dido? How do we read the Carthaginians? Some traction is afforded by reading Naevius' Dido in relation to her Latin epic predecessors, the *Odusia*'s Circe and Calypso, figures whose delaying and confrontational relationships with the journeying male hero are somewhat better understood by scholars (e.g. Dido as a Punic Circe).[31] But to answer these questions in terms of *pietas*, we will need to turn to the epic journeys not of Anchises, Aeneas, and the Trojans, but of Dido and some of her Carthaginian descendants.[32]

Before the late third century witnessed a boom in Latin literature and the attendant capacity for self-presentation that this entailed, the Roman past was an object of Greek historiographical interest. Rome would ultimately gain its "own" Greek historian in Polybius, but in the fourth and third centuries BCE it was the Sicilian Timaeus who first treated Rome as a significant historical player in its own right.[33] And it is Timaeus' depiction of the history of Rome's great enemy Carthage that is of interest to our present line of inquiry. In an anonymous text on remarkable queens (*Anonymous Tractatus de Mulieribus*), a striking passage is partially preserved:[34]

> Theiosso. Timaeus tells us that she was called Elissa in the Phoenician language. She was the sister of Pygmalion, the king of Tyre. Timaeus says that she founded Carthage in Libya (τὴν Καρχηδόνα τὴν ἐν Λιβύῃ κτισθῆναι). For when her husband was killed by Pygmalion, she put all her riches on a ship and fled (ἔφευγε) with some fellow citizens. And after she had suffered much (πολλὰ κακοπαθήσασα), she arrived in Libya, and she was called Deido by the Libyans in their native language because of her travels (καὶ ὑπὸ τῶν Λιβύων διὰ τὴν πολλὴν αὐτῆς πλάνην Δειδὼ προσηγορεύθη ἐπιχωρίως). After the foundation of the aforementioned city, the king of the Libyans wanted to marry her, which she refused. Because she was forced by her own citizens, she pretended to perform a rite to absolve her of a vow: she built an enormous pyre close to her house and lit it. Then she threw herself from her palace into the fire. (*FGrH* 566 F82)

For Timaeus, the story of Dido is similar to Odysseus' fate in the *Odyssey* and Aeneas' journey as shaped in the Roman tradition. Forced to flee her

---

be circumvented." See Barchiesi 1962: 479; Horsfall 1990: 138–44; Jahn 2007: esp. 68. Goldberg 1995: 54 is skeptical of the episode, but cf. Goldberg 2005: 35.

[31] Barchiesi 1962: 479. Consider the remarks in West's review of Rudd (West 1978): "This is a Roman Odyssey and Dido is Circe with a difference."

[32] For a discussion of the importance of gender for Dido and Aeneas' respective journeys, see Keith, Chapter 7 in this volume.

[33] In particular during the era of the Pyrrhic Wars; see Hartog 2001: 164. On Timaeus, see Baron 2013.

[34] After Haegemans trans. (2000: 279). See also Gera 1997: esp. 5–64 on the text in general; Kowalski 1929. On Timaeus in this regard, see Hornblower 1981; Pearson 1987; Baron 2013: 224, 258.

homeland (ἔφευγε) with a small band of companions, she suffers much on the way to Libya (πολλὰ κακοπαθήσασα), the site of her ktistic destiny. Ascribed by Timaeus to the native Libyans, the Phoenician Elissa is renamed Deido (Dido) since in their language the word means to wander/flee/travel.[35] Dido, then, is the "wanderer" incarnate, a figure whose travails embody the very essence of the ancient journey. While a shocking act of familial *impiety* prompted the voyage, it is the *pietas* to come that resonates most strongly with later descriptions of her encounter with Aeneas.[36] Dido's display of spousal fidelity, brought on by the demand that she remarry, leads to her suicide. While her death in the tradition is most strongly shaped by its later casting as a response to Aeneas' departure – along with the moment of her famous Vergilian curse of the Punic Wars to come – in Timaeus' telling it is a marked display of *pietas* to her husband and the oaths she had made.[37] As Haegemans remarks, "several motives for her suicide have been suggested, one of which was definitely faithfulness to her husband. Typical Roman virtues as piety, loyalty, duty, and devotion could be claimed by the Carthaginians for their founder."[38]

Dido's journey and her own life's *finis* lend her a martyr-like character, which perhaps unsurprisingly made her a symbol within later Christian literature and conceptions of the *univira*.[39] What we must note presently, however, is the presence of this particular narrative before the emergence of a defined Latin literary culture and a strongly canonized Roman perspective on Carthage and its founder. In fact, several scholars believe that Timaeus here preserves Phoenician sources, hence providing us with a momentary glimpse of the view from Tyre, perhaps even the view from

---

[35] Gera 1997: 138–9; Haegemans 2000: 284, 290: "Names that contain a reference to the world of the gods, like Theiosso or Elissa, are particularly fitting for a person with a divine mission, just as the name Dido seems to be connected with her journey." Serv. ad *Aen.* 1.340 also provides an exploration of the name. See Keith, Chapter 7 in this volume.

[36] Horsfall notes the impiety at the origin of Dido's voyage, but reads it as a general smear on the Carthaginians and, so too, as a feature that contrasts sharply with the origin of the Trojan journey, an opposition I find wanting; we must recall that deception is what prompts the fall of Troy, that of Paris, and that of the Greeks (1990: 134–5). If certain obscure variants are followed, Aeneas may even have sold the city out for his own survival (and gold), or exploited his ties of friendship with certain Greeks.

[37] Horsfall 1990 focuses on the negative elements of Timaeus' version, yet I follow Haegemans 2000 in finding the positive characteristics a bit more resonant. On the Vergilian Dido's curse and *pietas* see Syson 2013: 39: "Dido's immortal *fama*, for instance, is partly constituted through her condemnation of Aeneas' failure in *pietas*, which she expresses in her prophetic curse of Aeneas and his descendants."

[38] Haegemans 2000: 289. Cf. Baron 2013: 224. Desmond 1994: 24: "Even in this synopsis, Dido is a heroic figure; her suicide is an act of defiance that testifies to the nobility of her nature."

[39] See Lord 1969 on the "chaste Dido" tradition; Horsfall 1990: 138; Hexter 1992: 340.

Carthage.⁴⁰ When authors such as Naevius took up the task of shaping the lives of Aeneas and, perhaps, Dido, at least one characterization of the queen already existed that is in many ways antithetical to a depiction of her as Rome's impious proto-enemy.

There are, of course, aspects of Timaeus' tale that display a particular penchant on Dido's part for trickery and deception. While her slyness is levied for the good of her people and the preservation of her marital honor, the rumblings of stereotypes against the Phoenicians, well known since Homer (e.g. *Od.* 14.288–97), and of those later cast at the Carthaginians can be felt (*Punica fides* included), even if they are not activated to serve a fully negative characterization.⁴¹ Fortunately, this short paraphrase of Timaeus is not the only surviving text that preserves pre-Vergilian depictions of Dido. If we turn to a later author who is a close contemporary of Vergil and representative of a tradition built upon variants of the Dido legend, further light can be shed on Carthage's first ruler before we turn to her descendants in Plautus' *Poenulus*.

Justin's *Epitome* of Pompeius Trogus devotes several sections of Book 18 to the origins of Carthage, with significant focus given to Dido, her journey, and the founding of the city (Just. *Epit.* 18.4.1–6.8).⁴² Since the text survives only in Justin's third- or fourth-century *Epitome*, it is impossible to be sure how many features reflect the emphasis of the Augustan original and the various earlier traditions it preserved. Nevertheless, the marked focus on relevant themes throughout several sections is a strong indication that Trogus viewed Dido in a somewhat ambivalent, if not occasionally positive, light, especially concerning concepts related to her *pietas*.⁴³

---

[40] A view based largely on Polybius and testimony concerning Menander of Ephesus. *FGrH* T19 F7 (= Polybius 12.28–29a). Gera 1997: 127 n. 6; Haegemans 2000: 287, 290; Baron 2013: 224. Dido's departure from Tyre is recorded by Menander of Ephesus, who apparently quotes from the "Tyrian Annals" (Gera 1997: 130). Hexter 1992: 378 n. 102 points to similarities between Isis' story and that of Dido, while Gera 1997 also shows connections with the Egyptian Nitocris. Cf. also Sommer 2014.

[41] For Gera, the emphasis on the queen's riches in the tradition is probably related to the avarice or love of luxury ancient writers often attribute to the Carthaginians and Phoenicians. As she notes, Timaeus himself elsewhere speaks of greedy Carthaginians (1997: 131): *FGrH* 566 F106 (= Diodorus 13.108.4). On *Punica fides*, Horsfall 1990: esp. 134; Prandi 1979.

[42] Translation throughout is after Yardley 1994 (modified slightly). On Trogus, see Yardley 2003 and esp. the treatment in Yarrow 2006; Budin 2008: 236–9. Other attested depictions of Dido before Vergil (all lost) notably included that of Varro, who is remembered for his apparent decision to have Aeneas and Anna engage in a love affair, correcting the version perhaps implied by the chronological play attendant upon Dido appearing in Naevius (traditionally Carthage was founded many years after the Trojan war). Cf. Horsfall 1990: 141–2.

[43] I disagree with Haegemans' largely negative reading of Trogus' Dido (Haegemans 2000: 288). Gera 1997 also focuses on the negative valence of Trogus' telling.

Upon the ascent of young Pygmalion to the throne, Elissa (Dido) marries her rich uncle Acerbas. Because of Pygmalion's lust for money, this marriage was not to last. As Trogus puts it (18.4.7): "This excited Pygmalion who, in total disregard of the laws of humanity, put to death the man who was both his uncle and brother-in-law, with no thought for family obligations (*sine respectu **pietatis***)." This clear act of impiety prompts Elissa, under the shadow of complacency, to assemble a band of willing exiles opposed to his rule – an outcome achieved by dissembling and secrecy. Elissa here employs deception, but such tools are surely what remain for her after the impious actions of her brother and the impending threat of death. Following a ruse that allows Acerbas' wealth to be spirited away with the travelers, they set sail toward the west.

One of their most striking layovers during the journey to Libya is on Cyprus, which provides an important episode for my reading of Plautus' *Poenulus* later in this chapter. On Cyprus, the priest of Jupiter with his wife and children offer themselves as companions for the Tyrian voyage. Moreover, about eighty daughters of the Cypriots are taken on board so that the band of exiles – clearly stated to be mainly male – might have wives and their new city a future. This quasi-"Rape of the Sabine women" is shaped by the famous tale of Romulus, as well as other notable bride-snatchings from authors such as Herodotus (see *Histories* 1.1), but it is the particulars of these young women's plight that deserve our attention.[44] Trogus recounts (18.5.4): "It was a custom in Cyprus to send young girls down to the sea-shore on specific days before their marriage to earn money for their dowry by prostitution, and to offer Venus libations for the preservation of their virtue in the future." The sacred sexual activity of these young women, conducted under the aegis of Venus (patroness of Cyprus), is cut short by Dido's intervention.[45] She, the proto-Carthaginian traveler, appropriates the fertility and chastity of the young women for her own people, redirecting them to her city's future. While this may seem a detail redolent of the aetiological bent of recherché Hellenistic reporting or the antiquarian impulse of Trogus' day, there is something else to this episode and its focus on sacred sex, Venus, preserved virginity, and the fate of Carthage. These very themes – specifically the

---

[44] See Budin 2008: 238 for brief discussion of these parallels and bibliography. See the interesting comparison of the lives of Romulus and Dido at Sommer 2014: 167–9.
[45] Budin 2008: 239 offers a rather different translation of this passage aligned with her view that "sacred prostitution" does not exist in Classical antiquity as such.

rescue of daughters of Carthage from prostitution in honor of Venus – inform the plot of Plautus' *Poenulus*, where the *pius* Hanno displays his *pietas* by performing a nearly identical deed of last-minute virginal salvation in the creation (or recreation) of family and home. I discuss below the connections between these plotlines and their implications.

We must also briefly note that prostitution and the cult of Aphrodite became components of the Trojan journey at some point before it was recounted by Dionysius of Halicarnassus around the same time Trogus composed his work. Several times throughout *Ant. Rom.* 1.49–53 the Trojans found temples to Aphrodite, highlighting Aeneas' (and thus the later Romans') descent from the goddess, but also marking her as an omnipresent deity during the journey. Although she does not actively guide and protect the Trojans as they travel, it is clear from their actions that she is viewed as central to their success. Indeed, at 1.50.1 they dedicate temples to her at Actium and on Cyprus, introducing a competing sacral structure to the Cypriot landscape already defined by the famous temple Dido had visited (in certain chronologies) only a few years earlier. At 1.51.3 a shrine to Aphrodite is dedicated at Ambracia close to a hero-shrine of Aeneas. Dionysius tells us that priestesses called *amphipoloi*, who may even evoke the institution of sacred sex workers, attended the cult statue of Aphrodite in this shrine.[46] If so, Aeneas and the Trojans are recorded creating a ritual site for Venus and perhaps establishing the role of something akin to prostitution in her cult while on their journey west. Conversely, Dido frees young Cypriot girls from sacred sexual acts and establishes them as the first female Carthaginians – a pointed contrast. Several temples later, the Trojans complete their pre-peninsular adventures with the dedication of an altar built by Aeneas for Aphrodite Aeneias at Eryx (1.53.1), thus tying together the most significant of the goddess' sites for the narratives in this chapter; Eryx will soon emerge as key for Plautus' play, for female sexual acts tied to the goddess, and for the cultural interactions of Carthage and Rome.

While Aeneas continues on to Italy at this point in Dionysius' narrative, Dido's journey takes her to North Africa. And back in Trogus' account, after arriving in Libya with their new female companions Dido and the Phoenicians acquire land (through the famous deception of the cowhide) and found Carthage. Things appear to be going smoothly for the new western *oikistes*, whose journey in flight has achieved a new *nostos*; but

---

[46] On the potential ambiguity of the title in other resonant contexts, see Cyrino 2010: 43.

a storm is brewing in the hinterland (18.6.1): "Successful enterprises brought material prosperity to Carthage. Then Hiarbas, king of the Maxitani, summoned ten of the leading Carthaginians and asked for Elissa's hand in marriage, threatening war if they refused." Hiarbus (Iarbas) is known mainly from his role in the *Aeneid*, where he is the paradigmatic spurned suitor. Nevertheless, the differences between Trogus and Vergil are the most telling. Dido will commit suicide in each version, and her actions are similarly prompted by the doings of men. Yet for Trogus it is the specter of infidelity to her former husband, the prospect of a new marriage and the dishonor of Acerbas, that leads her to end her life:

> Caught in this trap, Elissa long called out the name of her husband, Acerbas, with streaming tears and sorrowful lamentation, finally replying that she would go where her destiny and that of her city called her. To carry out this undertaking she set aside a period of three months. She built a pyre on the outskirts of the city and sacrificed many animals, as if to placate the spirit of her dead husband and send him offerings before her marriage. Then, taking a sword, she mounted the pyre. She looked back at her people and declared that she was departing to join a husband, just as they had directed, and ended her life with the sword. As long as Carthage remained unconquered, Elissa was worshiped as a goddess. (18.6.5–8)

In this telling, Dido's suicide, though couched in deception, is a poignant act and strong symbol of *pietas* preserved. The Phoenician traveler's journey ends not in happy homecoming through the foundation of a new city and the creation of a future with an imperial destiny, but through death marked by devotion to her impiously slain husband.[47] Dido's voyage was prompted by the rending apart of family and home *sine respectu pietatis*, and it is the prospect of dishonoring the shadow and sustained memory of that now severed relationship, a prospect presented as her incipient new home takes shape, that proves too much for her. This Dido is something different than Vergil's tragic, elegiac, maenadic, and, at times, intractable obstacle. The female delayers and hurdles of the Odyssean, male-driven journey and the magical and seductive resonance of a Medea make up many of the models for the *Aeneid*'s Carthaginian queen; for the version of Dido's tale in Justin's account the gender relations are reversed. Men and their often sexualized and appropriative actions shape and sunder Dido's voyage and life, which in large part is preserved and guided, so long as it is, by *pietas*.

---

[47] For a different view on this matter, cf. Gera 1997: 135.

9.2 Plautus' *Pius Poenulus*

Among Dido's Carthaginian descendants, one man and his lost family shed the most light on the curious concept of *Punica pietas* in the Roman cultural imaginary. Naevius' Dido provides us with little to grasp, but the conjunction of *pietas* and travel in the epic may connect with the wandering Dido seen in Timaeus and, later, in Justin's Trogus. These layers complicate any simple view of Dido as a character modeled primarily on Circe or Calypso, one occasionally reduced to serve simply as a roadblock on the way west. Admittedly, we cannot know what influence or resonance, if any, the preexisting Greek and perhaps Phoenician versions of a pious Dido had on the shaping of the Aeneas legend, Trojan *pietas*, and Dido's own role in Naevius' poem, but it is not long after his composition of that foundational epic that another Roman author tackles some highly germane themes in a very different genre.

Plautus' *Poenulus*, like many Greek and Roman comedies – not to mention the Greek novel – centers on a plot driven by enforced travel and the distance between home and away.[48] Journeys across the high seas, snatchings by pirates, and voyages in search of one's beloved permeate both of these genres, and the *Poenulus* is no exception. The play, likely performed around 189 BCE, emerges in the aftermath of the Second Punic War, in the years immediately following Rome's campaigns in Aetolia.[49] Set in Aetolian Calydon, although infused with the cultural forces of the Roman world, the play's four main characters are Carthaginian by birth. This, then, is a play driven by "foreigners" in a "foreign" setting. Agorastocles, the youth in love, and the sisters Adelphasium and Anterastilus were all, as children, abducted from Carthage by pirates and taken across the seas to Greece. A pimp now owns the girls but, as the play suggests, they have yet to lose their virginity to a client. Apart from the girls, Agorastocles fares well in his new Calydonian life; he was adopted by the guest-friend and cousin of Hanno, the girls' father and the play's main *Poenus*. Much of our present interest in the play concerns Hanno, whose arrival in Calydon after years of searching for his daughters contains a telling mixture of themes central to understanding *pietas* and the journey.

---

[48] See Montiglio, Chapter 5 in this volume.
[49] Cf. De Melo 2012: 13. While De Melo's general dating is likely correct, I disagree concerning the inability of the play to be performed closer to the Second Punic War and the notion that the years between victory and performance would have lessened the social impact of Carthage on stage. For Nobilior's Aetolian campaigns and the play, see Fantham 2004: 237.

It is in the prologue that we first hear of Hanno's plight and, in particular, of his ongoing quest to restore his broken home back in Carthage:

> sed pater illarum Poenus, postquam eas perdidit,
> mari te\<rraque\> usquequaque
> quaeritat.
> ubi quamque in urbem est ingressus, ilico
> omnis meretrices, ubi quisque habitant, inuenit;
> dat aurum, ducit noctem, rogitat postibi
> und' sit, quoiatis, captane an surrupta sit,
> quo genere gnata, qui parentes fuerint.
> ita docte atque astu filias quaerit suas.
> et is omnis linguas scit, sed dissimulat sciens
> se scire: Poenus plane est. quid uerbis opust?
> is heri huc in portum naui uenit uesperi,
> pater harunc; idem huic patruos adulescentulo est:
> iamne hoc tenetis?
>
> (*Poen.* 104–16)

But ever since their Carthaginian father lost them, he's been looking for them everywhere by sea and by land. Whenever he enters a city, he immediately finds out where all the prostitutes live. He pays money, hires her for a night, and then asks where she's from and what country she comes from, whether she was captured in war or kidnapped, what family she comes from, and who her parents were. In this way he looks for his daughters cleverly and smartly. He also knows all languages, but he knowingly pretends not to know: he's an out-and-out Carthaginian. What need is there for words? Yesterday evening he came here into the harbor by ship, the father of these girls; the same man is the uncle of this young chap. Have you got it?[50]

The description of Hanno, called *pater illarum Poenus*, begins in a nearly epic tone as we learn that ever since he lost his daughters he has conducted his search "on land and sea" (*mari te\<rraque\>*), questioning young girls in a Homeric mode.[51] First and foremost Hanno is a *pater*; his "Punicness" is a secondary revelation. But it remains to be seen which characterization a reader ought to privilege in the shaping of sympathy for the character; how much historical and cultural baggage *Poenus* is meant to introduce.

Like *pater Anchises* in Naevius' epic, *pietas* and the paternal role guide Hanno's journey for the creation of home. Nevertheless, this is a Roman play performed in the long shadow of the Hannibalic War and very

---

[50] Trans. De Melo 2012 for all Plautus in this chapter.
[51] In this order (as opposed to *terra marique*) the collocation is rather rare. On the typical Homeric question repertoire, see Minchin 2007: 74–102. It is reflected above in lines 108–10.

close to a treaty with Carthage struck in 189 BCE – hence the implications of a pious Punic protagonist are complex. Indeed, in lines 104–16 we learn of Hanno's curious method of searching for his daughters,[52] and the speaker of the prologue relates that Hanno's "slyness" is perhaps his defining quality:

> ita docte atque astu filias quaerit suas.
> et is omnis linguas scit, sed dissimulat sciens
> se scire: Poenus plane est. quid uerbis opust?
>
> (111–13)

> In this way he looks for his daughters cleverly and smartly. He also knows all languages, but he knowingly pretends not to know: he's an out-and-out Carthaginian. What need is there for words?

His multilingual abilities and the anxiety they cause among some of the play's characters appear to align in these verses with the core ideological structures of *Punica fides*: *Poenus plane est* implies that trickery through linguistic play and subterfuge identify him beyond a doubt as Carthaginian.[53] Nevertheless, for all the negative views of Hanno that certain characters offer, his dealings are done in the service of his primary role as *pater*. All of the "deceptions" are not for the ruin of Rome but for the reclamation of his stolen daughters: this is not a tale of "Hanno at the gates." He is a compromised character, to be sure; this is a comedy after all, and he is meant to be funny. But, as Gruen remarks, "the persons who cast nasty aspersions upon Hanno are the more despicable characters in the play: the scheming slave and the swaggering soldier. If Plautus alludes to contemporary slurs against Carthaginians, he seems to subvert rather than to endorse them. Hanno, in fact, defies the caricatures."[54]

After the play's opening, a subplot designed by Milphio unfolds which is focused on tricking the pimp into losing his wealth and grip over the daughters, in turn allowing Agorastocles to marry Adelphasium.

---

[52] At times (e.g. Franko 1996: 428–9; Maurice 2004: 279) the passage is read with focus on the sexual implications of his overnight interrogations.

[53] Milphio remarks at 991, *nullus me est hodie Poenus Poenior*, appearing to appropriate and, in fact, surpass whatever is "Punic" about deception; but upon Hanno's initial use of Punic and subsequent switch to fluent Latin he insults him, "but you must be a swindler and a trickster since you've come here in order to catch us out, you double-tongued creature, with a forked tongue like a creeping beast" (1032–4). Cf. *Aeneid* 1.661–2. Horsfall 1990: 133: "*Ambiguam, bilinguis, mutet*, all hint at the characteristic conception of *Punica fides*."

[54] Gruen 2014: 609. Cf. Starks 2000: 176. Gratwick 1971: 32 n. 5: Hanno "is in fact by far the most pious character in the whole of Roman comedy"; critique at Maurice 2004: 268. Some readers have noted that the sisters are more compromised than Hanno in their often-meretricious worldview. Cf. Moodie 2015: 119.

The sisters are currently living as prostitutes, but, as noted above, the play makes it quite clear that they are still virgins capable of being restored to their previous social status without too much complication.[55] Nevertheless, for a "temporary" prostitute of Calydon, the date of the play is a very important mark on the festive calendar. Calydon is in the midst of celebrating the Aphrodisia, which the play casts as a festival of ritual prostitution carried out at the temple of Venus. And as Fantham correctly observes, the "festival dominates the action: If Agorastocles never quite manages to leave the stage for the temple, almost everyone else does."[56] Although Calydon historically appears to have had no such religious practice, other literary and historical analogues strike a note with Plautus' text, one of which is the Roman cult of Venus Erycina.[57]

In Pompeius Trogus' description of Dido's journey, we recall, the Phoenicians' layover on Cyprus (the island of Venus) included the snatching up of young women as future wives for their male-heavy crew, girls who were about to offer themselves up sexually for Venus. Adelphasium and Anterastilus, Carthaginian descendants of these same Cypriot girls, are in a nearly identical situation in the *Poenulus*. It is not Dido, however, who will arrive in the nick of time to carry the girls across the sea and away from a life of prostitution, but Hanno, their father. To my knowledge the connection between these texts and characters has yet to be made, but there is clearly a major dimension of the plot that binds these Carthaginian travelers, one that is fully driven home by the role of *pietas*.

There are also historical links between cults of Venus and the interfaces between Rome and Carthage under analysis. There may have been worship of a version of Venus/Astarte Erycina at Carthage; and it is clear that Carthaginian worship of Venus/Aphrodite/Astarte at Eryx in Sicily long antedated Roman involvement with the island and with the cult.[58] The First Punic War allowed the Romans to come face to face with the goddess

---

[55] Adelphasium states this later in the play (1185–6). Just as Hanno's method of searching has been read in ambivalent terms, so too the virginal state of the girls, even if the notion of their preserved chastity is maintained as the play resolves: see lines 232–6. See discussion of "The Chaste Prostitute of Calydon" in Dutsch 2008: 156–68.
[56] Fantham 2004: 238.
[57] Calydon actually had a particularly bloody cult of Artemis, not Aphrodite. See Richlin 2005: 188. On the Calydonian setting and Aphrodite, see e.g. Fantham 2004: 241; Fantham 2010: 178–83. Cf. Moodie 2015: 110 for a general summary of relevant Greek and Roman festivals.
[58] Schilling 1955: 235–9; Zucca 1989; Miles 2010: 274–5, 350, 403–4; Miles 2011: 276; Orlin 1997: 108–9. Budin 2008 argues against the practice of "sacred prostitution" at Eryx, but the Roman sources for the cult's second introduction to the city pose more issues for her take. Cyrino 2010: 43 less polemically summarizes a reasoned view of the evidence that accepts the problems with "sacred prostitution" per se.

on the eve of their expansion onto the world stage. A famous series of battles was fought at Eryx, and in time Venus became a patron of the Roman cause.[59] It is also widely attested that it was during this war that nearby Sicilian Segesta first claimed kinship ties with Rome through Aeneas' time on Sicily.[60] Venus of Eryx, then, emerged as a rather First Punic War goddess, ultimately symbolic of Rome's victory over Carthage while also performing her first widespread cultural work as Venus mother of Aeneas, representative of the Trojan influence throughout the West.[61] As Miles remarks:

> The rebranding of Aphrodite/Astarte as her Roman equivalent Venus, therefore, represented an attempt not only to "Romanize" the cult, but simultaneously to integrate Sicily within the Roman foundational myth associated with Aeneas ... the Roman promotion of the multi-valent cult of Venus Erycina thus emphasized resistance to the Carthaginians while simultaneously incorporating the contested island of Sicily within a Roman vision of history.[62]

What most immediately links this version of Venus to Plautus' Calydon and Trogus' Cyprus is the presence of sacred sex under the auspices of Venus. Venus at Eryx is reported to have been worshiped in this fashion, a factor that highlights her specific relevance for understanding the play, and perhaps for Trogus' telling of Dido's Cypriot episode. Scholars have explored the possible connections between the *Poenulus* and the introduction(s) of the cult of Venus Erycina at Rome.[63] Her first temple was finished in 215 BCE following a decision to call upon the goddess after the defeat at Lake Trasimene in 217 BCE (a fitting divinity to help, since she had already done so in the First Punic War).[64] A second temple to the goddess was erected at the Porta Collina in 184 BCE; Strabo informs us that it was a replica of that of Astarte in Eryx (6.2.6). The second temple was perhaps more open to the seemingly foreign practice of sacred sex, or at least somehow more connected to it (Ov. *Fast.* 4.863–72).[65] Regardless, Venus of Eryx, a goddess renowned for her role in Rome's first war with

---

[59] On Eryx, Roman literature, and the First Punic War, see recently Goldschmidt 2013: 119–22, with bibliography; on the battles, see Miles 2010: 99–100, 194–5; Lazenby 1996: 140–58.
[60] Cf. Erskine 2001: 178–84; Prag 2010.   [61] Cf. e.g. Galinsky 1969a: 160 ff.
[62] Miles 2010: 276. Although it is difficult to discern from the extant fragments, some scholars have even seen these very issues of Roman identity and Sicilian identity-negotiation at the core of Naevius' *Bellum Punicum* (Jahn 2007).
[63] Galinsky 1969b; Henderson 1999. Cf. Moodie 2015: 110, 112.
[64] See treatment of these temples in Ziolkowski 1992; Miles 2010, 2011.
[65] Cf. Fantham 2004: 242.

Carthage and tied to sacred sex, could surely have influenced Roman interpretations of Plautus' play.

Venus, as driving force and protector of Hanno and his Carthaginian family – not to mention provider of Carthage's first women from Cyprus in the Dido legend – is simultaneously Aeneas' mother and the patron of Rome, Carthage's conqueror. Plautus' play puts on stage this complex dialogue, wherein the forces of history and the divine guidance of the journeys that set it in motion are blurred; it erases any easy divisions between self and other, enemy and ally. Venus not only has her eye out for the wanderings of *pius Anchises*, but also for those of *pius Hanno* and *pia Dido*. In fact, the staging itself may have heightened such influence: "At Rome, *Poenulus* must have taken over Forum space beneath the Capitol of Jupiter Best and Greatest and of Venus Erucina."[66]

Venus and the voyage, Carthaginian and Trojan, permeate all the narratives under analysis. As Henderson puts it: "try to deny that a voyage in search of lost loved ones, brought safely to port across fluctuating oceans of Fortune by the unseen pilot Venus, makes reunion the requisite Happy Ending."[67] Propagator of the Trojan line and (perhaps as early as Naevius) helper and guide of their journey to Italy, Venus' Roman *bona fides* is solid. Concerning the *Aeneid*, Fratantuono has flagged the long reach of this particular characteristic: in the *Aeneid*, "Venus laments to Jupiter that *pietas* has not been duly honored, with reference both to Aeneas' exercise of the virtue and to her own (*A*. 1.253)."[68] But we must not overlook the various aspects of her Punic past. Like *pietas*, Venus crosses the aisle; she is the shaper of the future Carthaginians through her role in providing their first women; later, she acts as Hanno's guide, with her influence leading him to the festival in her honor where he will reclaim his "home." The goddess of love, whether Sicilian, Greek, Carthaginian, or Roman, is a unifier in these stories, one only outdone by *pietas* itself.

As I noted at the beginning of this section, the prologue introduces Hanno in two seemingly distinct ways – as *pater* and as *Poenus* – aspects of his characterization that emerge when he finally enters the stage. Following a long direct speech in Punic, a distancing factor that plays upon the textual cues that his trickery is lingual, Hanno switches to Latin and we, as readers, first learn of the man through his own words (950–60). Hanno's

---

[66] Henderson 1999: 8. For the significance of the Capitoline temple of Venus of Eryx, Warrior 2006: 82: "Since her temple in Rome was located on the Capitoline Hill, Venus of Eryx is the first known example of a foreign deity to be brought inside the *pomerium*."
[67] Henderson 1999: 8. [68] *VE* 3.1007.

pietas is immediately visible: his first actions are to pray to the gods and emphasize the justness of his cause. As Henderson remarks, "his utterances are prefaced with pious exclamations and peppered with religious invocations."[69] Some have seen an absurdity to his actions since the audience has only the prologue's somewhat negative portrayal to prepare it for Hanno's arrival.[70] Nevertheless, he here prays as Anchises did in the fragment discussed above from Naevius' *Bellum Punicum* that stressed his *pietas* as he called upon Neptune. Indeed, Gruen sees these lines as "a sublime paean to Jupiter," and Hanno's religiosity overall as sincere and, in general, superior to others in the play.[71] Several characters may present Hanno as a deceptive, fork-tongued trickster in luxurious dress, but his devotion and righteousness balance the negative perspectives.

His *pietas* is first explicitly mentioned at 1137. The nurse, Giddenis, our Carthaginian *Odyssey*'s new Eurycleia, recognizes Hanno and informs him of the situation in Calydon. Upon relating that it is the Aphrodisia and the girls have gone to the temple of Venus to pray for her favor, Giddenis remarks that they have clearly gained the goddess' support: Hanno has arrived just in time to save them before their full and final transformation into prostitutes. Moreover, Giddenis explicitly notes that Hanno's *pietas* is their salvation. The arrival of *pius Hanno* with the support of Venus seems to ensure the success of his mission. Like the actions of Dido before him, Hanno arrives in the nick of time to spirit these young Carthaginians away from prostitution ("Your piety has clearly helped us [*tua **pietas** nobis plane auxilius fuit*], since you've come here today in the nick of time; today their names would have been changed and they'd be earning a living with their bodies").[72] Hanno's imprecations later in the play define further how key *pietas* is to his voyage (1189–90): "restore their freedom to them, so that I may know that there is a reward for unconquerable piety (***pietati***)"; and at 1255–7:[73] "since the immortal gods approve of our **piety** [*nostram **pietatem***] and crown it. You're both my daughters and this is your relative, the son of [points to himself] this man's brother, Agorastocles." What the clearly marked verbal repetition of *pietas* indicates to a reader is certainly variable (some have seen it as sarcastic), but the characterization of Hanno

---

[69] Henderson 1999: 21.   [70] Cf. Maurice 2004 with Moodie 2015.   [71] Gruen 2014: 607.
[72] Within the numerous textual corruptions in the play this phrase reappears in several different locations, e.g. at 1279 in the mouth of Adelphasium: *mi pater, tua pietas plane nobis auxilio fuit*. It is, one must confess, a bit unclear how troubled the sisters were by their approaching induction into the life of Venus. See Moodie 2015: 185.
[73] Cf. Franko 1996 on these lines. For the statistics on piety-words in Plautus and their uniqueness in the *Poenulus*, see Moodie 2015: 191.

as a righteous journeyer, devoted to family and home, is unavoidable: *pietas* is what led Hanno across the sea and helped him to succeed in the restoration of his home, a restoration achieved with the guidance of Venus. This confluence of factors finds a clear parallel in Aeneas' own journey.

Hanno's *pietas* and *fides* are central to his success. And he is a figure in many ways more Roman than the play's other characters.[74] Such a characterization and its choice diction link Hanno to the Didos of Timaeus and Trogus; it also creates a Hanno whose resonance is found in the Anchises of the *Bellum Punicum* and the Aeneas of later Latin literature. Indeed, Naevius' Anchises was for Plautus' first audiences certainly one of if not the most defined Latin literary character with a connection to *pietas*; he is a potential model for understanding the more sincere side of the comedic Carthaginian. If Hanno can embody the voyager driven by *pietas*, and if the Didos of Timaeus and Trogus are also linked to such themes, perhaps Naevius' Carthaginian queen was also cast in a pious light. If Romans could accept a Hanno whose voyage is so described, proximity of the epic's composition to the Second Punic War would not by default demand a demonizing depiction of Carthage's founder.

As for the *Punica fides* side of things, at least in the *Poenulus* there are clear indications that audiences might consider such views subjective and perhaps misguided. For example, Milphio mocks Hanno for his Carthaginian appearance during his arrival scene, even though we know his master Agorastocles is in fact Carthaginian by birth. Furthermore, all of Milphio's attempts to engage Hanno in large-scale trickery betray a misreading of his intentions: he will do an enemy a bad turn, but that is about it. When Milphio wants him to lie to a judge about the girls in order to free them, his acquiescence to the plan is mistaken for a willingness to deceive: Hanno is telling the truth; it is Milphio who takes him for a trickster (1099–1111). Milphio thinks the tears starting to well up in his eyes indicate his use of *Punica fides*, but the suffering he has experienced and the unfolding truth that his voyage may now be at an end bring on his tears. For the clever slave, Hanno is a master deceiver. Yet this reading is Milphio's and is far more reflective of his own doings and the actions that were occurring in Calydon before Hanno's arrival.[75] With the *pius Poenus*

---

[74] Gruen 2014: 609: "Plautus subtly undermines the 'otherness' of Hanno. He associates the Carthaginian four times with *pietas*, that quintessentially Roman quality (Plaut. *Poenulus* 1137, 1190, 1255, 1277). Moreover, he has Hanno refer to an equally quintessential Roman virtue, that of *fides* (Plaut. *Poenulus* 967). By having a Carthaginian exemplify Roman values, Plautus sends a striking message. His audience will certainly have noticed that."
[75] Cf. e.g. Maurice 2004: 283.

comes the ability to free the girls legally and set all right that is rotten in Calydon. Before his entry it was up to Agorastocles and Milphio to employ methods rather easily characterized as *Punica fides*.

This marked ambivalence and ambiguity resurfaces in Vergil's Aeneas, who has been well shown to embody some of the negative values of *Punica fides*, especially in contrast to Dido, whom the reader would naturally expect to carry such qualities. Indeed, Dido emerges at times as the more sympathetic and, yes, perhaps even the more pious of the two.[76] Yet the tradition we have explored in this chapter undercuts the assumption that all Augustan readers would approach Vergil's epic with clear-cut expectations about its hero or about its heroine – not a novel point, but as it concerns the hero's *pietas* something little considered by scholars. While Dido's suicide in the *Aeneid* is perhaps lessened in terms of *pietas* since it is now caused by the departure of her new problematic lover, it is still predicated on a view of the poem's actions that can see the worst in Aeneas' deeds, at least momentarily. If anything, a reader's recollection of earlier narrative treatments of a Dido loyal to her husband until the end serves to highlight Aeneas' detrimental role in her legacy, his Jason-like status as a seducer and destroyer in the *Aeneid*'s perverted replay of her most typical storyboard from the earlier Greek and Roman accounts.

Nevertheless, the narrator conveys at *Aen*. 4.393–6 that Aeneas had love for Dido, although he suppressed it for the greater good of his divinely ordained national mission:

> at **pius Aeneas**, quamquam lenire dolentem
> solando cupit et dictis avertere curas,
> multa gemens magnoque animum labefactus amore
> iussa tamen divum exsequitur classemque revisit.
> (*Aen*. 4.393–6)

> But **pious Aeneas**, although he desires to soften her grieving by comforting her and to take away her concerns with words, groaning much and shaken in his heart by his great love, nevertheless follows the commands of the gods and returns to the fleet.

Aeneas' devotion to duty, divine and human, is often employed to "justify" his seemingly problematic abandonment of a developed and sympathetic character, but the famous meeting in the Underworld of Book 6 reactivates many of these suppressed complications. Dido is back with her husband, the reunion that her suicide had been designed to effect throughout the

---

[76] Cf. Starks 1999.

tradition attested before Vergil. Aeneas is now the third wheel, the one who complicates Dido's *Punica pietas*, whose visitation to Carthage made the very concept of *Punica fides* a historical possibility. *Punica fides* is, after all, a Roman-constructed necessary fiction; and Aeneas' process of self-justification reflects the rhetoric underpinning Rome's national discourse of defensive imperialism. Dido's tale of epic journey and pious end has, in Vergil's telling, been derailed and redirected as the retroactive engine for the creation of national stereotypes and trans-historical hatred. Vergilian characterization, always noted for its complexity, is in several key instances better understood when studied in the light cast by *pietas*' role in the epic journey. Throughout Latin literature, Trojan, Roman, and Carthaginian travelers engage with values and plotlines that are markedly transcultural. This factor brings the Roman world's greatest historical enemies closer together, even if distance always remains between them, a gap that – like Dido's silence herself in the Underworld – speaks louder than words.

CHAPTER 10

Defining Home, Defining Rome: Germanicus' Eastern Tour

Cynthia Damon and Elizabeth Palazzolo

For residents of the Roman Empire it was in some senses extraordinarily difficult to leave home, to take the epic journey that is the subject of this volume. A bizarre little passage from Tacitus' *Annals* makes this point succinctly. It comes in one of the ragbag collections placed at the end of a year's narrative, in this case the year 32 CE, thirteen years after the death of Germanicus, five years before that of Tiberius. An otherwise unknown Roman named Rubrius Fabatus turned up at the Sicilian strait, apparently en route to Parthia (6.14.2). When asked why, he could not come up with a believable reason for his voyage, so the authorities arrested him.[1] A journey beyond Rome's boundaries, Fabatus' *longinqua peregrinatio*, was, it seems, inexplicable and therefore suspect.[2] So this would-be traveler barely made it off the Italian peninsula.

The problem of leaving home if home was the Roman Empire is the topic of our chapter, broadly speaking. More specifically, we look at how Tacitus used that problem to add resonances to his narrative of Germanicus' journey to the East. In order to perceive the resonances and grasp their meaning we will consider Tacitus' narrative in light of literary convention, historical context, earlier journeys, and Germanicus' actual itinerary in 17–20 CE.[3] The narrative is a rather strange but appealing tale that

---
[1] *Ann.* 6.14.2: *at Rubrio Fabato, tamquam desperatis rebus Romanis Parthorum ad misericordiam fugeret, custodes additi. sane is repertus apud fretum Siciliae retractusque per centurionem nullas probabilis causas longinquae peregrinationis adferebat: mansit tamen incolumis obliuione magis quam clementia.* Woodman 2015: 259 n. 17 discusses a Tacitean passage that makes this same point from the Parthian perspective (*Ann.* 2.2.2: *petitum alio ex orbe regem*).
[2] Woodman (2017: ad loc.) notes that "from the forcible prevention of his alleged travel plans it is assumed that he was a senator" and adduces the travel ban instituted in 29 BCE by Augustus. For our purposes it is more important to observe that Tacitus leaves Fabatus' status obscure.
[3] Goodyear does not do the episode justice (1981: 352–3): "What are we to make of Germanicus' journey to the East? Obviously that he did not hurry to reach Syria or Armenia (55.6 hardly gainsays this), that he was keen on sight-seeing, and that he took pains to win popularity amongst the Greeks. This, I think, is all one can fairly assert." Halfmann's discussion is brief, as well (1986: 30–1, 168–70).

Defining Home, Defining Rome 195

illustrates, among other things, how hard it was for Germanicus to get away from Rome, but also, and conversely, how hard – indeed impossible – it was for him to come home, to achieve an epic *nostos*.

10.1 Home Away from Home

We begin with the episode's context in the *Annals*. The Eastern travels are set in opposition to the war of revenge and conquest that Germanicus had been conducting in Germany since before the death of Augustus. Germanicus' greatest success occurred at the battle of Idistaviso in 16 CE, where he soundly (but not finally) defeated Arminius (*Ann.* 2.9–22). After the campaign of 16 Germanicus pleaded for one more year in Germany "to complete his undertakings" (2.26.4: *efficiendis coeptis*), but Tiberius said no, firmly, and brought him back to Rome for the triumph that would declare the war "over" in 17 CE (2.41.2). Soon thereafter Tiberius sent Germanicus off to the other end of the empire, where his task was to "bring order to the troubled East with good sense" (2.43.1: *motum Orientem ... sapientia componi*). Further military exploits, it seems from *sapientia*, were off the table.[4]

The traditional historiographical antithesis to *militiae* is *domi*, and domestic affairs do dominate the first part of Germanicus' trip as presented by Tacitus – strangely so, given that Germanicus is not in fact "at home." He begins with family time, a visit to his adoptive brother Drusus in Dalmatia, where Drusus hopes to win some military glory for himself against the still-troublesome Arminius (2.53.1: *uiso fratre*; cf. 2.44–6). He then enters upon his second consulship in Nicopolis on the west coast of Greece: (2.53.1: *sed eum honorem Germanicus iniit apud urbis Achaiae Nicopolim*). Tacitus' *sed* reminds us, in case we were not paying attention, that this was supposed to happen in Rome.[5] While in Greece Germanicus visits Actium, doing so, according to Tacitus, "in remembrance of his forebears" (2.53.2: *cum recordatione maiorum suorum*). Tacitus again supplies context: "As I mentioned, his great-uncle was Augustus, his grandfather Antony, and Actium was a vast canvas of events both sad and happy," where "canvas" is a *faute de mieux* rendering of another

---

[4] The term *sapientia* returns at 2.64.1 in connection with the ovations awarded to Germanicus and Drusus for their diplomatic successes in 18–19 CE: *laetiore Tiberio quia pacem sapientia firmauerat quam si bellum per acies confecisset*. On *sapientia* see further n. 9 below.
[5] *Ann.* 2.53.1: "The following year, 18 CE, had Tiberius and Germanicus as consuls. **But** Germanicus entered office in an Achaean city, Nicopolis."

ancestor-word, *imago*.[6] Later he and Agrippina, who are traveling *en famille*, have a baby, their ninth and last, in Lesbos (2.54.2).[7] Her name? Julia. Germanicus also tried to go to Samothrace, which would have allowed him to follow his Julian roots even further back, since the island boasted a connection with Ilus' ancestor Dardanus. According to Vergil – or rather, to a story introduced by Vergil as an obscure but significant tale recounted by Latinus to his Trojan guests – Dardanus was an Italian by origin who spent time in Samothrace, presumably en route to the Troad (*Aen.* 7.205–11); he collected the Penates there, and according to Callimachus the island was even called Dardania (*ap.* Plin. *NH* 4.73).[8] Bad weather prevented Germanicus from visiting the *sacra Samothracum* (2.54.2), but he did make it to Ilium and "the sights there venerable for shifting Fortune and Rome's origin" (2.54.2: *a<dito I>lio quaeque ibi uarietate fortunae et nostri origine ueneranda*). In other words, the first few chapters about Germanicus' foreign mission are largely about family and Rome, a striking contrast with the narrative of his time in Germany, which ends with a triumph in which foreign goods, people, terrain, and events are exhibited at Rome (2.41.2: *uecta spolia, captiui, simulacra montium fluminum proeliorum*).

Germanicus' official business in this part of the journey occupies only nine words in the Latin: "Equally, he provided relief to provinces exhausted from internal quarrels and officials' abuses" (2.54.1: *pariterque prouincias internis certaminibus aut magistratuum iniuriis fessas refouebat*), where *pariter* introduces the official business as something of an afterthought. Furthermore, *refouebat* is a rather impressionistic word for his business, which was presumably responding to the provinces' request for a reduction to the tribute they owed the Treasury (cf. 2.42.5: *prouinciae Syria atque Iudaea fessae oneribus deminutionem tributi orabant*). The journey's other episodes are presented as inconsequential: a reception in

---

[6] *Ann.* 2.53.2: "He therefore spent a few days refitting his fleet, and approached the bays renowned for the Actian victory, the trophies dedicated by Augustus, and Antony's camp, in remembrance of his forebears. (As I mentioned, his great-uncle was Augustus, his grandfather Antony, and Actium was a vast canvas of events both sad and happy)." Memorials of Germanicus himself would later mark the landscape for his own posterity (2.82.2), in the form of arches on the Rhine and at Mt. Amanus near Antioch in Syria, together with a cenotaph at Antioch where he was cremated and a monumental bier at Epidaphne where he died. For discussion see, e.g., Schmitt 1997.

[7] *Ann.* 2.54.1: *Petita inde Euboca tramisit Lesbum ubi Agrippina nouissimo partu Iuliam edidit.*

[8] On the implications of the whole complicated tale see Horsfall 2000: ad loc., with ample bibliography; among many other things it figures Aeneas' arrival in Italy as a *nostos*.

Athens characterized by mutual ingratiation (2.53.3), a content-free stop in Euboea (2.54.1), sightseeing in Turkey (2.54.1–3), a storm and a demonstration of *mansuetudo* at Rhodes (2.55.3). Certainly the *sapientia* Tiberius called for at 2.43.1 and rewarded at 2.64.1 is not much in evidence, at least not until Germanicus gets to Syria and decides to attend to his Armenian mission rather than respond to Piso's provocations (2.55.6: *praeuerti ad Armenios instantior cura fuit*).[9]

The Rome-focused orientation is also visible in Germanicus' official actions later on the tour, which included converting Eastern kingdoms into Roman provinces (2.56.4) and keeping the deposed king of Armenia a virtual prisoner in Pompeiopolis, a significantly named city on the coast of Cilicia (2.58.2; cf. 2.4.2–3 and 2.2). Even in places where Germanicus himself tried to draw attention to otherness, Tacitus supplies Rome and Romanness. Thus in Athens, Germanicus reduced his honor guard to a single lictor "as a concession to the treaty of that allied [i.e. foreign] and ancient city" (2.53.3), but two chapters later we find the governor of Syria, Gnaeus Piso, putting Athens firmly back in its place as a not particularly distinguished dot on the map of the Roman Empire (2.55.1–2). And later in Alexandria, when Germanicus dresses Greek fashion in imitation of a polite gesture by Scipio Africanus to foreign allies, Tiberius himself erupts into the narrative, reproaching Germanicus' demeanor almost as it happened despite the fact that he, Tiberius, is in Rome (2.59.1–60.1); the artificiality of the intrusion is highlighted by Tacitean irony: "Germanicus, having not yet discovered his journey rebuked, sailed up the Nile" (2.60.1). The onward march of Romanness is marked in the text by Tacitus' last word on Germanicus' journey *qua* journey: "Then he went to Elephantine and Syene. These used to be the limits (*claustra*) of the Roman Empire, which **now** [i.e. at the time of writing, a century post-Germanicus] extends to the Red Sea."[10] The word *claustrum* originally signified, according to the *TLL*, an object used to lock the door of a building such as a house, and it is therefore a fitting finale to the "domesticity abroad" theme that we have been tracing.[11]

---

[9] For what Tacitus' Tiberius means by *sapientia* see, e.g., 2.47.4, 2.63.4–5, 2.64–7, the last of which is juxtaposed with Germanicus' failure to keep Vonones under control (2.69).
[10] *Ann.* 2.61.2: *exim uentum Elephantinen ac Syenen, claustra olim Romani imperii, quod nunc rubrum ad mare patescit.* See recently Schneider 2015.
[11] For *claustrum* "proprie" as a feature of houses see *TLL* 3.1319.58–70. For a complementary account of Germanicus among his family's monuments in the West – indeed, in Germany – see Woodman 2015: 262–5.

The short version of Part 1 is this: An imperial prince, as Tacitus tells the story, is *chez soi* over a vast stretch of territory.[12]

10.2 What is Wrong with this Picture?

But Tacitus' account of Germanicus' journey to the East in the *Annals* should not be studied as a purely literary artifact: Tacitus purports to represent real historical events, and the material record gives us additional insight into the relationship between Germanicus' journey and Tacitus' account of it.[13] More specifically, the gaps between the material record and the text reveal some of the unstated priorities that shaped Tacitus' narrative.[14] We focus on the epigraphic and numismatic evidence from Greece and Asia Minor, which sheds light on the journey *qua* journey, and on the aforementioned gaps in particular. The papyrus evidence from Egypt, which contributes greatly to the understanding of Germanicus' activities in Alexandria, is less useful for our purposes.[15]

The earliest portion of Germanicus' travels, from his visit to Drusus in Dalmatia and his assumption of the consulship for a second time in Nicopolis, is poorly represented in the material record. This is both surprising and disappointing, as evidence for the celebrations on the occasion of Germanicus' second consulship, which he held with Tiberius as colleague, might have provided a glimpse of the official status of their relationship at the beginning of Germanicus' journey, something to set against the dark backdrop of Tacitean rumor (2.42.1, 2.43.4, 2.55.6).[16] For the remainder of Germanicus' time in Greece, the epigraphic and numismatic material reinforces the importance of the stops included in Tacitus' narrative, but also expands our picture of Germanicus' activities in the region. Tacitus reports two stops in mainland Greece: a visit to Athens

---

[12] And not only an imperial prince. Compare Velleius' comments on his own travels as *tribunus militum*: *quem militiae gradum ante sub patre tuo, M. Vinici, et P. Silio auspicatus in Thracia Macedoniaque, mox Achaia Asiaque et omnibus ad Orientem visis provinciis et ore atque utroque maris Pontici latere, haud iniucunda tot rerum, locorum, gentium, urbium recordatione perfruor* (Vell. Pat. 2.101.3). He was with Gaius Caesar when he met the Parthian king on the Euphrates.

[13] The parallel narratives in Suetonius and Dio (Suet. *Tib.* 52 and Cass. Dio 57.18) are less informative. On Tacitus' literary sources for the reign of Tiberius see Martin 1994: 199–207. Sources for Germanicus' journey are listed by Halfmann (1986: 168–70).

[14] As should be clear from the discussion below, we recognize that those responsible for the material record of Germanicus' journey had their own priorities.

[15] On papyri relating to Germanicus' travels in Egypt, see Wilcken 1928; Post 1944; and Turner and Lobel 1959 (*P.Oxy.* XXV 2435).

[16] On the official relationship in numismatic evidence from Tiberius' principate more generally see Reinard 2015.

and a stop in Euboea, which is mentioned only briefly in passing as he departs the mainland for Lesbos (2.54.1: *petita inde Euboea*). The visit to Athens receives more attention from Tacitus, and is represented by a correspondingly significant material record related to Germanicus.[17] He is said to have been received there "with most extraordinary honors" (2.53.3: *excepere Graeci quaesitissimis honoribus*), where *honoribus* includes the sort of civic honors that might be recorded in an honorary inscription. There are also signs of Germanicus' presence elsewhere in mainland Greece, including inscriptions from Olympia related to Germanicus' chariot victory in the Olympic games of 17 CE.[18] Germanicus' Olympic victory, curiously absent from Tacitus' account, must be understood in juxtaposition with Tiberius' own victory in 4 BCE, during the period when Tiberius was living in Rhodes and had pointedly withdrawn from imperial politics.[19] Tiberius' participation seems to have reinvigorated the chariot races, which may have fallen out of fashion, and Germanicus may have been seen as following in the emperor's footsteps.[20] As a visiting imperial prince, however, his victory and the subsequent celebrations might have overshadowed the honors paid to Tiberius when he had participated not as the emperor's heir but as "Tiberius Claudius Nero, son of Tiberius" twenty years earlier.[21] Identified by his birth name and family, Tiberius has no visible connection to the imperial family in the inscription; in contrast, Germanicus' inscription names him, with all of the honors due to the emperor's heir, as "Germanicus Caesar, son of the Emperor Tiberius Caesar Augustus," and testifies to the imperial status with which he was traveling through Greece.[22]

In Tacitus' narrative, after departing mainland Greece, Germanicus next stopped on the island of Lesbos, where Agrippina gave birth to their youngest child, Julia Livilla. The island is the source not only of honorific

---

[17] Among the many inscriptions and fragments honoring Germanicus, see e.g. *IG* II² 3258–60 and *CIG* 316. It must be noted, however, that many fragments of inscriptions in honor of Germanicus dating to the approximate time of his travels in the East were not necessarily associated with his visit to the city (e.g. *IG* II² 3255, part of a group with *IG* II² 3254, for Tiberius, and *IG* II² 3256, for Drusus, who were never present in Athens together with Germanicus).

[18] *IvO* 221 commemorates Germanicus' victory, and is securely connected to Germanicus' journey eastwards in 17 CE by the Olympiad dating; *IvO* 372 is an honorary inscription for Germanicus and Drusus as benefactors of the city. See also *CIG* 1300, from Lacedaemon.

[19] *IvO* 220 records Tiberius' victory. [20] As suggested by Kaplan 1990: 259.

[21] *IvO* 220: Τιβέριον Κλαύδιον Τιβερίου υἱὸν Νέρωνα. Tiberius does seem to have taken issue with Germanicus' enthusiastic adoption of local customs while ostensibly traveling on official business; see, e.g., Tiberius' response to the news that Germanicus was attiring himself in Greek dress while in Alexandria (discussed above in Section 10.1, and further in Kaplan 1990: 363–5).

[22] *IvO* 221: Γερμανικὸν Καίσαρα, Αὐτοκράτορος Τιβερίου Καίσαρος Σεβαστοῦ υἱόν.

inscriptions for Germanicus, but also of inscriptions commemorating Agrippina in her own right and celebrating her fertility – which was, after all, to the benefit of both the imperial family and the empire – content that ties these inscriptions to the birth of their child on the island.[23] From Lesbos, Germanicus proceeded to Asia Minor. Tacitus describes Germanicus, having just reached the furthest outskirts of the province he had been sent to govern (2.54.1: *extrema Asiae*), as immediately setting off to see the sights in the storied regions of the Black Sea, and refers in general terms to Germanicus rendering assistance to unspecified "provinces" (2.54.1: *prouincias*). By the next sentence Tacitus already has Germanicus on his way back to the coast of Asia Minor (2.54.2: *in regressu*), but material evidence for Germanicus' presence in the Black Sea region is abundant, and implies a more extensive visit. The city of Caesarea Germanica, for example, took his name and celebrated his "re-founding" of the city with a coin naming him as κτίστης; this commemoration, tied as it is to Germanicus' benefactions to the city, can be linked with his physical presence in Caesarea Germanica and should not be attributed to posthumous opportunism.[24] Furthermore, the existence of a newly eponymous city hints at Germanicus' popularity in the region and the impact of his trip. This impact goes unheralded in Tacitus' account, where, as we have seen, the trip is reduced to generalities.

After Germanicus' circuit of the Black Sea region, Tacitus mentions stops in only two coastal cities in the province of Asia, Troy and Colophon, before Germanicus' arrival in Rhodes, but a number of other sites in the

---

[23] Eresus, Lesbos: *IGR* 4, 11 and *SEG* 52, 74=*IG* XII.2, 540; Mytilene, Lesbos: *IGR* 4, 99=*IG* XII.2, 232 and *IG* XII.2, 208. Agrippina is given titles assimilating her to Demeter on Lesbos, both in inscriptions and on coins issued by cities on the island (Methymna, Lesbos: *RPC* 2340; Mytilene, Lesbos: *RPC* 2347). Although these coins were minted under Caligula, based on the comparison to the contemporary coins from Mytilene that show Caligula and Julia Livilla (*RPC* 2348), they should be understood as commemoratives related to Germanicus and Agrippina's time on Lesbos.

[24] *RPC* 2017. The proliferation of commemorations of Germanicus under Caligula complicates the picture of references to Germanicus' travels: the majority of coins depicting Germanicus, for example, were posthumous commemoratives minted under Caligula's authority. The coins of Germanicus minted under Tiberius are all provincial issues; most depict Germanicus and Drusus together as heirs, in the same tradition as the coinage of Gaius and Lucius Caesar under Augustus, or Germanicus with both Drusus and Tiberius. The majority of the provincial coin types from Tiberius' reign depicting Germanicus were issued in Eastern mints, which may be connected to Germanicus' popularity in the region. On the coinage of Germanicus, see Panvini Rosati 1987; Piatelli 1987; and recently Reinard 2015. For our purposes, the most relevant material evidence is that which provides evidence of Germanicus' actions during his life, whether that takes the form of contemporary commemorations or later objects referencing events specifically tied to Germanicus' physical presence in the region, though the abundance of material from the Greek East honoring Germanicus provides general evidence for his popularity in the region, which may plausibly be connected to the time he spent in the area.

province of Asia have evidence of the time he spent in the region. Among the sites that could plausibly belong to a coastal route through Asia Minor, Ilium, Assos, Pergamum, Ephesus, Clazomene, Metropolis, Aphrodisias, Sardis, Eumenia, and Samos, have honorary inscriptions that may be associated with Germanicus' travels.[25] Germanicus' presence is also attested in Assos by an inscription of Caligulan date in which the people of Assos refer to Caligula's former visit to the city "with his father, Germanicus."[26] Where Tacitus narrates a journey that seems almost frivolous and motivated by personal interest – having failed to see the mysteries at Samothrace, Germanicus visits the site of Troy and consults the oracle at Colophon, as if doing a "greatest hits" tour of Asia Minor – the material sources attest to a journey of diplomatic visits and a warm reception by the cities of Asia Minor for the visiting imperial prince.[27]

In Armenia, Germanicus completed the first diplomatic task mentioned by Tacitus since his stop at Athens: crowning a new king for the Armenians. This event was commemorated on a didrachm minted in Caesarea in Cappadocia, which has an obverse with the head of Germanicus and a reverse showing Germanicus crowning Zeno as Artaxias III, and thus specifically commemorates an act inextricably tied to his travels in the area.[28] This incident represents the best example of the literary and

---

[25] Ilium: *IGR* 4, 206; Assos: *SEG* 60, 1313; Pergamum: *IGR* 4, 326 and *IGR* 4, 327; Ephesus: *CIL* 3, 426; Clazomene: *IGR* 4, 1549; Metropolis: *SEG* 56, 1235; Aphrodisias: *SEG* 30, 1252; Sardis: *IGR* 4, 1504; Eumenia: *IGR* 4, 723; Samos: *IGR* 4, 979–80. Admittedly, the presence of a single honorific inscription for Germanicus from a given city does not prove that he made a stop there in his official tour of the province; as Halfmann 1986: 169 notes, Germanicus' popularity, especially in the Greek East, makes it difficult to demonstrate that any given monument must be evidence of his presence in the city. Halfmann concludes that these inscriptions should not be used to add any stops to Tacitus' itinerary (unless, as he concedes in the case of the inscription from Assos in the note below, they explicitly refer to Germanicus' presence in the city). While it is true that honorific inscriptions alone cannot establish that Germanicus stopped in a particular city, the abundance of material related to Germanicus and his family members in the area suggests the importance placed on his presence by the cities of the province.

[26] *IGR* 4, 251=*IvAssos* 26=*IMT* 573: αὐτὸς μετὰ τοῦ πατρὸς Γερμανικοῦ.

[27] The frivolous quality of Germanicus' trip, as Tacitus presents it, is highlighted by the contrast with his description of Piso's journey: starting out on his plans hastily (2.55.1: *quo properantius destinata inciperet*), Piso inveighs against Germanicus in Athens before rushing to meet him in Asia via the swift direct route through the Cyclades (2.55.3: *nauigatione celeri per Cycladas*). Not only does Tacitus downplay Germanicus' diplomatic efforts en route to Asia, the official visit of state he does discuss is swiftly undermined by Piso, who condemns the honors Germanicus had shown to the Athenians. Moving on to Syria, Piso begins his governorship as a foil to Germanicus, gaining popularity in part through his and Plancina's jibes against Germanicus and Agrippina, which were rumored to be not unwelcome to the emperor (2.55.6: *quod haud inuito imperatore ea fieri occultus rumor incedebat*).

[28] *RPC* 3629. The dating of this coin is controversial: early proposals of a Tiberian date have largely been rejected in favor of minting under Caligula or Claudius. See most recently Reinard 2015: 177, who places the coin in the early years of Caligula's reign. Although the coin itself is certainly not

material evidence in close concord – both Tacitus' narrative and the minting of this coin acknowledge the political significance of this event.[29] By contrast, Tacitus does not mention Germanicus visiting Palmyra, although the lasting political significance of his visit to the city is attested by a much later inscription referring to changes to tariff regulations that apparently persisted from their institution during Germanicus' stay.[30] Some time thereafter Germanicus departed for Egypt.[31]

Examining the material record in juxtaposition with Tacitus' account both clarifies and obscures the picture of Germanicus' journey. Inscriptions and coins referring to places absent from Tacitus' account provide new information about Germanicus' time in the East, reveal the presence of other material potentially available to Tacitus, and allow us further insight into Tacitus' depiction of Germanicus. The presence of several stops not mentioned by Tacitus requires that we consider why the events that appear in *Annals* 2.53–70 *are* mentioned. How are we to account for the absence of some sites from Tacitus' narrative? Tacitus may not have had access to information about some of Germanicus' destinations, but his time as provincial governor of Asia argues against the possibility that he was unaware of *all* the aforementioned evidence. Perhaps, then, he deliberately excluded some stops. A number of the sites in Asia Minor for which there is material evidence of Germanicus' presence are inland, and it is difficult to draw an efficient route accommodating all of them.[32] If they were all visited on one trip, he made a circuitous journey. So it is possible that some of these cities were visited on a separate trip, and not during Germanicus' initial sea voyage eastward; perhaps they were stops on the journeys Tacitus alludes to when he says of the summer of 19 CE that Germanicus spent it "throughout many provinces" (2.62.1: *dum ea aestas*

contemporaneous with Germanicus' travels in Asia Minor, it nevertheless presents an example of a material source that confirms a formal stop along his journey by virtue of commemorating an event contingent on Germanicus' physical presence in the region.

[29] The event itself is undermined in Tacitus' narrative by the beginning of the next chapter, as Germanicus is unable to enjoy the fruit of this diplomatic success in light of growing defiance from Piso, who refuses an order that he or his son conduct part of his legions into Armenia. And soon thereafter Piso makes an ominous comment at a banquet at the Nabataean court criticizing Germanicus and Agrippina for accepting gold crowns more fit for Parthian kings than for Roman princes – a dangerous accusation to level against a Roman leader, let alone a member of the imperial household.

[30] *IGR* 3, 1056=*OGI* 629.

[31] See note 33 below on the chronological problems of Tacitus' narrative at this juncture.

[32] While discussing an inscription referencing Germanicus from Perge, Sahin (1995) summarizes the issues involved in generating a coherent itinerary that accounts for Tacitus' narrative and epigraphic evidence for Germanicus' presence at distant sites.

Germanico plures per prouincias transigitur).³³ The absence of detailed dating criteria makes it impossible to differentiate between stops made along Germanicus' initial journey eastward and travels completed after his arrival in the area but before his untimely death. What is more important than isolating individual points of disagreement between Tacitus' text and the other sources, however, is that the material data demonstrates the degree to which Tacitus is obscuring large portions of Germanicus' actions in the East when he groups many locations and many separate episodes under the general statements *prouincias . . . refouebat* (2.54.1) and *plures per prouincias transigitur* (2.62.1). Regardless of whether these sites are left out of the narrative of Germanicus' initial journey eastward, as it seems that some of them must have been (e.g. the sites in the Pontic region that Tacitus does not name), or are glossed over by the one-sentence reference to an entire summer of provincial governance, it is clear that Tacitus presents a selective narrative of Germanicus' time in the East.

The fact that Tacitus chooses to include even the thwarted trip to Samothrace while leaving out places that Germanicus demonstrably did visit prompts us to look for a thematic connection among the episodes mentioned in Tacitus – a theme absent in some real locations and highlighted by certain planned stops, even if they never occurred. A notable trend in Tacitus' description of Germanicus during these chapters is the emphasis on personal motivations rather than diplomatic and political goals.³⁴ The sort of public business that is amply recorded in honorary inscriptions and celebrated in coin issues is presented in general terms and with trivializing contextualization by Tacitus. Furthermore, in Tacitus' narrative there is no mention of positive responses to Germanicus between the honors at Athens and the gold crowns offered to him and Agrippina by the Nabataean king. The material sources, by contrast, convey a sense of pomp and prestige following the imperial retinue along the whole journey: a series of honorific inscriptions commemorating his journey after the fact suggests the existence of celebrations that served to

---

[33] *Ann.* 2.62.1: *ea aestas Germanico plures per prouincias transigitur.* This passage is a notorious chronological crux; *plures per prouincias* is puzzling if *ea aestas* refers to 19 CE, since Tacitus only mentions Egypt for the summer of 19 CE. This discrepancy and others involving the ovations he and Drusus were awarded for these achievements (2.64.1, 3.11.1) incline some to place 2.62–7 immediately after 2.58, thereby moving these travels to 18 CE, the year of Germanicus' journey from Rome to his Eastern command. For discussion see Goodyear 1981: ad loc. For our purposes the compression of the narrative is more significant than its chronology.
[34] A point made briefly by Halfmann 1986: 30.

commemorate the event at the time it occurred. Tacitus' account of the portion of Germanicus' journey in Asia Minor is explicitly a trip of sightseeing in between two "official" diplomatic episodes: his stop in Athens and his installation of a new king in Armenia. These episodes, which bookend Germanicus' stops in Asia Minor, are simultaneously domestic and foreign: they highlight both the extent of Rome's power and importance and the fact that a Roman from the very center of Rome, the imperial family itself, is deeply involved in diplomacy and governmental administration even when away from home. The other proximate stop on Lesbos picks up similar themes; giving birth on the road must have been nothing new for Agrippina, who was having her ninth child, but it is nevertheless an episode that takes the fundamentally domestic and places it in a very foreign setting. The political maneuverings and indeed the *sapientia* that must underlie the general expression "he provided relief to provinces exhausted from internal quarrels and officials' abuses" are nowhere to be found in Tacitus' account of Germanicus in the East, at least not before he reaches Armenia and deals with the leadership crisis there. Instead, we are presented only with sightseeing and a perhaps dangerous forbearance in the face of Piso's growing hostility. Germanicus appears not as a shrewd tactician or a skilled diplomat, but as a somewhat oblivious tourist – obsessed with the glory of the past and unable to see the growing threats to his own future.

Tacitus' account adds context and content to the material evidence, providing narrative and motive that connects the disparate episodes represented by individual pieces of material evidence for Germanicus' travels. In doing so, Tacitus highlights the apex of Germanicus' near-tragic rise and fall with the hindsight available only to the historian. The stops that Tacitus narrates in Asia Minor all have some significance for Germanicus' future: at Troy, the site of the origins of Rome's glory, Tacitus reminds us that the remains there also emphasize "ever-changeable fortune" (2.54.2: *uarietate fortunae*), and in Colophon Germanicus is said to have received hints of his imminent demise (2.54.4: *et ferebatur Germanico . . . maturum exitum cecinisse*). His next stop after these is Rhodes, where he has his first encounter with Piso, who would be the major antagonist of the brief remainder of his life – and the arrivals of Piso and Germanicus at Rhodes are presented in contrasting terms that suggest Germanicus' failure to recognize Piso as a viable threat. Unlike Germanicus, the reader understands that the *extrema Asiae* are still firmly within the grasp of the emperor at home in Rome, and that the political concerns that have come to characterize survival in Tiberius' court must also inform behavior abroad.

10.3 Neither Home nor Rome

An unusual feature of Germanicus' journey is its premature ending. The oracle at Claros that foretold his "imminent departure" spoke only too truly (2.54.4: *maturum exitum*).[35] Only Germanicus' ashes completed the last legs of the journey, by boat from Antioch to Corcyra[36] and then Brundisium, and overland, ever more slowly, from Brundisium up the Appian Way through Calabria, Apulia, and Campania to Tarracina, then on to Rome and eventually the Mausoleum of Augustus (3.1–4).[37] Woodman and Martin characterize the journey as an extended funeral procession,[38] and the contrast with his departure in 17 as one of the Roman people's heart-throbs (*amores*, 2.41.3; cf. 2.43.5–6) and the dedicator of a temple to "Hope" (2.49.2) could hardly be greater.[39] As is suggested by the decreasing distance between the named stops, the text zooms in on the final legs of the journey. Given Tacitus' selectivity in reporting earlier stages, the detail here is striking, which prompts the question: Is the end of this journey more important for the story than the beginning?

The journey's end is one aspect that differentiates Germanicus from Alexander, a figure who is evoked at Germanicus' funeral for, among other things, the "nearby location in which he died" (2.73.2), and who is in the air at several other spots on the journey – at Troy, for example, and of course in Egypt (2.54.2, 2.59.2).[40] Macedon did not see her most famous son again, or receive his relics. The end also differentiates Germanicus from Antony, another figure who shadows Germanicus on his travels, being mentioned by name at Actium and Athens and inextricable from

---

[35] The reading *exitum* is Heraeus' emendation, based on *praematuro exitu* at 2.71.1, for the manuscript's *exitium*, which, as a prophecy, is too precise to be described as *per ambages, ut mos oraculis*.

[36] Agrippina pauses for a few days at Corcyra to "settle her spirit" (3.1.1: *paucos dies componendo animo insumit*), very close to where Germanicus spent a few days refitting his fleet (2.53.2: *paucos dies insumpsit reficiendae classi*). Woodman and Martin (1996: ad loc.) note the parallel.

[37] According to Tacitus, contemporaries compared this cortège unfavorably with that of his father (3.5.1–2). Since the funeral of the elder Drusus seems to have been the final event of Livy's final book (cf. *Per.* 142), the historiographical stakes were very high. Tacitus also provides copious details about Piso's return to Rome, which seems to replicate some of Germanicus' outbound journey, visiting "the pleasure-spots of Asia and Greece" (3.7.1) and Drusus in Dalmatia (3.8), then crossing the Adriatic to Ancona (3.9.1), traveling down the via Flaminia through Picenum to Narni (3.9.1–2) and thence by boat to Rome, where he docked near the Mausoleum of Augustus (3.9.2) and crossed the city to his house overlooking the Forum (3.9.3).

[38] Woodman and Martin 1996: 85.

[39] Germanicus' promise and hopes in 17 also figure in Tacitus' depiction of his triumph, at which his success and attractive person were complemented by the promise represented by his children (2.41.3). Cf. 2.43.4 for Piso's understanding of his mission as being *ad spes Germanici coercendas*.

[40] See, recently, Gissel 2001 and Kelly 2010.

the recent history of both Armenia and his erstwhile capital, Alexandria.[41] Alexandria, of course, was the last stop for his corpse as well as Alexander's.[42] Furthermore, the journey's end distinguishes Germanicus in different ways from two predecessors who did return home and indeed to supreme power – namely Caesar, whose visits to Troy and Alexandria were given literary resonance by Lucan (among others), and Tiberius, whose Armenian mission received multi-media renown in Augustan celebrations of the return of the standards lost with Crassus.[43] Germanicus' story matches none of these paradigms: he dies but returns, and returns but does not rule.[44]

The alignment with Alexander is the most fully developed of the four parallels. At Germanicus' funeral, for example, the crowd in Antioch compares the two men on various criteria: appearance, age, manner and place of death, character, marital history, heirs, and military achievements.[45] Their stories intersect with a particular point in Egypt, and around the concept of antiquity. Germanicus' objective in making this highly provocative trip, says Tacitus, was "to become acquainted with antiquity" (2.59.1: *proficiscitur cognoscendae antiquitatis*).[46] This echoes

---

[41] On Antony's *ciuilis* demeanor in Athens see App. *B Civ.* 5.322–3. The whole story of Antony's initial post-Philippi tour of the East related at the beginning of Appian's *B Civ.* 5 seems highly relevant to Germanicus' tours. In Armenia Antony's treachery left a legacy of distrust and his subsequent military failure a belief in Parthian superiority (Tac. *Ann.* 2.53.2, 2.55.1, 2.3.1–2, 2.2.2).

[42] The tomb has not yet been found but is attested in Plutarch (*Ant.* 82.1, 84.2–4).

[43] Tiberius' outbound journey (to judge by Suetonius' brief report at *Tib.* 14.3) may also have some significant points of difference – and similarity. Tiberius led an army east, but revisited the civil war site of Philippi and consulted an oracle, leaving traces of his presence there that, according to Tacitus' contemporary, Suetonius, "are still visible today."

[44] The end of his father's story provides the closest historical parallel – see Woodman and Martin (1996: 85) – but the evocations of the elder Drusus in our section of the narrative are not tied to the journey theme (2.41.3, 2.82.2, 3.5.1–2). Likewise downplayed is the journey of Augustus' grandson C. Caesar, who was sent *ad res Orientis* in 1 BCE and, like Germanicus, died during his tour after extensive travels (Vell. Pat. 2.101; Cass. Dio. 55.10.18–21); see Tac. *Ann.* 2.4.1, 2.42.2.

[45] Gissel 2001: 292–3 suggests that the issue of the golden dinner accessories offered to Germanicus in Nabataea is a glancing reference to Alexander via the theme of Oriental luxury: Piso objects that they are more fit for a Parthian prince than for the son of the Roman *princeps* (2.57.4). Woodman 2015: 265 also detects an Alexander-echo in Tacitus' report of the German campaign, where Germanicus, like Alexander, fights bareheaded (*Ann.* 2.21.2).

[46] As we saw earlier, Tacitus downplays Germanicus' official acts in the Turkey segment of the trip, too. But a less innocent, if rather vaguely expressed, objective has been in the air from the beginning of the journey narrative. Piso, for example, believed that he was sent to Syria *ad spes Germanici coercendas* (2.43.4), and described Germanicus' moves against him as tantamount to revolution: *seque pulsum ut locus rebus nouis patefieret* (2.78.1); before he left for the East Germanicus consecrated a rebuilt temple of Spes (2.49.2). For Drusus the picture is much clearer: he is sent to Illyricum *ut ... studia ... exercitus pararet* (2.44.1) and as *paci firmator* (2.46.5); according to Goodyear (1981), Drusus was to secure peace *for Rome* by fomenting trouble amongst the Germans

the rather frivolous motivation Tacitus supplied for Germanicus' sightseeing in Turkey, where he was "moved by desire of acquaintance with places ancient and storied" (2.54.1: *cupidine ueteres locos et fama celebratos noscendi*). We do hear of some official business in Egypt, but it is downplayed as a pretext for seeing the ancient sites (2.59.1: *sed cura prouinciae praetendebatur* . . .) and untethered geographically (. . . *leuauitque apertis horreis pretia frugum multaque in uulgus grata usurpauit*); the ten words that Tacitus devotes to the opening of granaries omit much that we know from other sources, papyri in particular. However, if *cognoscendae antiquitatis* seems like a dubious assertion, historically speaking, that gives all the more salience to its evocation of Alexander. This we can see most clearly via Curtius' report about Alexander's Egyptian sightseeing tour, where a renowned monument is said to have attracted Alexander as a man "eager to become acquainted with old times" (Curt. 4.8.3: *Memnonis Tithonique celebrata regia **cognoscendae uetustatis auidum** trahebat*). You would have expected the eyes of both young men to be firmly fixed on a brilliant future rather than drawn to the distant and foreign past, however venerable its surviving monuments. The imperial prince was no Menelaus, the story of whose detour to Egypt was presumably told to Germanicus at Canopus, a town named for Menelaus' helmsman, and gets twenty words from Tacitus (2.60.1). Nor indeed is Germanicus a Hercules, who gets another twenty-four (2.60.2).[47] And yet their stories are given more narrative space than the passing allusions to Alexander and Antony, and more explicit attention than the potential alignments with Tiberius and Caesar.

But perhaps that is precisely the point. From the epic journey of Germanicus' Eastern tour as Tacitus tells it there could be no real *nostos*, because for him the past was home. In fact, it traveled with him in the person of his wife. The woman who saw to it that Germanicus returned to Rome, and who made the journey undeterred by the wintry sea, is uniquely associated with *antiquitas* as the public bids farewell to Germanicus at the

---

(2.62.1). As for the visit to Alexandria, there was a precedent in C. Caesar's visit two decades earlier (Goodyear cites Charlesworth *CAH* 10.621). But Oros. 7.3.4 (*ad ordinandas Aegypti Syriaeque prouincias*) suggests that Gaius' trip was authorized by Augustus.

[47] The "backstory" of the oracle at Colophon occupies a similarly disproportionate number of words (2.54.3). The story of Menelaus is an element of the Egypt narrative where Tacitus goes beyond what is found in Herodotus. See Goodyear 1981: ad loc. for the extant sources; Herodotus does discuss the Egyptian claims to Hercules (2.43–5). The reference to Tiberius' malicious intentions in sending Germanicus may evoke the model of Hercules (2.42.1: *amoliri iuuenem specie honoris statuit*; cf. 2.5.1). If so, the "monsters" Germanicus encounters in the East are mostly Roman: Piso, Plancina, and perhaps the *amici* . . . *callidi* of 2.57.2 (the contrary *aquilones* of 2.54.2 are the exception). The Armenians and Parthians, by contrast, are all smiles and diplomacy (2.56.3, 2.58.1).

Mausoleum. Agrippina is lauded, to Tiberius' intense irritation, as "Rome's jewel, the only blood relative of Augustus, a unique embodiment of antiquity!" (3.4.2: *decus patriae, solum Augusti sanguinem, unicum antiquitatis specimen*).[48]

The contrast with Germanicus' previous "return" is telling. The story of Germanicus' command in the West ended with and is recapitulated in the triumph that Tacitus reports as the first item under 17 CE, even though it occurred mid-year. He stresses its geographical extent and the terrain Germanicus mastered (2.41.2): "On 26 May Germanicus celebrated a triumph over the Cherusci, Chatti, Angrivarii and other nations as far as the Elbe, parading plunder, prisoners and representations (*simulacra*) of mountains, rivers and battles." This would seem to be the conclusion of an exemplary *nostos*. However, complications ensue when the report's conventional *res gestae* categories are confronted by the deadpan sarcasm of the subsequent sentence: "Since finishing the war was forbidden, it was considered finished" (2.41.2). And the meaning of Germanicus' triumph acquires additional parameters as we observe the five children in the triumphal chariot, and, with the Roman crowd, shudder remembering the fate of Germanicus' father Drusus and his uncle Marcellus (2.41.3). Not even Germanicus' successful *nostos* was an unqualified success.

Pursuing the comparison between Western and Eastern tours a bit further, if we try to identify the *res gestae* that would have been represented on the *simulacra* for Germanicus' Eastern triumph – he was awarded an ovation and three quasi-triumphal arches, after all (2.64.1, 2.83.2: *arcus . . . cum inscriptione rerum gestarum ac mortem ob rem publicam obisse*) – we get very different results depending on whether we draw on the material record or Tacitus' text. The coins and inscriptions would give us numerous scenes in which Germanicus was going about the state's business (*res publica*), addressing local problems and fostering civic pride in the many cities he visited: Corcyra, Olympia, Tanagra, Pergamum, Ephesus, Clazomene, Sardis, Palymra, etc. There would also be a splendid scene showing him crowning the king of Armenia (*RPC* 3629). This hypothetical Eastern triumph might also have been paired, at least in the imagination of the viewers, with a parallel parade celebrating Germanicus *Olympionikes*. The crowning scene would also be represented on the *simulacra* derived from Tacitus' account of the tour (2.56.3: *Germanicus in urbe Artaxata*

---

[48] For the expression cf. *Ann.* 2.46.1 on Inguiomerus, Arminius' uncle: *illo in corpore decus omne Cheruscorum*, tendentious praise by Maroboduus that needs to be read in light of the debacle narrated by Tacitus at 1.68.1–5.

adprobantibus nobilibus circumfusa multitudine insigne regium capiti eius imposuit). But of the remaining public business only his visit to Athens comes into focus (2.53.3: *hinc uentum Athenas* ...); the rest is blurry (*refouebat, leuauit*) or trivialized (*praetendebat*). The other images would look more like a tourist's photo album: Nicopolis, Byzantium, Troy, Colophon, Nabataea, Canopus, Thebes, etc. The disquiet aroused in the spectators of the German triumph when they reflected on the parallels between Germanicus, Drusus, and Marcellus would have been intensified by the addition of new analogues to ponder, none of them comforting: Alexander, Antony, Caesar, Tiberius. The spectators would also have a new criterion to puzzle over, namely, *antiquitas*.

Pelling draws a useful contrast between Germanicus' historical reference points (Troy, Scipio Africanus, Actium), and those of Cn. Piso (at 2.55.1 Mithridates, Sulla, Antony; at 2.43.2–3 his own father).[49] One might also contrast Germanicus' attachment to antiquity with Tiberius' attention to the recent past, in the form of Augustus' *instituta*, such as the ban on entering Egypt (2.59.2), and in the form of enemies such as the recently defeated Maroboduus, a more dangerous opponent, as Tiberius tells the Senate at 2.63.3, than Philip V, Pyrrhus, or Antiochus. Wilamowitz brings the issue nicely into focus when he notes that in one and the same year, 19 CE, Germanicus is touring the *miracula* of Egypt and Tiberius is overseeing the expulsion of Egyptian rites from Rome (2.85.4: *actum et de sacris Aegyptiis ... pellendis*).[50] *Annals* 2, which contains so much of Germanicus' story, concludes with Tacitus' most explicit criticism of nostalgia, "we extol antiquity and give to recent times no attention" (2.88.3: *uetera extollimus recentium incuriosi*), a critique prompted by consideration of other historians' failure to give Arminius, a relatively recent problem, his due.[51] In considering Tacitus' story of Germanicus' Eastern tour in its

---

[49] Pelling 1993: 72–4. Woodman 2015: 266, in light of the striking parallels between *Ann.* 2.53–4 and Livy 45.27, would add Aemilius Paullus to the list of the historical reference points for the Tacitean Germanicus. Tacitus seems to be interested in the different versions of the past that people carry with them. By all accounts Alexander's were as old as the oldest of Germanicus' (Achilles, Heracles, Memnon, Tithonus, etc.).

[50] Wilamowitz and Zucker 1911: 817.

[51] For Tacitus' dislike of nostalgia see also 2.53.3 on the *uetera ... facta* trotted out by the Athenians. Cf. also his celebration of <*in*> *maiores certamina* at 3.55.5. The installation of Italicus as king in Germany (11.16–17) brings many of the relevant themes to the surface: family tradition (Flavus vs. Arminius), cultural conditioning (Rome vs. Germany), personal qualities (*uirtus*), political slogans (*libertas* vs. *fides*), etc. Apropos of Tiberius, he has him privilege Augustus and Caesar over *uetustiora exempla* (3.6.2). But he also shows that Tiberius allows people such as Furius Camillus to amuse themselves with nostalgia, so long as they are harmless (2.52.4–5), and notes that Tiberius on occasion cites *prisci imperatores* as exemplary for himself (2.88.1).

narrative context, and against the backdrop of what can be discovered of the underlying historical reality and relevant historical parallels, we have highlighted the elements of "home" and "away" that convey significant aspects of the historian's representation of the problematic nature of Germanicus' situation as heir apparent to Tiberius. As we suggested with the hypothetical Eastern triumphs sketched just above, the story could have been told very differently. For Tacitus' reader, Germanicus' attempts to go away evoke reminders of home, and his attempts to peer into, or even take hold of, his future gravitate to the past. In the first outburst of grief upon news of Germanicus' death, Tacitus tells us, contemporaries described his mission as a "banishment" to the ends of the earth (2.82.1: *in extremas terras relegatum*). But Tacitus' readers know that he encountered many forms of home and Rome out there.[52] The Rome and home(s) that Germanicus' epic journey defines, in Tacitus' hands at least, are peculiar to the imperial prince and a long long way from the here and now of Tacitus' readers.[53] Unlike Rubrius Fabatus, Germanicus succeeded in reaching the border with Parthia, and he also made it to the *claustra* of the Roman Empire at Elephantine and Syene, but he seems to have taken home along with him. Home, however, whether construed as family, city, or past, was a place in which Tacitus' Germanicus had no future.[54]

---

[52] The interpenetration of home and not-home, or Rome and not-Rome, also manifests itself via a confusion of *aliena* and *domestica*. On a tiny scale, with accessories fit for a Parthian prince at a dinner honoring the Roman emperor's son (2.57.4). On a large scale, in the uncanny mirroring of the messy dynastic politics of an Armenia or a Parthia in the *domus Augusta* (see, e.g., Keitel 1978). And in between, with the Parthian prince Vonones, who was raised in Rome under Augustus' protection and installed as the king of Parthia, only to be ejected by the Parthians for being "infected with enemy ways" (2.2.2, 2.3).

[53] Pelling 1993: 77 reached a similar conclusion: "[Tacitus] can regard Germanicus ... as he regards the past: nostalgically attractive, brilliant, the sort of thing it is good to write about; but out of keeping with the real needs of the modern world." To judge from the epigram inspired in Germanicus by the thought (and perhaps sight) of Hector's tomb at Troy, Tacitus was not entirely off the mark in this (*Anth. Lat.* 708 Riese): *Martia progenies, Hector, tellure sub ima / (fas audire tamen si mea uerba tibi) / respira, quoniam uindex tibi contigit heres, / qui patriae famam proferet usque tuae. / Ilios en surgit rursum inclita, gens colit illam / te Marte inferior, Martis amica tamen. / Myrmidonas periisse omnes dic Hector Achilli, / Thessaliam et magnis esse sub Aeneadis.* Giancarlo 2010 is a recent discussion of the Latin epigram and its Greek counterpart. But see also Woodman's caveat (2015: 256 n. 3): "In fact I can detect no sign that Tacitus had read any of Germanicus' extant verse."

[54] Halfmann notes that Germanicus' journey was the last trip of this sort by a member of the imperial household (1986: 31).

CHAPTER 11

Odyssean Wanderings and Greek Responses to Roman Empire

Andrew C. Johnston

11.1 Introduction

Late in the year 355 CE, the young Julian, fresh from his studies in Athens, was preparing to embark on a westward journey, from which he would not return for some years. Commensurate with his new position as junior emperor, Caesar, he was to set out for the war-torn provinces of Gaul, to take up command of the Roman armies on the Rhine frontier. In a panegyric on the occasion addressed in Greek to his cousin, the senior emperor Constantius, he recalled Constantius' own formative experience as a young man sojourning among the Gauls, which, for the bookish prince, seemed to conform to an epic paradigm:

> Your interactions with the leaders of the βαρβάροι in that country provided you with an understanding of foreign manners, customs, and lifestyles. Homer, intending to highlight the wisdom of Odysseus, said that he was "much-traveled" (πολύτροπον), and that he had come to an understanding of the mentalities of many peoples and had visited their cities, so that he might choose what was very best from them all and be able to interact with people of all sorts. (Julian. *Or.* 1.12D)

But Odysseus, continued Julian, had never ruled an empire; the ethnographic knowledge that he acquired of the outlandish customs of the Homeric thought-world was, unlike that of Constantius, never to be applied to the governance of the real world of the Mediterranean. It is striking that, in the mirror of princes that Julian holds up before Constantius, the reflection of the "much-wandering man" is clearly discernible: the ideal Roman emperor, confronted by a disorientatingly diverse array of peoples

---

I am very grateful to the editors for their invitation to present at the original conference out of which this volume has emerged, and to my fellow participants for their helpful questions and suggestions. The two anonymous reviewers provided thoughtful feedback. Robert Cioffi generously read a draft of this chapter, and his learned comments and critiques greatly improved the finished version; any remaining errors or oversights are, of course, entirely my own. All translations are my own unless otherwise noted.

and customs scattered over a vast imperial space, must needs possess, in Julian's view, something of the character of the Odyssean interpreter.

That Odysseus should appear in this context ought, perhaps, not to surprise us; for the ancients he was, above all, the ἀνήρ πολύτροπος: more than simply "much-turned" or "much-traveled," the adjective conveys his quintessential adaptability.[1] His afterlife in antiquity reveals this mental adaptability – both as versatile actor himself and as malleable intellectual subject – to be his most enduring legacy, one which guaranteed his continual relevance in constructions and performances of Greek identity (or identities), well into the late Roman world. Odysseus was, in short, good to think with. Of the many facets of the complex Odyssean personality, the primary interest of this chapter is in the poet's original and primary characterization of him as ὃς μάλα πολλὰ πλάγχθη: the man who wandered far and wide (*Od.* 1.1–2).[2] My goal is to trace, in broad strokes, the tortuous *Nachleben* of Odysseus the wanderer in the writings of Greeks under Roman rule, from the middle Republic through the intellectual movements of the Second and Third Sophistic;[3] in particular, I hope to demonstrate that, far from being simply a learned but hollow game of allusion among the literary elite, the reception of Odysseus in this period – specifically his comparatively neglected encounters with Rome – was an important site of cultural negotiation and resistance.[4] The first part of this discussion will focus on the historical and geographical writers of

---

[1] For the prominence of this aspect of the Odyssean personality during his afterlife in antiquity, see, among others, Pucci 1987 and Montiglio 2011: 1.

[2] Montiglio 2005 is an excellent survey of the idea of wandering in Greek culture, from Odysseus to the novel.

[3] For a general introduction to the Second Sophistic, the classicizing Greek literary culture that found self-confident expression under Roman rule *c.*50–250 CE, see Anderson 2005 and Whitmarsh 2005, who does much deconstruction of the term. The analogous term "Third Sophistic" was first coined by Pernot 1993, and, though still much debated, has now come into general currency to describe the period following the Second Sophistic, from roughly the late third through the sixth centuries, when rhetoric became less epideictic, and more engaged with the realities of politics and society; see Fowler and Quiroga Puertas 2014.

[4] Bär (2013: 234 n. 37) has noted that the question of Homer in the Second Sophistic "has received comparatively little scholarly attention, given Homer's immense significance for Greek culture of the Imperial period"; Kim 2010 is the only monograph-length treatment of the subject, and Odysseus the wanderer features mostly in relation to Strabo's geography (56–80), which will be discussed below. Whitmarsh (2013: *passim* but esp. 49–62) has recently explored the productive reception of Odysseus' *apologoi* to Alcinous on Phaeacia as a prototype for "fiction." In scholarship on the Greek novel there has been much recent work on the genre's intertextual relationship with the *Odyssey*: see, *inter alios*, de Temmerman 2012; de Temmerman and Demoen 2011; Whitmarsh 2011; and Elmer 2008. See also Zeitlin 2001, on the various visual aspects of Homeric encounters in the second and third centuries CE.

Odyssean Wanderings and Greek Responses to Roman Empire 213

the second and first centuries BCE who developed a framework in which Odysseus occupied a central place as a guide for thinking through imperial time, space, and power; building upon this, the second and third parts of the chapter will explore the further elaboration of these themes in the works of four Greek intellectuals of the Roman empire: Dio of Prusa, Aelius Aristides, Lucian of Samosata, and the emperor Julian.

11.2 Odysseus in the Late Hellenistic West

We begin, as do so many stories of Greeks and Rome, with Polybius, who was among the earliest Greek interpreters of Roman empire, and whose keen insights into the Roman character provided orientation for successive generations of scholars, sophists, and statesmen.[5] Writing the history of an empire of unprecedented scale, complexity, and dynamism presented certain unique challenges, and its careful study offered "knowledge of greater importance than other spectacles or intellectual pursuits" (Polyb. 1.1); accordingly it required, in Polybius' view, a historian with a particular constellation of qualities, experience, and objectives. Thus in the twelfth book of his work – which is, unfortunately, preserved only through the extensive quotations of later excerptors – he digresses from his narrative of the final years of the Second Punic War in order to discuss historical methodology, and to engage in extensive criticism of his more recent predecessors in the genre. Timaeus of Tauromenium – the early third-century writer on Sicilian affairs, whose *Italika* (or *Sikelika*) was the first work of Greek historiography to deal with Rome to any significant extent – is singled out by Polybius for especially damning treatment as a negative exemplum.[6] Although this historiographical excursus is usually studied in isolation, without attention to its context within the book, the frame and occasion of the digression are important for a full appreciation of its significance. It is situated at the point where the symplectic, annalistic narrative shifts geographically from the Asian to the African theater. To mark this transition, Polybius seems, based on the surviving fragments, to have given a general preliminary description of the *situs Africae* in order

---

[5] On Polybius and Rome, see most recently Baronowski 2011; for Polybius' ethnographic gaze at Rome, see, *inter alios*, Walbank 1998, an important reassessment of the famous discussion of Roman society and the Republican constitution in the sixth book of the history.

[6] For the place of Timaeus (*FGrH* 566) and his thirty-eight-book historical work – the *Sikelika* and *Italika* – in the development of Hellenistic historiography, see Meister 1989–90; Pearson 1987; and Baron 2013.

to highlight his own firsthand observations of the country, perhaps made when he accompanied Scipio Aemilianus on the campaign that culminated in the destruction of Carthage.[7] His autopsy – or, perhaps more precisely, autophagy – of the landscape is represented most evocatively by his detailed account of the lotus, a plant with unmistakable mythological resonance, which Polybius claims not only to have seen for himself, but even to have tasted in several different forms:

> The lotus is not a large tree, but it is rough and covered in thorns, and it has a green leaf similar to buckthorn, though a little thicker and broader. At first the fruit resembles the full-grown white myrtle berry in color and size, but as it grows it turns dark red and ends up roughly the size of a round olive. The stone is very small. The locals gather them when they are ripe, and they pound and pack in jars with salt the portion intended for slaves, while that meant for free persons is pitted first, before being stored in the same manner, and this is what they eat. As a food, it is somewhat like figs or dates, but with a slightly sweeter aroma. There is even a kind of wine made from it, after it has been soaked in water and pressed, which in taste is sweet and pleasant, similar to a nice honey-wine, and the custom is to drink this unmixed with water. But it does not keep for more than ten days, and thus they produce it in small batches to meet demand. They also make vinegar from it.[8] (Polyb. 12.2 (= Ath. 14.651D))

Previously in the history, Polybius had introduced the reader to the Homeric Lotus-Eaters, an encounter with whom is woven into the narrative of the ill-fated African campaign of the consuls Cn. Servilius and C. Sempronius in 253 BCE. There, the paradoxical arrival of the Romans upon the shores of their mythical island – effecting a collapse between the imaginary and the real, between fictional and historical space – highlights the profound disorientation of the Romans, for whom these were uncharted waters, culturally as well as navigationally. It was no easy task to follow in the wake of Odysseus: Roman inexperience (ἀπειρία) at sea precipitated two naval catastrophes in quick succession, and soon

---

[7] Little can be reconstructed of the *res Africae* that occupied the beginning of Book 12; all that is preserved is a series of names of cities on the African coast quoted by later geographers. But the conclusion of the Roman campaigns against the Carthaginians in Iberia with the battle of Ilipa (206 BCE) had been related toward the end of Book 11, along with Scipio Africanus' first preparations for an invasion of Africa (11.24a), and thus Book 12 probably set the stage for the narrative of the final phase of the war around Carthage. On the narratological function of such geographical and ethnographic digressions, see the discussion of Morstein-Marx 2001, which uses Sallust's African digression (*Iug.* 17–19) as a case study.

[8] Athenaeus' interest was, unsurprisingly, in the culinary peculiarities, but in the introduction to his quotation from Polybius' text he states that Polybius "had seen it firsthand" (αὐτόπτης γενόμενος), which likely reflects the historian's own emphasis of this fact in the original.

compelled the Senate to abandon its maritime policy altogether.[9] The expansion of empire halted in the land of epic.

Here in Book 12, the lotus tale similarly conjures up an array of Odyssean associations, through which the historian might meditate on the nature of Roman ὑπεροχή and its proper interpretation.[10] It marks the important transition between the geographical and methodological sections of the excursus, and serves primarily to establish an identity between Polybius and Odysseus, the historian and the wanderer; it is a powerful metaphor for the necessarily twofold practice of the historian, representing the defining crux of historiography: wandering and return, observation and narrative. Take away one or the other, and the writing of history, like the *Odyssey* itself, is either impossible or it is meaningless fiction. The fact that the critique of Timaeus, which takes as its starting point his amateurish depiction of Africa, follows directly upon the account of the lotus demonstrates still more clearly that there is something much greater at stake here than flora. Timaeus, according to Polybius, was only an armchair historian, who never left his study at Athens; he was

> not only uninformed about Africa but childish and entirely unreasonable, and was still caught up in the ancient reports handed down to us that the whole of Africa is sandy, dry, and barren ... [he] has no reliable information on the subject and seems of set purpose to relate the exact opposite of the actual facts. (Polyb. 12.3)

With these underlying Odyssean themes established, Polybius then moves into a more theoretical discussion in which he delineates his own vision of the practice and ends of history, and of the character of the ideal historian. This discussion culminates in the explicit alignment between the wanderings of Odysseus and the inquiry of the historian. For Polybius, Odysseus is the original and quintessential "man of action" (ἀνὴρ πραγματικός), and thus he is the model interpreter of events, the prototypical pragmatic historian: quoting the four opening lines of the poem – "Sing to me of the man, Muse, the man of twists and turns, driven time and again off course ... Many cities of men he saw and learned their minds, many pains he suffered, heartsick on the open sea" – Polybius concludes that "the

---

[9] Polyb. 1.39.1–7. The significance of the presence of the Lotus-Eaters and Odyssean markers in Book 1 vis-à-vis the Roman context is explored by Biggs (2014: 1–2 and 143–9). The lotus passage in Book 12 has been neglected, to my knowledge, in previous scholarship on this digression.

[10] For the voyages of Polybius and the role of the *Odyssey* especially in his comparative interpretation of constitutions, see Hartog 2001: 163–71, though he places rather less emphasis on Polybius' self-fashioning.

dignity of history also demands such a man" (Polyb. 12.27–8).[11] In light of the autoptic description of the lotus that frames the digression, it is clear that we are to understand Polybius to be the true intellectual heir to Odysseus; indeed, in *actually* going through with eating the lotus and still remembering to return and to tell the tale, Polybius becomes, in a way, more Odyssean than Odysseus himself. The inquiry of the hero had been constrained by the fear of suffering the same fate as his oblivious companions, but the historian's methodical autopsy supplants the irrational aspect of the ancient report – to which Timaeus still subscribed – with an authoritative, complete, and thoroughly pragmatic account. Moreover, when this anecdote is read against the other, Roman, confrontation with the lotus, Polybius emerges as, in some sense, a corrector of the consuls Servilius and Sempronius, failed commanders who could neither understand nor appropriately respond to the cues of Odyssean geography.

Outside of his histories, in his role as ambassador and advocate, the Odyssean aspect of Polybius' identity was prominent enough to be recognized and reflected back to him by Romans such as Cato the Elder, who famously joked in the wake of the return of the Achaean hostages to Greece that Polybius-Odysseus had ventured back into the cave of the Cyclops by requesting in addition the restitution of their honors.[12] Among those elite Achaean hostages handed over to the Romans in the aftermath of the Third Macedonian War, Polybius wrote from a state of involuntary displacement from his homeland, a circumstance which seems to have suggested to him a certain basic parallelism with Odysseus and his wanderings.[13] This must be at least part of the point of the sustained comparison of himself with Timaeus, who, not dissimilarly, produced his histories while living for some fifty years at Athens in political exile from his native Tauromenium.[14] The time that he spent in Rome among the Romans, like Odysseus in the land of the Cyclopes, prompted Polybius to reflect on questions of selves and others, on the transformation of the Mediterranean

---

[11] For the lines of the *Odyssey*, I quote the translation of Fagles 1996. Herodotus too had aligned himself with the character of the wandering Odysseus, though only implicitly (e.g. with the idea of ἄστεα ἀνθρώπων ἐπεξιών at 1.5); on Odysseus and Ionian *theoria* in the late Archaic and early Classical periods, see Montiglio 2005: 118–46.

[12] Polyb. 35.6 (= Plut. *Cat. Mai.* 9).

[13] Hartog 2001: 15 places emphasis on the involuntary nature of Odysseus' travels.

[14] For Timaeus' exile under Agathocles, see Diod. Sic. 21.17.1. The chronology of the fifty years that Timaeus claims to have spent at Athens composing his historical works is debated; see Champion's note on *FGrH* 566 T4a in *BNJ*.

from Homer's wine-dark sea into a Roman lake.[15] Although Polybius had tasted all too keenly its bitter aftermath, he nonetheless realized that, more than simply a reorganization of political power, the Roman Empire had ushered in a dramatic revolution in knowledge. In comparison to the situation in ancient times, when "a true inquiry (ἀληθής ἱστορία) into the aforementioned regions [in the western Mediterranean] was not only difficult, but almost impossible," the world had been fundamentally changed by Roman expansion, and "almost all places had become accessible by sea and by land." At the same time, the Greek elite were deprived of the opportunity to pursue meaningful distinction in political or military careers in their own country (Polyb. 3.59.1–5: ἡ περὶ τὰς πολεμικὰς καὶ πολιτικὰς πράξεις φιλοτιμία), and those who would now find a renegotiated role as πρακτικοὶ ἄνδρες under Roman rule must instead take up the quest for the advancement of knowledge (βέλτιον γινώσκειν καὶ ἀληθινώτερον). While Timaeus, artfully cast by Polybius as the anti-Odysseus, "spent his entire life in exile *in one place*, almost as if purposely denying himself... the *firsthand experience* gained by *wandering* and *seeing things*" (Polyb. 12.28.6: τὴν ἐκ τῆς πλάνης καὶ θέας αὐτοπάθειαν),[16] Polybius, on the other hand, turned his forced sojourn into something intellectually productive:

> For the sake [of intellectual inquiry], I underwent the dangers and sufferings (τοὺς κινδύνους καὶ τὰς κακοπαθείας) that befell me in the course of my wanderings (ἐν πλάνῃ) through Africa and Iberia, as well as Gaul and the sea that washes the furthest shores of these countries, so that by correcting the errors of previous generations I might impart knowledge of even these parts of the world to the Greeks. (Polyb. 3.59.7–8)[17]

---

[15] Marincola 2007 has rightly emphasized the originality of Polybius' elevation of Odysseus to the status of the ideal historian, and has analyzed many of the strands of Greek historical thought that are implicated therein. But there is less attention in Marincola's treatment to the contemporary Roman context within which Polybius was working, which differentiates him from his forerunners and thoroughly shapes his theory of history, together with his own self-fashioning. Erskine 2012, conversely, offers a treatment of the various aspects of Polybius' sojourn among the Romans, although he only alludes in passing to "Polybius as Odysseus" (n. 69).

[16] There are several specific correspondences, italicized in the quotation above, in Polybius' critique of Timaeus with the opening lines of the *Odyssey* (*Od.* 1.1–4): the emphasis on "experience" (αὐτοπάθεια v. πάθεν), "seeing" (θέα v. ἴδεν), and "wandering" (πλάνη v. πλάγχθη), and the sharp contrast implied between Timaeus' stay only "in one place" (ἐν ἑνὶ τόπῳ), Athens, among the "cities of many men" (πολλῶν ἀνθρώπων ἄστεα) visited by Odysseus. This passage is noted by Marincola (2007: 23) in his discussion of the prominent aspect of Odysseus the historian's character as "sufferer."

[17] This programmatic passage – a brief digression in Book 3 that interrupts the narrative of the events of the Second Punic War in Italy – is not discussed by Marincola 2007, although it initially introduces the central themes to which Polybius will return in the methodological excursus in Book 12.

Appropriating the persona of the *wandering* Odysseus, the only aspect of the hero's malleable character that remained intelligible in a *Graecia capta* now devoid in any real sense of τὰ πολεμικὰ and τὰ πολιτικὰ, and reinterpreting his own captivity as a kind of odyssey became an empowering way of reclaiming meaningful agency. Recasting himself in the role of the new "man of action" rather than the man acted upon, and self-consciously developing this as a paradigm for future generations of Greek historians of Rome to follow, Polybius staked out a new place for the Greek intellectual elite under Roman rule. Ultimately, it was as an Odyssean wanderer-narrator that Polybius wished to be remembered, for his epitaph, according to Pausanias, conspicuously claimed that "he wandered over every sea and land" (Paus. 8.30.8).

Another side of this complex cultural negotiation is found in the final, haunting scene of his history. As Polybius stands gazing upon the destruction of Carthage with his patron and pupil Scipio Aemilianus, the Roman commander, moved to tears, turns to him and quotes two lines of Homer: "a day will come when sacred Troy will meet its end, along with Priam and his people" (Polyb. 38.21–2).[18] When pressed for the meaning behind this cryptic allusion, Scipio confesses to have been thinking of the eventual, inexorable ruin of his own city. In this synthetic interpretation of the Greek myth-historical past, the Roman imperial present, and the precarious future in the field at Carthage, the sagacious Scipio shows himself not only to be "a great and perfect man, and worthy of memory," but also, in many respects, the fulfillment of Polybius' Odyssean ideal: as an eloquent speaker, world traveler, and knowledgeable investigator of peoples and places, as well as a powerful leader of men, Scipio epitomizes the "man of action," possessed of all the requisite qualifications and opportunities of the pragmatic historian, of which Polybius himself in the end, with no further possibility of πολεμικὰς καὶ πολιτικὰς πράξεις after the Romans dismantled the Achaean League in 146 BCE, falls short.[19] If "the discipline of history will be well off only when men of action attempt to write histories" (Polyb. 12.28.3), then Scipio, who succeeds Polybius as the authoritative interpreter of events at the end of the work and whose voice it is that echoes beyond its conclusion, represents the hope of history. As such, Scipio is also constructed as the ideal reader of history: there are good

---

[18] Polybius quotes *Il.* 6.448–9, a prediction spoken by Hector.
[19] The last meaningful opportunity for πολιτικὰς πράξεις for Polybius was his important role in 146 in assisting the Senatorial commission of ten in the organization of the Peloponnese into the province of Macedonia and creating new constitutions for the Greek *poleis* under Roman rule, for which he was widely honored throughout the region: see Paus. 8.30.8–9; Polyb. 39.3–5.

reasons to think that in the digression on generalship in Book 9, which praises especially the quality of foresight (πρόνοια) and sets up Odysseus as an exemplar thereof, the historian was thinking of the young Scipio, who was, at the presumed time of its composition, at a particularly formative stage of his political career at Rome. As his tutor, Polybius may have encouraged Scipio to emulate certain Odyssean qualities – such as like πρόνοια – that translated well into Roman public life, an image which he furthered in his text through the subtle conflation of epic hero and Roman *imperator*.[20] Indeed, Scipio was known to quote from the *Odyssey*, and his Roman contemporaries could intelligibly couch their praise of him in terms borrowed from that poem; just as he picked up on Polybius' own self-fashioning, even the affectedly Hellenophobic Cato may have been at least vaguely aware of the carefully wrought persona of Aemilianus as a "Roman Odysseus."[21]

Although it has generally gone unnoticed in scholarship, there is compelling evidence to suggest that this Odyssean identity of Scipio was taken up and further elaborated upon by other Greek observers of Rome in the generation following Polybius. Most prominent and influential among these was Posidonius, the Stoic philosopher and polymath, who composed a history in fifty-two books that was conceived of as a continuation of the work of Polybius. Like Polybius, there was something of the Odyssean in his own character as a historian and geographer: he had spent time traveling significant stretches of the western Mediterranean, observing firsthand, among other customs and wonders, the behavior of the tides beyond the Pillars of Heracles and of the Gallic elite at table and of Marius regnant at Rome.[22]

In the seventh book of his *History after Polybius*, which survives only in scattered fragments, Posidonius gave an account of the great Eastern embassy undertaken by Scipio at the behest of the Senate around 144–143 BCE, in the course of which the Roman statesman "visited most parts of the inhabited world" (Diod. Sic. 33.28b: τὰ πλεῖστα μέρη τῆς οἰκουμένης ἐπῆλθον), and "inspected cities, peoples, and kings" (Plut. *Mor.*

---

[20] The digression on generalship is found at 9.12–20. For this aspect of Polybius' rhetorical fashioning of Scipio as Odysseus, and the Odyssean elements of their historical and literary relationship more generally, see Battistin Sebastiani 2015.
[21] For Scipio's quotation of the *Odyssey* (1.47) at Numantia, see Plut. *Ti. Gracch.* 21.7, and the discussion below. Cato was reported to have quoted a line from the *Odyssey* (10.495) to characterize the exceptional wisdom of Aemilianus (Plut. *Mor.* 200A).
[22] On Posidonius and the *History after Polybius* (Ἱστορία ἡ μετὰ Πολύβιον), see FGrH 87. For his visit as an ambassador to Marius in 87–86 BCE, see T 7; for the tide on the Lusitanian coast, see F 84; for the Gauls, see F 116.

200F: πόλεων ἐθνῶν βασιλέων ἐπίσκοπον).[23] While this episode in Scipio's illustrious career was to some extent overshadowed for the Romans by the conquests of Carthage (146 BCE) and Numantia (133 BCE), by which it was bookended, it was of decidedly greater moment in the Hellenistic East, where it made a spectacular impression, and firmly established Scipio as a larger-than-life figure in the Greek popular consciousness.[24] He was accompanied on this journey by the Stoic philosopher Panaetius, whose eyewitness account was probably one of the principal sources of information for the vivid depictions rendered by Posidonius.[25] From the extant fragments relating to Scipio's travels through the cities of men, it is evident that the historian placed marked emphasis on autopsy, visibility, and the gaze. The most memorable episode of the Scipionic wanderings, which is described in consistent fashion across the various surviving summaries derived from Posidonius, was the visit to Alexandria and the Egyptian hinterland in the company of the contemptible king Ptolemy VIII Physcon. The set purpose of the Roman in coming to Alexandria was "to view" (κατασκεψόμενοι), but he is a discerning "observer" (ἐπίσκοπος), greatly concerned with distinguishing the empty wonders valued by the king from "things truly worth seeing" (τὰ θέας ἄξια πρὸς ἀλήθειαν). Upon disembarking from his ship with his head veiled, the Alexandrians begged him to "reveal himself" (ἀποκαλύψασθαι), and subject himself to their gaze. In the course of his visit Scipio is represented as constantly surveying his surroundings, but "while inspecting the city, he was himself a spectacle for the Alexandrians" (*dum inspicit urbem, spectaculo Alexandrinis fuit*).[26] There is an intriguing parallel for this carefully constructed visitation scene between foreign dignitary and luxurious monarch in an urban environment located at the intersection of the exotic and the

---

[23] These are demonstrably derived from the same source, Posidonius (*FGrH* 87) F 6; see Dowden's discussion in *BNJ*. For the historical details and dating of this Eastern embassy of Scipio, which is sometimes alternatively placed in 140–139 BCE, see Mattingly 1986. Its specific aims and achievements are poorly understood, but it certainly took Scipio throughout Greece, Asia, Syria, and Egypt.

[24] Although Scipio was accompanied by Sp. Mummius and L. Metellus, his fellow ambassadors are mentioned by name in only one source (Just. *Epit.* 38.8.8), demonstrating the extent to which contemporary report and historical memory associated the embassy first and foremost with Scipio. A century later, Cicero certainly remembered "that famous and distinguished embassy" (*legatio illa nobilis*) for Scipio's role (*Acad. Pr.* 2.5).

[25] So great was the vividness with which Posidonius imbued scenes of the journey that at least one later Greek author (Ath. 12.549D) mistakenly thought that, although the embassy had taken place before his birth, Posidonius had himself accompanied Scipio.

[26] The quotations come from Posidonius (*FGrH* 87) F 6+1 (= Just. *Epit.* 38.8.8–11) and F 6+2 (= Diod. Sic. 33.28b), as well as Plut. *Mor.* 200E–F (= Posidonius F 125b Th).

familiar, one which involves similarly complex dynamics of viewing and visibility, where the subject of the gaze becomes the object, the looker looked upon: Odysseus at the court of Alcinous on Phaeacia.[27] When he comes up from the famed harbor as an eager viewer, Odysseus' veil – an enchanted mist summoned by Athena – is at first impenetrable to the gaze of the Phaeacians as he discerns the key sights of the strange land: the ships, the agora, the fortifications. But soon, in the company of the king as he is paraded through the streets into the assembly place, he himself becomes a spectacle for the "crowds of onlookers" among the Phaeacians, who, like the Alexandrians looking upon the Roman commander fresh from the sack of his own "Troy" at Carthage, "gazed at the knowledgeable man" (*Od.* 8.17–18: πολλοὶ δ' ἄρα θηήσαντο ἰδόντες ... δαΐφρονα).[28]

Alongside these implicit parallels in Posidonius' narrative between the epic and the historical journeys, which seem to have suggested to later Latin-speaking readers such as Horace the value of Odysseus as a pragmatic "paradigm" (*utile exemplar*) for Romans, and perhaps to have evoked the image of Scipio as an imperial Odysseus,[29] it is clear that the historian introduced explicitly Odyssean elements into the account of the embassy.[30] Echoing the address of one of the suitors to the disguised Odysseus back on Ithaca, Posidonius stated that Scipio was sent "to inspect both the violence and the lawfulness of mankind" (*Od.* 17.487; Posidonius [*FGrH* 87] F 30 [=Plut. *Mor.* 777A]: ἀνθρώπων ὕβριν τε καὶ

---

[27] For the ethnographic gaze of the *Odyssey*, and the particular significance of the episode on Phaeacia, see Dougherty 2001: 81–157. On the "epic gaze," and the hero as both subject and object thereof, see Lovatt 2013.
[28] Too little remains of Posidonius' original to look for specific verbal echoes of the Homeric text, but there may very well have been marked intertextual allusions. It is perhaps worth further noting here that other decadent and gluttonous Hellenistic monarchs were conventionally compared to the Phaeacian king Alcinous, who was viewed in the later tradition as the mythical epitome of excessive luxury; among the other fragments of Hellenistic historiography, see, for example, Theopompus (*FGrH* 115) F 114, on Strato, king of Sidon, who "exceeded all humanity in pleasure-seeking and luxury." This aspect of the Odyssean comparison between Ptolemy and Alcinous may have been made – or at least implied – by Posidonius, or by his Stoic source, Panaetius.
[29] The resonance between the late first-century BCE characterization by Horace of Odysseus as "inspector" (*Epist.* 1.2.18–20: *urbis et mores hominum inspexit*) and the roughly contemporary account in Trogus' history, derived from Posidonius, of Scipio's Eastern embassy (Just. *Epit.* 38.8.8–11: ... *Scipioni Africano ... qui ad inspicienda sociorum regna veniebant ... Africanus, dum inspicit urbem* ...) is unmistakable, and suggestive of the potential overlap between the two men in Roman thought. This parallel, together with the notion of Scipio as an "imperial Odysseus," is noted briefly by Leigh 2013: 107 and n. 91).
[30] This suggestion goes somewhat against the argument of Montiglio 2011: 66, who claims that there was little or no middle Stoic engagement with Odysseus, including Posidonius. The Odyssean shaping of Aemilianus with respect to the Eastern embassy is not mentioned by Astin (1967: 127, 138–9, 177), the standard biography of Scipio.

εὐνομίην ἐφορῶντα).³¹ Odyssean moments are found outside of the Eastern travels of Scipio as well: under the influence of the powerful conclusion of Polybius' history at Carthage, his continuator Posidonius staged a similar Homeric interpretation scene in the far western Mediterranean, at Numantia. Upon hearing the report of the death of the revolutionary tribune Tiberius Gracchus back at Rome, Scipio replied with a quotation from the *Odyssey*: "So perish any other who should do such things" (*Od*. 1.47: ὡς ἀπόλοιτο καὶ ἄλλος ὅτις τοιαῦτά γε ῥέζοι).³² In these works of Hellenistic historiography, the reader is meant not only to see Scipio through the lens of the *Odyssey*, but to watch Scipio himself interpret profoundly important historical moments through that same lens. While the loss of the greater part of the work of Posidonius, of his predecessor (Polybius), of his source (Panaetius), and of his contemporaries (Cleitomachus) precludes us from detailing further rhetorical uses of the image of Scipio as a Roman Odysseus, it seems to have been an idea that was very much in the air, fostered in part, perhaps, by Scipio's own careful and collaborative self-representation.

Since the third century, when Roman *imperium* had first begun to expand into the Hellenistic world, the Greeks had, in various ways, worked to accommodate and assimilate the extraordinary power of individual Roman commanders and politicians within their own traditions. Flamininus received divine honors at Chalcis, was hailed by the royal title of *soter*, and his portrait supplanted that of the Macedonian king on subsequent issues of gold coinage; some two generations after he had organized the province of Asia there was a revival of the cult of M. Aquillius at Pergamum; M. Claudius Marcellus in Sicily and Mucius Scaevola in Anatolia were remembered by the local Greek inhabitants for decades after their campaigns with annual eponymous festivals celebrated in their honor; statues of Aemilius Paullus took the place of those of the vanquished king Perseus at Delphi; crowns were routinely offered by Greek *poleis* to consuls in lieu of kings.³³ As the fragments of Hellenistic literary discourse

---

[31] This quotation, as with much of the texture of the embassy narrative, may have been borrowed from Panaetius, as it is also quoted, apparently independently of Posidonius, by the contemporary late second-century Carthaginian philosopher Cleitomachus (Plut. *Mor*. 200E), who was a pupil of Carneades and head of the Academy after 129 BCE.

[32] This line is spoken by Athena concerning the just demise of Aegisthus at the hands of Orestes; Posidonius (*FGrH* 87) F 110f (= *Excerpta de Sententiis* 387.13).

[33] For Flamininus, see Plut. *Flam*. 10, 16; for the cult of Aquillius at Pergamum, originally established in the 120s BCE, see Jones 1974; the Marcellia and Mucia festivals are mentioned by Cic. *Verr*. 2.2.51; Paullus' statues are known from Livy 45.27; for Manlius Vulso being offered a crown at Cibyra, see Livy 38.14.

concerning Scipio Aemilianus suggest, however, alongside these more easily recognizable strategies for fitting powerful Roman commanders into well-established roles and patterns of interaction, and thus normalizing the otherwise disjunctive experience of conquest, the rhetorical shaping of the historical narratives of the deeds of these Romans to conform to familiar Greek cultural paradigms – none more meaningful than the ἀνήρ πολύτροπος, Odysseus – was an important means by which Greeks came to terms with Roman Empire. This was, in part, self-interested protreptic: Polybius and Julian, separated by half a millennium, both saw the utility of fostering certain Odyssean qualities in Roman *imperatores*. But such subaltern strategies also contain an element of chauvinistic retreat into the past, which would only become more pronounced in the succeeding centuries of the Greek experience under Roman rule.

As he prefigured the agents of imperial expansion, the Homeric hero also anticipated imperial geography. In the thirty-fourth book of his histories, now almost entirely lost, Polybius devoted his attention to theories of the description of space rather than of time, and here too the shadow of the much-wandering man looms large. Homeric geography was a central concern of late Hellenistic scientific writers, who found themselves inevitably compelled to define their own positions with respect to the world as mapped by Odysseus; while some, like the learned Alexandrian librarian Eratosthenes, rejected this map, most, like Polybius himself, accepted at least a rationalized version of it.[34] Prominent within the camp of Odyssean apologists was Asclepiades of Myrleia, one of the first Greek intellectuals whom we know to have been active in the far western provinces of the Roman Empire. At some point toward the end of the second century BCE he traveled westward from Asia Minor and settled in the southern Iberian Peninsula, where he became a teacher of language and literature (γραμματικά) among the people of the Turdetani. Heavily influenced by the work of the Homeric critic Crates of Mallus during his studies at Pergamum, he was particularly interested in finding evidence to support a reading of the *Odyssey* that located the wanderings of the hero beyond the Pillars of Heracles and credited to the poet the articulation of a kind of proto-scientific worldview; for Crates and his followers,

---

[34] Polyb. 34.2–4 (= Strabo 1.2.15–17). Eratosthenes had derisively stated that "we may determine where Odysseus traveled when we find the cobbler who stitched the bag of the winds," a statement that Polybius found entirely too skeptical; it is particularly with regard to Meninx, the island of the Lotus-Eaters, and Sicily, the supposed location of Scylla and Charybdis, that Polybius attempted to defend and rehabilitate Odysseus' geography. Geus 2001 is the most thorough study of Eratosthenes in the context of the history of Hellenistic science.

Homer, via the firsthand "researches" of Odysseus, became a geographer *avant la lettre*.[35]

In the travelers' guide to the region of southern Iberia and its peoples that emerged out of Asclepiades' research and teaching – the περιήγησις τῶν ἐθνῶν – he presented a fascinating and provocative interpretation of the meanings of spaces now dominated by Roman power. With its title Asclepiades situated his work within the antiquarian genre of post-Homeric periegetic literature that had become increasingly popular during the Hellenistic period,[36] and, like the most famous of the periegetes, Pausanias, Asclepiades too had local "experts" as his guides. Nevertheless, he seems, as far as we can tell from the surviving fragments of the work, to have ignored the kinds of authentic local histories that might still have been recoverable in the western provinces of the Roman Empire, and instead to have imposed his own cultural narrative and his own intellectual map of the Homeric *nostoi* onto the landscape and its monuments.[37] Two examples will suffice to illustrate his methods and conclusions: at a city in the mountainous hinterland of the former Phoenician settlement of Abdera called "Odysseia" (a place which is otherwise unattested) he discovered a temple of "Athena," in which he claimed that shields and the prows of ships had been hung as memorials of the wanderings of Odysseus.[38] He further deduced that the eponymous founder of the small town of Ocelum in Lusitania must have been an otherwise unknown Trojan companion of Antenor, Ocelas.[39] The erasure by Asclepiades of both a Roman present and an authentic local past in his description of southern Iberia leaves the reader-traveler in a purely Greek landscape of memory, the meanings of which are redefined by the wanderings and works of Odysseus and his ilk. This selective reading of the landscape and its monuments is the same periegetic methodology found two-and-a-half centuries later in the writing of Pausanias, whose archaeology of

---

[35] On the importance of the Homeric *nostoi* in Spain for the Pergamene school, see Pérez Vilatela 1995.

[36] On the genre of periegetic literature, and Asclepiades' Hellenistic contemporaries such as Heliodorus, who wrote a guide to the Athenian acropolis in fifteen books, and Polemon of Ilium, who was famous for his zeal for the study of inscriptions, see Bischoff, s.v. Perieget, *RE* 19; Bowie 1974: 184–9.

[37] For two different perspectives on Asclepiades' project and relationship with local peoples, see Woolf 2011: 17–31 and Johnston 2017: 146–8.

[38] Asclepiades of Myrleia (*FGrH* 697) T 4 and F 7 = Strabo 3.4.3.

[39] The text of Strabo seems to be corrupt here, and reads *Opiscella*; but the town of Ocelum is attested in this vicinity in both Ptolemy (2.5.7) and Pliny (*NH* 4.118), and in a recently discovered inscription set up by the *vicani Ocelonenses* (*AE* 2002, 676).

mainland Greece whitewashed virtually all signs of a Roman presence.[40] The kinds of imaginary Odyssean geographies constructed and populated by Asclepiades and his contemporaries – intellectually totalizing in their combination of an authoritative mythological tradition and a malleable expansiveness – were powerful tools in the hands of Greek writers of the late Hellenistic period. This "irksome attitude of Greek scholarship," as Bickerman once called it, operated independently of Roman power, at the same time as it attempted to come to terms with the Roman impact on the meanings of Mediterranean space.[41]

Other late Hellenistic Homeric critics reconciled these altered meanings with Greek culture by remaking the past in the image of Rome, rather than stubbornly ignoring the imperial present. One of the more radical attempts in this vein to accommodate epic and empire was made by the distinguished grammarian and rhetorician Aristodemus, who had spent some time resident at Rome in the middle of the first century BCE, as the tutor of the children of Pompey the Great. Such a close and collaborative relationship with the Roman aristocracy seems to have influenced his scholarship. For centuries, cities and intellectuals had debated the question of the place of origin of Homer, basing their claims on local traditions or on internal evidence from the epics. The learned Aristodemus favored none of the typical candidates for the poet's hometown, such as Smyrna; he argued that Homer could only have been a Roman.[42] This sycophantic expropriation of the fountainhead of Greek cultural authority is profoundly disorienting. As narrated by the original *Roman* poet, Odysseus' wanderings take on entirely different connotations: reconnaissance for Roman imperial expansion, the pioneering survey of *mare nostrum*.

This tension between the power of culture and the power of empire can be further observed among the next generation of Greek geographical writers in the work of Strabo, who had been a pupil of Aristodemus at Nysa.[43] While he did not share his teacher's attitude toward Rome, Odysseus' wanderings are central to the geographical theory that Strabo

---

[40] On Pausanias' use of "myths of the ancient Greek past to shield himself from the full implications of being a subject," see Elsner 1992.
[41] Bickerman 1952: 70.
[42] [Plut.] *Vit. Hom.* 7 West (*Vita Romana*) 2; see M. L. West 2003. Two of the observed customs at Rome upon which Aristodemus based his argument for a "Roman Homer" were the Roman game of *pessoi* (a kind of chess-like strategy game, mentioned at *Od.* 1.107) and the way in which more humble Romans rise from their seats when their social betters arrive. For the political dimension of Aristodemus' argument, see Dubuisson 1987.
[43] For his relationship to Aristodemus, see Strabo 14.1.48.

develops in a lengthy introduction in the first book. He credits Odysseus with pioneering knowledge of the science of geography:

> I again refer to the fact that the poet is an expert in geography, and generalship, and agriculture, and rhetoric, knowledge of which subjects the poetic performance seems to pass on to the listeners. Certainly Homer has ascribed all knowledge of these subjects, at least, to Odysseus, whom he equips, to a greater extent than all Odysseus' contemporaries, with excellence in every field; for his Odysseus "saw many cities of men and learned their minds." (Strabo 1.2.3–4)[44]

Greek geography, as we see clearly expressed by Strabo in his introduction and throughout his mapping of the world in the next sixteen books, extended simultaneously on two axes – the spatial and the temporal – and Odysseus was instrumental in plotting values on both axes. Phrased differently, the wanderings were as significant because of *when* they took place as they were for *where* they took place. The growth of Roman power fundamentally affected the way in which the world was mentally mapped and structured: in spatial terms, Rome came to occupy the center of the οἰκουμένη, and could be conceived to be more or less coextensive with it.[45] But on the equally important temporal axis, Rome had – for Greek geographers – no depth. In this sense, the Roman Empire was flat.[46] Though it was the Romans who now gave meaning to the contemporary physical extent of space, it was the returns of Odysseus that filled out its deep historical dimension. The tension between these two axes was variously reconciled by Greek writers in the Roman Empire: Asclepiades, as we have seen, overlooked the Roman present to focus exclusively on the geographical meanings imbued by the mythical past, Aristodemus flatteringly reimagined Homer as a Roman, while Strabo and others attempted a rather more judicious balance between the various schools of thought. But this memory-scape remained, into late antiquity, a crucial site of debate and negotiation.

For writers of the late Hellenistic world confronted with the unprecedented power of Rome – Polybius, Posidonius, Asclepiades, Strabo – the figure of Odysseus, ever the ἀνὴρ πολύτροπος, had great evocative potential in the formulation of a cultural response. In particular, the wanderings

---

[44] Cf. the discussion of Strabo's relationship to Homeric geography in Kim 2010: 47–84, esp. 83–4 for the all too brief discussion of the Roman context.

[45] On the impact of the Roman Empire on conceptions of space and geography, see, *inter alios*, Nicolet 1991 and Clarke 1999.

[46] Dueck 2000: 75–6 also notes that in Strabo's account of the Roman Empire the Greeks "have chronological precedence, being more ancient, and cultural superiority in the world of scholarship and in the domain of visual art."

were a fruitful thought-world through which to reflect on time and space, and the location of power and culture therein. As a wanderer who saw the cities of men, he paved the way intellectually and geographically for Greek thinkers, writers, and speakers to move freely about the world of the Roman Mediterranean, with the confidence that they had, with Odysseus, already been there once before.

11.3 Odysseus in the Empire: Rome-Comings and Returns

Dio Cocceianus was among those imperial Greeks who found such liberation in the model of Odysseus. From Prusa, in Bithynia, Dio was active first in his native place as a sophist, and then at Rome as a student of Musonius Rufus in the early Flavian period.[47] But in the first years of Domitian's principate, Dio, like so many philosophers, ran afoul of the emperor on account of his open criticism, and was sent into exile, barred from both Rome and his homeland of Bithynia. Already by the early third century the story of Dio's exile and return had taken on a kind of legendary quality; the best information, apart from what can be gleaned from the corpus of Dio's own speeches, comes from the biography included by Philostratus in his *Lives of the Sophists*. In this account, the very end of Dio's exile – the powerful moment of his reintegration into the Roman community – was staged in dramatic fashion:

> He often visited the military camps in the rags he was accustomed to wear, and after the assassination of Domitian, realizing that the troops were on the verge of an uprising, he did not contain himself at the sight of the disorder that had broken out, but taking off his clothes he leapt on to a high altar, and began his address with the verse: "Then Odysseus of many counsels stripped himself of his rags," and having said this he revealed that he was no beggar, nor him whom they assumed him to be, but rather Dio the sage. He raised a mighty storm of invective against the tyrant, and explained to the soldiers that executing the will of the Roman people was in their best interests. And indeed the persuasiveness of the man was such as to be able to hold spellbound even those who lacked a thorough understanding of Greek culture (τοὺς μὴ τὰ Ἑλλήνων ἀκριβοῦντας). (Philostr. *VS* 1.7)

This story of the disguised Dio among the soldiers, cast in the role of Odysseus among the suitors, though most likely apocryphal, is an engaging and useful starting point for an investigation of the Odyssean self-fashioning of Dio, which – even if elaborated upon by Philostratus – was certainly not

---

[47] The fundamental study of Dio and his cultural and historical context is Jones 1978.

a biographical fiction.[48] If we examine Dio's own writings, it seems that he was already working to associate himself with Odysseus during his exile, a persona which was to become still more prominent after his return.

In two speeches delivered to the citizens of Prusa upon his reunion with the community, Dio compares his own recent experience of exile and reintegration to that of Odysseus: after so many years his fellow citizens had despaired of his return and thus, like the hero, he had suffered the ruin of his domestic affairs.[49] Public addresses to other Greek communities around this period reflect the same performance of identity; we find it most clearly articulated in the thirteenth discourse, which is, in large part, a retrospective on his own initial reaction to his exile. It was delivered in Athens, probably in 101 CE. After reflecting on the hardships and opportunities presented by exile through a consideration of Odysseus sitting on the shore of Ogygia, longing to see the smoke of Ithaca once again, Dio concluded that he, like the hero, would embrace his lot:

> Therefore I considered that Odysseus, after such far-flung wanderings, did not shrink from roaming yet again, when he carried an oar on the advice of Teiresias, a dead man, until he should encounter people who did not know the sea, even by rumor. Should I not do this same thing at the command of the god? And so, after I had encouraged myself not to fear nor to be ashamed of this course of action, having put on humble clothes and in other respects gotten myself into the right frame of mind, I set out to wander everywhere. (Dio Chrys. *Or.* 13.10)[50]

It was, perhaps, a reading of this passage that inspired Philostratus to invent the recognition scene among the soldiers, which allowed the biographer to craft a compelling and satisfying ring composition for Dio's roleplaying of an imperial Greek Odysseus. As with the Hellenistic examples of Polybius and Scipio Aemilianus discussed previously, there was a dynamic interplay between the rhetorical shaping of historiographical (or biographical) narratives and individuals' own self-fashioning.

As we have already noted in the case of Polybius, the idea of "Odysseus the exile" is not one peculiar to Dio: indeed, from the writings of contemporary Greek intellectuals at Flavian Rome, where the subject of exile was particularly current, it seems that Odysseus' wanderings were often analogized to the experience of the political refugee in the Roman

---

[48] On this episode and the historical difficulties, see Jones 1978: 48, 51–2; see also Gleason 1994: 153–6; Whitmarsh 2001a: 240–2.
[49] Dio Chrys. *Or.* 45.11 and 47.6–7.
[50] On Dio's manipulation of the persona of Odysseus in this oration, see Whitmarsh 2001a: 160–2.

world, especially in the Stoic circles around Musonius Rufus and Epictetus.[51] As Whitmarsh has demonstrated, across imperial Greek literature of the first and second centuries "there was considerable interest in exploring and expressing issues of cultural identity through the language of exile."[52] This was partly a function of the complex nexuses of identity that were developing in the Greek world under Roman rule, as the relationship between senses of belonging to *polis* communities and to other, imagined Panhellenic communities shifted. But it was also clearly a polemical response to Roman power; performing the identity of exile was an important elite cultural strategy. In this milieu, the wanderings of Odysseus were more than just subject material for learned sophistic *mimesis*; reinterpreted as a kind of paradigmatic exile, they allowed intellectuals such as Dio to come to terms with separation from the *polis* community, which otherwise involved social death and loss of identity. Odysseus represents a unique kind of "Greekness" that transcends the confines of the *polis*, one which continues to be intellectually and culturally productive even when displaced: "for a wise man, everything is Greece" (Philostr. *VA* 1.35.2: σοφῷ ἀνδρὶ Ἑλλὰς πάντα).[53]

The beginning and end of Dio's exile – at least in the retrospective shaping of the narrative of his life by Dio himself, and later by his biographer Philostratus – thus seem to have been of programmatic importance for defining the vision of his travels during that period of political separation as an Odyssean wandering. But the activities of this period itself merit at least brief discussion. One of the fictionalized adventures of Dio's exile is the subject of the seventh, or Euboean, discourse, which falls into two parts.[54] The first half of the work is, in some respects, reminiscent of a Greek novel in miniature: Dio, stranded by a shipwreck on Euboea, happens upon a huntsman on the shore, who offers him generous hospitality and introduces him to the life of happy simplicity lived by poor rustics, isolated from the unintelligible practices of the city. While the

---

[51] In his lectures in exile, Epictetus discussed the need for men to wander, either on business or merely to see the world, and, quoting the opening lines of the *Odyssey*, set Odysseus up as a paradigm (Arr. *Epict. diss.* 3.24.13). Cf. Montiglio 2011: 138–40. Ovid in exile at Tomis (*Tr.* 1.5.45–84) is among the first to exploit the potential of Odysseus to explore the coercive and arbitrary exercise of Roman monarchic power. With Ovid, however, there is also a sense of rivalry between Roman present and Greek past: in comparison with the *Neritius dux*, the poet suggests that his own wanderings are more distant, more bitter, and separate him from a far greater homeland, thus constituting an altogether more worthy subject for *docti poetae*.
[52] Whitmarsh 2001b: 270.   [53] Cf. Whitmarsh 2001a: 133.
[54] Dio Chrys. *Or.* 7; on public speech and community in late first-century Greece as illuminated by the *Euboicus*, see Ma 2000; for its narrative aspects, see Anderson 2000: 145–50.

tale shares its urban elite idealization of the countryside and of social marginality with the genre of the novel, the whole episode is, more fundamentally, modeled on Odysseus' encounter with the herdsman Eumaeus upon his return to Ithaca, with Dio again cast in the role of the wandering hero. In case the audience missed the Odyssean parallel, however, at the beginning of the second half of the work – which transitions from the novella into philosophical reflections on wealth, poverty, society, and the *polis* – Dio explicitly identifies Eumaeus and Odysseus as the epic counterpart for his own "true" story of a wanderer's autoethnographic observation of the familiar.[55] The end of the wanderings becomes a paradigm for serious social critique: just as Odysseus learns through inquiry what has become of his household in his absence, and of the predatory economic practices of the suitors who drain the resources of the rural producers, through conversation with the huntsman Dio comes to understand the problematic social and economic dynamics of city and countryside in Roman Greece, and witnesses the breakdown of the traditional ideology of the *polis*. While this is a highly stylized encounter, invented and retrojected for the purposes of an epideictic performance, it does seem that the real wanderings of Dio's exile too may have been part of a kind of Odyssean project of social and political commentary on the Roman world.

Particularly thought provoking in this respect is his long sojourn among the Getae, a Dacian people of the middle Danube who factored exigently into Roman imperial policy under Domitian and Trajan.[56] This extended visit was apparently undertaken with an eye toward researching and compiling material for an intended ethnographic work on the inhabitants of the region, which he would ultimately publish early in the rule of Trajan as the *Getica*.[57] While the Getae on the Danube would perhaps not have fulfilled the requirements of the quest assigned to Odysseus by Teiresias for "a people who did not know the sea, even by rumor," alluded to by Dio elsewhere as the objective of his own wanderings (Dio Chrys. *Or.* 13.10), the choice to blend the experience of exile with the composition of an ethnographic narrative can be understood as a further facet of his adoption

---

[55] Dio Chrys. *Or.* 7.83. At the beginning of the discourse (7.1) Dio acknowledges the turning of his ethnographic gaze upon the very heart of the Hellenic world, stating that, in a manner "appropriate for a wanderer" (ἀλητικόν), he would relate "what kind of people I met and what kind of lives they live at almost the center of Greece."

[56] On the history of the region and Roman relations with the trans-Danubian peoples, see Batty 2007.

[57] For the handful of surviving fragments of the *Getica*, all derived from Jordanes' later work on the Goths, see *FGrH* 707.

of the epic persona: as Odysseus served Polybius as the model interpreter of Roman history, he might serve Dio as the paradigm for ethnographic observation on the Roman imperial frontier. The remains of the broader ethnographic discourse in which the *Getica* was situated suggest that, like Asclepiades, Greek periegetes moving around an ever-expanding empire continued to envision themselves as following not only in the intellectual tradition, but also quite literally in the footsteps of the ἀνήρ πολύτροπος. In his contemporary account of another region on the northern frontier, Germania, the Roman historian Tacitus – who smiled at the chauvinism of imperial Greek intellectuals, "interested only in their own traditions" (Tac. *Ann.* 2.88: *qui sua tantum mirantur*) – alludes to traces of the wanderings of Odysseus "discovered" across the Rhine by certain (presumably Greek) writers.[58] Even as the Romans pushed the limits of geographical knowledge, the Greeks found that there was nowhere in the οἰκουμένη that Odysseus had not already been; and if he had crossed the Rhine, then Dio may have found him on the Danube. Frustratingly few fragments of the *Getica* survive, and it is difficult to reconstruct even a basic outline of the work; but Odysseus does seem to have made an appearance in the account of the ancient history of the Getae.[59] It was critical of Domitian,[60] and probably belongs in conversation with the four important discourses *On Kingship* addressed to Trajan in the first years of his rule, shortly after Dio's return.[61] In these works as well, especially in the first of the *Kingships*, Dio aligns himself with the cultural authority of Odysseus in the narrativization of his exile, and uses that persona to great effect in the complex rhetorical exploration of his symbouleutic and paideutic role in regard to the *princeps*.[62] Thus, in the end, his Odyssean self-fashioning was central to the definition and negotiation of identity with respect to both Greek culture and Roman power.

Few representatives of the Second Sophistic embody this kind of negotiation between the poles of culture and empire better than Aelius

---

[58] Tac. *Germ.* 3 (written *c.*98–100 CE): at Asciburgium, which these authors claimed had been founded and named by Odysseus, there was supposedly an altar inscribed in Greek characters with the name of Odysseus and his father, Laertes. Cf. the discussion of Tacitus' critique of the mentality of imperial *Graecorum annales* vis-à-vis their representation of the west in Johnston 2017: 125–32, esp. 131–32.
[59] Dio (*FGrH* 707) F 2 (= Jord. *Get.* 9.58–60). Their king Telephus, a son of Heracles, met Odysseus in combat, apparently when Odysseus had traveled to the region of the Danube within the borders (*fines*) of the Getae.
[60] Dio (*FGrH* 707) F 5 (= Jord. *Get.* 13.76), which discusses how the *avaritia* of Domitian eroded the longstanding *foedus* on the Danube that the Getae had observed with other *principes*.
[61] Dio Chrys. *Or.* 1–4.
[62] On this aspect of the *Kingships*, see Whitmarsh 2001a: 198–200, 243–6.

Aristides, who rose to prominence in the generation after Dio. As was the case for most successful sophists, Aristides' career involved travel both throughout the cities of the Greek East and occasionally to the emperor at Rome or in the provinces, in the role of ambassador and panegyrist.[63] Aristides' success before both of these audiences, *poleis* and *princeps*, is eloquently summed up in one of the last speeches of his career, an address to his patron divinity Asclepius in the late 170s CE:

> There is no city, no private person, no holder of public office, who after even a brief interaction with us did not welcome us and sing our praises as much as possible, which had nothing to do, I think, with my oratory, but was rather your doing, my patron. But in fact the greatest achievement in this respect is putting me on such friendly terms with the divine Emperors, and, besides just by my communication with them by mail, by providing me the opportunity to speak before them in person and to earn a degree of respect that no one had ever gained previously. (Aristid. *Or.* 42.13)

The speech to which Aristides here refers was a declamation before the emperors Marcus Aurelius and Commodus, which had been delivered at Smyrna in 177, on the occasion of the imperial visit to this long-important seat of sophistic education. Further on in this passage Aristides finds an interesting parallel for his epideictic performance: "Odysseus received from Athena the ability to give an oratorical display in the palace of Alcinous and before the Phaeacians – this was certainly a great thing and very opportune; my business as well was accomplished in this fashion" (Aristid. *Or.* 42.14). In this epic analogy the sophist is reenvisioned as Odysseus, with the divine patronage of Asclepius following in the epic tradition of Athena; the Roman emperor and his court collapse together with Alcinous and his Phaeacians.[64] There is much interesting cultural work being done here: two of Odysseus' primary identities – as clever speaker and world traveler – are made to prefigure the complex role of Greek sophists in the Roman Empire. Moreover, Odysseus and his *apologoi* among the Phaeacians provide an important means of reconceptualizing in the traditional terms of Greek culture, and thus naturalizing, the kinds of steeply hierarchical speech situations in which Greek intellectuals of the first and second centuries increasingly found themselves.

---

[63] On the various political and social roles of sophists in the period, see Bowersock 1969.
[64] Holmes 2008 has demonstrated how, in his *Hieroi Logoi*, Aristides aligns himself with another internal narrative episode in the *Odyssey*, Helen in Book 4. See also Schröder 1987 for the Odyssean self-fashioning of Aristides in this work (*Or.* 47–52).

During a visit to Rome twenty years earlier, Aristides had found himself in just such a situation, and on the occasion he delivered before the emperor Antoninus Pius one of his most famous orations, *On Rome*, which casts into sharp relief the perceived discrepancies between Roman power and Greek culture. One compelling and complex passage that comes toward the end of the lengthy address is particularly worth dwelling upon, in which Aristides meditates upon the impact of the Roman Empire on travel in the Mediterranean and beyond:

> It is you again who have best demonstrated the truth of the universal saying, that Earth is mother of all and common homeland. Now indeed it is possible for Greeks and non-Greeks (βαρβάρῳ) easily to travel wherever they wish, with or without their property, just as simply as passing from one homeland to another ... for security, it is enough to be a Roman citizen, or rather to be one of those united under your empire. It was said by Homer that "Earth is common of all" [*Il.* 15.189], and you have made it a reality. You have measured and recorded the land of the entire inhabited world; you have spanned the rivers with bridges of all varieties and excavated highways through the mountains and filled the wilderness and the deserts with rest stops; you have, in short, brought order and a settled way of life to all the places of the world ... There is no need whatsoever now to write a travel guide (περιήγησις) to lands and peoples or to catalog the customs (νόμοι) that each country practices. You yourselves have instead become universal guides (περιηγηταὶ κοινοὶ) for all, having thrown wide all the gates of the inhabited world and provided the opportunity to those who so desired to see everything for themselves (αὐτόπται πάντων γίγνεσθαι). You established common laws for all and you put an end to the previous conditions that, although they were entertaining to describe, were intolerable, if one looked at them reasonably. (Aristid. *Or.* 26.100–2)

This section of the speech is suffused with "memories of Odysseus";[65] with the pervasive themes of travel, autopsy, description, and the confrontation of selves and others, Aristides challenges the reader-listener to rethink the place of the hero in a fundamentally changed world.

Ushering in the homogenization and sanitization of the Mediterranean, the universalization of Roman power and the perfection of Roman knowledge – a state of affairs already adumbrated by Polybius three hundred years before – seem now to preclude entirely the possibility of Odyssean wanderings. The recurring question of the epic, ὦ ξεῖνοι, τίνες ἐστέ – "strangers, who are you?" – is no longer a meaningful one: there are no

---

[65] See generally Hartog 2001. He discusses Aristides and this oration only briefly (193–6), and raises more questions than he answers about its purpose and sincerity.

strangers in the Roman world, no pirates bringing evil to men of other lands, no real distinctions between Greeks and non-Greeks.[66] Even the *nostos* is now pointless: in the undifferentiated space of the Roman Empire as depicted by Aristides, one πατρίς fades into another; the smoke rising from Ithaca is no longer distinguishable.[67] Furthermore, the Odyssean narrative – the pioneering περιήγησις – is unwritten by imperial power, rendered obsolete. The once-entertaining ethnographic observations of Odysseus are trivial and ridiculous in light of the present state of affairs, where, with the Romans as the authoritative interpreters (περιηγηταὶ κοινοί) of the οἰκουμένη that they have inventoried, transformed, and dominated, everyone has now become a firsthand observer (αὐτοπταὶ γίγνεσθαι) of the universalized νόμοι of Rome.

This seemingly dramatic marginalization of the place of Odysseus, and thus the reevaluation of one of the fundamental points of orientation for the Greek experience of time and space, ultimately raises the question of Aristides' sincerity and motives in this effusive panegyric of Roman imperialism. Deeply and problematically engaged in the cultural debates of the Second Sophistic, it is carefully constructed to be a provocative and challenging text, which demands to be read against the grain, as well as against the views articulated by Aristides in other public speeches, especially the *Panathenaicus*, delivered at Athens within a year of this address. As a panegyric of an empire, rather than an emperor, the Roman oration is more truly a mirror of cultures than a mirror of princes, and in the sublime image of the unified and "flattened" Roman world reflected in this mirror there is a disquieting void, "the absence carved out by empire where a polis would have stood."[68] Among the many vacancies with which Aristides' fantasy of empire is punctuated is the possibility of meaningful participation in the political community, something mourned by Polybius already centuries before. But while the historian had nonetheless found a productive, renegotiated place for Odysseus in the empire, the sophist is overcome by its vast emptiness, in which memory fades and from which there could be no return.

As a means of commenting on Rome, Odysseus is used rather differently by Aristides' contemporary Lucian of Samosata. Odysseus is perhaps best known from Lucian's works as the object of the author's scathing

---

[66] See e.g. *Od.* 9.252–5.
[67] See Damon and Palazzolo, Chapter 10 in this volume, for more on this distinctly imperial "fade."
[68] Jarratt 2016: 223, who also emphasizes the importance of the Homeric themes in the speech, and interprets them as contributing to an "anti-sublime" that produces a whole (the empire) that is ruptured, failed, full of "holes or absences."

criticism at the beginning of the *True Stories*, where, as narrator of his travels at the court of Alcinous, Odysseus is accused of being – quite in contrast to Polybius' "father of history" – the originator of the worst kinds of historiography and ethnography.[69] Whether or not we are to take Lucian's polemic seriously is certainly open to debate, but it is clear that, in other writings, Lucian aligns himself much more collaboratively with Odyssean narratives. One such example is the comparatively underappreciated dialogue, *Nigrinus*.[70] The *Nigrinus* is set, from a narratological perspective, within a double frame: the exterior frame is a letter of Lucian to the otherwise unknown (and perhaps fictional) philosopher Nigrinus, which recounts in the form of a quasi-Platonic dialogue a discussion between Lucian, recently returned from a visit to Rome, and an unnamed friend, within which is embedded an account of a second conversation that Lucian claims to have had at Rome with Nigrinus.[71] After a brief introduction to Nigrinus' cultural attitudes, which found harmonious expression during the time that he spent in Athens, Lucian relates the philosopher's speech to him about his return thence to Rome:

> "For my part," he said, "when I first came back from Greece, as I drew somewhat near Rome, I stopped and I asked myself the reason for my return, quoting those words of Homer,
>
> 'Why, unhappy man, have you left the light of day …'
> meaning Greece, and the happiness and freedom there,
> 'and come to see …'
> (*Od.* 11.93–4)
>
> in this city the crowds, and the professional informers, and those arrogant routine morning greetings, and the lavish dinners, and the flatterers, and the murders, and the hopeful attempts to get written into wills, and the false friendships? And what have you even decided to do here, given that you can neither escape nor enjoy these established customs? … If it is necessary to speak in praise of evils, do not imagine that there is any better training ground for virtue or truer test of the soul than this city and living here. For it is no small accomplishment to resist such temptations, such sights and sounds grabbing your attention and pulling you in all directions, but you just have to imitate Odysseus and sail past them all, but not with your hands tied or your ears plugged with wax (that would be cowardly), but listening freely and openly looking down on it all." (Lucian, *Nigr.* 17–19)

---

[69] Lucian, *Hist. Ver.* 1, 3. See Kim 2010: 140–74.
[70] One of the most interesting recent readings of this dialogue is Whitmarsh 2001a: 265–79.
[71] For an attempt at understanding the eccentric form of the dialogue, see Anderson 1978.

What follows is a hilariously derisive, almost ethnographic lampoon of Roman society, in which the wanderings of Odysseus are translated into struggles of the philosopher to navigate the moral dangers of the urban landscape of Rome. The elaborate customs of the *salutatio* and the system of patronage, dining, baths, the theater, monumental statues, funerary rituals – all are dangers sailed past by Nigrinus, and mocked along the way. The Odyssean narrative is appropriately bookended by a conflation of the two audiences, with Nigrinus' interlocutor, Lucian, finding himself at the end in the same position as the Phaeacian listeners to the Homeric wanderer's tale: "Having gone through these arguments and many others like them, he brought his speech to an end. All the while I listened to him awestruck, worried that he would become silent. And when he did stop talking, I felt just like those Phaeacians" (Lucian, Nigr. 35). The "conversion experience" of Lucian to philosophy as a result of Nigrinus' story possessed simultaneously the power of the Sirens' song and the lotus' fruit: forgetful of all else, he was called down the path of the philosopher.[72]

Such sustained, explicit social and cultural critique of Rome is a relative rarity within the Second Sophistic, a movement that is usually so self-consciously and artificially oblivious to the ruling power. The themes of Lucian's dialogue have much more in common with the concerns of Roman satire – especially Juvenal – than with those of sophistic declamation. Swain has convincingly argued that Lucian's primary target in the *Nigrinus* is those who possess money without true culture;[73] he is in this dialogue, as so often in his other writings, concerned with the defense of the Greek culture, *paideia*, that he has – as a native Syrian but a Greek *pepaideumenos* – so laboriously acquired. The successful return of Odysseus, for Lucian's Nigrinus, is a metaphor for the resistance of the philosopher to the misappropriation, contamination, and degradation of "Greekness" under the powerful influence of the city of Rome and its wealthy but uncultured patrons.

11.4 Odysseus as Emperor

In the final stage of my own wanderings in this chapter I would like to come full circle, and to return briefly to Julian in the age of the Third Sophistic. After the murder of his family in the political purge carried out by his cousin Constantius, Julian grew up in a state of internal exile, locked away on an imperial estate in Cappadocia; possessed of an insatiable

---

[72] Lucian, *Nigr.* 3, 37–8. [73] Swain 1998: 315–21.

academic curiosity, he received a traditional Greek education – first in private, and only later, with some suspicion on the part of Constantius, at the great centers of Greek learning: Nicomedia, Pergamum, Ephesus, and Athens. He proudly professed to have very little knowledge of Latin, and self-identified as a Greek throughout his public life.[74] The merging of these two formative threads – the trauma of his exilic childhood and his thorough inculcation in Greek literature – seems to have encouraged an early and lifelong self-identification with the figure of Odysseus, who became for Julian an important point of mediation in his constructions of Hellenism. This is detectable already in his earliest writings, the three imperial panegyrics, delivered around the time he was sent to Gaul: two addressed to Constantius, and one to Constantius' wife Eusebia.

These texts have traditionally been read as empty, if rhetorically masterful, pieces of flattery, devoid of any real value for the historian.[75] But within the last two decades of scholarship there has begun a gradual rehabilitation of these speeches as sophisticated, nuanced, and even subversive texts, which are deeply engaged in rhetorical self-fashioning and covert critique of the regime of Constantius.[76] The panegyric of Eusebia is of particular interest for the way in which Julian aligns himself with Odysseus in order to simultaneously find a model for the praise of a noble woman and to reflect on the uncertainty of his own position. In 354 CE, in the wake of the execution of his brother Gallus, Julian had been summoned by Constantius to the court at Milan to respond to allegations that he had been complicit in Gallus' treason. It was the empress who had reconciled Julian with Constantius, a kindness which had perhaps saved his life, and which certainly placed him in her debt.

Toward the opening of the panegyric Julian identifies his former precarious position when recently arrived at the court of the emperor at Milan with that of Odysseus washed ashore on Phaeacia. While this is an epic analogue that had been developed by Julian's sophistic predecessors, the scene seems to be deployed here not only in the self-conscious construction of social and cultural distance from the center of Roman power, but also to subtly critique Constantius, whose Poseidon-like wrath is the ultimate cause of the wanderings of the tempest-tossed Julian-Odysseus. As Odysseus was hospitably received by Arete, the wife of Alcinous, who diffused potential conflict between the two men, thus Julian found himself dependent upon

---

[74] For Julian and Hellenism, see Elm 2012.
[75] For a survey of this line of scholarship, see Curta 1995: n. 8.
[76] Tougher 2012, for example, reads carefully veiled critique in the *First Panegyric* on Constantius.

the intercession of Eusebia. Moreover, the fact that "Homer did not hesitate to praise ... the wife of Alcinous, and other women of outstanding goodness," and that Athena, in disguise, had spoken to Odysseus "an encomium of Arete, just like an orator who has perfected the art of rhetoric" justifies and authorizes Julian's choice to deliver an uncustomary panegyric of the empress (Julian. *Or.* 3.104C–105A). Remarkably, Julian even goes so far as to structure his own speech explicitly according to the order and themes of Athena's proto-panegyric, beginning with her native land and ancestors, before moving on to her marriage to Constantius, who is disingenuously cast in the role of Alcinous.[77] As we have seen in previous case studies, Julian, exiled and marginalized by the abusive exercise of imperial power, subversively appropriated, in an act of resistance, an Odyssean identity in order to come to terms with his own marginality, and to reassert an active role in shaping his own political fate.

As his relationship with Constantius gradually soured in the late 350s, and eventually turned into open hostility, Julian continued to develop this self-image as Odysseus in his writings. Well educated and widely read, he was at times demonstrably inspired in the adoption of this persona by literary encounters with his imperial Greek predecessors who had seen themselves as following in the footsteps of the much-wandering man. At one of the emotional low points in his extended sojourn in the West, stranded on his own Ogygian isle far from the Greek culture to which he so longed to find a way back, he found strength in the model of the exiled Dio of Prusa. The self-consolatory address that he wrote from Gaul to his friend Sallust on the occasion is thoroughly influenced by the previously discussed thirteenth oration of Dio, including his identification with Odysseus the exile.[78] But the hero did not remain on Ogygia forever. Julian, the Odyssean emperor, would have his *nostos*. From what remains of his wartime propaganda as he marched eastward against Constantius, it seems that parallels with the epic journey factored into his public communication with the most ancient *poleis* of Greece. The idea of Corinth as Phaeacia – a civilized haven for Julian's father Julius Constantius during

---

[77] Julian. *Or.* 3.105A–106B; the qualities upon which Julian dwells are prudence (σωφροσύνη), justice (δικαιοσύνη), mildness (πραότης), fairness (ἐπιείκεια), love for her husband (ἡ περὶ τὸν ἄνδρα φιλία), generosity with her resources (ἡ περὶ τὰ χρήματα μεγαλοψυχία), and respect for her people and her relatives (ἡ περὶ τοὺς οἰκείους καὶ ξυγγενεῖς τιμή). On this speech, see Tougher 1998: esp. 111–14 and James 2012, who finds covert criticism of Eusebia alongside the overt praise. Given that Arete has a more direct claim to the Phaeacian throne (previously held by her father) than Alcinous, the epic analogy, carried to its logical conclusion, may contain a comment on the legitimacy of Constantius' rule.

[78] Julian. *Or.* 8.249D–250C.

his own wanderings through an otherwise hostile empire – was one of the salient themes quoted back to the emperor by Libanius from the letter that Julian had sent to the Corinthians during the campaign in the hope of winning their support for his cause by invoking their hereditary friendship.[79] Even after his untimely death in Mesopotamia, Libanius faithfully reproduced the emperor's Odyssean image in his funeral oration: in his youth, Julian, separated from Greece, "the land that he loved," and tempest-tossed in the Roman West like Odysseus on his raft, had wanted only to return (Lib. *Or.* 18.27).

11.5 Conclusion

As we have traced across five centuries, from Polybius to Julian, there was an important tradition in the imperial Greek reception of the wanderings of the Homeric Odysseus that found, in his quintessential character as ἀνήρ πολύτροπος, a suitably adaptable figure for meaningfully exploring a range of issues at the heart of debates surrounding Greek cultural identity under Roman rule: time, memory, and the construction of historical narrative; space, geography, and ethnography; imperial power, marginality, and resistance; and the role of the intellectual in society. Odysseus visited the cities of men and came to know their minds, but this is only part of his story; the story of the cities of men who continued to revisit Odysseus in order to come to know their own minds is one equally worth telling.

---

[79] Lib. *Or.* 14.30. The letter itself is lost, but the contemporaneous *Letter to the Athenians*, of comparable content, survives.

PART IV

Unearthly Journeys

Introduction

The final part of this volume takes us to the limits of time and space. From late antiquity to the lunar landing, Martin Devecka and Karen ní Mheallaigh productively push the temporal and geographical boundaries of our study. They mix expected and unexpected objects of analysis with a similar range of methods. Both display a comparative eye for cultural critique, and drive to the core of travel's potential manifestations. By the part's closing pages, the temporal distances of our exploration begin to collapse.

For Devecka, Rutilius Namatianus' *De reditu suo* is a multiform travel poem. It depicts a voyage between physical homes while also conveying a learned poet's intellectual journey into the lost, "Classical," past. This journey takes readers to the ends of the Roman Empire, spatially at the tidal flux of the Atlantic, and temporally at the era of Gothic rule. The Italian city of Luna provides Rutilius with an unearthly rest stop, and the poem's conflation of geography and tidal activity is shown to serve several literary purposes. Indeed, tides in Roman thought appear as the ends of the earth, a feature at odds with imperial knowledge but central to the ideology and cultural traditions encoded in "ancient" texts. As Devecka persuasively conveys, the poem's focus on flux and ruination constructs an often mournful and introspective meditation on Rome's past and a present where Rome itself after the sack could fade into history, becoming nothing but the shadow of a great name. Not all is so bleak, however, since for Devecka Rutilius' focus on tides betrays more than melancholy nostalgia: there is hope for an improved future. Cities and tides rise and fall, they ebb and flow, and Rome's recent decline may very well be followed naturally by a return to the top. In his observation of these features, Rutilius is also up to something else. He participates in a complex game of literary reference, wherein his knowledge of the world allows for the poetic self-construction of a "Rutilius" who is master of the political and cultural landscapes he inhabits, which are themselves in serious flux during his voyage home. Devecka concludes with an intriguing comparison between Rutilius Namatianus and Augustine that brings to the fore many themes explored throughout the chapter that resonate with wider cultural debates of the period.

Rutilius may bring us to the ends of the known world, but beyond the Roman Empire is the infinite expanse of the cosmos. Ní Mheallaigh takes us there through two parallel voyages of her own. The first reads Lucian's depictions of lunar travel and their moon-to-earth perspective within ancient traditions of the "view from on high" and the potential ethnographic implications of such a distanced perspective, a viewpoint already explored in part by O'Sullivan. Travel always affects one's experience of home, but the departure from Earth may forever impact home's ability to sit at the center of one's identity. For an author grappling with Greek identity in a Roman world, what could be more attractive than the perspective granted from a lunar vantage, one that encompasses the entire Earth and the vastness of its paradoxically minuscule histories? In her own journey through the tradition of *gaiaskopic* texts, ní Mheallaigh also makes meaningful stops at the ekphrasis of Achilles' shield in the *Iliad* and the *Somnium Scipionis* of Cicero's *De republica*, wherein she engages directly with intellectual currents that span the temporal and cultural scope of the volume. Much of this chapter, however, pushes readers beyond the direct reach of the "Greek and Roman" found in the volume's title, and in the process offers a series of reflections on what must have made the journey and the very idea of "home" so powerful throughout history; on what drove countless individuals to wonder at the expanse of the known and unknown worlds. Lucian could only imagine the moon, so ní Mheallaigh takes us to the twentieth century to experience the impact of lunar travel in the age of NASA. Through detailed analysis of interviews with astronauts and the cultural reception of photographs taken from space, Classical depictions of lunar visitation are cast in a new and surprising light. Together, the two chapters of this final part invite us to reconsider the reference points with which we plot our concepts of "home" and "away," and through which we map our own journeys.

CHAPTER 12

From Rome to the Moon: Rutilius Namatianus and the Late Antique Game of Knowledge

Martin Devecka

Rutilius Namatianus' *De reditu suo* is a poem written in elegiac couplets that describes, over the course of two books, its author's 417 CE journey by sea from Rome to his family plantation somewhere in Gallia Narbonensis. Eduard Norden called its author "the last classical poet," which is a debatable judgment; it would be eminently reasonable, however, to think of *De reditu* as the last travel poem of antiquity. My aim in this chapter will be to justify both parts of this claim: first, to explain in what sense *De reditu* should count as an antique or Classical travel poem, and then, by setting it alongside some contemporary Christian writings with which it was in polemical engagement, to show why the tradition in which Rutilius wrote was coming to an end.[1]

In what follows, I will be focusing on the poem's use of tidal flux, which I argue it adopts as a controlling metaphor in more than one sense. *De reditu* is a journey from Rome to the moon, bound together by its author's ability to interpret the landscape in terms of a rubric of "Classical" knowledge. The purpose of Rutilius' lunar voyage is to allow him to assimilate a historiographical narrative of Roman defeat and recovery to the rhythm of the tides, thus naturalizing it and allowing him to predict, on the basis of a kind of metaphoric science, that Rome will rebound from its recent sack by the Goths. But this astronomical allegory also hints, as we will see, at the emergence in the early fifth century CE of forms of "local Romanness" that were already transforming the Roman world from an empire into a polycentric political system.[2]

---

[1] For a long time there was considerable scholarly disagreement on the precise date of the journey recorded in the poem; see Cameron 1967 for a summary of the then-current opinions, as well as for Cameron's proposal of 417 CE. With the discovery in the 1970s (Ferrari 1973) of additional fragments from Book 2 that indicate for the poem a dramatic date after the signal successes of Constantius Florus, this last proposal now enjoys a plurality of critical support: Fo 1992: viii–ix, with Fo 1989: 51 and Wolff 2005: 66. Rutilius as the "last classical poet": Norden 1927: 85.
[2] For the concept of "local Romanness," see originally Heather 2005: 437–50. I employ it here in the sense developed by Peter Brown, as reflecting a certain distributed loyalty to Roman

The content of this allegory – and the rest of the poem, too – should be taken as an intervention in a fifth-century "debate over providence" that saw Christian authors, most notably Augustine, blame the capture of the eternal city on the sins of its inhabitants, supposedly in reply to a pagan polemic that blamed the disaster on Rome's abandonment of the old gods. Rutilius travels through a landscape that argues, at almost every point, for Rome's fated recovery from a disaster that will, in retrospect, prove to have been no disaster at all. The landscape speaks to Rutilius in a language of allusion and elite "scientific" knowledge. This knowledge, however, was – as I will conclude by arguing – itself the target of an ultimately successful Christian polemic that invalidated, for future generations, the modes of interpretation by which Rutilius situated himself within the landscape through which he moved. Consequently, no one was going to be able to travel in quite the same way again.[3]

12.1

I began by saying that *De reditu suo* (hereafter *DRS*) is a travel poem. Without further qualification, though, this may be a claim that obscures more than it explains, since, as the other chapters in this volume have shown, the coherence of the ancient travel poem as a genre conceals a bewildering array of competing forms and tendencies. Composed in elegiacs though it is, *DRS* describes a journey that is in many important senses an epic one – sufficiently so, indeed, that François Paschoud has devoted an article to arguing that Rutilius ought to have written in hexameter. Since the beginning of the twentieth century, scholars have noticed a self-consciously Odyssean patterning in the poem, which claims to chronicle the author's long-delayed return to the humble land of his birth. Rutilius flags this intertext both directly, via quotation, and indirectly, via a complex play of linguistic and structural allusions to Homeric citations by earlier Latin poets – chiefly Ovid. These, for instance, are the terms in which Rutilius evokes the environs of Rome:

> Nec locus ille mihi cognoscitur indice fumo,
>   qui dominas arces et caput orbis habet
> (quamquam signa leuis fumi commendat Homerus,
>   dilecto quotiens surgit in astra solo),

---

institutions and patterns of life in an empire that was increasingly able to do without Rome: Brown 2012: 392–407.

[3] For the debate over providence, see Cameron 2010: 209–11 with Paschoud 2012: 380–8.

> sed caeli plaga candidior tractusque serenus
>   signat septenis culmina clara iugis.
>   (*DRS* 1.193–7)

> Nor was the place known to me by the evidence of smoke, that place which holds the commanding towers and headship of the world (although Homer commends the sign of a thin smoke, whenever it rises from a beloved land to the stars), but a shining and clear piece of sky indicates those heights, famous for their seven hills.

The poet's explicit mention of Homer directs us toward *Od.* 1.57, where Odysseus pines for the καπνὸν ἀποθρῴσκοντα. But Ovid has traveled this ground already: at *Pont.* 1.3.33–4 he invokes Odysseus' desire to see *fumum de patriis . . . focis* in defense of his own "pious or womanish" wish to return to Rome. The mediated character of allusions like this one has led at least one scholar to wonder whether Rutilius had direct access to the text of Homer at all.[4]

Ovid's *Tristia* is the *DRS*'s other major intertext – compare especially the drawn-out departure at *DRS* 1.155–216 with Ovid's techniques of poetic delay in *Tr.* 1.3 – and it is immediately apparent what a challenge the poet has set himself in bringing together these very different sources of inspiration: on the one hand, an epic of a hero's return; on the other, a series of smaller laments over an exile's departure. Suffice it to say, the doubled poetic affiliations of the *DRS* can hardly be explained by reason of convenience.[5]

I do not plan to say much more about these affiliations, except to remark that one result of their interplay is to throw into question the valences both of the end and of the beginning of Rutilius' journey. In *DRS*, Rutilius' Rome is Ovid's Rome but also Homer's Troy; conversely, the family plot at Toulouse is at once Homer's Ithaca and Ovid's Tomis. One can never be sure which end of Rutilius' journey is home, and which is away.[6]

---

[4] Fo 1992: ad loc. For a more in-depth study of this allusory chain, see Squillante 2005: 173–98, and, for a treatment that emphasizes Rutilius' dependence on Ovid, Fo 1989: 52. Tissol 2002 offers a full account of Homeric/Ovidian double allusions in the poem. *DRS* as epic: Paschoud 1979: 319–22, a series of observations repeated and expanded upon by Fo 1989: 54 and finally by Soler 2006, who offers a concise but thorough summary of the poem's generic affiliations. Vergil is another important source of language and allusive content for Rutilius, and on this basis it has sometimes been argued that Aeneas is one of the poet's identificatory avatars: e.g. Wolff 2005: 68 and Clarke 2014: *passim*. For the purposes of this chapter, however, the choice between Odysseus and Aeneas ends up being an insignificant one.

[5] For a treatment of the conflicts inherent in Rutilius' intertextual program, see again Squillante 2005: 173–5.

[6] On this Homeric smoke as an echo both of Ithaca and of Troy, see Privitera 2004: 45. For the paradoxical nature of the poem's allusory frame, see Clarke 2014: 93; although Clarke's interest lies

In short, then, we cannot rely on Rutilius' structural models to make our interpretive decisions for us. Beneath the careful and loving portrait of Rome with which the poem begins lies, as Maria Squillante has argued, an echo of burning Ilium justified, at least in part, by the then all-too-recent sack of the city under Alaric: if Rutilius goes out of his way to tell us that there is no smoke in the Roman sky, then, to paraphrase Freud, the text of the poem knows no negation. Its end, if we had it, would probably present similar ambiguities. In any case, we know that the family estates to which Rutilius is returning are *laceri*, marred by *saeua incendia* (*DRS* 1.29). A close look at the midpoint of the poem will shed some light, I think, on this strange bivalent structure. As we will see, it is exactly here that the poet most clearly builds his poem around the reciprocal back-and-forth sloshing of the tides.[7]

What we have, at the conclusion of Book 1, is a kind of "end in the middle." It marks a terminus, as I shall argue, in a double sense of the word – the insertion of a border – but it also makes a point of passage into the vast unknown of the second book. Here is how Book 1 of *DRS* concludes:

> Interea madidis non desinit Africus alis
>   continuos picea nube necare[8] dies.
> Iam matutinis Hyades occasibus udae;
>   iam latet hiberno conditus imbre Lepus,
> exiguum radiis, sed magnis fluctibus, astrum,
>   quo madidam nullus navita linquat humum;
> namque procelloso subiungitur Orioni
>   aestiferumque Canem roscida praeda fugit.
> Uidimus excitis pontum fauescere arenis
>   atque eructato uertice rura tegi,
> qualiter Oceanus mediis infunditur agris,
>   destituenda uago cum premit arua salo,
> siue alio refluus nostro conliditur orbe,
>   siue corusca suis sidera pascit aquis.
> (*DRS* 1.631–44)

---

mainly in the poem's Vergilian echoes, she reaches much the same conclusion as I do about its author's ambiguously double-ended journey.

[7] Squillante 2005: 176. For the "family estates" and some background on Rutilius' historical situation, see Vesserau 1904: 194–222 and, more briefly, Paschoud 1993: 16, with some intriguing but speculative additions made by Heather 2005: 249–50.

[8] For *necare*, most modern editions have *negare*; but see Rocchi 2016 for a convincing argument in favor of preserving the manuscript reading.

Meanwhile, Africus does not cease, with its dampened wings, to stifle the daylight with pitch-dark clouds. Now the moist Hyades are setting in the morning, now the Rabbit hides behind winter rain, a star with puny rays, but great fluxes of water, under which no sailor would leave the moist land; for it sits beneath gusty Orion and, a dewy prey, it flees heat-bringing Sirius. We saw the sea grow yellow with stirred up sands, the land get covered with vomited peaks of water, just as the Ocean drowns the inland fields, when it presses the deserted acres with wandering seawater, whether it strikes as a reflux from another world than ours, or whether it nourishes the shining stars with its waters.

A storm has kept Rutilius' boat in harbor at Triturrita for several days. The surge from this storm has caused a confusion of sea and land that reminds the poet of tidal floods, for which, accordingly, he provides two different explanations.

One of Rutilius' etiologies, the one that begins *sive corusca suis*, has always been well understood by scholars and editors. Seneca, Pliny, and Lucan, among others, all discourse at rather more length on the theory that the sun and the other fiery bodies of the heavens sustain their burning by drawing water up from the oceans to use as fuel. This is a Stoic theory, I should note, and therefore not bound by conditions of plausibility or explanatory accuracy.[9]

The other aetiology has occasioned rather more controversy, or at least confusion. Early editors, including the Duffs, to whom we owe the Loeb translation, were sure that Rutilius' *alio . . . orbe* referred to the moon – not an unreasonable conclusion, given the tidal context in which it appears. Etienne Wolff and most others who have edited the text in recent decades have taken a different approach, preferring to translate *alio nostro orbe* as "a different part of the world." There are good reasons for accepting this second interpretation. First, a theory of tides according to which water sloshes down from the poles was an established hypothesis in ancient astronomy; and second, there is no ancient theory of lunar influence on tides that Rutilius' *refluus* precisely fits. It may also be argued that *orbis*, in good classical Latin, is almost never used to describe a terrestrial sphere, although this is how Rutilius' use of the word would have to be read by those who plump for Duff et al.'s reading of the passage.[10]

---

[9] A Stoic theory: Doblhofer 1977: ad loc., following Mueller 1882: 4, which provides a fuller account of the theory's Stoic affiliations. cf. Plin. *HN* 2.212–18, Sen. *QNat.* 3.28, and Lucan, *BC* 9.311–18 *inter alia*.

[10] For the moon: Duff and Duff 1934: 821 (in agreement with Doblhofer 1977: ad loc, and following Zumpt 1837: ad loc., who was the first to notice a passage of Claudian that might be taken to provide a parallel for this interpretation: *Dixit et antiquae muros egressa Ravennae / Signa movet;*

Against all these respectable philological arguments, there is one objection which is to my mind decisive in favor of reading *orbis* here as "moon": the next stop on Rutilius' itinerary after Triturrita, where he's trapped by the storm, is almost certainly the Ligurian city of Luna. Scholars can agree on this, although the town is nowhere named in what remains of *DRS*, for geographical reasons but also because Rutilius tags the first port of call in Book 2, otherwise anonymous, with some obvious allusive clues:

> Aduehimur celeri candentia moenia lapsu;
>   nominis est auctor sole corusca soror.
> indigenis superat ridentia lilia saxis
>   et leui radiat picta nitore silex;
> diues marmoribus telus, quae luce coloris
>   prouocat intactas luxuriosa niues.
>   (*DRS* 2.63–8)

> We are borne with a swift transit beneath the shining walls; the source of the name of the place is the sister of the bright sun. Shining lilies overtop the native rocks and the veiny flint gives off a light sheen; a land rich in marble, which with the brightness of its color challenges, luxuriant, the virgin snows.

Supposing that this identification is secure, we may venture to suggest that Rutilius' discussion of the tides is a kind of proleptic gloss, a gesture entirely in keeping with what Squillante aptly calls his "manierismo neoalessandrino." Luna's name is suppressed in the verse so that the poet can point to it using a series of clues of decreasing difficulty, for the delectation of a cultured readership.[11]

But this identification of an Alexandrian device at work in Rutilius' account of tides does not really explain very much. There were plenty of options for encoding the name of Luna in the text without putting it there explicitly; so why choose tides? After all, what Rutilius is really describing

---

iamque ora Padi portusque relinquit / Flumineos, certis ubi legibus aduena Nereus / Aestuat et pronas puppes nunc amne retuso, / Nunc redeunte uehit nudataque litora fluctu / Deserit, Oceani lunaribus aemula damnis (*Cons. Hon.* VI 495–9)). Claudian is evoking the head of the Adriatic Sea, one of the few locations in the Mediterranean basin that experiences significant tides. Against the moon: Wolff 2007 (in agreement with Castorina 1967: ad loc., apparently also winning the assent of Fo); for a treatment of all the difficulties involved in identifying *alio . . . orbe* with the moon, see Fo 1992: ad loc. The most recent edition, Pozzato and Rodighiero 2011: ad loc., remains agnostic on the question. For a discussion of the moon in which *orbis* probably needs to be translated "sphere," see Lucr. 5.751 ff.

[11] For the identification of this town with Luna, see Fo 1992: ad loc. and Vesserau 1904: 271. "manierismo di marco neoalessandrino": Squillante 2005: 166; see Heather 2005: 232–4 for a similar opinion, and for further discussion of Rutilius' program as a purely literary one, Fo 1989: 53–4. On Rutilius' route, see Franceschelli and Dall'Aglio 2014: 18 and Soler 2006.

here is a storm; tides get thrown in as a sort of digressive–descriptive bonus. What are tides doing in this poem, and why has Rutilius used them to end his first book while bridging a gap to the second? The answer to these questions is complicated, and it is, I am afraid, going to throw what seemed like a stable reading of *alio nostro orbe* as *Luna* into doubt once again.

12.2

Rutilius' invocation of the tides should be understood against the background of a Roman literary tradition. In an echo of our modern notion that to know nature is to control it, Roman writers demonstrated their knowledge of the secret mechanics behind tidal flux in order to show that they had, one way or another, mastered the content of a narrative in which tidal fluxes were embedded. Like those tropes of ancient *gaiaskopia* discussed by Karen ní Mheallaigh in the next chapter, discussions of the tides in Roman poetry served both to situate narrators at a privileged vantage point and to integrate these narrators within a literate tradition.[12] As we will see, this kind of knowledge game could take a characteristically "imperial" form, in histories and geographies that chronicled Rome's mastery of peoples and spaces – a topic highly pertinent to Rutilius' project in the *DRS* which is, among many other things, a sustained reflection on the future of Roman territory as a Roman world.

In the Roman epic tradition, tides had served since at least the time of Vergil as a figure for the excess of the poet's knowledge over the knowledge of the characters who were trapped in the poem. Silius Italicus' *Punica* shows us how the trope could work: in the third book of that poem Hannibal goes to see the temple of Hercules/Melqart at Gades. There he notices that the sea, rising suddenly, has invaded the dry land. After a vivid description of tidal action that shifts us from Hannibal's viewpoint to that of the poet – from the flood tide to the ebb tide, which would have taken place many hours after Hannibal had split the scene but which traces for us, since we know where to look, the eventual course of his career – Silius concludes the episode by giving an account of causes. It was the moon all along, he says:

> Cymothoes ea regna uagae pelagique labores
> Luna mouet, Luna, immissis per caerula bigis,
> fertque refertque fretum, sequiturque reciproca Tethys.
> (Sil. *Pun.* 3.58–60)

---

[12] See ní Mheallaigh, Chapter 13 in this volume.

> These kingdoms of wandering Cymothoe and the laborings of the sea are moved by the moon; the moon, driving her chariot through the heavens, brings and draws back the sea, and Tethys follows each way in turn.

The poet knows the ultimate reasons that lie behind a phenomenon that Hannibal, trapped in the poem's onward-rushing narrative, can only naively watch. As Eleni Manolaraki has skillfully shown, the tidal trope will continue to haunt Hannibal through the poem's remaining fourteen books, where descriptions of tides and shifting currents keep cropping up at moments when Hannibal has made a miscalculation or failed to observe something vital. His ignorance of the nature and causes of tides somehow translates into an ignorance about destiny, its cyclicality, the alternating rise and fall of kingdoms – matters regarding which the poet, who understands that the moon is in control, has no illusions.[13]

The tides thus belong to a range of tropes, derived from ancient "astrological" science, that demonstrate the superiority of elite over demotic knowledge by showing how the former, just by way of its notionally otiose obsession with celestial bodies, can give a causal and predictive account of what happens on Earth. Compare Silius' treatment of tides, for instance, with Cicero's account of how Aemilius Paullus calmed Roman troops before the battle of Pydna by predicting, and explaining, a solar eclipse. As Scipio Aemilianus there recounts:

> memini me admodum adulescentulo, cum pater in Macedonia consul esset et essemus in castris perturbari exercitum nostrum religione et metu, quod serena nocte subito candens et plena luna defecisset. tum ille ... haud dubitauit postridie palam in castris docere nullum esse prodigium, idque et tum factum esse et certis temporibus esse semper futurum, cum sol ita locatus fuisset ut lunam suo lumine non posset attingere. (Cic. *Rep.* 1.23)

> I remember when I was just a lad, and my father was consul in Macedonia and we were in camp there, the army was stirred up by superstition and fear because, on a clear night, the shining full moon suddenly disappeared. Then he ... hardly hesitated to teach in the camp, the next day, how this was no prodigy at all, and that it had happened then, and would happen at known times always in the future, when the sun was so positioned that its light could not reach the moon.

In this case, Aemilius actually deploys his knowledge of astronomy as a form of social control. Both here and at the hands of Rutilius, though, the distinction between knowledge and ignorance is mapped onto the distance

---

[13] Manolaraki 2009: *passim*.

that separates the heavens from the earth below. Rutilius borrows freely from this repertoire, loading his poem with astronomical observations at a density unusual even for an author writing self-consciously in an Alexandrian tradition. A longstanding debate among modern readers about the precise date of the poem has been the predictable consequence. But, as Alan Cameron showed convincingly in a 1967 article, any attempt to take Rutilius' astrology literally will find itself mired in inconsistencies. The point of these learned references is not to give an accurate calendar of Rutilius' journey. It is, as Cameron says, "to make a display of the poet's knowledge."[14]

The position adopted by Rutilius in respect to the heavens – one of "scientific" control over his subject matter – is his default pose throughout *DRS*, and it structures his passage through a landscape that comes to be marked as Roman just by its connection to the literate culture of Rome's elites. Rutilius places himself within this landscape through a continuous act of learned interpretation. Consider this example, from about midway through Book 1:

> Stringimus †expugnatum† et fluctu et tempore Castrum:
>   index semiruti porta uetusta loci.
> Praesidet exigui formatus imagine saxi,
>   qui pastorali cornua fronte gerit.
> Multa licet priscum nomen deleuerit aetas,
>   hoc Inui Castrum fama fuisse putat,
> seu Pan Tyrrhenis mutauit Maenala siluis,
>   siue sinus patrios incola Faunus init;
> dum renouat largo mortalia semina fetu,
>   fingitur in Uenerem pronior esse deus.
>   (*DRS* 1.227–36)

We anchor at Castrum, overthrown by time and waves: The old gate is a sign of the half-ruined palace. A little image, formed of rock, sits upon it, which bears goat horns on its forehead. Although much time has obliterated its ancient name, the story goes that this is Castrum Inui, either because Pan swapped Maenala for Tuscan woods, or because Faunus "enters" the laps of his native land; when the seeds of things are renewed with great growth, it is imagined that the god is prompter to desire.

---

[14] Cameron 1967: 31–3, at 33. Other examples of Rutilian astrological marking: *DRS* 1.183–8, 371–6, 429–30, 631–8. On the non-realism of Rutilius' text in general, see Wolff 2005: 66–7. Rutilius' elite status: Vesserau 1904: 165–9. For a discussion of tides that is functionally parallel to Scipio's treatment of eclipses, see Sen. *Prov.* 1.2–4.

Here Rutilius is, to say the least, in close engagement with Vergil, reporting on the disappearance of a *nomen* whose rise the *Aeneid* had predicted:

> hi tibi Nomentum et Gabios urbemque Fidenam,
> hi Collatinas imponent montibus arces,
> Pometios Castrumque Inui Bolamque Coramque;
> haec tum nomina erunt, nunc sunt sine nomine terrae.
> (*Aen.* 6.773–6)
>
> These will erect Nomentum and Gabii and the city of Fidena, these will put Collatine fortresses on the mountains, and Pometii and Castrum Inui and Bola and Cora; these will be their names then, but now they are lands without name.

But two further complications bear noting. First, Rutilius' deployment of the Vergilian allusion is plainly archaeological; he is using the *Aeneid* as a source of information about a site whose ruined state makes it difficult to identify directly. And, second, Rutilius supplements or corrects the Vergilian reference with a series of hypotheses. One, the etymological remark about Inui, comes from Servius; the other, a demythologizing explication of this etymology as reflecting the turning of the seasons, appears to have been of the poet's own invention.[15]

In this case – as, I would argue, in most cases throughout the poem – the apparently literary and intertextual character of *DRS* is more or less a side effect of the poet's self-presentation as One Who Knows. Rutilius turns the landscape into poetry, not by trapping it in a web of literary allusions, but, perhaps more simply, just by telling us what he knows about it. Nor was this practice unique to *DRS*; Ausonius does essentially the same thing in the opening twenty-two lines of his *Mosella*. A few decades after *DRS* the Gallic poet, lawyer, and accidental bishop Sidonius Apollinaris could use knowledge as a technique for narrating his journey in prose according to a rubric that closely parallels Rutilius' own. As Sidonius explains in an introductory note:

> Litteras tuas Romae positus accepi, quibus an secundum commune consilium sese peregrinationis meae coepta promoueant sollicitus inquiris, uiam etiam qualem qualiterque confecerim, quos aut fluuios uiderim

---

[15] Fo 1992: ad loc. Here is the Servian passage: *castrumque inui una est in Italia ciuitas, quae castrum nouum dicitur: de hac autem ait "castrum Inui," id est Panos, qui illic colitur. Inuus autem latine appellatur, Graece Πάν: item Ἐφιάλτης Graece, latine Incubo: idem Faunus, idem Fatuus, Fatuclus. dicitur autem Inuus ab ineundo passim cum omnibus animalibus, unde et Incubo dicitur. "castrum" autem ciuitas est; nam castra numero plurali dicimus, licet legerimus in Plauto "castrum Poenorum" quod etiam diminutio ostendit; nam "castellum" dicimus* (Serv. *Aen.* 6.775). For a perceptive reading of this Vergilian allusion, see Clarke 2014: 100.

poetarum carminibus inlustres aut urbes moenium situ inclitas aut montes numinum opinione uulgatos aut campos proeliorum replicatione monstrabiles, quia uoluptuosum censeas quae lectione compereris eorum, qui inspexerint, fideliore didicisse memoratu. (Sid. Apoll. *Epist.* 1.5.1)

I received your letters at Rome, in which you asked, solicitously, whether the affairs that brought me have proceeded according to our common hope, and also that I should set down carefully which road I had taken and how, and what rivers I had seen that were famous from the songs of poets or cities famous from the arrangement of their walls or mountains generally believed to house divinities or fields noteworthy for the battles that had happened there, because you thought pleasurable what you had discovered from reading the writings of those who had seen them firsthand.

This way of traveling and reflecting on traveling was, to all appearances and at least for a certain kind of Roman, conventional. Not by inventing the real, but by properly identifying and classifying it, was how the traveler could demonstrate his descriptive art. The approach is perhaps characteristic of a "late" culture that saw itself as inheriting a landscape already rich in time-depth and signification beyond anything a poet might freshly invent.[16]

12.3

If it is true, as I have just been arguing, that Rutilius "travels" by means of a constant process of learned interpretation, then we have reason to think that the tidal simile that ends Book 1 of the *DRS* should also be read in this literate register. We should be prepared to see it functioning not only within the architecture of the poem – by way of a playful signpost pointing toward Luna – but also as another in a series of quilting points that binds the *DRS* to the poet's own elite Roman culture.

To understand this binding, we should begin by appreciating that tides were in an important way constitutively alien to that culture. The Mediterranean was, and still is, almost entirely a tideless sea; where the Romans did have to reckon with tides was in the north, along Atlantic and North Sea coasts that were distant, both culturally and spatially, from the imperial center. When Rutilius imports to the heartland a set of tidal forces that

---

[16] Squillante 2005: 198–208; Fo 1989: 55. On the "local" or Gallic character that Rutilius and Ausonius might be thought of as sharing, see Paschoud 1993: 15–18. On Rutilius' "creation" of the landscape in *DRS*, see Clarke 2014. Readers who wish to see for themselves should compare *Mos.* 1–17 with some of the passages I have cited from Rutilius, especially the latter's description of and departure from Rome.

were only supposed to affect the margins of the empire, he is using the languages of geography, astrology, and natural history to advance a forceful claim about both that empire's present state and its eventual fate.[17]

The establishment of the moon's influence on tides can be dated no later than Posidonius, the late second-century BCE polymath whose work, though now lost, was in this respect as in many others to leave a distinctive trace upon the intellectual culture of Rome.[18] It is at least superficially surprising that an astrological culture already capable by 500 BCE of decoding the causes and periodicity of solar eclipses should have waited another three centuries before systematizing the much more regular correspondences between tides and lunar phase. On the other hand, the Mediterranean and Black Seas are not strongly tidal bodies of water; the daily flux is barely noticeable in all but a few coastal locations, and so it is understandable that tides should not have concerned Greek astronomers. Silius Italicus, as we saw, sets his tidal *miraculum* at Gades; he is right to do so, since the Pillars of Hercules are where the more powerful tides of the Atlantic begin to exert their influence.[19]

With the extension of Roman control to Spain, Gaul, and eventually Britain, tides became a matter of practical import as they had not been in an earlier period. At the same time, historians also began to treat them as a trope of empire. Consider this passage of Tacitus, an evocative treatment of tides on the Southern end of Britain:

> Britanniae situm populosque multis scriptoribus memoratos non in comparationem curae ingeniiue referam, sed quia tum primum perdomita est. Ita quae priores nondum comperta eloquentia percoluere, rerum fide tradentur ... Naturam Oceani atque aestus neque quaerere huius operis est, ac multi rettulere: unum addiderim, nusquam latius dominari mare, multum fluminum huc atque illuc ferre, nec litore tenus adcrescere aut resorberi, sed influere penitus atque ambire, et iugis etiam ac montibus inseri uelut in suo. (Tac. *Agr.* 10.4–6)

> I include the geography of England and its peoples, which have already been recounted by many writers, not to compete with them in scrupulousness or wit, but because they were first fully conquered at that time. And so, those things that earlier writers ginned up with eloquence before they had

---

[17] Small tides in the Mediterranean: Marmer 1922: 209–10. An exception for certain harbors on Sicily: Strabo 1.3.11. Greek Atlantic exploration and interest in the tides: Roller 2013: 17–20.
[18] See Johnston, Chapter 11 in this volume.
[19] Posidonius corrects Aristotle on this point (Strabo 3.3.3), and seems to have simply opted for lunar responsibility outright: fr 10 (Strabo 1.3.1–12), with the commentary of Thieler 1982: ad loc. For the early history of Greek speculation about the tides, see Aldersley-Williams 2016: 25–40.

been discovered, let them now be transmitted with better fidelity ... An inquiry about the nature of the ocean and the tides does not belong to this work, and many have already written on this topic: I would add this one thing, that the sea nowhere stretches her domain more widely, extending willy-nilly in many river-like streams, not only swelling and receding along the shore, but indeed winding its way among mountains and ridges as though in its own domain.

This vivid and energetic description comes at the end of a treatment of the geography of Britain, which the historian explicitly associates with Rome's "first conquest" of that island. The position of this passage in Tacitus owes much to a precedent established by Caesar and continued by Pliny the Elder: no conquest is complete without a topographical account, and no account of a geographical *topos* is complete without some discussion of the tides that nibble away at its borders.[20]

It seems impossible to doubt that Rutilius wrote with an awareness of this cultural geography, especially since the most direct poetic precedent for the "tidal digression" that ends Book 1 of *DRS* highlights exactly the foreign or barbarian connotations of extreme tidal flux. In the middle of the first book of the *Bellum Civile*, Lucan gives an enumeration of the Gallic and Germanic tribes that have been left in peace by Caesar's departure for Rome with his legions. The catalog also names several "barbarian" bodies of water that have thus been freed from "Roman keels." The one that Lucan describes at greatest length is the Northern Ocean, where

> ... iacet litus dubium quod terra fretumque
> uindicat alternis uicibus, cum funditur ingens
> Oceanus uel cum refugis se fluctibus aufert.
> uentus ab extremo pelagus sic axe uolutet
> destituatque ferens, an sidere mota secundo
> Tethyos unda uagae lunaribus aestuet horis,
> flammiger an Titan, ut alentes hauriat undas,
> erigat Oceanum fluctusque ad sidera ducat,
> quaerite, quos agitat mundi labor.
> (Luc. *BC* 1.408–17)

There lies the doubtful shore, which sea and land claim in turn, when the great ocean sweeps in or departs with backward-flowing waves. Whether a

---

[20] For the traditional Roman association of Britain and northern Europe with tidal digressions, see Kraus and Woodman 2014: ad loc. For some historical anecdotes regarding early Roman encounters with the dramatic tides of the Atlantic world, see Aldersley-Williams 2016: 41–52. Tacitus again associates (wind-driven?) tidal fluxes with barbarians (this time the Hiberi and Sarmatae) at *Ann.* 6.33.

wind from the far-off pole stirs up the sea and calms it with its departure, or whether, moved by the motion of the second star, Tethyos sweats and swells at lunar seasons, or whether flame-bearing Titan, so that it may slurp up the waves, raises up the sea and draws its flux to the stars – investigate, you in whom the world's labors plant unease.

Tides are geographically "barbarous" for this most historiographical of poets just as we saw they were for historians. The filiation between this passage and Rutilius' much shorter treatment of tides is obvious and has long been recognized by commentators.[21]

The allusion makes it impossible for us to avoid recognizing what was already implicit in Rutilius' "displacement" of this *topos*: if tides do not belong in the Mediterranean, then they have come there from the "barbarian" north. As simile, they have gotten into the DRS along much the same trajectory by which Alaric's Goths, who cast a long shadow over the poem, came into Italy. Jacqueline Clarke has argued that Rutilius carefully describes a landscape in the DRS that is on the edge of slipping beyond its author's control; here would seem to be an example of the same phenomenon on the level not of description but of simile.[22]

Rutilius' Luna thus pulls us, so to speak, in two different directions. On the one hand, the poet gives a "learned" causal account of tides that accords with his general practice of overwriting local events with his own, superior, knowledge. On the other hand, the extreme flood tides that the poet describes seem out of place in the Mediterranean heart of the empire. They belong to the landscape of the provinces, and particularly to the landscape of a North Atlantic coast that, by Rutilius' time, had already fallen out of the Roman orbit. The surges that flood these Italian shores are indeed, on this account, "refluxes from another world."

Rutilius would thus seem to have envisioned, or have been unable to escape, encoding *two* theories of tides in the phrase *alio refluus . . . nostro orbe*; the *alius orbis* in question is at once the moon and the post-Roman space of northern Europe. In this case, *orbis* would have to carry a heavy

---

[21] Castorina 1967: ad loc; Doblhofer 1977: ad loc; Fo 1992: ad loc. As further evidence that Rutilius has this kind of geographical dislocation in mind, I cite his description of salt-pans from a hundred-odd lines before: *Subiectas uillae uacat aspectare salinas; / Namque hoc censetur nomine salsa palus, / qua mare terrenis decliue canalibus intrat / multifidosque lacus paruula fossa rigat. / Ast ubi flagrantes admonuit Sirius ignes, / cum pallent herbae, cum sitit omnis ager, / tum cataractarum claustris excluditur aequor, / ut fixos latices torrida duret humus. / Concipiunt acrem natiua coagula Phoebum / et grauis aestiuo crusta calore coit; / haud aliter quam cum glacie riget horridus Hister / grandiaque adstricto flumine plaustra uehit* (DRS 1.475–87). On such dislocations in DRS more generally, see Wolff 2005: 70–2.

[22] Clarke 2014: 105–6.

and rather awkward semantic burden, representing at the same time a part of our world and something utterly distinct from it. To the attentive reader, moreover, this shift in meaning comes as something of a shock. From the beginning of the poem, Rutilius has been training us to read *orbis* as referring to a comfortable whole, and in particular a *Roman* whole: the homogeneous world that the empire has made. This late semantic shift, I think, constitutes the master key to the poem's tidal vocabulary and to the historiographical program which that vocabulary encodes.

Prior to this point in the poem, *orbis* has appeared four times – in each case, apparently, with a sense something like "the whole world." Such is Rutilius' usage, for instance, in a couplet from near the beginning of the poem that has often, and misleadingly, been quoted out of context:

> dumque offers uictis proprii consortia iuris,
>   Urbem fecisti, quod prius orbis erat.
>   (*DRS* 1.65–6)
>
> And, while you grant the defeated a share in your own laws, you have made a city out of what was once a world.

In the Loeb edition, the Duffs translate these lines with characteristic bombast: "by offering to the vanquished a share in thine own justice, thou hast made a city of what was erstwhile a world." Rutilius seems, in a conventional way, to be praising Rome for its extension of citizens' rights to all (free) inhabitants of its imperial space; that is what it means to turn an *orbis* into an *urbs*.[23]

He uses *orbis* several times over the course of *DRS* in exactly this sense, always asserting the identity of Roman space with the globe. The distinction between them only becomes apparent at the end of Book 1, where Rutilius highlights it, in his discussion of tides, by making reference to another *orbis* that is *alius nostro*. This last and strikingly different use of *orbis*, then, would seem to be an exercise in retrospective recharacterization, a jarring gesture toward the partiality of what we could earlier, reading briskly, have assumed was the whole.[24]

---

[23] Duff and Duff 1934: 769. To list the dozens or perhaps hundreds of texts in which this quotation has appeared either as a summary of imperial Rome's actual function or as an uncomplicated epitome of Rutilius' own views would be otiose. One unfortunate instance occurs at Pozzato and Rodighiero 2011: 24.

[24] At 1.145 (*altricemque suam fertilis orbis alat*) Rutilius uses *orbis* to describe the area from which food is transferred to Rome for annonarial purposes. We have already seen him calling Rome *caput orbis* at 1.194. An important transitional moment is at 1.609, where Rutilius analogizes corrupt Roman officials to *Harpyias, quarum discerpitur unguibus orbis*. The "world" being referred to here is still an entirely Roman one, but it seems to be in the process of self-inflicted dissolution.

Here is some corroborating evidence for these suggestions. Toward the beginning of the poem, Rutilius avers that:

> Obruerint citius scelerata obliuia solem
>   quam tuus e nostro corde recedat honos.
> Nam solis radiis aequalia munera tendis,
>   qua circumfusus fluctuat Oceanus
>   (*DRS* 1.53–6)

> Let evil forgetfulness overwhelm the sun before your honor ever leaves our heart. For you proffer gifts equal to the sun's rays, limited by the wavy ocean.

He thus makes Rome the sun, so to speak, of the world, a figure that scholars have long recognized lies beneath much of his description of the eternal city. At the outset, again, this will strike us as nothing more than a commonplace imperial trope, where the benefits of Roman rule fall invisibly, like the rays of the sun, on a world that is nourished by it – an apparently "dead" metaphor, at which, again, Rutilius' treatment of tides makes us take a second look. When part of the world is the moon, Rome's characterization as the sun indicates not only its importance but also its partiality, and – for the provincial traveler – its distance. By this point in Rutilius' journey the skies are dark, and the light, as he says, is scant indeed.

As the moon wanes and waxes in cycles, however, so it goes with the empire of Rome. Pushing this analogy, Rutilius writes:

> Aduersis solemne tuis sperare secunda:
>   exemplo caeli ditia damna subis.
> Astrorum flammae renouant occasibus ortus;
>   Lunam finiri cernis, ut incipiat.
>   (*DRS* 1.121–4)

> It is your habit to look for better fortunes in bad times: and, following celestial example, you undergo losses that enrich you. The fires of heaven repeat their rise by way of setting; you see the moon finish up as it began.

Rutilius mentions the moon twice more in the first book of *DRS*. Not surprisingly, it appears there first in its new (1.205–6) and then in its crescent phase (1.433–4). Just as the moon does, Rome too will come out of occlusion.

The flood and ebb tides follow the regular cycles of the moon. Looking back toward the beginning of the poem, we can now see that Rutilius had "planted" a certain amount of tidal imagery there that takes on a new significance in light of the lunar divagation with which Book 1 concludes. For instance, this further analogy for the inevitable recovery of Rome:

> Quae mergi nequeunt, nisu maiore resurgunt
> exiliuntque imis altius acta uadis.
> (*DRS* 1.129–30)
>
> What cannot be submerged resurfaces with greater force, and what has been driven down to the depths leaps up all the higher.

Rome will not be drowned in this barbarian tide – a flood that will eventually withdraw to the unknown reaches of the north, where, according to the rules of nature, it belongs.

These aquarian observations come near the beginning of the poem, in the midst of a well-known passage where Rutilius confidently predicts Rome's recovery from a recent series of Gothic depredations that had ended in the sack of the eternal city itself, an event unprecedented since the Gallic incursions of the late fourth century BCE. He mentions the Gauls themselves, the Samnites, Pyrrhus, and Hannibal, noting in each case that Rome came to subjugate those who had defeated it.[25]

This chain of Livian *exempla* points inexorably toward the conclusion that Rome, in the wake of the Gothic invasions, will not only survive but thrive. Roman success in the past had been characterized by the empire's ability to outlast whatever enemies it could not overcome at first; by the time the *DRS* was being composed the Goths had also been starved out of Italy and dispersed in the north. Scholars who read *DRS* as a poem of optimism – whether propagandistic or essentially justified by the remarkable successes of Constantius Florus after 412 CE – have naturally tended to take these lines as an explicit and comprehensive statement of Rutilius' historiographical position – a reading that will turn out to need a good deal of qualification.[26]

Are the tidal allusions in this passage just a "scientific" analogy for a basically historiographical claim? Or are they supposed to lend Rutilius' historiographical arguments something *more* than rhetorical support? In my view, the latter reading is to be preferred – not just because late antique beliefs about astrology gave ample grounds for supposing that there could be a real relation between celestial bodies and earthly events, but because Rutilius is, as I have shown, playing a game of knowledge in which the poet's learned assertions are the only accurate description of the world. His

---

[25] *DRS* 1.121–30.   [26] Cameron 2010: 211; Sarris 2011: 50–1.

tidal analogies go to show that never-ending cycles of collapse and recovery really do exist in nature, and that the history of the Roman Empire might well turn out to be one of these cycles.[27]

Rutilius would thus indeed seem to be making an "optimistic" projection about the future of Rome, as most scholars have understood him to be doing. To read him in this way, though, would be in an important sense to miss his point. Whether the Roman Empire would survive and thrive was a live question in the literary debates of the early fifth century, but the more pressing issue was what kind of an empire would survive – and for whom?

12.4

In answer to this question, as we have seen, the *DRS* uses the science of tides to evoke a vision of Rome as a distributed system of political centers, each exerting its own attraction. If Rome is the sun, then Luna – even if its light is borrowed – still stands as an *alius orbis*, one perhaps of many. The Rome of the future, for Rutilius, is a system of many bodies; *DRS* thus gives a premonition of something like the "local Romanness" invoked by Peter Heather and others to explain the shape of the post-Roman world in the sixth century and after. What Rutilius uses tides to depict is a Roman Empire that can, in a sense, do without Rome – an empire united by laws, by a way of life, by the solidarity of its aristocrats, rather than by loyalty to a central place. Looked at from this perspective, the polemical value of Rutilius' natural-cyclical view of history may come into sharper focus.[28]

Indeed, it is on just this point that Rutilius can be seen to engage most directly with some of his contemporaries. In a 1905 article Albert DuFourcq proposed that the opening of *DRS* should be read as a response to the first several books of *City of God*, an intriguing suggestion that Pierre Courcelle and Alan Cameron have corroborated with convincing textual evidence. The point of conflict between Augustine and Rutilius would appear, on the accounts of these scholars, to be this: Augustine reads Rome's history as a series of disasters that Rome's gods failed to prevent, while Rutilius interprets the same disasters as trials from which Rome emerged all the stronger. We can recognize this as one of the "providentialist debates" that Paschoud, in a recent reply to Cameron's *Last Pagans of*

---

[27] "Influence" in late antique astrology: Barton 1994: 107–10.
[28] Heather 2005: 437–50; Brown 2012: 392–407.

Rome, identifies as a flashpoint of pagan–Christian conflict in the intellectual sphere.[29]

What is at issue in these debates is not just whether Rome will survive its recent troubles, but how the responsibility for those troubles ought to be doled out. Do they stem from a "failure" of the values, religious and otherwise, of a "pagan" state that Christians have been divinely ordained to save and inherit? Or, as Rutilius argues, was the invasion of the Goths just part of the cyclical character of Roman history – a disaster from which, as from the Gallic sack of 390 BCE, Rome would emerge transformed, but all the stronger?

Augustine sets forth his side of the argument in an extended critique of a Roman historiography that, as he professes to show, refutes pagan claims of a providential destiny for the empire. This is well known. What is less well appreciated is that Rutilius – the only representative we have of the anti-Christian party in this controversy – conducts his defense of Rome through a travel poem. For him, as I have argued in some detail above, the landscape itself comes to count as an argument in favor of a "providential" Roman recovery from the disasters of the early fifth century CE.

This is strange. Augustine and Rutilius hardly seem to be arguing on the same level – and, as I will soon suggest, they really are talking past each other in at least one meaningful sense. Rutilius does, however, have techniques to make the landscape signify. His travel poem is an argument in space, with the tides at its center. As a simile, the tides mediate his apperception that some part of the non-Roman world has found a place within the empire. As a tidal displacement, this disruption can only be temporary: when the barbarian tides withdraw, the old landscape of Roman control will reemerge from underneath the flood. The simile of the tides, however, also marks the central point in an astrological allegory that extends, not in time, but in space. Rome is the sun, Luna the moon; the ferocious tides that end Book 1 of the *DRS* mark a midpoint in Rutilius' passage from one to the other. This speaks to the poet's appreciation of Rome's future as a system of bodies rather than a homogeneous, centrally governed empire: *orbes*, not *orbis*.

All this, I have been arguing, is an effect of the superposition of Rutilius' authorial knowledge over the space through which he travels.

---

[29] Dufourcq 1905; Courcelle 1948: 83; Cameron 1967: 35–8; Paschoud 2012: 380–8. For a treatment of Rutilius' initial *laus Romae* that elaborates its significance for these providentialist debates within a setting of pagan-Christian conflict, see Ratti 2006: 240–3. Ratti takes an extreme position with regard to the religious, as opposed to the historiographical, content of these debates (cf. Cameron 2010: 211–14).

This knowledge obscures the landscape in a way that demonstrates its status as superior to mere observation or to local knowledge, and as capable of structuring a journey that would otherwise have been a dull and decentered account of one place after another. Nowhere is this clearer than in the poem's evocation of tides at a point in space where they never, in fact, take place.

In this regard, I have suggested, Rutilius' procedure was characteristic of travel writing in his time and among members of his social class. His was an "argument in space" that would have been well understood by those of his contemporaries who could recognize themselves in the author of the *DRS*. Augustine's critique of Roman providence in the *City of God* was at least meant to be understood – if not necessarily appreciated – by this same audience. One upshot of this critique, however, was that the kind of knowledge by which members of this class distinguished themselves was of no ultimate value for understanding or interpreting the world. For Augustine, the Christian God was the master sign by which everything else had to be interpreted. It was in a similar spirit that Ambrose, Augustine's friend and teacher, could say in his *Hexameron* that the tides represent "the mystery of Christ and the church" (*Hex.* 4.31). Far from constituting a piece of astral knowledge through which the terrestrial world can be interpreted, tides themselves now called for interpretation through monotheistic dogma: the wonder had become a sign.

With his knowledge of tides to guide him, Rutilius set out to travel from Rome to the moon; in so doing, he also set out to demonstrate that Roman providence had not yet failed. He was one of the last to be able to journey in this way. With him, a whole epoch of travel poetry draws to a close.

CHAPTER 13

Looking Back in Wonder: Contemplating Home from the Iliad *to* Pale Blue Dot

Karen ní Mheallaigh

Extraterrestrial travel provides the ultimate experience of what it is to be "away," and, in doing so, radically reconfigures our sense of what "home" means. Humans finally achieved the technological means to propel us from the Earth in the 1960s, but we dreamed of leaving our terrestrial home long before we could accomplish the ambition. In this chapter I explore the extraordinary dialogue between this ancient imaginary tradition and the documented experience of the first actual astronauts – a dialogue that reveals how ancient thought-experiment and fantasy not only preempted but even shaped modern reality. My focus will be on the defamiliarizing experience of looking back at our homeworld from the vastest distances imaginable, in both the real tradition of space exploration and the imaginary tradition of *gaiaskopia* – of gazing at the Earth from outer space – that stretches back to the earliest Greek literature.

I will begin with the apex of the ancient tradition, the extended *gaiaskopia* in Lucian's *Icaromenippus*, a philosophical fantasy from the second century CE, whose narrator Menippus flies to the Moon and looks down on the entire Earth from there. This text is a watershed moment as Lucian creates a genealogy for his *gaiaskopia* that invites us to read Menippus' vision in light of comparable thought-experiments in Homer's *Iliad*, Aristophanes' *Peace*, Plato's *Phaedo*, and Cicero's *Dream of Scipio*. In this way, Menippus' view back toward the Earth becomes a view over the expanse of Greek literature. Through the motif of *gaiaskopia*, Lucian exercises his commanding vista on the literary canon, and the view from

---

This chapter was written whilst I was a Marie Curie research fellow at the Aarhus Institute of Advanced Studies, and I gratefully acknowledge both the funding and the resources of AIAS and Aarhus University. I am also very grateful to the volume editors, Tom and Jess, both for their original invitation to join the conference at Yale, and for their exemplary patience and efficiency throughout the editing process. My thanks, too, to the Press readers for their insightful and helpful comments. Translations, unless otherwise indicated, are my own.

the Moon becomes an extraterrestrial visualization and *précis* of the literary home-world by this alien author.[1]

I will then turn to the modern *gaiaskopiai* of our first astronauts and the shared experience of these that was provided by the first photographs of our planet from outer space. The first wave of Earth images was generated mainly in the context of the Apollo missions in the 1960s and early 1970s, and includes photographs of Earth taken by robotic and human agents from both Earth orbit and the Moon itself. The second wave (1990s–early 2000s) comprises images taken by probes from far more remote distances in our solar system. My aim is to reveal certain common themes that emerge from ancient and modern responses to seeing our planetary home from afar, whether in reality or the imagination, and to explore here how these journeys away influenced – or radically changed – our sense of what "home" is.

13.1 Lucian, *Icaromenippus*, and the Ancient Gaiaskopic Tradition

Icaromenippus is a philosophical satire, and one of the earliest surviving fantasies of lunar exploration.[2] Finding himself disillusioned with his fellow-citizens' greed and ambition, Menippus, the protagonist and intellectual rebel, turns his mind to astronomy, hoping to escape sordid everyday concerns by contemplating the heavens instead. However, he quickly finds himself disappointed again: each of the philosophers he consults outbids the next in his claims to know the truth, and as a result, Menippus finds himself lost in a cacophony of conflicting theories which hopelessly confuse him. Not one of them, he realizes, has the answers to his questions; they are all charlatans and frauds. If he wants to know how the universe works, he must consult the gods directly (*Icar.* 2–3). And so, inspired by the flying mechanism in the myth of Daedalus and Icarus, Menippus flies to heaven and breaks his journey by landing on the Moon.

Paradoxically, the truly magical moment of *Icaromenippus* is not the point when Menippus first lands on the Moon, but when, after meeting the spirit of the deceased philosopher Empedocles there, he learns a

---
[1] On travel narrative as an intertextual experience, compare Martin Devecka's chapter, Chapter 12, in this volume.
[2] See Gómez Alcalde-Diosdado 2010. Competitors for this prestige include Lucian's other lunar narrative in *True Stories*, and (probably) Antonius Diogenes' novel, *The Wonders beyond Thule*, both of which I explore in a forthcoming book, *The Moon in the Greek and Roman Imagination: Selenography in Myth, Literature, Science, and Philosophy*.

method for enhancing his eyesight, and looks back down on the Earth. Suddenly, the entirety of human existence far below is revealed to him in one panoptic vision. Menippus struggles to convey the overwhelming sense of confusion he experienced at seeing the whole world in this way:

ΜΕΝΙΠΠΟΣ πάντα μὲν ἑξῆς διελθεῖν . . . ἀδύνατον, ὅπου γε καὶ ὁρᾶν αὐτὰ ἔργον ἦν· τὰ μέντοι κεφάλαια τῶν πραγμάτων τοιαῦτα ἐφαίνετο οἷά φησιν Ὅμηρος τὰ ἐπὶ τῆς ἀσπίδος· οὗ μὲν γὰρ ἦσαν εἰλαπίναι καὶ γάμοι, ἑτέρωθι δὲ δικαστήρια καὶ ἐκκλησίαι, καθ᾽ ἕτερον δὲ μέρος ἔθυέ τις, ἐν γειτόνων δὲ πενθῶν ἄλλος ἐφαίνετο· καὶ ὅτε μὲν ἐς τὴν Γετικὴν ἀποβλέψαιμι, πολεμοῦντας ἂν ἑώρων τοὺς Γέτας· ὅτε δὲ μεταβαίην ἐπὶ τοὺς Σκύθας, πλανωμένους ἐπὶ τῶν ἁμαξῶν ἦν ἰδεῖν· μικρὸν δὲ ἐγκλίνας τὸν ὀφθαλμὸν ἐπὶ θάτερα τοὺς Αἰγυπτίους γεωργοῦντας ἐπέβλεπον, καὶ ὁ Φοῖνιξ ἐνεπορεύετο καὶ ὁ Κίλιξ ἐλῄστευεν καὶ ὁ Λάκων ἐμαστιγοῦτο καὶ ὁ Ἀθηναῖος ἐδικάζετο. ἁπάντων δὲ τούτων ὑπὸ τὸν αὐτὸν γινομένων χρόνον ὥρα σοι ἤδη ἐπινοεῖν ὁποῖός τις ὁ κυκεὼν οὗτος ἐφαίνετο. ὥσπερ ἂν εἴ τις παραστησάμενος πολλοὺς χορευτάς, μᾶλλον δὲ πολλοὺς χορούς, ἔπειτα προστάξειε τῶν ᾀδόντων ἑκάστῳ τὴν συνῳδίαν ἀφέντα ἴδιον ᾄδειν μέλος, φιλοτιμουμένου δὲ ἑκάστου καὶ τὸ ἴδιον περαίνοντος καὶ τὸν πλησίον ὑπερβαλέσθαι τῇ μεγαλοφωνίᾳ προθυμουμένου – ἆρα ἐνθυμῇ πρὸς Διὸς οἵα γένοιτ᾽ ἂν ἡ ᾠδή;
ΕΤΑΙΡΟΣ Παντάπασιν, ὦ Μένιππε, παγγέλοιος καὶ τεταραγμένη.
(*Icar.* 16–17)

MENIPPUS: It would be impossible . . . to go through it all in sequence, given that it was a challenge even to take it in with my eyes. But the principal details appeared just as Homer describes on the shield: for there were feasts and weddings here, courts and assemblies there, and in another quarter someone was offering sacrifice, while someone else nearby appeared to be grieving. Whenever I cast my eye toward the land of the Getae, I would see the Getae waging war. And whenever I'd switch to the Scythians, they could be seen wandering about on their wagons. Turning my eye a little to one side, I spied the Egyptians farming, whilst the Phoenician was engaged in trade, the Cilician in piracy, the Spartan was being flogged and the Athenian sitting in court. With all of this going on at the same time, you should picture what a hotchpotch it looked like. It was as if someone stood many singers – or rather, many choirs together – then ordered each of the singers to abandon the harmony and sing his own tune instead. With each individual competing to finish his own song and eager to outdo his neighbour by singing loudly, do you perceive, by Jove, what the song would be like?
COMPANION: Totally ridiculous and confused, Menippus.

The cluster of similes – the hotchpotch, the choral cacophony, the *imago mundi* on the shield of Achilles – captures the chaos of Menippus' experience very effectively. The image of the hotchpotch, which appeals to the sense of taste and smell as well as sight, and the choruses which appeal directly to the sense of hearing, trigger, imaginatively, a multisensory experience which recreates the impression of aesthetic overload at the sight of the whole world.[3]

Lucian is the first writer in the European tradition to use the Earth-view to explore the crisis of infinity. Menippus attempts to describe the sensory overload of infinity, which proved almost too much for his eye to take in (ὁρᾶν αὐτὰ ἔργον ἦν). Syntactic narrative is inadequate for the task, since it imposes too rigid a straitjacket on what the eye sees (παντα ... ἑξῆς διελθεῖν ... ἀδύνατον). Instead, he resorts to reporting merely "a summary of things" (τὰ ... κεφάλαια τῶν πραγμάτων), which appear just as they did on the Homeric shield. Menippus' distinction between the moment of sensory reception and the slower cognitive process of converting what one sees into impressionistic pastiche or ordered narrative is a fascinating analysis of what the ekphrastic eye does.[4]

His allusion to the Iliadic shield is significant, given the shield's long association with the ineffability of vision. Here it is shorthand for a sight that he finds otherwise impossible to describe. The shield's intertextual presence therefore interlaces this *ekphrasis*-to-beat-all-*ekphrases* (a description, not of an individual item or scene, but of the whole world) with the problems of *ekphrasis* itself, thereby imbuing it with a meta-ekphrastic edge and reinforcing the sense of language's deficiency as a vehicle for the infinite.[5]

This theme would recur in both the literature of the modern era and the documented experiences of the astronauts themselves. In his short story "The Aleph," Jorge Luis Borges confronts the problem of converting the

---

[3] The contemporary Roman emperor Marcus Aurelius contemplates the chaos of the world when viewed from above in terms that are similarly reminiscent of the Iliadic shield (*Med.* 7.48): Καὶ δὴ περὶ ἀνθρώπων τοὺς λόγους ποιούμενον ἐπισκοπεῖν δεῖ καὶ τὰ ἐπίγεια ὥσπερ ποθὲν ἄνωθεν κάτω· ἀγέλας, στρατεύματα, γεώργια, γάμους, διαλύσεις, γενέσεις, θανάτους, δικαστηρίων θόρυβον, ἐρήμους χώρας, βαρβάρων ἔθνη ποικίλα, ἑορτάς, θρήνους, ἀγοράς, τὸ παμμιγὲς καὶ τὸ ἐκ τῶν ἐναντίων συγκοσμούμενον (And so, when you are making judgments about people, you should survey earthly matters as if looking down from some height at herds, armies, farms, weddings, divorces, births, deaths, noisy courts, lonely spaces, the varied tribes of barbarians, festivals, funerals, marketplaces ... the great medley of things mingled together out of opposites). On the "view from above" as a philosophical exercise, see Hadot 1995: 238–50.

[4] For discussion, *inter alia*, of the mechanics of the ekphrastic gaze in the literature of the imperial period, see Goldhill 2001.

[5] On the literature and art of infinity, see Eco 2009, which takes as its starting point the description of Achilles' shield in *Il.* 18 (pp. 9–13). The discussion of meta-ekphrasis in Webb (2009: 167–91, esp. 174–5) and Squire 2013 are particularly apposite here.

Looking Back in Wonder 267

infinite into a narrative, or even into language itself. The "aleph" in his tale is a panoptic device, which compresses the entire universe into a single eyeshot. As the narrator attempts to describe what he saw in this one moment, he struggles – like Menippus – with the breakdown of narrative and language:

> And here begins my despair as a writer ... How ... can I translate into words the limitless Aleph, which my floundering mind can barely encompass? ... In that single gigantic instant I saw millions of acts both delightful and awful; not one of them amazed me more than the fact that all of them occupied the same point in space ... What my eyes beheld was simultaneous, but what I shall now write down will be successive, because language is successive.

Borges' distinction between the instantaneous, sensory experience and the slower cognitive process of description echoes Menippus' difficulties closely. In a postscript, Borges would later acknowledge the influence of Lucian's *True Stories* on his story (though *Icaromenippus* resonates more closely, in fact).[6]

By alluding to Achilles' shield, Lucian also situates his *gaiaskopia* within a tradition of telescopic Earth-viewing that (as we shall see) includes Trygaeus' aerial view in Aristophanes' *Peace*, Socrates' magnificent vision of the Earth in Plato's *Phaedo*, and Cicero's *Dream of Scipio*. The Homeric shield has been recognized since antiquity as a model of the cosmos (the term *kosmou mimēma* occurs in a scholion on Aratus' *Phainomena*).[7] In *Iliad* 18, the smith-god Hephaestus fashions for Achilles a circular shield, on which he carves a representation of the cosmos, exploiting his privileged view of the universe as a divinity (*ll*. 483–608). Although the poet's description does not allow us to reconstruct the positioning of the decorative motifs on this imaginary object with any certainty, it does invite us to envisage, in an impressionistic way, the diverse activities of human culture (marriages, disputes, war, urban life, agriculture, etc.) framed by the everlasting elements of the natural cosmos (the celestial bodies and the all-encompassing ocean that traces the shield's outer rim). One very important effect of this disposition is to assert the importance of human culture within the universe: no matter how small we are as individuals,

---

[6] Borges 1999. The passage quoted is from Borges 1945/1970: 26–7. Excellent discussion of the *Icaromenippus* passage can be found in Squire 2011: esp. 330–1; Purves 2010a: 51.
[7] Schol. ad Arat. 26.15–16 Martin; cf. also ps.-Heraclitus, *Allegories* 43.2; Clement of Alexandria, *Stromata* 5.14.101.4 and *Paedagogus* 3.12.99.3. On this ancient allegorical tradition, see Hardie 1985: 15–17. For discussion of the poetic and especially ekphrastic dimensions of the shield description, see Squire 2013, with extensive bibliography in n. 1.

collectively, on a cosmic scale, humans *matter* in the Homeric world view. At the same time, however, the enclosure of the entire cosmos as an artifact within a poem about one man – Achilles – generates a crisis of interpretation for the poem's audience or readers: how are we to evaluate the importance of the poem's theme against that of the shield? Or to put it another way: what does *one* life matter, on a universal scale? This imagined remote view of our home estranges it and poses profound and unsettling questions about both the quotidian (the anonymous human characters that are represented on the shield's surface) and the extraordinary (Achilles, who will take up the shield and eventually meet his death, leaving all that is familiar) in relation to one another.

Another important intertext for Lucian's *Icaromenippus* is Socrates' vision of the upper Earth in Plato's *Phaedo*. Although it is not evoked in the same explicit manner as the *Iliad* in the passage quoted earlier on p. 265, Lucian has already provided the reader with several clues to its intertextual presence in the dialogue. Menippus' epistemological trajectory from commitment to natural philosophy to disillusionment with it is modeled on Socrates' selfsame trajectory in the *Phaedo* (97b8–98c2). There are even verbal echoes between the two works: Menippus' avowed frustration with the philosophers' "principles," "final causes," "atoms," "voids," and "materials and forms and things of that sort" closely echoes Socrates' disappointment with Anaxagoras' reliance on "'airs' and 'aithers' and 'waters' and many other strange things" (*Phd.* 98c2). Finally, the "multi-coloured spheres" that Menippus mentions at *Icar.* 6 evoke Socrates' extraordinary vision of the Earth as a "multi-coloured ball." In this way, Lucian has primed the reader to recall Socrates' vision as Menippus looks down from the Moon.

In *Phaedo* Socrates describes his adventurer's vision of the Earth as a network of huge, interconnected, dimly lit craters (108e–111c). We may believe that we inhabit the surface of the Earth, but actually we dwell deep down in one of these crater-like depressions. The people of the Mediterranean, in fact, are like frogs clustered around a pond (109b). We have no idea what the world actually looks like, for we have never yet emerged from our crater to contemplate it. Deep in our mist-filled crevasse, we see things dimly. Like fish looking up from the sea-bed toward the surface of the ocean and believing *that* is the sky, in a similar way, what we call the "sky" is in fact merely the sediment of the upper world's surface (109c–d). If one of us, however, climbed up to the rim of our crater-world and looked out over the top, he would behold a world that is more exuberantly bright and beautiful than he has imagined possible, and the world he has left behind would seem murky in contrast, just like the world underwater (110a). Socrates says this world would appear like a ball of twelve leather strips: a patchwork of crimson and gold and dazzling white, and swirled with many other colours that we have never before seen. From this distance, our dank craters dapple its surface with dimples of mist and glinting hints of the water far below. The people of this upper world dwell on islands which are buffeted on the air, breathing in pure ether. As a result, they are longer living and healthier, and all of their senses are vastly superior to ours. They see the Sun, Moon, and stars as they *really* are, and not just "through a glass darkly," as we troglodytes do (111a–c).

Another relevant, parallel passage – albeit one that is not explicitly evoked by Lucian here – is from the sixth book of Cicero's *Republic*, better known as the *Dream of Scipio* (*Somnium Scipionis*). Here the Roman general Scipio Aemilianus, a leader of the Third Punic War, experiences a dream in which his dead grandfather and a leader of the Second Punic War, Scipio Africanus, leads him on a tour through the universe. Fictionally, the dream takes place prior to the younger Scipio's final destruction of Rome's great enemy Carthage in 146 BCE; the elder Scipio therefore offers his grandson a glimpse of the glory that awaits him, provided he shows genuine statesmanlike qualities throughout his life. Scipio is taken to the Milky Way, which, the elder Scipio explains, is the celestial destination for all great souls after death. From this place, "a circle shining out among the flames with the most dazzling brilliance," Scipio gets a clear view of the wonders of the cosmos, including stars of unimaginable size which he had never before seen from Earth, the Moon, and finally – dwarfed by the stellar orbs – our own planet, which looks so tiny that Scipio feels the pointlessness of his imperial conquests, through which he had acquired a mere dot in space: *iam ipsa terra ita mihi parua uisa est, ut me imperii nostri, quo quasi punctum eius attingimus, paeniteret.*[8] Listening to the harmony of the cosmos, Scipio's eyes are drawn to the Earth again and again, and his grandfather explains what he sees:

> Uides habitari in terra raris et angustis in locis et in ipsis quasi maculis, ubi habitatur, uastas solitudines interiectas ... hic autem alter subiectus aquiloni, quem incolitis, cerne quam tenui uos parte contingat! Omnis enim terra, quae colitur a uobis, angustata uerticibus, lateribus latior, parua quaedam insula est circumfusa illo mari, quod "Atlanticum," quod

---

[8] Cic. *Rep.* 6.16. For discussion of Scipio's cosmic panorama, especially the model that Cicero follows here, see Büchner 1984: 470–7 and Zetzel 1995: 235–7. For Scipio's response to the view, see Luck-Huyse 1997: 191–2. On the episode, see also Johnston's discussion in this volume, Chapter 11.

"magnum," quem "Oceanum" appellatis in terris; qui tamen tanto nomine quam sit paruus, uides. (*Rep.* 6.19–21)

You see that the Earth is inhabited in disparate and confined places, and in these inhabited "spots" (*maculae*), so to speak, vast wildernesses are interposed ... But this northern part, which you inhabit – look at what a slender portion is allotted to you! For the whole territory inhabited by you is narrow at top and bottom, wider at the sides, and surrounded, like a little island, by that sea, which you in different lands call the "Atlantic" or the "Great Sea" or "Ocean" – though you see how small it is, despite a name of such grandeur.

There are similarities between Scipio's vision of the Earth and Socrates' vision in Plato's *Phaedo*: in particular, the microcosmic "patches" of inhabited spaces hark back to the crater-worlds that mottled Socrates' globe.[9]

Lucian's *gaiaskopia* in *Icaromenippus* incorporates several *topoi* from these earlier narratives. Menippus' comparison of the minuscule humans far below with swarms of ants (and their cities with mere ant-hills, *Icar.* 19) is modeled on Plato's *Phaedo* 109a–b, where (as we have seen) Socrates compares the human race to ants or frogs around the Mediterranean pond.[10] In Aristophanes' *Peace*, similarly, the aerial traveler Trygaeus describes how humans appeared "tiny" to him from above, and also increasingly wicked, the higher he ascended.[11] It is a common feature of such Earth-views to invite us to ponder the futility of our quotidian preoccupations in this way.[12] In fact, this lies at the foundation of the entire tradition, for when Hephaestus in the *Iliad* translates his god's view of the cosmos into the design on the shield, the image nudges us to realize how small and fleeting, against the backdrop of eternity, the tragedies that

---

[9] For a similar image, see Arist. [*Mund.*] 392b30.
[10] This connection is noted also by Camerotto 2014: 207 n. 43. In Lucian's *Charon* 15, Charon, looking down on the Earth from a height, compares humans to wasps. At *Hermot.* 5, the Stoic Hermotimus claims that, from the summit of the Hill of Virtue, all people appear tiny like ants.
[11] See Luck-Huyse 1997: 190. *Peace* 821–3:

μικροὶ δ' ὁρᾶν ἄνωθεν ἦστ'. ἔμοιγέ τοι
ἀπὸ τοὐρανοῦ 'φαίνεσθε κακοήθεις πάνυ,
ἐντευθενὶ δὲ πολύ τι κακοηθέστεροι.

You were tiny to look at from above.
From Heaven, you seemed terribly wicked to me,
and from that position onwards even wickeder still.

[12] Luck-Huyse (1997: 187–92) briefly discusses the variety of emotional responses to views of the Earth from above in ancient literature, but does not include the Iliadic shield in her discussion.

engulf the humans at Troy actually are.[13] In *Icaromenippus* Lucian combines the poignancy of these realizations with the Aristophanic seed of satire, and uses his *gaiaskopia* not only to expose the greed and skulduggery that is endemic in humankind, but also to reflect on the pointlessness of our conflicts great and small which, from the remote lunar perspective, seem trivial indeed.

13.2 Modern Gaiaskopic Tradition: The First Wave, 1966–1972

Lucian's fantasy was realized in 1969 – over 1,800 years later – when the astronauts of the Apollo 11 mission became the first humans to land on the Moon and look back from there at planet Earth. But before that event, three photographs kick-started a brand-new cycle of gaiaskopic narratives for the modern world. The first photograph of our world from outer space had been taken in August 1966 by the unmanned NASA spacecraft *Lunar Orbiter 1*. However, it had little impact. The original image was grainy, streaked, and dark (Figure 1); as one journalist recalls, "it looked like a newsprint version of a high-contrast snapshot from space, a stark scattering of whites and blacks."[14] The second photograph, taken two years later, was dramatically different. It was taken by astronaut William Anders, one of the crew of the *Apollo 8* spacecraft as it orbited Earth, and it showed our planet rising in spectacular colour above the lunar horizon on December 24, 1968 (Figure 2). The image became known as *Earthrise*. This was followed by *The Blue Marble*, the first image of the whole Earth, which was taken on December 7, 1972 by the crew of *Apollo 17* and released by NASA on December 23 that year (Figure 3). With these early pictures, a millennia-long imaginary tradition of Earth-viewing was converted into reality, albeit a reality that was to a degree fictional and mediated, with some deception, through photography.[15] In profound and surprising ways, the ancient *gaiaskopic* tradition had already preempted the photographic reality.

---

[13] *Il.*18. 478–608; see Taplin 1980 for the classic humanist interpretation within the context of the *Iliad*.
[14] The quotation is from an editorial, "The Moon view," which appeared in print on page A34 of the *New York Times* on November 19, 2008. A version of this article can be retrieved at www.nytimes.com/2008/11/19/opinion/19wed3.html.
[15] For some of the ways in which photographs of what the astronauts saw were edited to conform to terracentric expectations, see notes on Figures 2 and 3. Lucian's allusion to the Iliadic ekphrasis constitutes a reminder to the reader of the mediated nature of his description.

Fig. 1 The first ever photograph of Earth, taken by *Lunar Orbiter 1* in August 1966. The image in the upper register is the original photograph, which was published in 1966. The lower register shows the same image, restored by the Lunar Orbiter Image Restoration Project (LOIRP), and published in November 2008. (Image credit: NASA, Lunar Orbiter)

The crisis of expression, which Menippus experiences upon seeing the Earth in *Icaromenippus*, was itself a well-documented experience among the first men who *actually* saw the Earth from the Moon.[16] The "rhetorical failure" of the early years of space exploration has been explained partly as a

---

[16] Poole 2008 is an excellent analysis of the subject. Weber 1985 examines literary responses to "seeing the Earth."

Fig. 2 *Earthrise*, December 24, 1968. This was the first extraterrestrial photograph of our world to have major impact on the public consciousness. In fact, the original image issued by NASA had a different orientation: Borman saw the Moon on the right, with the Earth appearing to emerge over its side. For publication, however, the press altered the orientation to meet terracentric expectations, so that the lunar surface should appear as the "ground" below our feet, and the Earth now appears to rise vertically above the lunar horizon, thus adapting the astronautical experience to a more familiar terrestrial one; see Poole 2008: 76–7. For the colour version, please refer to the plate section.
(Image credit: NASA)

result of the training of the astronauts themselves, who were mainly test pilots in those days, and whose experience therefore had taught them *not* to emote.[17] Partly, too, it was a result of their cramped working conditions and densely packed schedules, which left very little time or space for deeper

---

[17] As Michael Collins (1974: 54) complained: "It was like describing what Christiaan Barnard wore while performing the first heart transplant … we weren't trained to emote, we were trained to

Fig. 3 *The Blue Marble*, the first photograph of the whole Earth taken by a manned spacecraft, in this case the crew of *Apollo 17*. The photo was taken en route to the Moon on December 7, 1972, at a distance of *c.*45,000 km from the Earth. As with the *Earthrise* image four years previously, the orientation of *The Blue Marble* was changed for publication, in order to conform with terracentric expectations of "up" and "down." In the original orientation Antarctica was at the top of the globe, but in the published image, seen here, it appears at the bottom; see Poole 2008: 95. For the colour version, please refer to the plate section. (Image credit: NASA, Johnson Space Centre)

contemplation anyway. NASA had not prepared their astronauts for the potential psychological impact of their experience; as a result, they could only exclaim at the beauty and wonder of what they were witnessing, in terms which seemed hopelessly jejeune to the millions waiting on

> repress emotions ... If they wanted an emotional press conference, for Christ's sake, they should have put together an Apollo crew of a philosopher, a priest, and a poet – not three test pilots."

Fig. 1 The first ever photograph of Earth, taken by *Lunar Orbiter 1* in August 1966. The image in the upper register is the original photograph, which was published in 1966. The lower register shows the same image, restored by the Lunar Orbiter Image Restoration Project (LOIRP), and published in November 2008. (Image credit: NASA, Lunar Orbiter).

Fig. 2   *Earthrise*, December 24, 1968. This was the first extraterrestrial photograph of our world to have major impact on the public consciousness. In fact, the original image issued by NASA had a different orientation: Borman saw the Moon on the right, with the Earth appearing to emerge over its side. For publication, however, the press altered the orientation to meet terracentric expectations, so that the lunar surface should appear as the "ground" below our feet, and the Earth now appears to rise vertically above the lunar horizon, thus adapting the astronautical experience to a more familiar terrestrial one; see Poole 2008: 76–7. (Image credit: NASA).

Fig. 3   *The Blue Marble*, the first photograph of the whole Earth taken by a manned spacecraft, in this case the crew of *Apollo 17*. The photo was taken en route to the Moon on December 7, 1972, at a distance of *c.*45,000 km from the Earth. As with the *Earthrise* image four years previously, the orientation of *The Blue Marble* was changed for publication, in order to conform with terracentric expectations of "up" and "down." In the original orientation Antarctica was at the top of the globe, but in the published image, seen here, it appears at the bottom; see Poole 2008: 95. (Image credit: NASA, Johnson Space Centre).

Fig. 4 *Pale Blue Dot*, taken by *Voyager 1*, from the suite of images known as the Solar System "family portraits." The tiny speck which is visible near the middle of the bright streak farthest right is Earth, seen from a distance of *c*.6 billion km. (Image credit: NASA/JPL–Caltech).

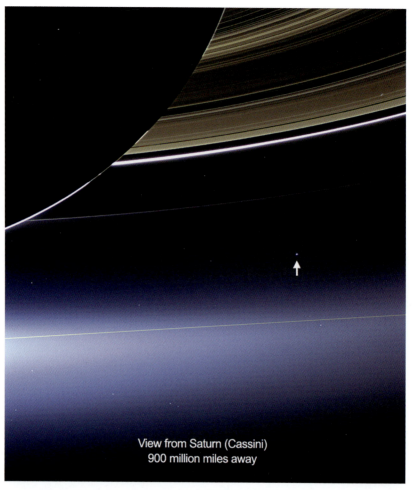

Fig. 5 *The Day the Earth Smiled*, taken by NASA's *Cassini* spacecraft on July 19, 2013. Saturn and its rings are in the foreground, and below these in the same frame we can see Earth with its Moon, 1.44 billion km in the distance. Close-up, the Moon appears as a faint protrusion to the right of the Earth. (Image credit: NASA/JPL–Caltech/Space Science Institute).

Earth.[18] Their frustration was exacerbated by the "almost unbearable responsibility to communicate what they had learned to the rest of the human race."[19] *Apollo 15* astronaut Dave Scott felt "unable even to begin to convey the wonder I felt looking back at the Earth from this distance."[20] Prince Sultan Bin Salman Al Saud of Saudi Arabia, a payload specialist on the fifth flight of the space shuttle *Discovery* in 1985, described his first view of the Earth as "really one of the most memorable moments of my entire life. I just said, in Arabic, 'Oh, God,' or something like 'God is great' . . . *It's beyond description*."[21] According to NASA astronaut Nicole Stott, "'Indescribable' is a word that is used a lot, but I think it's accurate. You look out the window and pictures just don't do justice to what you see."[22]

Others described, like Lucian, their struggle to process their experience. Michael Collins, the command module pilot for the first lunar landing with Apollo 11, remarked: "It is a pity that my eyes have seen more than my brain has been able to assimilate or evaluate, but like the Druids at Stonehenge, I have attempted to bring order out of what I have observed, even if I have not understood it fully."[23] Just as Menippus' allusion to the Iliadic shield invited us to read his words within the tradition of *mimēmata tou kosmou*, by inviting us to view his work as a descendant of the structure at Stonehenge Collins converts it into a sort of textual monument: both structures seek, in different ways, to make sense of the universe and to represent it for others here on Earth. For Collins, the massive, silent stones convey something of the ineffability of his experience.

Given these difficulties of finding adequate words, it was common to resort to music instead. Ronald McNair, a mission specialist on *Challenger* who was killed in a subsequent mission, played his saxophone in orbit to express ideas that he felt he could not articulate in words.[24] Ken Mattingly recalled selecting particular pieces of music to enhance his experience of visual wonder on *Apollo 16*: "I had Berlioz's 'Symphonie Fantastique' and some other things that I really liked that just matched the mood of seeing this unbelievable scene of things floating by."[25] Russell Schweickart was

---

[18] For a thorough examination of this "rhetorical failure," see Poole 2008: 97–115, whose account I draw on liberally here.
[19] Poole 2008: 97.   [20] Poole 2008: 102.   [21] Quoted from White 2014: 18 (emphasis mine).
[22] Quoted from White 2014: 18.
[23] Collins 1974: 474. Collins records how he subsequently tried to express what he had seen through painting, but considered his attempts "a total flop" (1974: 474–5). Al Bean, an astronaut with Apollo 12, became a well-known artist in later life.
[24] See White 2014: 212–13.
[25] Quoted from NASA's oral histories: www.jsc.nasa.gov/history/oral_histories/MattinglyTK/MattinglyTK_11-6-01.htm.

also noted for his careful selection of music to create a soundtrack for the Apollo 9 mission.[26] More recently, in 2013, a video which went viral on YouTube featured astronaut Chris Hadfield performing David Bowie's "Space Oddity" on board the International Space Station, whilst he gazed at our home-world through the window.[27] Bowie's famous, plaintive lyric captured, in an instantly recognizable way, the existential loneliness of a man "floating in a tin can, far above the world." Music has played an evocative role in imaginative recreations of outer space as well. Well-known examples include Vangelis' theme to Carl Sagan's television series *Cosmos*, and director Stanley Kubrick's use of both Johann Strauss II's "Blue Danube" and Richard Strauss' overture from *Also sprach Zarathustra* at significant moments in his 1968 film *2001: A Space Odyssey*. Each of these pieces seems to express, respectively, the serenely unfolding infinity of space, the synchrony of the interplanetary dance, or the absolute command of the astrophysical laws that bring Earth, Moon, and Sun into alignment. And in fact, there is a rich ancient tradition underlying this tendency to exploit music's more direct expressive power in this context. The idea that musical harmony is the language of celestial order goes back to the Pythagoreans and even earlier. In Cicero's *Dream of Scipio*, as Scipio's gaze wanders around the universe, a strange music fills his ears, which his grandfather explains by expounding, briefly, the Pythagorean doctrine of the harmony of the spheres: as each of the heavenly spheres rotates (the ninth sphere, the Earth, is at the centre of the cosmos, and does not move), it produces its own particular sound. These notes produce the notes of the musical octave.[28] Heard, imaginatively, in the backdrop to Scipio's speech, this harmonious music would seem like a celestial ratification of Scipio's predictions for his grandson's glorious future. In quite the opposite way, when Menippus evokes the dissonant voices of a multitude of choirs as he gazes on the Earth, he generates a soundtrack of cacophony for his *gaiaskopia*, which expresses not the serenity of the heavens, but the chaos and complexity of our world. Given the prevalence of the Pythagorean theory in antiquity, Lucian's imaginary soundscape would have been striking indeed.

---

[26] Poole 2008: 104.

[27] From the very start, music has been central to our mission of cosmic outreach. Each of the *Voyager* probes carries a golden phonograph record containing, among other sounds of the Earth, ninety minutes of the greatest terrestrial music, including a Navajo chant, a Peruvian wedding song, Beethoven, Bach, and Chuck Berry's rock'n'roll hit "Johnny B. Goode" (Sagan 1994: 124–5).

[28] Cic. *Rep.* 6.18–19. For elucidation of this difficult passage and the theory it contains, see Büchner 1984: 478–84 and Zetzel 1995: 239–41.

It is a leitmotiv of both ancient and modern gaiaskopic narratives to pronounce on the surprisingly small appearance of our world when viewed from a distance. Modern narratives emphasize its astonishingly beautiful but ultimately fragile appearance, which seems at odds with our experience of the planet beneath our own feet: "As we walk its surface, it seems solid and substantial enough, almost infinite as it extends flatly in all directions. But from space there is no hint of ruggedness to it; smooth as a billiard ball, it seems delicately poised in its circular journey around the sun, and above all it seems fragile."[29] *Earthrise* and *The Blue Marble* cast the Earth's vivid colours into sharp contrast with the dead, grey Moon in the foreground and the deep black of space. Collins recalled this contrast from space, and how he didn't quite appreciate the beauty of Earth until he saw the Moon: "The moon is so scarred, so desolate, so monotonous, that I cannot recall its tortured surface without thinking of the infinite variety the delightful planet earth offers: misty waterfalls, pine forests, rose gardens, blues and greens and reds and whites that are missing entirely on the gray-tan moon."[30] Scipio's view of the Earth, with its icy caps and scorched equatorial zone, hints – in a very restrained way – at such contrasts in the terrestrial landscape, but the closest to this vision is Socrates' description of the Earth as a ball of mesmeric colour and glamor, light and shade, which seems astonishingly prescient of *The Blue Marble*.

Both *Earthrise* and *The Blue Marble* revealed Earth's isolation in the infinite expanse of space, which dwarfs it. In a similar way, Collins recalled having to search for Earth on the journey home from the Moon:

> I looked out of my window and tried to find Earth. The little planet is so small out there in the vastness that at first I couldn't even locate it ... I looked away for a moment and, poof, it was gone. I couldn't find it again without searching closely. At that point I made my discovery. Suddenly I knew what a tiny, fragile thing Earth is.[31]

Neil Armstrong, on the same mission, would recall how, from the Moon, *he could block out the entire Earth with his thumb*. Russell Schweickart remembered this when describing his own experiences during a spacewalk on Apollo 9, as the spacecraft orbited the Earth:

> The contrast between that bright blue and white Christmas tree ornament and the black sky, that infinite universe, really comes through ... It is so

---

[29] Collins 1974: 471.   [30] Collins 1974: 469.
[31] Michael Collins, "Our planet: fragile gem in the universe," *Birmingham Post-Herald*, March 1, 1972, cited in Poole 2008: 99.

small and so fragile and such a precious little spot in that universe that *you can block it out with your thumb*, and you realize than on that small spot, that little blue and white thing, is everything that means anything to you – all of history and music and poetry and art and death and birth and love, tears, joy, games, all of it *on that little spot out there that you can cover with your thumb*.[32]

Stuart Roosa, the command module pilot of Apollo 14, remembered looking at the Earth "like a jewel in the sky," reflecting that everything he knew was contained there, then covering it up with the palm of his hand.[33] In an allusion to these experiences, in the 1995 film *Apollo 13* (directed by Ron Howard), the character of astronaut Jim Lovell (played by Tom Hanks) uses his thumb early in the film to block the Moon from his position on the Earth – and subsequently to block the Earth from his view as he orbits the Moon. All of these gestures hark back to Menippus' claim that, from his vantage point on the Moon, "the whole of Greece looked *no bigger to me than four fingers' breadth*."[34] Evidently, human beings have been marveling at the Moon with their hands for millennia; the history of this gesture is a long one.

Humans are invisible from outer space. This worried philosophers such as Hannah Arendt, who – incidentally – used similar analogies to our ancient authors (comparing humans to rats or snails, instead of frogs or ants) to articulate her anxieties about how the view from outer space would reduce all traces of human output to a minuscule scale.[35] In the end, however, it was the invisibility of political boundaries – at a time when disastrous wars were being fought over them on Earth – that struck viewers hard. "You can't see the boundaries over which we fight wars," remarked Don Lind, an astronaut on the Spacelab-3 science mission.[36] Russell Schweickart's essay "No frames, no boundaries" – which later became a film of the same name – was one of the most famous explorations of this theme.[37] The absolute absence of humans from outer space provoked greater awareness of the disparity between the appearance of our world from afar and the experience of it close up. For the audience of the Apollo years in particular, it was just as impossible to square *The Blue Marble* with

---

[32] Schweickart 1977: 12 (emphasis mine).
[33] Quoted from Poole 2008: 112, citing the *Washington Post*, December 13, 1994 (a report on Roosa's death).
[34] *Icar.* 18.
[35] Arendt 1968: 279. For an overview of Arendt's critical response to the mission of space exploration, see Weber 1985: 20–3.
[36] Quoted from White 2014: 43.   [37] See Poole 2008: 165–6.

the chaos of the Vietnam War, racial conflict, and environmental devastation as it was to separate them; one view of Earth seemed poised in tragic contrast and mutual dialogue with the other. Upon seeing *The Blue Marble*, Kurt Vonnegut remarked: "Earth is such a pretty blue and pink and white pearl in the pictures NASA sent me. It looks so *clean*. You can't see all the hungry, angry earthlings down there – and the smoke and the sewage and trash and sophisticated weaponry."[38] People protested at the millions that were spent to send a few men into space.[39]

In the ancient *gaiaskopiai*, in contrast, humans tend *not* to disappear from view. On the contrary, on the Iliadic shield and in both of Lucian's Earth-views, humans play a prominent and visible role. The *Phaedo* is more ambivalent, comprising two distinct views of Earth, one which features humans and the other which excludes them. We begin with the Earth-bound perspective of the crater-dweller, who looks up for the first time and sees the color and richness of the upper world, including humanoids who live aloft on islands of cloud. But then we switch to a remote (and unidentified) perspective from outer space, where the world appears as a multicoloured ball, devoid of individual presences. In Cicero's more scientific *gaiaskopia*, cities and features of the physical geography are visible (Scipio points out Carthage, the Caucasus, and the Ganges, for example), but humans are not. Despite this variation in the visibility of humans, most of the ancient Earth-views comment, implicitly or explicitly, on the futility of fighting over boundaries in a way that is directly analogous to the modern tradition. This is explicit in *Icaromenippus* and *The Dream of Scipio*, and implicit in the Iliadic shield. The exception, paradoxically, is the *Phaedo*, whose visual vocabulary is closest to *The Blue Marble*, but which (for reasons connected with Socrates' philosophy, as we shall see) explores none of the poignant ideas which that photograph raised. In general, however, because humans are more visible in ancient Earth-views, the contrast between appearance and reality is less sharply delineated in the ancient images than in the modern ones. In fact, this contrast is a distinct feature only of the Iliadic shield, for only here is there a sense in which the generic scenes of human activity seen on the shield – in the remote, god's-eye view of humanity – are in conflict with the close-up reality in which Achilles himself and the other actors at Troy are soon to be embroiled – in a (not un-ironic) meditation on the difference

---

[38] Vonnegut 1969/1976: 83.
[39] Gil Scott-Heron's poem "Whitey's on the Moon," from the album *Small talk at 125th and Lenox* (Flying Dutchman records, 1970), is a well-known example of this theme in contemporary poetry.

between art and life.⁴⁰ Paradoxically, Menippus' remote *gaiaskopia* in *Icaromenippus* reveals more detail to him about everyday life at home on Earth. This is because Menippus' magical eye and panoptic position enable him to see events that are ordinarily concealed from him as a human actor below. It is characteristic of Lucian to suggest that art or fiction is more real than reality itself. There is a similar reversal in *True Stories* where the reality of our home planet is seen only as a mirror-image, a pale reflection of the real world.⁴¹ By stepping outside the narrative of life – quite literally, off the planet – Menippus has entered into a zone of zero-degree focalization on the Moon, and become an omniscient narrator.⁴² However, there is still a tension between Menippus' global view and local interpretation, which confines the infinite variety of the world's nations to a sequence of stereotyped activities. Menippus reads the world through the eyes of the Greek literary tradition. This contrasts vividly with the experience of astronauts such as Tom Stafford of Apollo 10, who declared "You don't look down at the world as an American but as a human being."⁴³

No ancient Earth-view seems to have provoked contemplation on the reality beneath the clouds in as grittily topical a manner as the modern photographs did, either. From the *Iliad* to Lucian, human activities are envisaged in a generic way. Lucian comes closest to offering us a historicized snapshot of our world from outer space, but even here the world that Menippus sees is explicitly not Lucian's society of the second century CE, but the Hellenistic world of some five hundred years or so before. Alexander's successor kings and their troubled dynasties are in evidence (*Icar.* 15), and the Colossus of Rhodes is still standing (*Icar.* 12).⁴⁴ Lucian selects this

---

[40] Ironic, because the *Iliad* itself is a poem, and therefore the "reality" of the world that it presents is just as much a product of detached artifice as the images on the shield. The metapoetics of the *Iliad* therefore embroil the audience/reader in questions about the representational nature of art. *The Blue Marble* generates similar ironies: as a photograph, the image that it presents is rhetorically "real," yet this "reality," we know, has been manipulated artificially to conform to our expectation that "north" means "up" etc., which means that *The Blue Marble* is not precisely what the astronauts themselves saw.

[41] For fuller discussion of the interplay between reality and representation on Lucian's Moon in *True Stories*, see ní Mheallaigh 2014: 216–27.

[42] By doing this, Lucian reifies and exaggerates the cartographic (or "eusynoptic") thrust of the narrative of the *Iliad* – on which, see Purves 2010a: 24–64.

[43] See Poole 2008: 104 with n. 18.

[44] The Colossus of Rhodes was completed in 280 BCE and stood for a little over half a century. It collapsed in the earthquake of 226 BCE, but thereafter its gargantuan ruins remained *in situ* for centuries and became a tourist attraction (Strabo 14.2.5; Plin. *HN* 34.41). According to Pliny, the thumb was so enormous that visitors could not close their arms around it, and each finger was larger than most statues. The lighthouse on Pharos (also mentioned at *Icar.*) was built a little later in the third century BCE, and stood erect throughout antiquity.

view because it is to this period that the historical Menippus of Gadara, inventor of Menippean satire, belongs, but the choice could also reflect an awareness of the importance of the period of the Hellenistic *megalopoleis* for the development of a more global type of consciousness that is represented by the *gaiaskopia* itself, since this was a time when Greeks all over the world – in Egypt, Gaul, and along the Black Sea – could claim homogeneity of culture.[45] But in spite of the retro time-shift, what Menippus saw might have resonated with contemporary events in Lucian's world too. It does not stretch the imagination too far, I think, to suggest that Menippus' comments about the futility of war (for example) could have had a more pointed resonance for some of Lucian's readers in Marcus Aurelius' war-troubled reign, even though the nature of the comment is itself generic.[46]

A final point of contact – and difference – between the two *gaiaskopic* traditions lies in their effects on the viewer. The Earth photographs changed the way humans think about our home, and awakened a new global consciousness which was seminal to nascent New Age and environmental movements in the 1960s and 1970s.[47] *Earthrise* has been described as "the most influential environmental photograph ever taken," while *The Blue Marble* is reputedly the single most reproduced image in human history.[48] At the level of the individual, the effects of leaving Earth and looking back at it remotely were dramatic; many astronauts from the Apollo years experienced a new dawning of spiritual, ecological, or humanitarian thought as a result of their journey into space; some became artists, in their struggle to express what they had seen; some experienced religious conversions or psychological breakdown.[49]

Of the ancient Earth-views, several (as we have seen) imply a more detached way of evaluating earthly matters as a result of looking at things from afar, and in each case this is in keeping with the narrator's own

---

[45] Pitts and Versluys 2014: 16–17.
[46] The Parthian Wars of 161–6 CE were a popular theme for contemporary historiographers, to judge from Lucian's essay *How to Write History*.
[47] For a fascinating exploration of these connections, see Poole 2008 and White 2014.
[48] The claim about *Earthrise* was made by photographer Galen Rowell, in *Life* Magazine's *100 Photographs that Changed the World* edition (2003). The assertion about *The Blue Marble* is made by Poole 2008: 82, and widespread in other sources as well, though I cannot find any official statistical analyses or source references to support it; cf. Lazier 2011: 606 on the globalization of the image.
[49] For a survey and discussion of these experiences, see Poole 2008: 97–115, esp. 105 ff.

natural inclinations. This is clear in the following speech by Lucian's Menippus, as he looks down on Earth from the Moon:

> Μάλιστα δὲ ἐπ' ἐκείνοις ἐπῄει μοι γελᾶν τοῖς περὶ γῆς ὅρων ἐρίζουσι καὶ τοῖς μέγα φρονοῦσιν ἐπὶ τῷ τὸ Σικυώνιον πεδίον γεωργεῖν ἢ Μαραθῶνος ἔχειν τὰ περὶ τὴν Οἰνόην ἢ Ἀχαρνῆσι πλέθρα κεκτῆσθαι χίλια· τῆς γοῦν Ἑλλάδος ὅλης ὡς τότε μοι ἄνωθεν ἐφαίνετο δακτύλων οὔσης τὸ μέγεθος τεττάρων, κατὰ λόγον, οἶμαι, ἡ Ἀττικὴ πολλοστημόριον ἦν. ὥστε ἐνενόουν ἐφ' ὁπόσῳ τοῖς πλουσίοις τούτοις μέγα φρονεῖν κατελείπετο· σχεδὸν γὰρ ὁ πολυπλεθρότατος αὐτῶν μίαν τῶν Ἐπικουρείων ἀτόμων ἐδόκει μοι γεωργεῖν. ἀποβλέψας δὲ δὴ καὶ ἐς τὴν Πελοπόννησον, εἶτα τὴν Κυνουρίαν γῆν ἰδὼν ἀνεμνήσθην περὶ ὅσου χωρίου, κατ' οὐδὲν Αἰγυπτίου φακοῦ πλατυτέρου, τοσοῦτοι ἔπεσον Ἀργείων καὶ Λακεδαιμονίων μιᾶς ἡμέρας. καὶ μὴν εἴ τινα ἴδοιμι ἐπὶ χρυσῷ μέγα φρονοῦντα, ὅτι δακτυλίους τε εἶχεν ὀκτὼ καὶ φιάλας τέτταρας, πάνυ καὶ ἐπὶ τούτῳ ἂν ἐγέλων· τὸ γὰρ Πάγγαιον ὅλον αὐτοῖς μετάλλοις κεγχριαῖον ἦν τὸ μέγεθος. (*Icar.* 18)

> Most of all, I was overcome with laughter at those who were quarreling over land-boundaries and those who prided themselves for farming the Sicyon plain or owning a thousand yards of land around Oenoe at Marathon or at Acharnae – because at that moment in time, from my vantage point above, the entirety of Greece looked to me no bigger than four fingers' breadth, and Attica, proportionately, was a mere fraction of that. So I reflected how little was left for these wealthy men to pride themselves on, for it seemed to me that even the man with the most acreage was farming no more than one Epicurean atom. Looking toward the Peloponnesus, and seeing the territory of Cynouria, I recalled how many Argives and Spartans had fallen in one day over such a meager patch of land, no broader than an Egyptian bean. And whenever I caught sight of someone preening himself on his gold because he owned eight rings and four dishes, I laughed out loud at him, for the whole of Pangaeum along with its mines was the size of a millet-seed.

Menippus' thoughts echo those of Socrates in Plato's *Theaetetus* where, following the anecdote about the astronomer Thales falling into the well, Socrates expounds on the otherworldly nature of those who are dedicated to philosophy. Wealth matters very little to such a person, Socrates explains, for "Whenever he hears that someone who owns ten thousand or more acres of land possesses a marvellous fortune, this sounds very small indeed to him, *since he is accustomed to looking at the entire earth.*"[50] Menippus' ventriloquizing of this perspective from his lunar position,

---

[50] Pl. *Tht.* 174e: γῆς δὲ ὅταν μυρία πλέθρα ἢ ἔτι πλείω ἀκούσῃ ὥς τις ἄρα κεκτημένος θαυμαστὰ πλήθει κέκτηται, πάνσμικρα δοκεῖ ἀκούειν <u>εἰς ἅπασαν εἰωθὼς τὴν γῆν βλέπειν</u>. This similarity is noted by Camerotto 2014: 208.

where he is afforded a literal view of the entire Earth, suggests that, through his fantastic experiment, he is now becoming a true philosopher and astronomer in this Socratic sense, in contrast with the venal and pusillanimous pseudo-intellectuals he has left behind. His departure from Earth, and the sense of detachment from worldly matters that goes with it, are an outgrowth of the natural contempt that he had already expressed for such things – which is what had prompted him toward astronomy in the first place. Given Menippus of Gadara's associations with Cynicism, Lucian's *gaiaskopia* is usually interpreted as a variation of the Cynic motif of *kataskopia* or the "view from above," in which the viewer exploits his position to deride those below.[51] However, Menippus' more thoughtful contemplation of the smallness of earthly territories and the futility of the wars that are fought over them draws his *gaiaskopia* closer to the more general philosophical exercise of adopting a "view from above," which was advocated especially by Stoics as a method for disentangling oneself from mundane distractions and gaining a clearer perspective on human affairs. This recommendation recurs often in the *Meditations* of the Stoic emperor Marcus Aurelius, who was contemporary with Lucian himself.[52]

Some astronauts reported a similar increase in philosophical outlook as a result of their travels in outer space. Michael Collins denied having attained "complete guru-like detachment" from the world, but nevertheless acknowledged a sense of "earthly ennui," which he describes as a minor version of the "Buzz syndrome." This term is a reference to astronaut Buzz Aldrin's well-documented series of psychiatric difficulties after walking on the Moon, because life thereafter could be nothing but an anti-climax. For Collins, this took the form of a "mild melancholy about future possibilities" instead; he no longer experienced excitement the way he had before Apollo 11, but he was also "more impervious to minor problems," such as two people squabbling:

> When two of my people come to me red-faced and huffing over some petty dispute, I feel like telling then, "Well, the earth continues to turn on its axis, undisturbed by your problem; take your cue from it, and work it out by yourselves; it really doesn't amount to much anyway." Of course, I don't say that … but not many things seem quite as vital to me any more. My threshold of measuring what is important has been raised.[53]

---

[51] Helm (1906: 80–114) examines Menippean elements in *Icaromenippus*.
[52] M. Aur. *Med.* 7.47–8, 9.30, 11.1–2. For further Stoic advocacy of this mental exercise, cf. Sen. *QNat.*, preface 7–11, with discussion, including this passage of *Icaromenippus*, in Hadot 1995: 238–50.
[53] Collins 1974: 462.

Menippus experiences a similar deepening of philosophical feeling, and a confirmation of his convictions, not a transformation of them. What he formerly suspected, he now knows is true.

Only one ancient Earth-view talks about a radical change in world-outlook: this is the *Phaedo*. The theory of an epistemological paradigm shift is in fact interwoven into Socrates' *gaiaskopia* because its narrative and imagery are so richly entangled with Socrates' allegory of the Cave from *Republic* 7 (514a–520a).[54] There is a clear analogy between the experience of Socrates' crater-dweller in the *Phaedo* as he discovers the upper world for the first time and the experience of the cave-dweller in the *Republic*, who emerges from the subterranean darkness into the sunlit world beyond the cave, only to realize that the reality that he had believed before was nothing but a play of shadows on the cave wall; *this* is the true reality. As a result of this discovery, he is filled with the desire to return to his cave, to inform the others in there about the truth, and to set them free. Socrates does not provide us with a postscript to the story of the crater-dweller in the *Phaedo*, but, on the basis of the analogy with the cave-dweller, we may surmise that this individual would similarly have been inspired to impart his new knowledge to his fellow troglodytes, causing a massive paradigm shift in the crater-dwellers' conceptualization of their world. Now the crater, in comparison with the upper world, will seem dank, isolated, and so much more limited than they had previously imagined. Presumably, the next step will be a mass exodus from the crater and exploration of the upper world. In short, both are narratives about leaving one's home-world, only to experience a profound cognitive transformation as one views one's home from outside, with new eyes. Both are stories about paradigm shifts in the way we see reality.

There are striking resonances also between Socrates' imagined experience in the *Phaedo* and people's responses to seeing our world from outer space for the first time in the modern era. In both cases the world we formerly knew now seems a much smaller, isolated, and more delicate place. In fact, the Platonic metaphor of the cave underlies much of the imagery used to describe the experience of leaving the Earth, whose confinement was likened

---

[54] In an interview with astronaut Gene Cernan – the last man on the Moon – Frank White, author of *The Overview Effect*, suggested Plato's cave allegory as an analogy for the experience of the astronaut who tries to explain what he saw to those left behind on Earth: "One of the things this research has shown me is that the problem is not that the astronauts aren't articulate about their experiences, but that we have no context for hearing what you are saying" (White 2014: 180, 166–7).

to a "prison," "cradle," or even a "womb."[55] But there is a fundamental difference between the ancient and modern narratives of *gaiaskopia*. The crater-dweller in *Phaedo* discovers a brighter, better world outside. *The Blue Marble* inverted this experience by revealing the darkness that envelops us utterly; as a result, our own little world appeared isolated and small, yes, but suddenly by far the most beautiful place to be. Leaving the known world, both in reality and in the ancient imagination, tends to imbue the adventurer with a sense of evangelistic duty to those left behind, but the message, it turns out, could vary greatly. When the astronauts returned home, it was not, on the whole (like Socrates' fugitive) to urge a mass exodus into space, but to impart instead the sobering truth that our terrestrial "cave" is all we have, and "good planets are hard to find."[56] "The Earth, it turns out, is lovely, and to see it is to wish also to return."[57]

13.3 Second-Wave *Gaiaskopiai*: *Pale Blue Dot* and *The Day the Earth Smiled*

In the second wave of remote Earth-views, cameras point at our world from much vaster distances than the lunar surface. Since the heady years of the Apollo program, two such photographs have impinged on human consciousness in a comparable way. The first of these was taken on February 14, 1990, when NASA commanded the space probe *Voyager 1* to turn its camera toward Earth from the edge of interstellar space, about 6 billion kilometers away, just as it was about to leave our solar system forever. The resulting image was *Pale Blue Dot*, so called because the Earth, at this enormous distance, is almost undetectable; it appears less than a pixel in size, no more than a mote of dust (Figure 4).

---

[55] For the Earth as prison, see the following optimistic claim from the newspaper *Kansas City Star*, December 7, 1972 (cited in Poole 2008: 94): "Man ... escaped the prison of his planet. And in looking back across the void, understood that it was a prison only if he let it be." For the Earth as cradle, cf. the quote attributed to Russian rocket engineer Konstantin Tsiolkovsky: "The earth is the cradle of humanity, but mankind will not stay in the cradle forever." For the Earth as womb, see Russell Schweickart on the "Cosmic Birth Phenomenon" in White 2014: 186.

[56] The latter phrase was a well-known slogan on contemporary bumper stickers in the USA (see Lazier 2011: 621). Michael Collins recalls: "I determined in that moment that I would do all I could to let people know what a wonderful home we have – before it is too late. So I have a personal, simple message to pass on: There is only one Earth. It is a tiny, precious stone. Let us treasure it; there is not another one." Collins, "Our planet," quoted from Poole 2008: 107. On "Earth Day" and the "Whole Earth" movement, see Poole 2008: 147–69.

[57] Lazier 2011: 620.

Fig. 4 *Pale Blue Dot*, taken by *Voyager 1*, from the suite of images known as the Solar System "family portraits." The tiny speck which is visible near the middle of the bright streak farthest right is Earth, seen from a distance of $c.6$ billion km. For the colour version, please refer to the plate section. (Image credit: NASA/JPL–Caltech)

It may have been scientifically useless, but such a remote view of our planet turned out to have immense rhetorical power.[58] Visually, there is nothing to match it in the ancient gaiaskopic tradition, for no ancient thinker on record ever conceived of our Earth in this way. And yet we find continuities of thought even between the ancient tradition and the response to *Pale Blue Dot*, for in the wake of its publication the astronomer Carl Sagan, whether he knew it or not, echoed, with uncanny precision, the sentiment and even the very imagery of Lucian's imaginary *gaiaskopia* in *Icaromenippus*, from the passage quoted earlier on p. 282:

> The Earth is a *very small stage* in a vast cosmic arena. *Think of the rivers of blood spilled by all those generals and emperors so that in glory and triumph they could become the momentary masters of a fraction of a dot*. Think of the endless cruelties visited by the inhabitants of one corner of this pixel on the scarcely distinguishable inhabitants of some other corner. How frequent their misunderstandings, how eager they are to kill one another, how fervent their hatreds. Our posturings, our imagined self-importance, the delusion that we have some privileged position in the universe, are challenged by this point of pale light. Our planet is a lonely speck in the great enveloping cosmic dark. In our obscurity – in all this vastness – there is no hint that help will come from elsewhere to save us from ourselves ... There is perhaps no better demonstration of the folly of human conceits than this distant image of our tiny world. To me, it underscores our responsibility to deal more kindly with one another and to preserve and cherish the pale blue dot, the only home we've ever known.[59]

The italicized phrases here mark my emphasis, and indicate points of intersection between Sagan's and Lucian's texts. Both authors use the same theatrical metaphor of the world as a "stage" to express the feeling of zooming out on human existence.[60] Both reflect upon the pointlessness of warfare and the meaninglessness of human pride in conquest, and are struck in different ways by our petty divisions: for Sagan this is a poignant realization; for Menippus it is largely an absurd one, but regrettable too. Both authors use imagery of the infinitesimally small to help visualize the paradoxical tininess of our world: Sagan's "fraction of a dot," "pixel," "point of pale light," "tiny world," and "dot" correspond to Lucian's "mere fraction" of four-fingers' breadth, "one Epicurean atom," "Egyptian bean," and "millet-seed."

---

[58] Poole 2008: 182–6.   [59] Sagan 1994: 6–7.
[60] At *Icar.* 17 Menippus describes the ridiculous scenes in the "motley and manifold drama" of humanity (ἐν αὐτῷ γε ποικίλῳ καὶ πολυειδεῖ τῷ θεάτρῳ).

There are important differences too, of course. Sagan emphasizes the lonely darkness that engulfs our world, which is the dominant feature, visually, of *Pale Blue Dot*. This in turn prompts him to reflect on our apparent isolation within the universe, and our responsibility to care for our home. There is no such sense of existential loneliness or global fragility in any ancient Earth-view, though the closest analog, arguably, is the Homeric shield, where human life is framed by the emptiness of the natural world: the heavens and the oceanic ring. Scipio in Cicero's *Dream of Scipio* points out the vast stretches of emptiness that separate small pockets of human civilization on Earth. But ancient Earth-views do not focus on the void, which is such an overwhelming and disturbing feature of the reality of space.

The second of these significant second-wave *gaiaskopiai* was a photograph taken on July 19, 2013 by the *Cassini* probe as it orbited Saturn. It is known as *The Day the Earth Smiled*, as the entire Earth's population was invited to smile at the sky on the day it was taken. From the vast distance (1.44 billion kilometers) none of this detail can be seen, and the Earth appears no more than an indiscriminate point of light in the suffocating black of space (Figure 5). Yet we *know* we are assembled in our billions on that tiny scintilla, where thousands of smiling faces have turned toward the sky. Uniquely, *The Day the Earth Smiled* converted outer-space telescopy into a cosmic drama in which we could all participate, connecting humans with our technological offspring orbiting a distant world.[61] It was described as "a day of cosmic self-awareness, celebrated planet-wide and marked by an interplanetary salute between robot and maker,"[62] and many activities were planned all around the world to mark the occasion.

In Lucian's view from the Moon in *True Stories*, the viewer through the telescope sees not only all the cities and peoples of the world, but also his own household and homeland, and he can also hear everything that is being said by everyone.[63] The narrative, albeit brief, suggests a more controlled process of "zooming in" on such detail than the panoptic chaos of *Icaromenippus*. For reasons to do with the nature of *True Stories* itself,

---

[61] For details, see the official website at thedaytheearthsmiled.com/.
[62] diamondskyproductions.com/recent/index.php#mmw.
[63] *Ver. hist.* 1.26: ἂν μὲν οὖν εἰς τὸ φρέαρ καταβῇ τις, ἀκούει πάντων τῶν παρ' ἡμῖν ἐν τῇ γῇ λεγομένων, ἐὰν δὲ εἰς τὸ κάτοπτρον ἀποβλέψῃ, πάσας μὲν πόλεις, πάντα δὲ ἔθνη ὁρᾷ ὥσπερ ἐφεστὼς ἑκάστοις· τότε καὶ τοὺς οἰκείους ἐγὼ ἐθεασάμην καὶ πᾶσαν τὴν πατρίδα (Now if someone goes down into the well, he hears everything that is being said by our people on the earth, and if someone looks into the mirror, he sees all the cities and all the peoples, just as if he were standing over them. On that occasion I watched my family and my entire homeland).

Fig. 5 *The Day the Earth Smiled*, taken by NASA's *Cassini* spacecraft on July 19, 2013. Saturn and its rings are in the foreground, and below these in the same frame we can see Earth with its Moon, 1.44 billion km in the distance. Close-up, the Moon appears as a faint protrusion to the right of the Earth. For the colour version, please refer to the plate section. (Image credit: NASA/JPL–Caltech/Space Science Institute)

there is far less detail about the Earth here than in *Icaromenippus*; instead, the technological apparatus – the mirror and the well – is the prominent feature (and notably absent from *Icaromenippus*). This device enhances both the observational realism and the patina of exactitude with which Lucian invests his fantasy, in a manner that is characteristic of, and thematically central to, this narrative of "plausible lies."[64] A unique consequence of this is that Lucian awakens in our imagination the possibility of a remote viewing technology that is constantly there on the Moon, watching us. In all other ancient Earth-views we see through the eyes of a temporary viewer-in-the-text: fleetingly, through the smith-god Hephaestus' mind's eye in the *Iliad*, as he works in his forge on the shield; furtively, through the eyes of Socrates' explorer, peeping out over the rim of our crater-world in *Phaedo*; in passing, through Scipio's dream in Cicero, or the magically enhanced eye of Menippus, who is only a temporary visitor to the heavens in Lucian's *Icaromenippus*. In each case, as soon as our textual accomplice moves on to some other business, our view of the Earth vanishes with him. But *True Stories* generates a rather different sort of scenario. Here, Lucian installs a permanent viewing apparatus on the Moon, with specific directions about where to find it (the palace of King Endymion), should we ever go there. Even after Lucian, our viewer-in-the-text, leaves the Moon, that remote telescope remains after him – and who knows what other lunar spies are looking down on us, right now? Furthermore, Lucian also invites us on Earth to imagine the possibility of seeing *the other way*, for he explicitly wonders, as he looks into the mirror, if those on whom he is spying can see him too. Not only does *True Stories* create for the first time, therefore, an uncannily prescient sense of a satellite, it also generates an imaginary optical drama across outer space, which unites viewers on the Earth with viewers on the Moon. In this sense, Lucian's fiction preempts the scenario underlying *The Day the Earth Smiled*, which "marked the first time that inhabitants of Earth knew in advance that their planet was being imaged."[65]

13.4 Conclusion

Famously, when the crew of *Apollo 8* first saw the Earth rising over the lunar horizon on Christmas Eve 1968, they quoted a passage from the King James edition of the book of Genesis: "In the beginning God created the heaven and the earth."[66] A version of this had been done before. When man first gazed at the Earth from the Moon in ancient literature, Lucian evoked a creation story too: the story of the smith-god hammering away

---

[64] My thanks to Emily Greenwood, who suggested this connection between technology and precision to me, when I presented a version of this chapter at the conference "Home and Away: the Epic Journey" (Yale, April 2014).
[65] photojournal.jpl.nasa.gov/catalog/PIA17171.
[66] On the preparation for this reading, and its controversial aftermath, see Poole 2008: 128–40.

in his forge, carving an image of the cosmos. Millennia and cultures apart, both *Icaromenippus* and Apollo 8 represent profoundly important moments in our shared human experience of our home, and marked it in similar ways.

It may have taken two thousand years before Lucian's fictions of extraterrestrial travel would become historical fact, but the vision of Earth had its roots very far back in the Greek literary imagination. In their piecemeal fashion, these visionaries foresaw the beauty and iridescence of our globe, and the crisis of expression that astronauts would feel when confronted with everything they know. They predicted that the world would look much smaller from space, and the ways that this would affect our perceptions of our ordinary preoccupations. They even anticipated the irrevocable cognitive transformation that would come about as a result of leaving our planetary home and looking back, even if the nature of the conversion was not at all the optimistic experience Socrates had envisaged. Nothing would quite prepare us for the shock of seeing our home as a globe suspended in space or as a tiny scintilla of light adrift in the great void. Nevertheless, the continuum of cognitive experience, both real and imagined, is extraordinary, converting the most audacious voyages away from home into *nostoi* to ancient thought.

References

Alcock, S. E. (1993) *Graecia Capta: The Landscapes of Roman Greece*. Cambridge.
Alcock, S. E., Cherry, J. F., and Elsner, J. (eds.) (2001) *Pausanias: Travel and Memory in Roman Greece*. Oxford.
Alden, M. J. (2000) *Homer beside Himself: Para-Narratives in the Iliad*. Oxford.
  (2017) *Para-Narratives in the Odyssey: Stories in the Frame*. Oxford.
Aldersley-Williams, H. (2016) *The Tide: The Science and Stories behind the Greatest Force on Earth*. New York.
Alexiou, M. (1974) *The Ritual Lament in Greek Tradition*. Cambridge.
  (2002) *The Ritual Lament in Greek Tradition*, 2nd ed. revised by D. Yatromanolakis and P. Roilos. Lanham, Boulder, New York, and Oxford.
Allan, W. (2008) "Performing the Will of Zeus: The Διὸς βουλή and the Scope of Early Greek Epic," in M. Revermann and P. Wilson (eds.), *Performance, Iconography, Reception: Studies in Honour of Oliver Taplin*. Oxford: 204–16.
Anderson, G. (1978) "Lucian's *Nigrinus*: The Problem of Form," *Greek, Roman and Byzantine Studies* 19: 367–74.
  (2000) "Some Uses of Storytelling in Dio," in S. Swain (ed.), *Dio Chrysostom: Politics, Letters, and Philosophy*. Oxford: 143–60.
  (2005) *The Second Sophistic: A Cultural Phenomenon in the Roman Empire*. London.
Arendt, H. (1968) "The Conquest of Space and the Stature of Man," in *Between Past and Future: Eight Exercises in Political Thought*. New York: 265–80.
  (1998) *The Human Condition*. Second edition. Chicago.
Astin, A. E. (1967) *Scipio Aemilianus*. Oxford.
Austin, R. G. (1964) *P. Vergili Maronis Aeneidos Liber Secvndvs*. Oxford.
  (1971) *P. Vergili Maronis Aeneidos Liber Primus*. Oxford.
Bachelard, G. (1964) *The Poetics of Space*. (tr.) M. Jolas. Boston.
Bakker, E. J. (2013) *The Meaning of Meat and the Structure of the* Odyssey. Cambridge.
Bär, S. F. (2013) "Odysseus' Letter to Calypso in Lucian's *Verae Historiae*," in O. Hodkinson, P. Rosenmeyer, and E. Bracke (eds.), *Epistolary Narratives in Ancient Greek Literature*. Leiden: 221–36.
Baragwanath, E. (2002) "Xenophon's Foreign Wives," *Prudentia* 33.2: 125–58.
  (2008) *Motivation and Narrative in Herodotus*. Oxford.
Barchiesi, A. (1978) "Il lamento di Giuturna," *Materiali e Discussioni* 1: 99–121.

(1997) *The Poet and the Prince: Ovid and Augustan Discourse*. Berkeley.
(2001) *Speaking Volumes: Narrative and Intertext in Ovid and Other Latin Poets*. London.
Barchiesi, M. (1962) *Nevio Epico: Storia, Interpretazione, Edizione critica dei frammenti del primo epos latino*. Padua.
Baron, C. A. (2013) *Timaeus of Tauromenium and Hellenistic Historiography*. Cambridge.
Baronowski, D. W. (2011) *Polybius and Roman Imperialism*. Bristol.
Barton, T. (1994) *Ancient Astrology*. London.
Bartsch, S. (1998) "*Ars* and the Man: The Politics of Art in Virgil's *Aeneid*," *Classical Philology* 93: 322–42.
Battistin Sebastiani, B. (2015) "Scipio Aemilianus and Odysseus as Paradigms of *pronoia*," in A. Nascimento Pena, M. de Jesus, C. Relvas, R. C. Fonseca, and T. Casal (eds.), *Revisitar o Mito: Myths Revisited*. Vila Nova de Famalicão: 483–94.
Batty, R. (2007) *Rome and the Nomads: The Pontic–Danubian Realm in Antiquity*. Oxford.
Beissinger, M., Tylus, J. and Wofford, S. (eds.) (1999) *Epic Traditions in the Contemporary World*. Berkeley.
Benton, C. (2003) "Bringing the Other to Center Stage: Seneca's *Medea* and the Anxieties of Imperialism," *Arethusa* 36: 271–84.
Bernstein, N. W. (2013) *Ethics, Identity and Community in Later Roman Declamation*. New York.
Bessone, F. (2015) "Love and War: Feminine Models, Epic Roles, and Gender Identity in Statius's *Thebaid*," in J. Fabre-Serris and A. Keith (eds.), *Women and War in Antiquity*. Baltimore: 119–37.
Bickerman, E. J. (1952) "*Origines Gentium*," *Classical Philology* 47: 65–81.
Bierl, A. (2008) "Die Abenteuer des Odysseus," in J. Latacz, T. Greub, P. Blome, and A. Wieczorek (eds.), *Homer: Der Mythos von Troia in Dichtung und Kunst*. Munich: 171–9.
Biggs, T. (2014) "A Roman *Odyssey*: Cultural Responses to the First Punic War from Andronicus to Augustus," Ph.D. dissertation, Yale University.
(2017) "*Primus Romanorum*: Origin Stories, Fictions of Primacy, and the First Punic War," *Classical Philology* 112.3: 350–67.
Billerbeck, M. (1986) "Aspects of Stoicism in Flavian Epic," in F. Cairns (ed.), *Papers of the Liverpool Latin Seminar: Fifth Volume 1985*: Liverpool: 341–56.
Bonifazi, A. (2009) "Inquiring into *Nostos* and its Cognates," *American Journal of Philology* 130: 481–510.
Borges, J. L. (1970[1945]) "The Aleph," in *The Aleph and Other Stories, 1933–1969*. Ed. and trans. N. T. di Giovanni. New York: Dutton, 15–30.
Bowersock, G. (1969) *Greek Sophists in the Roman Empire*. Oxford.
Bowie, E. (1974) "The Greeks and their Past in the Second Sophistic," in M. I. Finley (ed.), *Studies in Ancient Society*. London: 166–209.
(2000) "The Reception of Apollonius in Imperial Greek Literature," in M. A. Harder et al. (eds.), *Apollonius Rhodius*. Leuven: 1–10.

Bradley, P. J. (2010) "Irony and the Narrator in Xenophon's *Anabasis*," in V. J. Gray (ed.), *Xenophon*. Oxford: 520–52; first published in E. I. Tylawsky and C. G. Weiss (eds.), *Essays in Honor of Gordon Williams*. New Haven, 2001: 59–84.

Brennan, S. (2012) "Mind the Gap: a 'Snow Lacuna' in Xenophon's *Anabasis*," in F. Hobden and C. Tuplin (eds.), *Xenophon: Ethical Principles and Historical Enquiry*. Mnemosyne Supplements 348. Leiden: 307–39.

Briggs W. W. Jr. (1980) *Narrative and Simile from the* Georgics *in the* Aeneid. Leiden.

Brooks, P. (1984) *Reading for the Plot: Design and Intention in Narrative*. New York.

Brown, P. (2012) *Through the Eye of a Needle: Wealth, the Fall of Rome, and the Making of Christianity in the West*. Princeton.

Brownson, C. (1992) *Xenophon:* Anabasis. Cambridge, MA; rev. J. Dillery (1998).

Büchner, K. (1984) *M. Tullius Cicero* De Re Publica: *Kommentar*. Heidelberg.

Buckley, E. (2014) "Valerius Flaccus and Seneca's Tragedies," in M. Heerink and G. Manuwald (eds.), *Brill's Companion to Valerius Flaccus*. Leiden and Boston: 307–25.

Budin, S. L. (2008) *The Myth of Sacred Prostitution in Antiquity*. Cambridge.

Burgess, J. (2001) *The Tradition of the Trojan War in Homer and the Epic Cycle*. Baltimore.

(2011) "Intertextuality without Text in Early Greek Epic," in Ø. Andersen and D. T. T. Haug (eds.), *Relative Chronology in Early Greek Epic*. Cambridge: 168–83.

(2012) "Belatedness in the Travels of Odysseus," in F. Montanari, A. Rengakos, and C. Tsagalis (eds.), *Homeric Contexts: Neoanalysis and the Interpretation of Oral Poetry*. Berlin: 269–90.

Burkert, W. (1985) *Greek Religion*, trans. J. Raffan. Cambridge, MA.

Burnett, A. M., and Oldman, D. (2015) "Roman Coins and the New World of Museums and Digital Images," in K. M. Coleman (ed.), *Images for Classicists*. Cambridge, MA: 91–115.

Cameron, A. (1967) "Rutilius Namatianus, St. Augustine, and the Date of the *De Reditu*," *Journal of Roman Studies* 57: 31–9.

(2010) *The Last Pagans of Rome*. Oxford.

Camerotto, A. (2014) *Gli Occhi e la Lingua della Satira: Studi sull' Eroe Satirico in Luciano di Samosata*. Milan and Udine.

Casali, S. (1999) "Facta Impia (Virgil, *Aeneid* 4.596–9)," *Classical Quarterly* 49.1: 203–11.

Casson, L. (1959) *The Ancient Mariners: Seafarers and Sea Fighters of the Mediterranean in Ancient Times*. Princeton.

(1974) *Travel in the Ancient World*. London.

Castelletti, C. (2014) "A Hero with a Sandal and a Buskin: The Figure of Jason in Valerius Flaccus' Argonautica," in M. Heerink and G. Manuwald (eds.), *Brill's Companion to Valerius Flaccus*. Leiden and Boston: 173–91.

Castorina, E. (ed.) (1967) *Claudius Rutilius Namatianus:* De Reditu. Florence.

Ceccarelli, P. (1996) "L'Athènes de Périclès: un 'pays de cocagne'? L'idéologie démocratique et l'αὐτόματος βίος dans la comédie ancienne," *Quaderni Urbinati di Cultura Classica* 54: 109–59.

Chantraine, P. (1953) *Grammaire Homérique*, vol. II: *Syntaxe*. Paris.
  (1999) *Dictionnaire étymologique de la langue grecque: histoire des mots*. Paris.
Clare, R. J. (2002) *The Path of the Argo: Language, Imagery and Narrative in the Argonautica of Apollonius Rhodius*. Cambridge.
Clarke, J. (2014) "The Struggle for Control of the Landscape in Book 1 of Rutilius Namatianus," *Arethusa* 47.1: 89–107.
Clarke, K. (1999) *Between Geography and History: Hellenistic Constructions of the Roman World*. Oxford.
Clauss, J. J. (1993) *The Best of the Argonauts*. Berkeley.
  (1997) "Conquest of the Mephistophelian Nausicaa: Medea's Role in Apollonius' Redefinition of the Epic Hero," in J. J. Clauss and S. I. Johnston (eds.), *Medea: Essays on Medea in Myth, Literature, Philosophy, and Art*. Princeton: 149–77.
  (2010) "From the Head of Zeus: The Beginnings of Roman Literature," in J. J. Clauss and M. Cuypers (eds.), *A Companion to Hellenistic Literature*. Chichester: 463–78.
  (2012) "The Argonautic Anabasis: Myth and Hellenic Identity in Apollonius' *Argonautica*," in C. Christophe Cusset, N. Le Meur-Weissman, and F. Levin (eds.), *Mythe et pouvoir à l'époque hellénistique*. Lyon: 417–37.
Clay, J. S. (1985) "Aeolia, or under the Sign of the Circle," *Classical Journal* 80: 289–91.
  (1999) "The Whip and Will of Zeus," *Literary Imagination* 1: 40–60.
Colini, A. M. (1979) "La torre di Mecenate," *Rendiconti dell'Accademia dei Lincei* 35: 239–50.
Collins, M. (1974) *Carrying the Fire: An Astronaut's Journey*. New York.
Cook, E. F. (1995) *The* Odyssey *in Athens: Myths of Cultural Origins*. Ithaca.
  (1999) "'Active' and 'Passive' Heroics in the *Odyssey*," *The Classical World* 93: 149–67.
Corbeill, A. (2004) *Nature Embodied: Gesture in Ancient Rome*. Princeton.
Courcelle, P. (1948) *Histoire litteraire des Grandes Invasions Germaniques*. Paris.
Cowan, R. (2014) "My Family and Other Enemies: Argonautic Antagonists and Valerian Villains," in M. Heerink and G. Manuwald (eds.), *Brill's Companion to Valerius Flaccus*. Leiden and Boston: 229–48.
Curta, F. (1995) "Atticism, Homer, Neoplatonism, and Fürstenspiegel: Julian's Second Panegyric on Constantius," *Greek, Roman, and Byzantine Studies* 36: 177–211.
Cyrino, M. S. (2010) *Aphrodite: Gods and Heroes of the Ancient World*. London and New York.
Dalby, A. (1992) "Greeks Abroad: Social Organisation and Food among the Ten Thousand," *Journal of Hellenic Studies* 112: 16–30.
Danek, G. (1998) *Epos und Zitat: Studien zu den Quellen der* Odyssee. Vienna.
de Certeau, M. (1984) *The Practice of Everyday Life*. (tr.) S. Rendall. Los Angeles.
de Jáuregui, M. H. (2011) "Priam's Catabasis: Traces of the Epic Journey to Hades in *Iliad* 24," *Transactions of the American Philological Association* 141: 37–68.
de Jong, I. J. F. (2001) *A Narratological Commentary on the* Odyssey. Cambridge.

de Jong, I. J. F. (ed.) (2012) *Space in Ancient Greek Literature: Studies in Ancient Greek Narrative*. Leiden.
De Lauretis, T. (1984) *Alice Doesn't*. Bloomington.
Deleuze, G. and Guattari, F. (1987) *A Thousand Plateaus: Capitalism and Schizophrenia*, (tr.) B. Massumi. Minneapolis.
De Melo, W. (2012) "The Little Carthaginian," in *Plautus, vol. IV*. Loeb Classical Library.
Derderian, K. (2001) *Leaving Words to Remember: Greek Mourning and the Advent of Literacy*. Leiden and Boston.
Desmond, M. (1994) *Reading Dido: Gender, Textuality, and the Medieval Aeneid*. Minneapolis.
de Temmerman, K. (2012) "Achilles Tatius," in I. J. F. de Jong (ed.), *Space in Ancient Literature*. Leiden: 517–35.
  (2014) *Crafting Characters: Heroes and Heroines in the Ancient Greek Novel*. Oxford.
de Temmerman, K., and Demoen, K. (2011) "Less than Ideal Paradigms in the Greek Novel," in K. Doulamis (ed.), *Echoing Narratives: Studies of Intertextuality in Greek and Roman Prose Fiction*. Groningen: 1–20.
Dillery, J. (1995) *Xenophon and the History of his Times*. London and New York.
Doblhofer, E. (1977) *De reditu suo; sive, Iter Gallicum: Kommentar*. Heidelberg.
Dougherty, C. (1993) *The Poetics of Colonization: From City to Text*. Oxford.
  (2001) *The Raft of Odysseus: The Ethnographic Imagination of Homer's Odyssey*. Oxford.
Dougherty, C., and Kurke, L. (eds.) (2003) *The Cultures within Ancient Greek Culture: Contact, Conflict, Collaboration*. Cambridge.
Dowden, K. (1996) "Heliodoros: Serious Intentions," *The Classical Quarterly* 46: 267–85.
Dubuisson, M. (1987) "Homèrologie et politique: le cas d'Aristodémos de Nysa," in J. Servais et al. (eds.), *Stemmata: Mélanges de philologie, d'histoire et d'archéologie grecques offerts à Jules Labarbe*. Liège: 15–24.
Dué, C. (2002) *Homeric Variations on a Lament by Briseis*. Lanham, MD.
  (2006) *The Captive Woman's Lament in Greek Tragedy*. Austin, TX.
Dueck, D. (2000) *Strabo of Amaseia: A Greek Man of Letters in Augustan Rome*. London and New York.
Dufallo, B. (2013) *The Captor's Image: Greek Culture in Roman Ecphrasis*. New York.
Duff, J. W. and Duff, A. M. (eds.) (1934) *Minor Latin Poets, Volume 2*. Cambridge, MA.
DuFourcq, A. (1905) "Rutilius Namatianus contre saint Augustin," *Revue d'histoire et de littérature religieuses* 10: 488–92.
Dunsch, B. (2015) "'Why Do we Violate Strange Seas and Sacred Waters?' The Sea as Bridge and Boundary in Greek and Roman Poetry," in M. Grzechnik and H. Hurskainen (eds.), *Beyond the Sea: Reviewing the Manifold Dimensions of Water as Barrier and Bridge*. Cologne: 17–42.
Dutsch, D. M. (2008) *Feminine Discourse in Roman Comedy: On Echoes and Voices*. Oxford.

Dyson, J. T. (2001) *King of the Wood: The Sacrificial Victor in Virgil's* Aeneid. Norman, OK.
Easterling, P. E. (1991) "Men's *kleos* and Women's *goos*: Female Voices in the *Iliad*," *Journal of Modern Greek Studies* 9: 145–51.
Eco, U. (2009) *The Infinity of Lists*, trans. A. McEwen. New York.
Edwards, C. (1993) *The Politics of Immorality in Ancient Rome*. Cambridge.
  (1996) *Writing Rome: Textual Approaches to the City*. Cambridge.
Eisenberger, H. (1973) *Studien zur* Odyssee. Wiesbaden.
Elliott, J. (2014) "Space and Geography in Ennius' *Annales*," in M. Skempis and I. Ziogas (eds.), *Geography, Topography, Landscape: Configurations of Space in Greek and Roman Epic*, Trends in Classics Supplementary vol. 22. Berlin and Boston: 223–64.
Elm, S. (2012) *Sons of Hellenism, Fathers of the Church: Emperor Julian, Gregory of Nazianzus, and the Vision of Rome*. Berkeley.
Elmer, D. (2008) "Heliodoros' 'Sources': Intertextuality, Paternity, and the Nile River in the *Aithiopika*," *Transactions of the American Philological Association* 138: 411–50.
  (2013) *The Poetics of Consent: Collective Decision Making and the* Iliad. Baltimore.
Elsner, J. (1992) "Pausanias: A Greek Pilgrim in the Roman World," *Past & Present* 135: 3–29.
Erskine, A. (2001) *Troy between Greece and Rome: Local Tradition and Imperial Power*. Oxford.
  (2012) "Polybius among the Romans: Life in the Cyclops' Cave," in C. Smith and L. M. Yarrow (eds.), *Imperialism, Cultural Politics, and Polybius*. Oxford: 17–32.
Fagles, R. (1996) *The Odyssey*. Introduction and notes by B. Knox. New York.
Fantham, E. (2004) "Maidens in Other-land or Broads Abroad: Plautus' *Poenulus*," in T. Baier (ed.), *Studien zu Plautus' Poenulus*. Tübingen: 235–51.
  (2010) *Roman Readings: Roman Response to Greek Literature from Plautus to Statius and Quintilian*. Berlin.
Fantham, R. E. (1999) "The Role of Lament in the Growth and Eclipse of Roman Epic," in M. Beissinger, J. Tylus, and S. Wofford (eds.), *Epic Traditions in the Contemporary World*. Berkeley and Los Angeles: 221–35.
Fantuzzi, M. (1988) *Ricerche su Apollonio Rodio*. Rome.
Feeney, D. (1986) "Following after Hercules in Virgil and Apollonius," *Proceedings of the Virgil Society* 18: 47–85.
  (1991) *The Gods in Epic: Poets and Critics of the Classical Tradition*. Oxford.
  (2014) "First Similes in Epic," *Transactions of the American Philological Association* 144: 189–228.
  (2016) *Beyond Greek: The Beginnings of Latin Literature*. Cambridge, MA.
Fehr, B. (1990) "Entertainers at the Symposion: The *Akletoi* in the Archaic Period," in O. Murray (ed.), *Sympotica: A Symposium on the Symposion*. Oxford: 185–95.
Ferenczi, A. (2014) "Philosophical Ideas in Valerius Flaccus' Argonautica," in M. Heerink and G. Manuwald (eds.), *Brill's Companion to Valerius Flaccus*. Leiden and Boston: 136–53.

Ferrari, M. (1973) *Frammenti Ignoti di Rutilio Namaziano: La Tradizione Manoscritta di Rutilio Namaziamo*. Padua.
Feuillâtre, E. (1966) *Études sur les* Éthiopiques *d'Héliodore*. Paris.
Finkelberg, M. (1995) "Odysseus and the Genus 'Hero'," *Greece & Rome* 42.1: 1–14.
Flower, M. (2012) *Xenophon's* Anabasis, *or The* Expedition of Cyrus. New York.
Fo, A. (1989) "Ritorno a Claudio Rutilio Namaziano," *Materiali e Discussioni* 22: 49–74.
Fo, A. (ed.) (1992) *Claudius Rutilius Namatianus:* Il Ritorno. Turin.
Foley, H. P. (1995) "Penelope as Moral Agent," in B. Cohen (ed.), *The Distaff Side*. New York: 93–115.
  (2001) *Female Acts*. Princeton.
Ford, A. (1999) "Odysseus after Dinner: *Od*. 9.2–11 and the Traditions of Sympotic Song," in N. Kazazis and A. Rengakos (eds.), *Euphrosyne: Studies in Ancient Epic and its Legacy in Honor of Dimitris N. Maronitis*. Stuttgart: 109–23.
Fornara, C. W. (1971) *Herodotus: An Interpretative Essay*. Oxford.
Foster, J. (1973–4) "Some Devices of Drama used in *Aeneid* 1–4," *Proceedings of the Virgil Society* 13: 28–41.
Foucault, M. (1986) "Of Other Spaces: Utopias and Heterotopias," trans. J. Miskowiec, *Diacritics* 16.1: 22–7.
Fowler, D. (2007) "Laocoon's Point of View: Walking the Roman Way," in S. J. Heyworth, P. G. Fowler, and S. J. Harrison (eds.), *Classical Constructions: Papers in Memory of Don Fowler, Classicist and Epicurean*. Oxford: 1–17.
Fowler, R. C. and Quiroga Puertas, A. J. (2014) "A Prolegomena to the Third Sophistic," in R. C. Fowler (ed.), *Plato in the Third Sophistic*. Berlin: 1–30.
Franceschelli, C. and Dall'Aglio, P. (2014) "Entre voies de terre et voies d'eau: l'évolution du voyage en Italie Padane, entre l'itinerarium Burdigalense et le témoignage de Sidoine Apollinaire," *Belgeo* 2: 2–14.
Franko, G. F. (1996) "The Characterization of Hanno in Plautus' *Poenulus*," *American Journal of Philology* 117.3: 425–52.
Frazer, J. G. (1921) *Apollodorus:* The Library. Cambridge, MA and London.
Fusillo, M. (1989) *Il Romanzo Greco: Polifonia ed Eros*. Venice.
Gaca, K. L. (2008) "The Little Girl and her Mother: *Iliad* 16.7–11 and Ancient Greek Warfare," *American Journal of Philology* 129: 145–71.
  (2010) "The Andrapodizing of War Captives in Greek Historical Memory," *Transactions of the American Philological Association* 140: 117–61.
  (2010–11) "Telling the Girls from the Boys and Children: Interpreting παῖδες in the Sexual Violence of Populace-Ravaging Ancient Warfare," *Illinois Classical Studies* 35–6: 85–109.
  (2011) "Girls, Women, and the Significance of Sexual Violence in Ancient Warfare," in E. Heineman (ed.), *Sexual Violence in Conflict Zones*. Philadelphia: 73–88.
  (2011–12) "Manhandled and Kicked Around: Reinterpreting the Etymology and Significance of *Andrapoda*," *Indogermanische Forschungen* 116: 110–46.

(2014) "Martial Rape, Pulsating Fear, and the Sexual Maltreatment of Girls (*paides*), Virgins (*parthenoi*), and Women (*gynaikes*) in Antiquity," *American Journal of Philology* 135: 303–57.
(forthcoming) *Sexual Warfare against Girls and Women: Ancient History, Modern Witness, Overpowering Injustice*. Oxford.
Gale, M. (ed.) (2004) *Latin Epic and Didactic Poetry: Genre, Tradition and Individuality*. Swansea.
Galinsky, K. (1969a) *Aeneas, Sicily, and Rome*. Princeton.
  (1969b) "Plautus' *Poenulus* and the Cult of Venus Erycina," in J. Bibauw (ed.), *Hommages à Marcel Renard*, vol. I. Brussels: 358–64.
  (1996) *Augustan Culture: An Interpretive Introduction*. Princeton.
Ganiban, R. (2014) "Virgilian Prophecy and the Reign of Jupiter in Valerius Flaccus' *Argonautica*," in M. Heerink and G. Manuwald (eds.), *Brill's Companion to Valerius Flaccus*. Leiden and Boston: 249–68.
Gardner, H. H. and Murnaghan, S. (eds.) (2014) *Odyssean Identities in Modern Cultures: The Journey Home*. Columbus, OH.
Garrison, J. D. (1992) *Pietas from Vergil to Dryden*. University Park, PA.
Garvie, A. F. (1994) *Homer: Odyssey. Books VI–VII*. Cambridge.
  (2014) "Sunshine over the Strymon," in E. Vintró, F. Mestre, and P. Gómez (eds.), *Som per mirar*, vol. I. Barcelona: 111–40.
Gautier, L. (1911) *La Langue de Xénophon*. Geneva.
Gera, D. L. (1997) *Warrior Women: The Anonymous* Tractatus de Mulieribus. Leiden.
Germain, G. (1954) *Genèse de l'Odyssée: le fantastique et le sacré*. Paris.
Geus, K. (2001) *Eratosthenes von Kyrene: Studien zur hellenistischen Kultur- und Wissenschaftgeschichte*. Munich.
Giancarlo, B. (2010) "Gli Epigrammi di Germanico," *Rivista di Cultura Classica e Medioevale* 52.1: 81–106.
Gildenhard, I. (2012) *Virgil, Aeneid 4.1–299*. Cambridge.
Gildenhard, I. and Zissos, A. (eds.) (2013) *Transformative Change in Western Thought: A History of Metamorphosis from Homer to Hollywood*. Oxford.
Gilhuly, K. and Worman, N. (eds.) (2014) *Space, Place, and Landscape in Ancient Greek Literature and Culture*. Cambridge.
Gissel, J. (2001) "Germanicus as an Alexander Figure," *Classica & Mediaevalia* 52: 277–301.
Gleason, M. W. (1994) *Making Men: Sophists and Self-Presentation in Ancient Rome*. Princeton.
Glenn, J. (1971) "The Polyphemus Folktale and Homer's *Kyklôpeia*," *Transactions of the American Philological Association* 102: 133–81.
Goldberg, S. M. (1995) *Epic in Republican Rome*. New York.
  (2005) *Constructing Literature in the Roman Republic: Poetry and its Reception*. Cambridge.
Goldhill, S. (2001) "The Erotic Eye: Visual Stimulation and Cultural Conflict," in S. Goldhill (ed.), *Being Greek under Rome: Cultural Identity, the Second Sophistic and the Development of Empire*. Cambridge: 154–94.

Goldschmidt, N. (2013) *Shaggy Crowns: Ennius' Annales and Virgil's Aeneid*. Oxford.
Gómez Alcalde-Diosdado, A. (2010) *El Hombre en la Luna en la Literatura*. Granada.
Goodyear, F. R. D. (1981) *The Annals of Tacitus, Books 1–6: Vol. II, Annals 1.55–81 and Annals 2*. Cambridge.
Gowers, E. (1994) "Horace, Satires 1.5: An Inconsequential Journey," *Proceedings of the Cambridge Philological Society* 39: 48–66.
  (2010) "Augustus and 'Syracuse'," *Journal of Roman Studies* 100: 69–87.
  (2012) *Horace: Satires Book I*. Cambridge.
Graham, J. (1964) *Colony and Mother City in Ancient Greece*. Manchester.
Granger, H. (2007) "Poetry and Prose: Xenophanes of Colophon," *Transactions of the American Philological Association* 137: 403–33.
Gratwick, A. S. (1971) "Hanno's Punic Speech in the *Poenulus* of Plautus," *Hermes* 90: 25–45.
Graverini, L. (2010) "'Amore, 'dolcezza', stupore: Romanzo antico e filosofia," in R. Uglione (ed.), *Lector intende: laetaberis: il Romanzo dei Greci e dei Romani*, Atti del Convegno Nazionale, Turin, April 27–28. Alessandria: 57–88.
Greenblatt, S. (ed.) (2010) *Cultural Mobility: A Manifesto*. Cambridge.
Grethlein, J. (2013) *Experience and Teleology in Ancient Historiography: Futures Past from Herodotus to Augustine*. Cambridge.
Gruen, E. (2014) "Roman Comedy and the Social Scene," in M. Fontaine and A. C. Scafuro (eds.), *The Oxford Handbook of Greek and Roman Comedy*. Oxford: 601–14.
Hackman, O. (1904) *Die Polyphemsage in der Volksüberlieferung*. Helsingfors.
Hadot, P. (1995) *Philosophy as a Way of Life: Spiritual Exercises from Socrates to Foucault*, trans. M. Chase and ed. A. I. Davidson. Oxford and New York.
Haegemans, K. (2000) "Elissa, the First Queen of Carthage, through Timaeus' Eyes," *Ancient Society* 30: 277–91.
Halfmann, H. (1986) *Itinera principum: Geschichte und Typologie der Kaiserreisen im römischen Reich*. Wiesbaden.
Hamilton, H. C. and Falconer, W. (trans.) (1854–7) *The Geography of Strabo*. London.
Harder, M. A. (1994) "Travel Descriptions in the *Argonautica* of Apollonius Rhodius," in Z. von Martels (ed.), *Travel Fact and Travel Fiction: Studies on Fiction, Literary Tradition, Scholarly Discovery and Observation in Travel Writing*. Leiden: 16–29.
Hardie, P. (1985) "*Imago mundi*: Cosmological and Ideological Aspects of the Shield of Achilles," *Journal of Hellenic Studies* 105: 11–31.
  (1986) *Virgil's Aeneid: Cosmos and Imperium*. Oxford.
  (1993) *The Epic Successors of Virgil: A Study in the Dynamics of a Tradition*. Cambridge.
  (2012) *Rumour and Renown: Representations of Fama in Western Literature*. Cambridge.
Harrison, E. L. (1972–3) "Why did Venus Wear Boots? Some Reflections on *Aeneid* 1.314f.," *Proceedings of the Virgil Society* 12: 10–21.

(1989) "The Tragedy of Dido," *Echos du monde Classique/Classical Views* 33: 1–21.
Hartog, F. (2001) *Memories of Odysseus: Frontier Tales from Ancient Greece*, trans. J. Lloyd. Chicago.
Heather, P. (2005) *Fall of the Roman Empire: A New History of Rome and the Barbarians*. Oxford.
Heerink, M. (2015) *Echoing Hylas: A Study in Hellenistic and Roman Metapoetics*. Madison and London.
Heirman, J. G. M. and Klooster, J. (eds.) (2013) *The Ideologies of Lived Space in Literary Texts, Ancient and Modern*. Ghent.
Helm, R. (1906) *Lucian und Menipp*. Leipzig.
Henderson, J. (1999) "Hanno's Punic Heirs: Der Poenulus-neid Des Plautus," in J. Henderson (ed.), *Writing Down Rome: Satire, Comedy, and other Offences in Latin Poetry*. Oxford: 3–37.
Heubeck, A., West, S., Hainsworth, J. B., Hoekstra, A., Russo, J., and Fernández-Galiano, M. (1988–92) *A Commentary on Homer's* Odyssey. 3 vols. Oxford.
Hexter, R. (1992) "Sidonian Dido," in R. Hexter and D. Selden (eds.), *Innovations of Antiquity: The New Ancient World*. New York and Abingdon: 332–90.
  (1999) "Imitating Troy: A Reading of *Aeneid* 3," in C. G. Perkell (ed.), *Reading Vergil's* Aeneid*: An Interpretive Guide*. Norman, OK: 64–79.
Hinds, S. (2000) "Essential Epic: Genre and Gender from Macer to Statius," in M. Depew and D. Obbink (eds.), *Matrices of Genre: Authors, Canons, and Society*. Cambridge, MA: 221–44.
Hobden, F. (2013) *The Symposium in Ancient Greek Society and Thought*. Cambridge.
Hollis, A. (2007) *Fragments of Roman Poetry c. 60 BC–AD 20*. Oxford.
Holmes, B. (2008) "Aristides' Illegible Body," in W. V. Harris and B. Holmes (eds.), *Aelius Aristides between Greece, Rome, and the Gods*. Leiden: 81–114.
Holst-Warhaft, G. (1992) *Dangerous Voices: Women's Laments and Greek Literature*. London.
  (2000) *The Cue for Passion: Grief and its Political Uses*. Cambridge and London.
Hopman, M. (2012) "Narrative and Rhetoric in Odysseus' Tales to the Phaeacians," *American Journal of Philology* 133: 1–30.
Hornblower, J. (1981) *Hieronymus of Cardia*. Oxford.
Horsfall, N. M. (1973–4) "Dido in the Light of History," *Papers of the Virgilian Society* 13: 1–13 (= Horsfall 1990).
  (1976) "Virgil, History, and the Roman Tradition," *Prudentia* 8: 73–89.
  (1989) "Aeneas the Colonist," *Vergilius* 35: 8–27.
  (1990) "Dido in the Light of History," in S. Harrison (ed.), *Oxford Readings in Virgil's Aeneid*. Oxford: 127–44.
  (2000) *Virgil,* Aeneid *7: A Commentary*. Leiden.
Hunter, R. L. (1989) *Apollonius of Rhodes.* 'Argonautica *Book III'*. Cambridge.
  (2005) "'Philip the Philosopher' on the *Aithiopika* of Heliodorus," in S. Harrison et al. (eds.), *Metaphor and the Ancient Novel, Ancient Narrative*, suppl. 4. Groningen: 123–38.

Hurst, A. (2012) "Préfigurations de Médée," *Gaia* 15: 81–96.
Jackson, S. (1997) "Argo: The first Ship?" *Rheinisches Museum für Philologie* 140: 249–57.
Jacobson, J. (2009) "A Developed Nature: A Phenomenological Account of the Experience of Home," *Continental Philosophy Review*. 42: 355–73.
Jacobson, K. (2010) "The Experience of Home and the Space of Citizenship," *The Southern Journal of Philosophy* 48.3: 219–45.
  (2012) "Philosophical Perspectives on Home," in S. J. Smith, M. Elsinga, L. Fox O'Mahony, O. Seow Eng, S. Wachter, and R. Dowling (eds.), *International Encyclopedia of Housing and Home*, Vol V. Oxford: 178–82.
Jaeger, M. (1997) *Livy's Written Rome*. Ann Arbor.
Jahn, S. (2007) *Der Troia-Mythos: Rezeption und Transformation in epischen Geschichtsdarstellungen der Antike*. Cologne.
James, L. (2012) "Is There an Empress in the Text? Julian's *Speech of Thanks* to Eusebia," in N. Baker-Brian and S. Tougher (eds.), *Emperor and Author: The Writings of Julian the Apostate*. Swansea: 47–60.
Jarratt, S. (2016) "An Imperial Anti-Sublime: Aristides' *Roman Oration*," in L. Pernot, G. Abbamonte, and M. Lamagna (eds.), *Aelius Aristide écrivain*. Turnhout: 213–29.
Jenkyns, R. (2013) *God, Space, and City in the Roman Imagination*. Oxford.
Johnston, A. C. (2017) *The Sons of Remus: Identity in Roman Gaul and Spain*. Cambridge, MA.
Jones, C. P. (1974) "Diodoros Pasparos and the *Nikephoria* of Pergamon," *Chiron* 4: 183–205.
  (1978) *The Roman World of Dio Chrysostom*. Cambridge, MA.
Jörgensen, O. (1904) "Das Auftreten der Goetter in den Buechern ι-μ der *Odyssee*," *Hermes* 39: 357–82.
Judge, E. A. (1974) "'*Res Publica Restituta*': A Modern Illusion?" in J. A. S. Evans (ed.), *Polis and Imperium: Studies in Honour of Edward Togo Salmon*. Toronto: 279–311.
Kaniewski, D. et al. (2010) "Late Second–Early First Millennium BC Abrupt Climate Changes in Coastal Syria and their Possible Significance for the History of the Eastern Mediterranean," *Quaternary Research* 74: 207–15.
Kaplan, M. (1990) *Greeks and the Imperial Court, from Tiberius to Nero*. New York.
Keitel, E. (1978) "The Role of Parthia and Armenia in Tacitus, *Annals* 11 and 12," *American Journal of Philology* 99: 462–73.
Keith, A. (1999) "Versions of Epic Masculinity in Ovid's *Metamorphoses*," in P. Hardie, A. Barchiesi, and S. Hinds (eds.), *Ovidian Transformations: Essays on the* Metamorphoses *and its Reception*. Cambridge: 214–39.
  (2000) *Engendering Rome: Women in Latin Epic*. Cambridge.
  (2008) "Lament in Lucan's *Bellum Ciuile*," in A. Suter (ed.), *Lament: Studies in the Ancient Mediterranean and Beyond*. Oxford: 233–57.
  (2016) "City Lament in Augustan Epic: Antitypes of Rome from Troy to Alba Longa," in M. Bachvarova, D. Dutsch, and A. Suter (eds.), *The Fall of Cities*

in the Mediterranean: Commemoration in Literature, Folk-Song, and Liturgy. Cambridge: 156–82.
- (forthcoming) "Women's Travels in Latin Elegy," in E. Z. Damer and M. Myers (eds.), *Travel and Geography in Latin Literature*. Madison, WI.
Kelly, B. (2010) "Tacitus, Germanicus and the Kings of Egypt (Tac. *Ann.* 2.59–61)," *Classical Quarterly* 60: 221–37.
Kilb, H. (1973) *Strukturen epischen Gestaltens im 7. und 23. Gesang des* Odyssee. Munich.
Kim, L. (2010) *Homer between History and Fiction in Imperial Greek Literature*. Cambridge.
Kirchhoff, A. (1879) *Die homerische* Odyssee. Berlin.
Kirk, G. S. (1970) *Myth: Its Meaning and Function in Ancient and Other Cultures*. Berkeley.
Kleywegt, A. J. (2005) *Valerius Flaccus,* Argonautica, *Book 1: A Commentary*. Leiden and Boston.
Klooster, J. J. H. (2012) "Apollonius of Rhodes," in I. J. F. de Jong (ed.), *Space in Ancient Greek Literature: Studies in Ancient Greek Narrative*. Leiden: 55–76.
Knight, V. (1995) *The Renewal of Epic: Responses to Homer in the* Argonautica *of Apollonius*. Leiden.
Knox, B. (1964) *The Heroic Temper: Studies in Sophoclean Tragedy*. Berkeley.
Kondratieff, E. J. (2014) "Future City in the Heroic Past: Rome, Romans, and Roman Landscapes in *Aeneid* 6–8," in A. M. Kemezis (ed.), *Urban Dreams and Realities in Antiquity: Remains and Representations of the Ancient City*. Leiden: 165–228.
Kowalski, J. (1929) *De Didone Graeca et Latina*. Cracow.
Kraus, C. and Woodman, A. J. (eds.) (2014) *Tacitus:* Agricola. Cambridge.
Kullmann, W. (1955) "Ein vorhomerisches Motiv im Iliasproömium," *Philologus* 99: 167–92.
Kuttner, A. L. (1995) *Dynasty and Empire in the Age of Augustus: The Case of the Boscoreale Cups*. Berkeley.
Lakoff, G. and Johnson, M. (1980) *Metaphors we Live by*. Chicago.
Lalanne, S. (2006) *Une éducation grecque: rites de passage et construction des genres dans le roman grec ancien*. Paris.
Landrey, L. (2014) "Skeletons in Armor: Silius Italicus' *Punica* and the *Aeneid*'s Proem," *American Journal of Philology* 135.4: 599–635.
Lattimore, R. (trans.) (1965, 1967) *The* Odyssey *of Homer*. New York.
Lazenby, J. F. (1996) *The First Punic War: A Military History*. Stanford.
Lazier, B. (2011) "Earthrise; or, the Globalization of the World Picture," *American Historical Review* 116.3: 602–30.
Lee, M. O. (1979) *Fathers and Sons in Virgil's* Aeneid: Tum genitor natum. Albany, NY.
Lefebvre, H. (1970) *La révolution urbaine*. Paris.
- (1991) *The Production of Space*. (tr.) D. Nicholson-Smith. Oxford.
Leigh, M. (2010) "Early Roman Epic and the Maritime Moment," *Classical Philology* 105.3: 265–80.

(2013) *From* Polypragmon *to* Curiosus: *Ancient Concepts of Curious and Meddlesome Behaviour*. Oxford.
Lindheim, S. H. (2010) "Pomona's *pomarium*: The 'Mapping Impulse' in *Metamorphoses* 14 (and 9)," *Transactions of the American Philological Association* 140: 163–94.
Littlewood, C. (2016) "Elegy and Epic in Lucan's *Bellum Ciuile*," in A. Keith and J. Edmondson (eds.), *Roman Literary Cultures*. Toronto: 159–84.
Loney, A. C. (2019) *The Ethics of Revenge and the Meanings of the* Odyssey. Oxford.
Loraux, N. (1990) *Les mères en deuil*. Paris.
Lord, A. B. (1960) *The Singer of Tales*, 2nd ed. Cambridge, MA; repr. 2000.
Lord, M. L. (1969) "Dido as an Example of Chastity: The Influence of Example Literature," *Harvard Library Bulletin* 17: 22–44.
Lossau, M. (1990) "Xenophons *Odyssee*," *Antike Und Abendland* 36: 47–52.
Louden, B. (1999) *The* Odyssey: *Structure, Narration, and Meaning*. Baltimore.
Lovatt, H. (2013) *The Epic Gaze: Vision, Gender, and Narrative in Ancient Epic*. Cambridge.
Luck-Huyse, K. (1997) *Der Traum vom Fliegen in der Antike*. Stuttgart.
Lumb, T. W., and Rattenbury, R. M. (eds.) (1960) *Heliodore:* Les Ethiopiques (Theagene et Chariclee), trans. J. Maillon. 2nd ed. Paris.
Ma, J. (2000) "Public Speech and Community in the Euboicus," in S. Swain (ed.), *Dio Chrysostom: Politics, Letters, and Philosophy*. Oxford: 108–24.
  (2004) "You Can't Go Home Again: Displacement and Identity in Xenophon's Anabasis," in R. Lane Fox (ed.), *The Long March: Xenophon and the Ten Thousand*. New Haven: 330–45.
Macleod, C. W. (1983) *Collected Essays*. Oxford.
Maehler, H. (1963) *Die Auffassung des Dichterberufs im frühen Griechentum bis zur Zeit Pindars*. Göttingen.
Malkin, I. (1998) *The Returns of Odysseus: Colonization and Ethnicity*. Berkeley.
  (2011) *A Small Greek World: Networks in the Ancient Mediterranean (Greeks Overseas)*. New York.
Manuwald, G. (1999) *Die Cyzicus-Episode und ihre Funktion in den* Argonautica *des Valerius Flaccus*. Göttingen.
  (2009) "What Do Humans Get to Know about the Gods and their Plans? On Prophecies and their Deficiencies in Valerius Flaccus' *Argonautica*," *Mnemosyne* 62: 586–608.
  (2013) "Divine Messages and Human Actions in the *Argonautica*," in A. Augoustakis (ed.), *Ritual and Religion in Flavian Epic*. Oxford: 33–51.
  (2015) *Valerius Flaccus*. Argonautica *Book III*. Cambridge.
Manolaraki, E. (2009) "Silius' Natural History: Tides in the *Punica*," in A. Augoustakis (ed.), *Brill's Companion to Silius Italicus*. Leiden: 293–322.
Marcovich, M. (1978) "Xenophanes on Drinking-Parties and Olympic Games," *Illinois Classical Studies* 3: 1–26.
Marincola, J. (2007) "Odysseus and the Historians," *Syllecta Classica* 18: 1–79.
Mariotti, S. (1955) *Il Bellum Poenicum e l'arte di Nevio: Saggio con edizione dei frammenti del* Bellum Poenicum. Rome.

References

Marks, J. (2008) *Zeus in the* Odyssey. Washington, DC.
Marmer, H. (1922) "The Problem of the Tides," *The Scientific Monthly* 14.3: 209–22.
Martin, R. H. (1994) *Tacitus.* London.
Martin, R. P. (1993) "Telemachus and the Last Hero Song," *Colby Quarterly* 29: 222–40.
Mattingly, H. B. (1986) "Scipio Aemilianus' Eastern Embassy," *Classical Quarterly* 36: 491–5.
Maurice, L. (2004) "The Punic, the Crafty Slave and the Actor: Deception and Metatheatricality in the *Poenulus*," in T. Baier (ed.), *Studien zu Plautus' Poenulus.* Tübingen: 267–90.
McGinn, T. J. (2004) *The Economy of Prostitution in the Roman World.* Ann Arbor.
Meister, K. (1989–90) "The Role of Timaeus in Greek Historiography," *Scripta Classica Israelica* 10: 55–65.
Meyer, D. (2012) "Apollonius as a Hellenistic Geographer," in T. D. Papanghelis and A. Rengakos (eds.), *Brill's Companion to Apollonius Rhodius*, 2nd ed. Leiden: 267–86.
ní Mheallaigh, K. (2014) *Reading Fiction with Lucian: Fakes, Freaks and Hyperreality.* Cambridge.
Miles, R. (2010) *Carthage Must Be Destroyed: The Rise and Fall of an Ancient Civilization.* New York.
  (2011) "Hannibal and Propaganda," in D. Hoyos (ed.), *A Companion to the Punic Wars.* New York and Chichester: 260–79.
Minchin, E. (2007) *Homeric Voices: Discourse, Memory, Gender.* Oxford.
Mitousi, I. (2014) "Valerius' *Argonautica* as an Ideological Epic of the Flavian Era," in A. Augoustakis (ed.), *Flavian Poetry and its Greek Past.* Leiden and Boston: 153–68.
Moles, J. L. (1984) "Aristotle and Dido's Hamartia," *Greece & Rome* 31.1: 48–54.
Monaghan, M. E. (2005) "Juno and the Poet in Valerius' *Argonautica*," in M. Paschalis (ed.), *Roman and Greek Imperial Epic Poetry.* Rethymnon: 9–27.
Mondi, R. (1983) "The Homeric Cyclopes: Folktale, Tradition, and Theme," *Transactions of the American Philological Association* 113: 17–38.
Monti, R. C. (1981) *The Dido Episode and the* Aeneid: *Roman Social and Political Values in the Epic.* Leiden.
Montiglio, S. (2005) *Wandering in Ancient Greek Culture.* Chicago.
  (2011) *From Villain to Hero: Odysseus in Ancient Thought.* Ann Arbor.
  (2013) *Love and Providence: Recognition in the Ancient Novel.* New York.
Moodie, E. K. (2015) *Plautus'* Poenulus: *A Student Commentary.* Ann Arbor.
Morgan, J. R. (2003) "Heliodoros," in G. L. Schmeling (ed.), *The Novel in the Ancient World*, rev. ed. Leiden: 417–56.
Morstein-Marx, R. (2001) "The Myth of Numidian Origins in Sallust's African Excursus (*Iugurtha* 17.7–18.12)," *American Journal of Philology* 122: 179–200.
Morwood, J. (1991) "Aeneas, Augustus, and the Theme of the City," *Greece and Rome* 38: 212–23.

Most, G. W. (1989) "The Structure and Function of Odysseus' *Apologoi*," *Transactions of the American Philological Association* 119: 15–30.
Muecke, F. (1983) "Foreshadowing and Dramatic Irony in the Story of Dido," *American Journal of Philology* 104.2: 134–55.
Mueller, F. (1882) *De Claudio Rutilio Namatiano Stoico*. Leipzig.
Mueller, M. (2007) "Penelope and the Poetics of Remembering," *Arethusa* 40.3: 337–62.
Muellner, L. (1976) *The Meaning of Homeric EUXOMAI through its Formulas*. Innsbruck.
Murnaghan, S. (1987) *Disguise and Recognition in the* Odyssey. Princeton.
  (1999) "The Poetics of Loss in Greek Epic," in M. Beissinger, J. Tylus, and S. Wofford (eds.), *Epic Traditions in the Contemporary World: The Poetics of Community*. Berkeley: 203–20.
Murray, A. T. (trans.) (1919) *The* Odyssey. Berkeley.
Nagy, G. (1979) *The Best of the Achaeans: Concepts of the Hero in Archaic Greek Poetry*, rev. ed. Baltimore; repr. 1998.
Neumann, J. (1993) "Climatic Changes in Europe and the Near East in the Second Millennium BC," *Climatic Change* 23: 231–45.
Newlands, C. (1996) "The Metamorphosis of Medea," in J. J. Clauss and S. I. Johnson (eds.), *Medea: Maiden or Murderess*. Princeton: 178–208.
Nicolet, C. (1991) *Space, Geography, and Politics in the Early Roman Empire*. Ann Arbor.
Nieto-Hernández, P. (2000) "Back in the Cave of the Cyclops," *American Journal of Philology* 121: 345–66.
Norden, E. (1927) *Die Romische Literatur*. Stuttgart.
Nugent, S. G. (1992) "Vergil's 'Voice of the Women' in *Aeneid* V," *Arethusa* 25: 255–92.
Oliensis, E. (2004) "Sibylline Syllables: The Intratextual *Aeneid*," *Proceedings of the Cambridge Philological Society* 50: 29–45.
Orlin, E. M. (1997) *Temples, Religion, and Politics in the Roman Republic*. Leiden.
O'Sullivan, T. M. (2011) *Walking in Roman Culture*. Cambridge.
Otte, J. P. (1992) "*Sanguis Iovis et Neptunia Proles*: Justice and the Family in Valerius' *Argonautica*." Ph.D. thesis, New York University.
Page, D. L. (1955) *The Homeric* Odyssey. Oxford.
Palmer, R. E. A. (1997) *Rome and Carthage at Peace*. Stuttgart.
Panvini Rosati, F. (1987) "La monetazione di Germanico nel quadro della politica monetaria Giulio Claudia," in G. Bonamente and M. P. Segoloni (eds.), *Germanico: la Persona, la Personalita, il Personaggio nel Bimillenario della Nascita*. Rome: 79–86.
Parker, G. (2008) "The Gender of Travel: Cynthia and Others," *Materiali e Discussioni* 61: 85–100.
Paschoud, F. (1979) "A quel genre littéraire le poème de Rutilius Namatianus appartient-il?" *Revue des Études Latines* 57: 315–22.
  (1993) "Les lettres en Gaule à la fin de l'Empire romain," *Antiquité Tardive* 1: 15–21.

(2012) "On a Recent Book by Alan Cameron: *The Last Pagans of Rome*," *Antiquité Tardive* 20: 359–88.
Pearson, L. (1987) *The Greek Historians of the West: Timaeus and his Predecessors*. Atlanta.
Pease, A. S. (1935) *Publi Vergili Maronis* Aeneidos *Liber Quartus*. Cambridge, MA.
Pelling, C. B. R. (1993) "Tacitus and Germanicus," in T. J. Luce and A. J. Woodman (eds.), *Tacitus and the Tacitean Tradition*. Princeton: 59–85.
  (2009) "Bringing Autochthony Up-to-Date: Herodotus and Thucydides," *Classical World* 102.4: 471–83.
Pérez Vilatela, L. (1995) "Los *nostoi* en Iberia, según la escuela de Pérgamo," *Cuadernos de Filología Clásica* 5: 321–44.
Perkell, C. (1997) "The Lament of Juturna: Pathos and Interpretation in the *Aeneid*," *Transactions of the American Philological Association* 127: 257–86.
  (2008) "Reading the Laments of *Iliad* 24," in A. Suter (ed.), *Lament: Studies in the Ancient Mediterranean and Beyond*. Oxford: 93–117.
  (2013) "Wandering," in R. F. Thomas and J. M. Ziolkowski (eds.), *The Virgil Encyclopedia*. Chichester: 1373–5.
Pernot, L. (1993) *La rhétorique de l'éloge dans le monde gréco-romain*. Paris.
Piatelli, S. (1987) "Le legende monetarie di Germanico," in G. Bonamente and M. P. Segoloni (eds.), *Germanico: la Persona, la Personalita, il Personaggio nel Bimillenario della Nascita*. Rome: 87–93.
Pitts, M. and Versluys, M. J. (2014) *Globalisation and the Roman World: Perspectives and Opportunities*. Cambridge.
Polleichtner, W. (2005) "Hercules' Nutzlose Keule: Valerius Flaccus (1,634f.) kommentiert Apollonios von Rhodos (1,532)," *Rheinisches Museum* NS 148: 349–60.
Pomeroy, S. (1994) *Xenophon*, Oeconomicus: *A Social and Historical Commentary*. Oxford and New York.
Poole, R. (2008) *Earthrise: How Man First Saw the Earth*. New Haven and London.
Post, L. A. (1944) "A New Reading of the Germanicus Papyrus," *American Journal of Philology* 65: 80–2.
Powell, B. B. (1970) "Narrative Pattern in the Homeric Tale of Menelaus," *Transactions of the American Philological Association* 101: 419–31.
Pozzato, S. and Rodighiero, A. (eds.) (2011) *Claudius Rutilius Namatianus. Il Ritorno*. Turin.
Prag, J. R. W. (2006) "Poenus Plane Est – But Who Were the 'Punickes'?" *Papers of the British School at Rome* 74: 1–37.
  (2010) "Kinship Diplomacy between Sicily and Rome," in D. Bonanno, C. Bonnet, N. Cusumano, and S. Péré-Noguès (eds.), *Alleanze e Parentele: Le "affinità elettive" nella Storiografia sulla Sicilia Antica*, Convegno internazionale, Palermo, 14–15 Aprile 2010. Caltanissetta: 179–206.
  (2014) "*Phoinix* and *Poenus*: Usage in Antiquity," in J. C. Quinn and N. Vella (eds.), *The Punic Mediterranean: Identities and Identification from Phoenician Settlement to Roman Rule*. Cambridge: 11–23.

Prandi, L. (1979) "La '*fides punica*' e il pregiudizio anticartaginese," in M. Sordi (ed.), *Conoscenze Etniche e Rapporti di Convivenza nell'Antichità*. Milan: 90–7.
Privitera, T. (2004) "Rutilio e il fil di fumo," *Rivista di Cultura Classica e Medioevale* 46.1: 41–50.
Pucci, P. (1987) *Odysseus Polutropos: Intertextual Readings in the* Iliad *and the* Odyssey. Ithaca, NY.
Purves, A. C. (2010a) *Space and Time in Ancient Greek Narrative*. Cambridge and New York.
  (2010b) "Wind and Time in Homeric Epic," *Transactions of the American Philological Association* 140: 323–50.
Quint, D. (1989) "Repetition and Ideology in the *Aeneid*," *Materiali e Discussioni* 23: 9–54.
  (1993) *Epic and Empire: Politics and Generic Form from Virgil to Milton*. Princeton.
Ratti, S. (2006) "Rutilius Namatianus, Aelius Aristide et les chrétiens," *Antiquité Tardive* 14: 235–44.
Redfield, J. (2009 [1983]) "The Economic Man," in L. E. Doherty (ed.), *Homer's Odyssey*. Oxford: 265–87.
Reece, S. (1993) *The Stranger's Welcome: Oral Theory and the Aesthetics of the Homeric Hospitality Scene*. Ann Arbor.
Reinard, P. (2015) "*Divisa namque et discors aula erat*: die Germanicus-Münzen des Tiberius, Caligula und Claudius: Beobachtungen zur Iulisch-Claudischen Dynastie," *Marburger Beiträge zur antiken Handels-, Wirtschafts- und Sozialgeschichte* 33: 157–212.
Reinhardt, K. (1960) *Tradition und Geist*. Göttingen.
Richlin, A. (2005) *Rome and the Mysterious Orient: Three Plays by Plautus*. Berkeley.
Rieu, E. V. (trans.) (1959) *Apollonius of Rhodes:* The Voyage of the Argo. New York.
Rinner, W. (1978) "Zur Darstellungsweise bei Xenophon, *Anabasis* III 1–2," *Philologus* 122.1: 144–9.
Ripoll, F. (1998) *La morale héroïque dans les épopées latines d'époque flavienne*. Paris.
Rocchi, S. (2016) "A Short Note on Rutilius Namatianus 1.632," *Classical Quarterly* 66.1: 419–21.
Rogerson, A. (2017) *Virgil's Ascanius: Imagining the Future in the* Aeneid. Cambridge.
Roller, D. W. (2013) *Through the Pillars of Herakles: Greco-Roman Exploration of the Atlantic*. London.
Roller, M. (2004) "Exemplarity in Roman Culture: The Cases of Horatius Cocles and Cloelia," *Classical Philology* 99.1: 1–56.
  (2009) "The Exemplary Past in Roman Historiography and Culture," in A. Feldherr (ed.), *The Cambridge Companion to the Roman Historians*. Cambridge: 214–23.
Rood, T. C. B. (2004) "Panhellenism and Self-Presentation: Xenophon's Speeches," in R. Lane Fox (ed.), *The Long March: Xenophon and the Ten Thousand*. New Haven: 305–29.
  (2006) "Advice and Advisers in Xenophon's *Anabasis*," in D. Spencer and E. Theodorakopoulos (eds.), *Advice and its Rhetoric in Greece and Rome*. Bari: 47–61.

Rose, G. P. (1969) "The Unfriendly Phaeacians," *Transactions of the American Philological Association* 100: 387–406.
Rowell, H. T. (1947) "The Original Form of Naevius' *Bellum Punicum*," *American Journal of Philology* 68.1: 21–46.
Rutherford, R. B. (1989) *The Meditations of Marcus Aurelius: A Study*. Oxford.
Sagan, C. (1994) *Pale Blue Dot: A Vision of the Human Future in Space*. New York.
Sahin, S. (1995) "Studien zu den Inschriften von Perge I: Germanicus in Perge," *Epigraphica Anatolica* 24: 21–36.
Saïd, S. (1979) "Les crimes des prétendants, la maison d'Ulysse et les festins de l'*Odyssée*," in S. Saïd, F. Desbordes, J. Bouffartigue, and A. Moreau (eds.), *Études de littérature ancienne*. Paris: 9–49.
Sandy, G. N. (1982) *Heliodorus*. Boston.
Sarris, P. (2011) *Empires of Faith: The Fall of Rome to the Rise of Islam, 500–700*. Oxford.
Schadewaldt, W. (1959) "Kleiderdinge: Zur Analyse der *Odyssee*," *Hermes* 87: 13–26.
Schilling, R. (1955) *La religion romaine de Vénus, depuis les origines jusqu'au temps d'Auguste*. Paris.
Schmitt, T. (1997) "Die drei Bögen für Germanicus und die römische Politik in frühtiberischer Zeit," *Rivista Storica dell'Antichità* 27: 73–137.
Schneider, P. (2015) "*Quod Nunc Rubrum ad Mare Patescit*: The *Mare Rubrum* as a Frontier of the Roman Empire," *Klio* 97.1: 135–56.
Schröder, H. O. (1987) "Das Odysseusbild des Aelius Aristides," *Rheinisches Museum für Philologie* 130: 350–6.
Schweickart, R. (1977) "No Frames, no Boundaries," in M. Katz, W. P. Marsh, and G. G. Thompson (eds.), *Earth's Answer: Explorations of Planetary Culture at the Lindisfarne Conferences*. New York: 2–13.
Scodel, R. (1982) "The Achaean Wall and the Myth of Destruction," *Harvard Studies in Classical Philology* 86: 33–50.
Scott, M. (2013) *Space and Society in the Greek and Roman Worlds*. Cambridge.
Segal, C. (1994) *Singers, Heroes, and Gods in the* Odyssey. Ithaca.
Sharrock, A. (2011) "Womanly Wailing? The Mother of Euryalus and Gendered Reading," *Eugesta* 1: 55–77.
Shipley, G. and Salmon, J. B. (eds.) (1996) *Human Landscapes in Classical Antiquity: Environment and Culture*. London.
Skempis, M. and Ziogas, I. (eds.) (2013) *Geography, Topography, Landscape: Configurations of Space in Greek and Roman Epic*. Berlin.
Skutsch, O. (1985) *The* Annals *of Q. Ennius*. Oxford.
Soler, J. (2006) "Le poème de Rutilius Namatianus et la tradition du récit de voyage antique: à propos du 'genre' du *De reditu suo*," *Vita Latina* 174: 104–13.
Sommer, M. (2014) "Elissas lange Reise: Migration, Interkulturalität und die Gründung Karthagos im Spiegel des Mythos," in A.-B. Renger and I. Toral-Niehoff (eds.), *Genealogie und Migrationsmythen im antiken Mittelmeerraum und auf der arabischen Halbinsel*. Berlin: 157–76.
Sourvinou-Inwood, C. (1995) *"Reading" Greek Death: To the End of the Classical Period*. Oxford.

Spaltenstein, F. (2002) *Commentaire des* Argonautica *de Valerius Flaccus (Livres 1 et 2)*. Brussels.
  (2004) *Commentaire des* Argonautica *de Valerius Flaccus (Livres 3, 4 et 5)*. Brussels.
Spencer, D. (2010) *Roman Landscape: Culture and Identity*. Cambridge.
Squillante, M. (2005) *Il Viaggio, la Memoria, il Ritorno: Rutilio Namaziano e le Transformazioni del Tema Odeporico*. Naples.
Squire, M. (2011) *The* Iliad *in a Nutshell: Visualizing Epic on the* Tabulae Iliacae. Oxford.
  (2013) "Ekphrasis at the Forge and the Forging of Ekphrasis: The 'Shield of Achilles' in Graeco-Roman Word and Image," *Word & Image* 29.2: 157–91.
Stanford, W. B. (ed.) (1947) *The* Odyssey. London.
Stanford, W. B. (1954) *The Ulysses Theme: A Study in the Adaptability of a Traditional Hero*. Oxford.
Starks, J. H. (1999) "*Fides Aeneia*: The Transference of Punic Stereotypes in the *Aeneid*," *Classical Journal* 94.3: 255–83.
  (2000) "*Nullus me est hodie poenus poenior*: Balanced Ethnic Humor in Plautus' *Poenulus*," *Helios* 27.2: 163–86.
Steinbock, A. (1995) *Home and Beyond: Generative Phenomenology after Husserl*. Evanston, IL.
Stephens, S. (2008) "Ptolemaic Epic," in T. D. Papanghelis and A. Rengakos (eds.) *Brill's Companion to Apollonius Rhodius*, 2nd ed. Leiden: 95–114.
Stover, T. (2012) *Epic and Empire in Vespasianic Rome*. Oxford.
  (2014) "Lucan and Valerius Flaccus: Rerouting the Vessel of Epic Song," in M. Heerink and G. Manuwald (eds.), *Brill's Companion to Valerius Flaccus*. Leiden and Boston: 290–306.
Strzelecki, W. (1964) *Cn. Naevii* Belli Punici *Carminis Quae Supersunt*. Leipzig.
Suter, A. (2003) "Lament in Euripides' *Trojan Women*," *Mnemosyne* 16.1: 1–28.
Swain, S. (1998) *Hellenism and Empire: Language, Classicism, and Power in the Greek World, AD 50–250*. Oxford.
Syson, A. J. R. (2013) *Fama and Fiction in Vergil's* Aeneid. Columbus, OH.
Tally, R. T. (2013) *Spatiality: The New Critical Idiom*. London.
Taplin, O. (1980) "The Shield of Achilles within the *Iliad*," *Greece & Rome* 27.1: 1–21.
Tarrant, D. (1960) "Greek Metaphors of Light," *Classical Quarterly* 10.3–4: 181–7.
Thalmann, W. G. (2011) *Apollonius of Rhodes and the Spaces of Hellenism: Classical Culture and Society*. New York and Oxford.
Thieler, W. (ed.) (1982) *Poseidonios: die Fragmente*, 2 vols. Berlin.
Thomas, R. F. (2004–5) "Torn Between Jupiter and Saturn: Ideology, Rhetoric and Culture Wars in the *Aeneid*," *Classical Journal* 100: 121–47.
Tipping, B. (2010) *Exemplary Epic: Silius Italicus'* Punica. Oxford.
Tissol, G. (2002) "Ovid and the Exilic Journey of Rutilius Namatianus," *Arethusa* 35.3: 435–46.

Topper, K. (2012) *The Imagery of the Athenian Symposium*. Cambridge.
Tougher, S. (1998) "In Praise of an Empress: Julian's *Speech of Thanks* to Eusebia," in M. Whitby (ed.), *The Propaganda of Power: The Role of Panegyric in Late Antiquity*. Leiden: 105–23.
  (2012) "Reading between the Lines: Julian's *First Panegyric* on Constantius II," in N. Baker-Brian and S. Tougher (eds.), *Emperor and Author: The Writings of Julian the Apostate*. Swansea: 19–34.
Tsagalis, C. C. (2002) "Xenophon *Homericus*: An Unnoticed Loan from the *Iliad* in Xenophon's *Anabasis*," *Classica & Mediaevalia* 53: 101–21.
Tuplin, C. J. (2003) "Heroes in Xenophon's *Anabasis*," in A. Barzanò, C. Bearzot, F. Landucci, L. Prandi, and G. Zecchini (eds.), *Modelli Eroici dall'Antichità alla Cultura Europea*. Rome: 115–56.
Turner, E. G. and Lobel, E. (1959) *The Oxyrhynchus Papyri, Part XXV*. London.
Van Wees, H. (1992) *Status Warriors: War, Violence, and Society in Homer and History*. Amsterdam.
Versnel, H. S. (1987) "Greek Myth and Ritual: The Case of Kronos," in J. Bremmer (ed.), *Interpretations of Greek Mythology*. London: 121–52.
Vesserau, J. (1904) *Sur son retour*. Paris.
Vidal-Naquet, P. (1986) *The Black Hunter: Forms of Thought and Forms of Society in the Greek World*. Baltimore.
Virilio, P. (1997) *Open Sky*. (tr.) J. Rose. London.
von der Mühll, P. (ed.) (1962) *Homeri* Odyssea. Stuttgart.
von Martels, Z. (ed.) (1994) *Travel Fact and Travel Fiction: Studies on Fiction, Literary Tradition, Scholarly Discovery and Observation in Travel Writing*. Leiden.
Vonnegut, K. (1976 [1969]) "Excelsior! We're going to the Moon! Excelsior!" *New York Times Magazine*, July 13, 1969: 9–11; repr. in *Wampeters, Foma & Granfalloons*. New York: 77–89.
Wacht, M. (1991a) *Juppiters Weltenplan im Epos des Valerius Flaccus*. Mainz.
  (1991b) "Zur Motivierung der Handlung im Epos des Valerius," in M. Korn and H. J. Tschiedel (eds.), *Ratis omnia vincet: Untersuchungen zu den Argonautica des Valerius Flaccus*. Zurich and New York: 101–20.
Walbank, F. W. (1998) "A Greek Looks at Rome: Polybius VI Revisited," *Scripta Classica Israelica* 17: 45–59.
Warrior, V. M. (2006) *Roman Religion*. Cambridge.
Webb, R. (2009) *Ekphrasis, Imagination and Persuasion in Ancient Rhetorical Theory and Practice*. Farnham.
Weber, R. (1985) *Seeing Earth: Literary Responses to Space Exploration*. Athens, OH and London.
Wecowski, M. (2002) "Homer and the Origins of the Symposium," in F. Montanari (ed.), *Omero: Tremilla Anni Doppo*. Rome: 625–37.
Welch, T. S. (2005) *The Elegiac Cityscape: Propertius and the Meaning of Roman Monuments*. Columbus, OH.
West, D. (1978) "Studies in Latin Poetry – Niall Rudd: *Lines of Enquiry: Studies in Latin Poetry*," *The Classical Review* 28.1: 76–8.

(trans.) (2003) *Virgil: The Aeneid*. London.
West, M. L. (2003) *Homeric Hymns. Homeric Apocrypha. Lives of Homer*. Loeb Classical Library 496. Cambridge, MA.
  (2014) *The Making of the* Odyssey. Oxford.
White, F. (2014) *The Overview Effect: Space Exploration and Human Evolution*, 3rd ed. Reston, VA.
Whitmarsh, T. (2001a) *Greek Literature and the Roman Empire: The Politics of Imitation*. Oxford.
  (2001b) "'Greece is the World': Exile and Identity in the Second Sophistic," in S. Goldhill (ed.), *Being Greek under Rome: Cultural Identity, the Second Sophistic and the Development of Empire*. Cambridge: 269–305.
  (2005) *The Second Sophistic*. Cambridge.
  (2011) *Narrative and Identity in the Ancient Greek Novel: Returning Romance*. Cambridge.
  (2013) *Beyond the Second Sophistic: Adventures in Greek Postclassicism*. Berkeley.
Wigodsky, M. (1972) *Vergil and Early Latin Poetry*. Wiesbaden.
von Wilamowitz-Moellendorff, U. and Zucker, F. (1911) "Zwei Edikte des Germanicus auf einem Papyrus des Berliner Museums," *Sitzungsberichte der Königlich Preussischen Akademie der Wissenschaften* 38: 794–821.
Wilcken, U. (1928) "Zum Germanicus-Papyrus," *Hermes* 63.4: 48–65.
Williams, G. D. (2012) *The Cosmic Viewpoint: A Study of Seneca's* Natural Questions. New York and Oxford.
Williams, R. D. (1960) *P. Vergili Maronis* Aeneidos *Liber Quintus*. Oxford.
  (1962) *P. Vergili Maronis* Aeneidos *Liber Tertius*. Oxford.
  (1972) *The* Aeneid *of Virgil, Books 1–6*. London.
Willis, I. (2011) *Now and Rome: Lucan and Vergil as theorists of politics and space*. London.
Winkler, J. J. (1982) "The Mendacity of Kalasiris and the Narrative Strategy of Heliodoros' *Aithiopika*," *Yale Classical Studies* 27: 93–158.
Wiseman, T. P. (1984) "Cybele, Virgil and Augustus," in T. Woodman and D. West (eds.), *Poetry and Politics in the Age of Augustus*. Cambridge: 117–28.
Wohl, V. (1993) "Standing by the Stathmos: The Creation of Sexual Ideology in the *Odyssey*," *Arethusa* 26.1: 19–50.
Wolff, E. (2005) "Quelques aspects du *De reditu suo* de Rutilius Namatianus," *Vita Latina* 173: 66–74.
Wolff, E. (ed.) (2007) *Claudius Rutilius Namatianus: Sur son retour*. Paris.
Woodman, A. J. (2015) "Tacitus and Germanicus: Monuments and Models," in R. Ash, J. Mossman, and F. B. Titchener (eds.), *Fame and Infamy: Essays for Christopher Pelling on Characterization in Greek and Roman Biography and Historiography*. Oxford: 255–68.
  (2017) *The* Annals *of Tacitus, Books 5 and 6*. Cambridge.
Woodman, A. J. and Martin, R. H. (1996) *The* Annals *of Tacitus, Book 3*. Cambridge.
Woolf, G. (2011) *Tales of the Barbarians: Ethnography and Empire in the Roman West*. Oxford.

Wright, T. L. (1998) "Valerius Flaccus and the Poetics of Imitation," Ph.D. Dissertation, University of Virginia.
Yardley, J. (trans.) (1994) *Justin:* Epitome of the Philippic History of Pompeius Trogus. Atlanta.
    (2003) *Justin and Pompeius Trogus:* A Study of the Language of Justin's Epitome of Trogus. Toronto.
Yarrow, L. M. (2006) *Historiography at the End of the Republic: Provincial Perspectives on Roman Rule.* Oxford.
Yavetz, Z. (1990) "The Personality of Augustus: Reflections on Syme's *Roman Revolution*," in K. A. Raaflaub and M. Toher (eds.), *Between Republic and Empire: Interpretations of Augustus and his Principate.* Berkeley: 21–41.
Zanker, P. (1988) *The Power of Images in the Age of Augustus.* Ann Arbor.
Zeitlin, F. I. (2001) "Visions and Revisions of Homer," in S. Goldhill (ed.), *Being Greek under Rome: Cultural Identity, the Second Sophistic and the Development of Empire.* Cambridge: 195–266.
Zetzel, J. E. G. (1995) *Cicero De Re Publica Selections.* Cambridge.
Ziołkowski, A. (1992) *The Temples of Mid-Republican Rome and their Historical and Topographical Context.* Rome.
Zissos, A. (2004) "Terminal Middle: The *Argonautica* of Valerius Flaccus," in S. Kyriakidis and F. de Martino (eds.) *Middles in Latin Poetry.* Bari: 311–44.
    (2006) "Sailing and Sea-Storm in Valerius Flaccus (*Argonautica* 1.574–642): The Rhetoric of Inundation," in R. Nauta, H.-J. Van Dam, and J. J. L. Smolenaars (eds.), *Flavian Poetry.* Leiden and Boston: 79–95.
    (2008) *Valerius Flaccus' Argonautica Book 1.* Oxford.
    (2012) "The King's Daughter: Medea in Valerius Flaccus' *Argonautica*," in A. J. Boyle (ed.), *Roman Medea. Ramus* 41.1–2: 94–118.
Zucca, R. (1989) "Venus Erycina tra Sicilia, Africa e Sardegna," in *L'Africa Romana: Atti del 6. Convegno di Studio,* 16–18 Dicembre 1988. Sassari: 771–9.
Zumpt, A. W. (1837) *Observationes in Rutilii Claudii Namatiani Carmen de Reditu Suo.* Berlin.

Index Locorum

Aelius Aristides
  Orations
    26.100–2 233
    42.13 232
    42.14 232
Anth. Lat.
  708 Riese 210
Apollonius Rhodius
  Argonautica
    1.1–2 62
    1.2–4 130
    1.17 94
    1.535 92
    1.773 138
    1.902–3 93
    2.541–6 95
    3.215 94
    4.11 95
    4.35–9 96
    4.186 93
    4.194–5 95
    4.361–3 96, 98
    4.368–9 96
    4.996–1000 97
    4.1030–41 97
    4.1147 93
    4.1290–7 99
Aristophanes
  Peace
    821–3 270

Catullus
  101.1–2 176
Cicero
  De republica
    1.23 250
  Academica Priora
    2.5 220

Claudian
  de Consulatu Honorii
    VI 495–9, 247–8
Q. Curtius Rufus
  4.8.3 207

Dio Chrysostom
  Orations
    13.10 228, 230

Ennius
  Annales
    Sk. *Ann.* 28–9 = Serv. Dan. ad G. 3.35 175
Epic Cycle
  Cypr. fr. 1, 29
Euripides
  Medea
    166 98
    255 98
    496 98

FGrH
  566 F82 178

Heliodorus
  Aethiopica
    1.22.4 100
    2.34.2 106
    2.34.4 106
    4.11.3 102
    4.18.2 103, 106
    4.18.5 105
    5.2.7 105, 107
    5.22.3 100, 103
    5.27.8 101
    6.7.9 103
    6.15.4 103
    8.5.15 105

Herodotus
  Histories
    7.142.3–144.1 118
    8.109.5 117
Hesiod
  W&D
    100–5 23
    109–19 12–13
    168–73 13
Homer
  Odyssey
    1.1–2 31, 130, 212
    1.1–21 111–12
    1.47 222
    1.84–95 39
    1.93–5 35–6
    1.204–5 51, 120
    1.345–59 120
    3.368–70 36
    3.447–54 123
    4.360–62 38
    4.557–60 42
    5.29–42 40
    5.151–2 92
    5.219–20 92
    5.306–10 66
    7.133–4 94
    7.189–96 50
    8.17–18 221
    8.28–33 51
    8.564–71 52
    9.2–11 17
    9.19–20 57
    9.106–15 18
    9.161–2 20
    9.269–78 21
    9.349–50 43
    9.357–9 22
    9.410–11 23
    9.475–9 24, 28
    9.517–19 45
    9.529–30 46
    9.532–34 46
    10.17–18 47
    11.93–4 235
    11.328–34 55
    11.352–3 32, 56
    13.42–3 120
    13.44–5 121
    13.418–19 37
    13.422–4 37
    15.64–6 120
    15.65–6 92, 120
    17.487 221
    21.293–306 25–6
    21.343–53 121
    21.406–11 26–7
    21.428–30 27
    22.17–19 27
    22.413–15 28
    23.248–9 121
    23.350–60 121
    schol. ad. Hom. *Il.* 24.804, 135
Horace
  Epistulae 1.2.18–20, 221

IGR
  IGR 4, 251=IvAssos 26=IMT 573, 201
IvO
  IvO 220, 199
  IvO 221, 199

Julian
  Orationes
    1.12D 211
    3.104C–105A 238
Justin
  Epitome
    38.8.8–11 220–1

Libanius
  Orations
    18.27 239
Livius Andronicus
  Odusia
    FPL 7, 177
    FPL 11, 176
    FPL 17, 177
    FPL 30, 175
    FPL 39, 174
Livy
  ab Urbe Condita
    1.1.3 177
Lucan
  Bellum Civile
    1.374–8 86
    1.408–17 255–6
Lucian
  Icaromenippus
    16–17 265
    18 278, 282
  Nigrinus
    17–19 235
    35 236
  Verae Historia
    1.26 234–5, 288

Gnaeus Naevius
  Bellum Punicum
    FPL 5, 173
    FPL 6, 173
    FPL 9, 171, 173
    FPL 20, 177
    FPL 22, 173
    FPL 24, 173
    FPL 50, 176
    FPL 51, 176

Rutilius Namatianus
  de Reditu Suo
    1.29 246
    1.53–6 258
    1.65–6 257
    1.121–4 258
    1.129–30 259
    1.145 257
    1.193–7 244–5
    1.227–36 251
    1.475–87 256
    1.631–44 246–7
    2.63–8 248

Ovid
  Metamorphoses
    8.161 134
  Epistulae ex Ponto
    1.3.33–4 245

Pausanias
    8.30.8 218
Philostratus
  Lives of the Sophists
    1.7 227
  Life of Apollonius
    1.35.2 229
Plato
  Republic
    6.19–21 269–70
  Phaedo
    98c2 268
  Theaetetus
    174e 282
Plautus
  Poenulus
    104–16 185–6
    111–13 186
    950–60 189
    991 186
    1032–4 186
    1137 190
    1185–6 187
    1187–90 190
    1251–7 190
Pliny the Elder
  Natural Histories
    36.13.19 § 2 134
Polybius
  Histories
    1.1 213
    3.59.1–5 217
    3.59.7–8 217
    12.2 (= Athenaeus 14.651D) 214
    12.3 215
    12.27–8 215–16
    12.28.6 217–18
    38.21–2 218
Pompeius Trogus
    18.4.7 181
    18.5.4 181
    18.6.1 183
    18.6.5–8 183
Posidonius (*FGrH* 87)
    F 6+1 (= Justin, *Epitome* 38.8.8–11) 220
    F 6+2 (= Diodorus 33.28b) 220
    F 30 (= Plutarch, Moralia 777A) 221
    F 125b Th (=ps.-Plutarch, *Moralia* 200E–F) 220
    F 110f (= *Excerpta de Sententiis* 387.13) 222

Sidonius Apollinaris
  Epistles
    1.5.1 252–3
Silius Italicus
    3.58–60 249–50
Strabo
  Geography
    1.2.3–4 226
    5.3.8 168

Tacitus
  Agricola
    10.4–6 254–5
  Annales
    2.2.2 194, 206, 210
    2.2.3 210
    2.26.4 195
    2.41.2 195–6, 208
    2.42.1 198, 207
    2.42.5 196
    2.43.1 195, 197
    2.43.3 206
    2.43.4 198, 205
    2.44.1 206
    2.46.1 208
    2.46.5 206
    2.53.1 195

Index Locorum

2.53.2 195–6, 205–6
2.53.3 197, 199, 209
2.54.1 196–7, 199–200, 203, 207
2.54.2 196–7, 200, 204–5, 207
2.54.4 204–5
2.55.1 197, 201, 206, 209
2.55.3 197, 201
2.55.6 197–8, 201
2.56.3 207–9
2.59.1 197, 206–7
2.60.1 197, 207
2.61.2 197
2.62.1 202–3, 207
2.64.1 195, 197, 203, 208
2.71.1 205
2.73.2 205
2.78.1 206
2.82.1 210
2.85.4 209
2.88.1 209
2.88.3 209
3.1.1 205
3.4.2 208
3.6.2 209
3.7.1 205
3.55.5 209
6.14.2 194
Germania
3 231
Theognis
757–68 14

Valerius Flaccus
Argonautica
1.1–4 62
1.71–8 65
1.100–2 66
1.212–26 67
1.227–39 68
1.240–9 70
1.252–3 72
1.531–5 63
1.544–5 64
1.558–60 63
1.561–7 64
1.621–6, 634–5, 73
2.369–73 74
2.373–7 75
2.378–84 76
2.384–92 76
2.639–47 77
2.659–62 78

3.74–5 79
3.80–2 79
3.186–9 79
3.262–6 80
3.362–8 80
3.375–6 81
3.488 81
3.545–51 81
3.551–61 82
3.604–10 84
3.628–32 84
3.667–81 85
3.712–14 85
3.719–21 87
4.5–8 82
5.171–3 87
8.50–1 107
Velleius Paterculus
2.101.3 198
Vergil
Aeneid
1.1–3, 130
1.31–3 153
1.92 175
1.126 156
1.148–56 156
1.180–94 159
1.193 160
1.199 160
1.198–207 71, 160
1.205 160
1.206 160
1.207 69
1.224 160
1.225–6 160
1.238 161
1.257–60 161
1.332–3 153
1.338–9 132
1.340 132, 179
1.341–2 134, 153
1.343 133
1.358–9 133
1.360 137
1.361–3 132–3, 137
1.365–8 133
1.384–5 153
1.418–26 161–2
1.437–8 161–2
1.490–7 135
1.628–9 154
1.661–2 186
1.754–5 158
2.289–90 158

Vergil (cont.)
  2.293–5 158
  2.314–17 154–5
  2.761–7 139
  2.796–804 138
  3.62–8 140
  3.75 173
  3.94–6 69
  3.121–37 141
  3.321–7 139
  4.175 164
  4.215 165
  4.393–6 192
  4.438–9 154
  4.449 154
  4.537–46 137
  4.569–70 155
  4.596 170
  4.644 137
  5.613–15 142
  5.622–9 142
  5.630–4 143
  5.709–18 143–4
  5.750 144
  5.755–7 144
  6.29 134
  6.687–8 170
  6.773–6 252
  7.10–14 131
  7.21–4 131–2
  7.375 155
  7.377 155
  7.496 82
  8.348 167
  8.680–1 163
  8.685–713 136
  8.704–5 163
  9.638–9 164
  9.641 63, 164
  10.261 164
  12.99 165
  12.940 166
  Georgics
    1.145 69
  Servius Auct. ad *Aen.* 1.148, 156
  Servius Auct. ad *Aen.* 1.149, 156
  Servius Auct. ad *Aen.* 6.775, 252

Xenophanes
  1.13–24W 15–16
Xenophon
  Anabasis
    3.1.3–4 118
    3.1.6 116
    3.1.11–13 110
    3.2.25 108
    4.1.23–4 115
    4.3.2–3 114
    4.3.10–12 125–6
    4.3.17–19 122
    4.4.14 115
    4.5.9–10 124–5
    4.6.3 115
    4.8.27 123
    5.1.2 108
    5.3.3 116
    5.3.6 116
    5.4.27–30 114
    6.5.24 109
    7.2.3 117
    7.6.32 109
    7.6.34 117
    7.8.1 116–17
    7.8.4 117
    7.8.19 117
    7.8.8–11, 22–4, 126–7
    7.139.5 117
  Oeconomicus
    3.10 121

General Index

Achilles, 34, 61–2, 106, 119, 123, 136, 138–9, 209, 242, 265–8, 279
Achilles Tatius, 99–100
Aeolus/Aiolos, 16, 46–8, 52, 54, 56, 58
Ages of Man
   Bronze/Heroic, 12, 25, 28–9, 59, 74
   Golden, 9, 12–30, 61
     meat, 14, 20, 25
   Iron, 7–8, 17, 19–24, 28–30, 63, 74
Agrippina the Younger, 148, 196, 199, 201–3, 205, 208
Ajax
   Lokrian, 35, 61
   Telamonian, 20, 61
Alcinous/Alkinoos, 17, 32, 35, 47, 49–57, 94
Alexandria, 94, 197–9, 206–7, 220, 223, 267
Amazons, 102, 134–6
   Penthesilea, 102, 134–6, 138
ambages. See under *Aeneid*
amor, 192, 205
Anchises, 142–3, 170–5, 185, 189–91
Andromache, 90, 96, 132, 139, 143–4
Andronicus, Livius
   Odusia, 174–8
Aphrodite (Venus), 132–6, 147, 153–4, 160–1, 171, 174, 181–2, 187–90
   Erycina, 187–9
Apollinaris, G. Sidonius, 252–3
Apollodorus, 91
Apollonius Rhodius
   Argonautica
     Aeetes, 94
     Hypsipyle, 93
     love/lovers, 91–9
aporia, 68, 84, 111, 119
Apuleius, L.
   Cupid and Psyche, 104
Ara Pacis Augustae, 166
Arete, 35, 47, 50, 121, 125, 237–8
Argo, 1–2, 10, 59–64, 69, 72–4, 92, 94, 98, 130
   primacy, 62–3

Aristides, P. Aelius
   Orations, 231–4
   and *Odyssey*, 231–4
   and Rome, 233–4
   Panathenaicus, 234
Aristodemus, 225–6
Asclepiades of Myrleia, 223–5
Athena (Pallas/Minerva), 34–43, 47, 50, 58, 120, 123, 128, 221–2, 224, 232, 238
Athens, 117–18, 197–8, 201, 203, 205, 209, 211, 215–17, 228, 234–5, 237
Augustus, x, 5, 138, 145–8, 152, 156–8, 161–9, 171, 180, 192, 195–6, 199–200, 206, 208–10
   Prima Porta, 166

Bellerophon, 33–5
Black Sea, 108, 116, 130, 200–1, 254, 281
Borges, Jorge Luis
   "The Aleph", 266–7
boundaries, 4, 10, 20, 124, 241, 278–9, 282
   violation of, 73
Brundisium, 5, 205

Calypso/Kalypso, 30, 32, 34, 39–43, 49, 51–2, 57, 92–3, 112, 128, 178, 184
Carthage
   foundation of, 132–3, 162, 183
catasterism, 70, 86, 157, 164
Centaurs/Centauromachy, 16, 25–6
Circe/Kirke, 17, 48–9, 52, 56–7, 131, 177–8, 184
civil war, 4, 28, 77, 79, 87, 114, 146, 206
Cleopatra, 136, 138, 144
Colchis, 10, 59, 65, 87, 95–9
collapse, 152, 157, 161, 169, 260
colonization, 4, 11, 19, 29, 118, 153
Crates of Mallus, 223–4
Cyclop(e)s, 17–25, 28–9, 44–5, 47, 94, 174, 177, 216, *See also* Polyphemus

319

Cypria, 29
Cyzicus, 77–84, 86

Delphi, 99–103, 105–6, 116, 222
Dido
  curse, 179
  etymology, 153, 179
  fidelity of, 179–83
  as *univira*, 179
Dio of Prusa (Dio Cocceianus), 227–31
  Getica, 230–1
  On Kingship, 231
Dionysius of Halicarnassus
  on the Trojan journey, 182
Dioscuri (Tyndaridae), 79, 86
distance, 2, 7, 78, 102, 114, 146, 184, 193, 205, 237, 241, 250, 258, 263–4, 269, 275, 277, 285, 288
domestic/foreign, 36, 121, 126, 146, 195, 197, 204, 210
Drusus (Nero Claudius Drusus Germanicus), 195, 198–200, 203, 205–6, 208–9

East/Eastern, 75, 136, 148, 203, 206–7, 219
Egypt, 11, 38–9, 44, 101, 136, 180, 198, 202–3, 205–7, 209, 220, 281
ekphrasis, 79, 172, 242, 266–8, 271
elegy, 5, 10, 15, 75, 77, 82, 142, 183, 243–4
empire
  Persian, 108, 119
  Roman, 59, 145–8, 194–7, 200, 210–11, 213, 215, 217, 223–36, 239, 241–3, 254, 256–62
Ennius, Quintus
  Annales, 174–5
Epictetus, 93, 229
epyllion, 83
ethnography, ix, 211, 213–14, 221, 230, 234–6, 239, 242
Euripides, 34
  Medea, 67, 98
exempla/exemplarity, viii, 10, 59–88, 208
exile, 35, 93, 95, 98, 110, 117, 128, 130, 132–3, 137–8, 140–1, 144–5, 153, 171, 181, 216–17, 227–31, 236, 238, 245

Fabatus, Rubrius, 194, 210
feminist theory, 130–2
Flavian dynasty, 59, 72, 227–8

gaiaskopia
  ancient, 263–71, 279–81
  modern, 271–91
gaze, 123, 220–1, 276

gender, ix, 2–4, 60, 74–5, 89–90, 99, 102, 106, 108, 119–29, 147, 155, 164, 178, 181–3, 187, 189, 238
genre, viii–ix, 1, 5, 10, 60–1, 73, 90, 130, 132, 134, 151, 184, 212–13, 224, 230, 244
Germanicus
  and the past, 205–10
  as tourist, 205–10
  civic honors, 199, 202–3, 208
  death of, 205–6
Giants/Gigantomachy, 16, 166

Hannibal, 249–50, 259
Hector, 96, 135, 143, 154, 158, 210, 218
Helen (of Troy), 39, 232
Heliodorus (*Aethiopica*)
  Chaereas, 103–5
  Chariclea, 89, 91, 99–107
  love/lovers, 103–7
  Theagenes, 101–7
Hera (Juno), 65, 75, 77, 81–3, 95, 135, 139, 142, 155, 162, 174
Hercules/Heracles, 64, 69, 72–8, 81–8, 136, 167, 207, 209, 219, 223, 249, 254
Herodotus (*Histories*), 16, 22, 59, 117, 128, 181, 207, 216
Hesiod
  Theogony, 13, 19
  Works and Days, 12, 18–19, 24
homeland, 12, 16, 29, 42, 46, 48, 50, 78, 81, 89, 91–3, 96–8, 102, 104–6, 109, 120, 133, 139, 142–3, 153, 172, 179, 216, 227, 229, 233, 288
homelessness, 91, 95–6, 98, 103, 105–7
Homer
  Iliad
    shield of Achilles, 242, 265–8, 275, 279–80
  Odyssey
    prophecy of Nausithous, 52–4
Horace (Q. Horatius Flaccus), 5, 221
Hypsipyle, 93

identity, 2, 4, 6–7, 46, 57, 75, 104, 106, 118–19, 124, 130, 145, 148, 172, 188, 212, 215–16, 219, 228–9, 231, 238–9, 242, 257
imperium, 59, 61, 132, 161, 164, 222
Ithaca, 9, 11–12, 18, 24, 31–2, 36–7, 39–42, 45, 48–9, 52–4, 56–8, 92–3, 96, 108, 112, 120, 138, 221, 228, 230, 234, 245
Iulus (Ascanius), 63, 82, 142, 164

General Index

Julian, Emperor
  and Constantius, 236–9
  and Odysseus, 211–12, 236–9

kataskopia, 283
kleos, 11, 62, 64–6, 70, 79, 109, 120, 129
Kronia, 14
Kronos, 12–15, 19, 21, 24

landscape, 1, 5, 61, 75, 79, 87, 131, 145, 158, 163, 175, 182, 196, 214, 224, 236, 241, 243–4, 251–3, 256, 261, 277
lawlessness, 15, 18–19, 21, 24
Lemnos, 74–7
Lotus-Eaters, 108, 214–16
Lucan
  Bellum Civile, 69, 77–8, 87, 144, 206, 247, 255
Lucian
  Icaromenippus, 264–75, 279–84, 287–91
  Nigrinus, 235–6
  Verae Historiae, 235

mapping impulse, 163
Marcus Aurelius, 232, 266, 281, 283
Meleager, 85–7
memory, 84, 109, 120, 122, 218, 220, 224, 226, 234, 239
Menelaus, 35, 37–8, 44, 47, 120, 207
migration, 29, 118, 145
moon (natural satellite), 7, 146, 242–3, 247–50, 254, 256, 258, 261, 263–6, 268–9, 271–80, 282–3, 288–91

Naevius, Gnaeus
  Bellum Punicum
    Anchises, 172–5, 185, 189
    Dido, 177–8
    First Punic War, 175–7
    pietas, 171–8, *See also* under *pietas*
Namatianus, Rutilius Claudius
  De reditu suo
    and Alexandrianism, 248, 251
    and Augustine, 260–2
    and Homer, 244–6
    and Ovid, 244–5
    date of composition, 243, 251
    Luna (Italian city), 241, 248
    tides/tidal flux, 241, 243, 246–62
NASA (National Aeronautics and Space Administration), 242, 271–9, 285, 290
Nausicaa/Nausikaä, 50, 121, 125–6
Nestor, 34–9, 61
Nobilior, Fulvius
  campaigns, 147, 184

nostalgia, 92–5, 104, 143, 209, 241
nostos, 1, 6–8, 29–30, 39–42, 53, 56, 60–1, 65–6, 70, 72, 75, 82–3, 87, 89, 92, 94, 99, 101–5, 107–12, 115–17, 119, 121, 146, 148, 175–7, 182, 195–6, 207–8, 234, 238
novel (Greek), 91, 99–107, 122, 184, 229–30

Odysseus
  as model, 60–1, 66–7, 72–3, 92–5, 98–102, 106–7, 113, 116, 119–21, 123, 126, 128–9, 131, 133–4, 137–8, 148, 153, 178, 211–39, 245
Odyssey
  as model. *See* under Odysseus as model
orbis, 6, 146, 244, 247–9, 256–8, 260–1
Ovid (P. Ovidius Naso), ix, 83, 134, 188, 229, 244–5

Pandora, 23, 30
Penelope, 25–6, 30, 34, 37, 90, 92, 112–13, 120–1, 126, 129, 136
Phaeacia, 31, 38, 41, 43, 46–8, 50–2, 54–5, 97–8, 108, 120, 212, 221, 237–8
Philostratus
  Life of Dio, 227–9
photography, 242, 264, 271–2, 279–81, 285, 288
pietas, 70, 76, 79, 131, 134, 147, 170–93
Pindar, 13
Plato
  Phaedo, 263, 267–70, 279, 284–5, 290
  Republic, 128, 284
  Theaetetus, 282
Plautus, Titus Maccius
  Poenulus
    Hanno, 147, 171–2, 182, 184–7, 189–92
    historical context, 147, 184–5
    Milphio, 186, 191–2
    pietas. *See* under *pietas*
Polybius
  as ambassador, 216
  Histories
    autopsy, 214, 216, 220, 233
    on Scipio, 218–19
Polyphemus, 17–25, 28, 39, 43–7, 53, 55, 57, 73, 174–5
pompē, 10, 31–58
  etymology and meaning, 32–4
  Menelaus/Menelaos, 38–9
  Odysseus, 39–58
  Telemachus/Telemachos, 36–8
Poseidon (Neptune), 35, 39, 42, 45–6, 49, 51–5, 112, 131, 156, 165, 173–4, 190, 237

Posidonius
  as historian and geographer, 219, 221, 254
  on Scipio, 219–22
Prometheus, 30, 87
Proteus, 38, 43
Punic Wars, viii, 63, 147, 172, 175–6, 178, 184, 187–8, 191, 213, 217, 269
Punica fides, 147, 171, 180, 186, 191–3
Punica pietas, 147, 171–2, 192
Pythagoras
  harmony of the spheres, 269–70, 276

refugee, 106, 153, 228
romance, 10, 89, 93, 102–3, 107, 151
Rome
  boundaries of, 194, 197, 210, 231, 278
  Campus Martius, 163, 168
  Mausoleum of Augustus, 168, 205, 208
  monuments, 5, 168–9, 187–8, 205

Sabine women, 181
sacred prostitution, 171, 181–2, 187–9
sacrifice, 14, 20, 25, 28, 30, 39, 43–5, 50, 116, 122, 127, 160, 183, 265
Sarpedon, 33
Scipio Aemilianus, 214, 218, 223, 228, 250, 269
  as Odysseus, 219
  Somnium Scipionis, 269–70
Scipio Africanus, P., 197, 209, 214, 221, 269
  Somnium Scipionis, 269–70
sea-storm (and epic), 42, 57, 73–4, 77, 86, 100–1, 155–7, 175–7
Seneca the Younger, 65, 69, 75, 83, 251
Silius Italicus, T.
  Punica, 63, 249, 254
Sophistic
  Second, 212, 231, 234, 236
  Third, 145, 212, 236
space
  theory and scholarship of, 1–6
Sparta, 36, 40, 117
Stoicism, 72, 75–6, 219–21, 229, 247, 270, 283
Strabo
  Odysseus and methodology, 212, 225–6
  on Augustan Rome, 168–9
Suitors, 25–9, 37
symposium, 8, 14–15, 17–18, 22–8, 124

Tacitus, P. Cornelius
  Agricola, 254–5
  Tiberius, 197–9, 207–10, 231
teichoskopia, 163

Telamon, 76, 85
Telemachus/Telemachos, 12, 92, 120–1, 177
telos, 5, 61, 89, 109, 146, 151
Theognis, 14
Thucydides, 117
Timaeus of Tauromenium, 145, 147, 153, 171–2, 178–80, 184, 191
  and historiography, 213–17
Titans/Titanomachy, 16, 19
topography, 158, 163
tragedy, 10, 59, 61, 63, 67–72, 77, 80–1, 83, 87, 95, 98, 107, 134, 142, 183, 204, 279
travel
  travel ban (Augustan, 29 BCE), 194
  unwilling, 7, 87, 103, 184
  willing, 7, 35, 94, 103, 145, 181
Trogus, Pompeius, Gn. (Justin *Epitome*), 147, 171, 221
  on Dido (see also Dido), 180–3

urbs, 146, 257

Valerius Flaccus, G.
  Argonautica
    amor, 75–7, 80, 82, 84–5
    amor rerum, 66, 75–6, 84–5
    and Lucan, 77
    exempla/exemplarity, 59–88
    Hylas, 68, 81–3
    Jason, 65
    and Aeneas, 71
    characterization of, 66, 70–2, 76, 78–9, 82, 89
    labor, 63, 69, 72, 75, 77, 79, 81, 87–8
    prophecy (prophecies of Idmon and Mopsus), 67–70
vegetarianism, 14, 20–2, 25
Vergil (P. Vergilius Maro)
  Aeneid
    ambages, 134
    exempla/exemplarity, 136, 138
    Hercules and Cacus, 167
    Lusus Troiae, 165
    movement
      chaotic, 146, 154–9, 164
      horizontal, 146, 152–8, 160–1, 164–6
      orderly, 146, 152, 155–7, 165, 167, 174
      vertical, 146, 152, 154, 157–64
    pietas. See under *pietas*
    shield of Aeneas, 136, 163–4
  Georgics, 69, 77

view
    cosmic, 7, 146, 267–70, 282, 287–91
    from above, 146, 152, 159–60, 163–4, 169, 266, 270, 283
    of epic hero, 159–64
virtus, 60, 63–6, 69, 72, 76–9, 81–2, 85–8

walls, city, 133, 139, 141–4, 146, 157–9, 161–2, 164
wandering, 11, 32, 35, 51, 57, 91–5, 97–100, 102–5, 107, 146, 151–5, 157–9, 167, 176, 179, 184, 211, 215–17, 223, 228–9, 238, 247, 250, 265, 276
women
    and lament, 106, 140–3, 183
    as opponents/obstacles, 108, 130, 132, 136, 143–4, 183
    as travelers, 95–107, 130–44, 152–5, 177–83

xenia (guest-friendship), 25, 33, 39, 43, 45, 47, 52, 54, 73, 78–80, 184

Xenophanes, 15–18
Xenophon
    Anabasis
        and the *Odyssey*. *See* under *Odyssey* as model
        Hellas (character), 126–8
        home
            harmony of, 111–13, 128–9
            security, 112–14, 117, 119, 126, 233
            women in, 111, 119–29
    Cyropaedia, 129
    Oeconomicus, 112, 119, 121–2
Xenophon (novelist)
    Ephesiaca
        Habrocomes, 103–5

Zeus (Jupiter), 12–14, 19, 21–4, 28–30, 36, 39–42, 44, 52–4, 59, 61, 63–4, 67, 69–75, 80, 86, 88, 110, 112, 116, 155, 159–61, 165–6, 181, 189–90
    Dios boulē, 29, 166
    Xeneios, 21